Irish Military Elites, Nation and Empire, 1870–1925

Loughlin Sweeney

Irish Military Elites, Nation and Empire, 1870–1925

Identity and Authority

Loughlin Sweeney
John Endicott College of International Studies
Daejeon, Korea (Republic of)

ISBN 978-3-030-19306-5   ISBN 978-3-030-19307-2   (eBook)
https://doi.org/10.1007/978-3-030-19307-2

Cover illustration: Lebrecht Music & Arts / Alamy Stock Photo

This Palgrave Macmillan imprint is published by the registered company Springer Nature Switzerland AG
The registered company address is: Gewerbestrasse 11, 6330 Cham, Switzerland

To my Grandparents

Acknowledgements

This book represents the culmination of six years of work in research, writing, and revision, and thus there are a great many people to whom I owe a debt of immense gratitude. I must thank my doctoral supervisor, Eugenio Biagini, who has been incredibly patient, kind, and giving of his immense insight and broad knowledge throughout this process. For their mentorship and guidance over these many years, I must also thank John Bew, Tim Wilson, Ian d'Alton, and the late Christopher Bayly and Keith Jeffery. I am particularly grateful to Enda Delaney, who has been intimately involved in this project at every stage and who very graciously hosted me at the University of Edinburgh in the final weeks of this manuscript's production.

I owe a huge debt of gratitude to my editors at Palgrave Macmillan, Molly Beck and Maeve Sinnott, for being so accommodating of my requests and for keeping me on track. I am grateful for the valuable assistance in funding this research provided by the Arts and Humanities Research Council, the University of Cambridge History Faculty, Queens' College Cambridge, the Royal Historical Society, and the Woosong Educational Foundation. A large share of gratitude must also go to my friends and colleagues in the Cambridge and Edinburgh Irish History research groups, for many years of stimulating discussions and enthusiastic feedback. A nicer group of colleagues could not be asked for.

To mention the names of all the friends and colleagues at Queens' and Endicott who made this experience such a pleasure would require a volume of its own—however, I must especially thank Kevin Kester, Shachi Amdekar, William King, and my head of department, Marilyn Lafay, for their comments on chapters and their enthusiastic support. I must also thank the staff of the many archives and research libraries in Ireland and the United Kingdom who facilitated my enquiries and made my research an absolute pleasure. Worthy of especial thanks are Mike Weaver at the Cambridge History Faculty, Jean Turner at the Glucksman Library in Limerick, and the staff of the National Library of Ireland. This list would not be complete without listing three formative mentors to whom I owe special gratitude: Jennifer Reagan-Lefebvre, Paul Doolan, and Chris Friendly. Finally, and very much not least, my heartfelt thanks to my parents, Joe and Katherine, my sister Laura, and my grandmother Mary. We may be scattered across the globe, but we're together when it counts.

I am grateful to Alamy image library's historical photograph archive and to the National Library of Ireland for permission to reproduce images from their collection. Some of the archival material in this book appears by permission of the Trustees of the Liddell Hart Centre for Military Archives at King's College London.

I must especially remember my grandfather, Loughlin Joseph Sweeney, who kindled in me a lifelong love of history and of Ireland, and who died while this manuscript was coming together. He is sorely missed.

CONTENTS

꜕

ABOUT THE AUTHOR

Loughlin Sweeney is a historian of Ireland and the British Empire. He conducted this research while pursuing a doctorate at Queens' College Cambridge, awarded in 2017. He is an assistant professor at the John Endicott College of International Studies in South Korea, where he lectures on global history and researches Irish communities in the nineteenth-century Pacific. He has been a visiting fellow at Queen Mary, University of London, and the University of Edinburgh, and publishes regularly in the fields of Irish history, the British Empire, the Irish diaspora, and imperial, colonial, and postcolonial studies.

ABBREVIATIONS

AMS	Assistant Military Secretary
ANZAC	Australia and New Zealand Army Corps
ASC	Army Service Corps
BMH	Bureau of Military History
CCA	Cork County Archives
CIGS	Chief of the Imperial General Staff
C-in-C	Commander-in-Chief
DIB	Cambridge Dictionary of Irish Biography
DNB	Oxford Dictionary of National Biography
GHQ	General Headquarters
ICS	Indian Civil Service
IMS	Indian Medical Service
IRA	Irish Republican Army
JP	Justice of the Peace
KBE	Knight of the British Empire
KCIO	King's Commissioned Indian Officer
KCL	Liddell Hart Centre for Military Archives, King's College, London
LUL	Limerick University Library
NCO	Non-commissioned officer
NLI	National Library of Ireland
OTC	Officers Training Corps
PRONI	Public Records Office of Northern Ireland
QAIMNS	Queen Alexandra's Imperial Military Nursing Service
RAF	Royal Air Force
RAMC	Royal Army Medical Corps
RFC	Royal Flying Corps
RHMS	Royal Hibernian Military School

TCD	Manuscripts and Archives Research Library, Trinity College Dublin
UVF	Ulster Volunteer Force
WAFF	West African Frontier Force

LIST OF FIGURES

LIST OF TABLES

CHAPTER 1

Introduction

When the Irish ambassador laid a laurel wreath at the Cenotaph in London on Remembrance Sunday 2014, it was the first time a representative of the Irish government had done so since 1946, when Ireland was still a member of the British Commonwealth. Ambassador Dan Mulhall said of the occasion that it demonstrated 'no contradiction between the rightful commemoration of our own struggle for independence … and remembering the Irish war effort a century ago'; rather, 'the coincidence of these two sets of events merely serves to highlight the complexity of our national history.'[1] The recognition by the State that Irishmen had fought and died in British uniform, and that this fact is worthy of remembrance, evinces a significant shift in public attitudes towards the long and complex relationship between Ireland and the British Army. The First World War has long represented different things in the popular mythologies and cultural traditions of the North and South of Ireland, as Catriona Pennell, Anne Dolan, and others have examined in detail.[2] Remembrance of British military service before 1914 evinced an uneasy complicity with the crimes of empire. For many years in the Republic, the British Army was a booming silence, its remains dotting the physical and mental landscape: its former forts strung along the coastline; the stentorian imperial architecture of its barracks and official buildings commanding Ireland's towns and cities; the whispers of forgotten campaigns in epigraphs on tombstones and monuments; the glinting symbols of British rule—medals and badges sporting crowned heads, crowned harps, elephants, and tigers—tucked away into drawers and

© The Author(s) 2019
L. Sweeney, *Irish Military Elites, Nation and Empire, 1870–1925*,
https://doi.org/10.1007/978-3-030-19307-2_1

forgotten. In Northern Ireland, the British Army was until very recently a painful and immediate presence.

When President Mary McAleese attempted, in the 1990s, to rehabilitate the memories of Irishmen who fell in the First World War, the political context of the Troubles was too present; the memory of catastrophe still too raw and current. In the intervening years, a remarkable change in public attitudes has taken place as increasingly confident Irish publics look to the foundational events of the modern Irish state a century ago.[3] Now, it appears that the public is hungry for a popular history that embraces the complexity of these events, and casts them not as legends within the national narrative, but as confused, ambiguous, and contested, paralleling contemporary struggles between religious and national identities in other parts of the world. Where once the commemorative rituals and signifiers of Irish nationality were framed as evidence for exceptionalism, now they are desired as explanations of context.

This book concerns the social history of one overlooked aspect of the British Army in Ireland: the Irish military elite. Three broad thematic areas are considered: social context, military identities, and moral authority. The officer corps is envisaged not simply as a British imposition, but as an organic component of the Irish establishment, characterised by strong ties to Ireland's civilian social elite, and by its position at a crucial intersection between Ireland, Britain, and the wider British Empire. In the opening chapters, officers will be shown to represent a key aspect of the increasingly close interconnections between the British Army and Irish society in the late nineteenth and early twentieth centuries. The evidence of hundreds of Irish officers is marshalled to illustrate the social, demographic, and imaginative boundaries of the Irish officer corps, and the sometimes surprising ways these seemingly monolithic boundaries could be moulded or stretched by Irish officers.

By examining questions of social advancement, elite socialisation, professionalism, and national identity, the middle chapters of this book identify a nineteenth-century tradition of 'military Irishness', and within this context, elaborate the role of Irish officers in the dislocating events of the Great War and Irish independence. In addition to examining prominent military Irishmen, the stories of Irish officers who have thus far been neglected by historians, or who have only been studied as part of a more general Irish 'establishment', will be placed to the fore. Studying these officers' forgotten voices can provide a new perspective on a crucial period of Irish history: the long maturation of Irish nationalism between the

1870s and the 1920s, culminating in the revolutionary period which created the contemporary political structures on the island of Ireland. The final chapters will portray the decline of Irish officers' social position, faced with the challenges of the War of Independence, partition, and the Irish Civil War. The Irish military establishment lost its moral authority in this period, though the identity of military Irishness nonetheless survived in small pockets in Ireland, persisted in the overseas British Empire, and attracted Irishmen to serve in the British Army around the world following southern independence.

This book is not a collection of accounts of battle, or a list of the births, deaths, and campaigns of a complete set of Irish officers of the Victorian and Edwardian officer corps. It does not pretend to complete objectivity in its reporting of these men's lives, which is, in any case, an impossibility due to the limitations of the available sources. It resists prescriptively assigning a definitive answer to the question of what 'Irishness' is. Rather, it intends to be an exploration of what a particular, privileged, if increasingly beleaguered segment of the Irish elite imagined itself to represent, and how this sense of identity coloured its interactions with other parts of Irish society, and with different conceptions and performances of Irishness. It is the collective biography of an elite out of place, faced with the erosion of its authority and the irrelevance of its sense of identity.

MILITARY CONTEXT

From the creation of a formalised, structured fighting force in the seventeenth century until the time of the Napoleonic Wars, the British Army had been constituted of aristocratic gentlemen who raised bodies of men from the locality, drilled and equipped them, and led them into battle. A centralised army administration emerged during the course of the nineteenth century, with the establishment and growth of training institutions (artillery and engineer officer training began at Woolwich in 1741, training for line officers was instituted at Sandhurst in 1801, and an Army Medical School was eventually established in 1860), and the increasing policymaking authority of the Commander in Chief and War Office. Eventually, an Imperial General Staff was created following the South African War. However, the fundamental ethos and relational paradigm of the British Army remained that of aristocratic officers with a paternalistic attitude to their men, whose essential qualification for their position was tied to their class. The officer class, like the Peerage, represented a sticky form of social distinction that resisted impulses to reform for a long period, and reproduced an archaic sense of identity. How this phenomenon operated in Ireland, in the period when the political and cultural idea of the Irish nation was moving increasingly rapidly in radical new directions, is the central question posed by this book.

At the turn of the nineteenth century, two events took place that prefaced the ever-closer connections between the British Army and Ireland. First, in 1793, the proscription on Catholics and dissenters serving in the British forces, one of the infamous Penal Laws, was abolished, and the era of the 'Wild Geese', Catholic gentry and aristocrats serving in the Irish Brigades of continental armies, drew to a close.[4] Many of these Catholic aristocrats' former holdings in Ireland had, in the meantime, been awarded to English officers in recognition of military service, and the male descendants of these Ascendancy officers inaugurated another strand of the Irish military tradition.[5] The other event that tied the military and Ireland together was the Napoleonic War, which necessitated the garrisoning of large numbers of troops in Ireland and the construction of new fortifications, stations, and barracks. A key location for organising and drilling soldiers was the Curragh in County Kildare, which was expanded with permanent facilities on the eve of the Crimean War, and which by the late nineteenth century was the largest military installation in the United Kingdom.[6] In the following decades, the creation of these institutions provided economic opportunities in garrison towns, a steady income for the young men of rural populations, and a way of life for Irish elites. The persistent poverty of the country ensured a large pool of potential recruits; crises in Ireland, like the Famine and the Fenian revolts, and wars in the empire, provided a steady demand for soldiers. From the eighteenth-century militia and fencible units, to the cavalry of Waterloo and the Crimea, to the dashing exploits of colonial adventurers, the army also provided a prestigious, exciting, and increasingly desirable career to the Irish upper classes.[7]

The civil and military reforms taking place in the latter half of the nineteenth century afforded many opportunities to Irish candidates for colonial service. From the 1870s, the eminent Victorian soldiers Garnet Wolseley and Frederick Roberts, both Irishmen, gathered around themselves 'rings' of talented officers with differing backgrounds and ideas about professionalisation.[8] The way in which the Irishness of these two men interacted with their public and professional roles, not only as imperial popular heroes but also as Commanders-in-Chief in Ireland in the

1890s, will be assessed, as will the extent to which the officer corps professionalised, and the potential for demographic change this afforded. The abolition of the purchase of commissions in 1871, the outcome of an early attempt at officer professionalisation, constitutes the starting point of the period under consideration. Its end point extends beyond the turmoil of the War of Independence, partition, and Civil War, to highlight the continuities that existed after partition. The popular militarism of the beginning of the twentieth century, which was a function of Ireland's connection to the wider British Empire and manifested itself in public ritual, consumer culture, military ceremonial, and other forms of imperial ornamentalism, began to release its hold on the population as Irish national politics took centre stage. It was to be replaced by different touchstones of identity, concurrent with the creation of two new political units on the island of Ireland in the 1920s. In this crucial period for the formation of modern Ireland, the relationship between the British army and Irish society was of central importance. Professionalisation, class, and empire defined that relationship, and the changing role played by army officers in Irish society reflects the changing nature of Irish identity.

According to Lawrence McBride's *The Greening of Dublin Castle*, the advance of constitutional nationalism in Ireland went hand in hand with the professionalisation of the elite spaces of the Irish social structure; the civil service bureaucracy and judiciary increasingly adopted professional norms which dislodged old-fashioned, aristocratic forms of the reproduction of privilege, allowing an increasing number of middle-class administrators into elite spaces. This, in McBride's analysis, allowed for a broadening of acceptable political opinions, lending a respectability to the moderate nationalism that many of these new middle class elites espoused.[9] *Contra* McBride, however, this relationship between professionalisation and constitutional nationalism does not appear to bear out within the officer corps. Rather, the opposite relationship between nationalism and privilege can be observed. The reproduction of aristocratic attitudes within the corps actually contributed to the decline of imperialist forms of militarism in Irish society, and undermined the ability of military elites to project moral authority. The lack of a 'greening' effect within the officer corps meant that it was increasingly marginalised as the political situation continued to evolve. As the national movement became popularised, Irish militarism was reclaimed by civilians, such as the members of the nationalist and unionist political militias which proliferated in the prelude to the First World War, and reproduced by their descendant communities of violence during the Irish Civil War and the Troubles.[10]

APPROACHES: IRELAND, BRITAIN, EUROPE, AND EMPIRE

Representatives of almost every political 'tribe' and conception of national identity in nineteenth-century Ireland were willing participants in the British military. The Irishmen who became officers in this diverse and highly institutionalised organisation were driven by the dictates of their convictions and obligations to king, country, family, faith, empire, and ambition. Their status as imperial officers not only affords an insight into Ireland as an imperial nation, but also invites parallels with the civil-military relations of other multiethnic European empires.[11] Their place in Irish history sits uneasily across traditional narratives of religion and nationality. Officers overlap the history of elites, empire, militarism, and Britishness in an Irish context, and taken as a group they can tell us a great deal about the significance of these factors to Irish history which goes beyond tired stereotype and untested assumption.

The methodology employed herein draws from prosopographical studies of military officers, like those of David Haire, David Fitzpatrick, and István Deák. A focus on social history has yielded fruitful results in an Irish context in the work of Barry Crosbie and Fergus Campbell. Crosbie's analysis of Irish imperial networks has brought light to the overseas soldier's 'attachment to—and continuing impact upon—the structures of society left behind' in the form of economic and social connections, and Campbell's spirited counterargument to McBride's 'greening' thesis makes innovative use of primary sources to draw important conclusions about Irish elites.[12] Studies covering various social classes and periods have utilised correspondence to draw useful conclusions about these groups, and the work of Crosbie and Fitzpatrick on professional and familial networks relies primarily on these kinds of sources.[13] David French's social history of the British Army provides an instructive example of how these methods might be applied in this research area.[14] Recontextualising military and political matters, and drawing out their social implications, has been the objective of a number of important studies by Alvin Jackson, George Boyce and Alan O'Day, Thomas Dooley, David Fitzpatrick, and others.[15] Apart from a handful of notable exceptions, biographies of military officers from this period do not spend a great deal of time focusing on their backgrounds, nor do they go into much detail about their private, non-professional lives—though this reflects a limitation in the source material, rather than a lack of perspective. Alvin Jackson and Keith Jeffery utilise personal correspondence and private papers as well as public documents to arrive at a more rounded understanding in their biographies of Anglo-Irish officers, while an assessment of the whole officer corps as an elite group has been drawn out by historians such as Gordon Craig, Elizabeth Muenger, Lawrence McBride, and (for Austro-Hungarian officers) István Deák, in the influential *Beyond Nationalism*.[16]

The hundreds of Irish officers in this study were identified in official papers, memorials, memoirs, membership lists, and other indicators of officer networking, and information was compiled concerning the characteristics of the networks in which they moved, in the manner of the previous thoroughgoing studies of Nicholas Perry, Jane Leonard, Peter Martin, Steven O'Connor, and others.[17] As is the case in those studies, there is no objective measure against which the representativeness of this sample of officers can be compared; however, in selecting the officers for inclusion steps were taken to limit the potential for selection bias, such as locating officers using public memorials, battle honours or army lists, which are not explicitly divided by class, religion, or political difference. It was for this reason, too, that Irish officers were not sought solely from the Irish regiments. The selection of officers, while necessarily a less than perfect snapshot of the Irish officer corps, is nonetheless consistent with expectations given the findings of other scholars. Accordingly, the findings which are derived from this dataset are adopted cautiously, and care has been taken not to brook needless conjecture.

This book sets its stride by the invaluable groundwork provided by the aforementioned scholars, but also questions some of the underlying assumptions of this previous work (we should, for example, be sceptical of David Haire's characterisation of military life in Ireland as evincing 'near-active-service conditions … [and] scarcity of social amenities among a partially hostile population').[18] It seeks to address a major problem common to much of the scholarship—an insufficient diversity of sources, over-emphasising the importance of a small number of officers and relying too heavily on the accounts of politicians and other elites, instead of the officers themselves. This study, therefore, seeks to foreground the testimony of officers who have been thus far neglected in the scholarship, attempting to capture both their contemporary attitudes, and how these changed in response to a mutable political context.

It is particularly important, as the mythology of Irish nationalism is being reappraised in the context of the centenary of the First World War and the War of Independence, that Ireland's global connections are explored. Irish history has recently discovered a new resonance in histories of interconnection and mobility: for instance the four-nations approach incorporates Irish experience into subjects traditionally thought of as 'British history', as well as highlighting Ireland's contribution to the British Empire. The new approaches and appraisals of diaspora history, furthermore, reveal multiple Irish 'worlds' and place Ireland within wider histories of connections across oceans and between communities.[19] In terms of numbers, and arguably in terms of public perception as well, the military was the largest conduit through which the colonial empire (outside colonies of settlement) was experienced by the Irish. It is also a pan-Irish story, due to the increasingly diffuse assortment of garrisons peppering the country which increased in size and number from the 1870s until the numerical peak of British soldiers garrisoned in Ireland was reached in 1914.[20] As a social history of military officers in Ireland, and the Irish military tradition they embodied from the abolition of commission purchasing through the upheavals of the land war, the professionalisation of the officer corps, labour unrest, world war, the emergence of radical republicanism, and partition, this book affords a unique perspective on aspects of Irishness and identity in this revolutionary period.

The gradually changing demographics and norms of the officer corps, and the vast diversity of situations confronting them in Ireland—from relative stability in the 1870s to the departure of the British Army from the twenty-six counties in 1922, and beyond—will be examined to explain how Irish officers found themselves in the midst of dual crises, of authority and identity, in the period of Irish independence.

NOTES

1. Dan Mulhall, 'At London's Cenotaph, 9 November 2014', Irish Department of Foreign Affairs <https://www.dfa.ie/irish-embassy/great-britain/about-us/ambassador/ambassadors-blog-2014/november-2014/ambassador-blog-12-november/>, created 12 November 2014. See also the preface to Eugenio Biagini and Dan Mulhall, eds., *The Shaping of Modern Ireland: A Centenary Assessment* (Sallins, 2016).
2. Catriona Pennell, *A Kingdom United: Popular Responses to the Outbreak of the First World War in Britain and Ireland* (Oxford, 2012), p. 171; Catriona Pennell, 'Going to War', in John Horne, ed., *Our War: Ireland and the Great War* (Dublin, 2008), p. 40; Paul Taylor, *Heroes or Traitors? Experiences of Southern Irish Soldiers Returning from the Great War 1919–1939* (Liverpool, 2015); Anne Dolan, *Commemorating the Irish Civil War: History and Memory, 1923–2000* (Cambridge, 2006), pp. 201–202.

3. For a discussion of what Fitzpatrick calls 'Irish commemorative expertise' and its boundaries, see David Fitzpatrick, 'Commemoration in the Irish Free State: A Chronicle of Embarrassment', in Ian McBride, ed., *History and Memory in Modern Ireland* (Cambridge, 2001); Richard S. Greyson, 'From Genealogy to Reconciliation: Public Engagement with Remembrance of the First World War in Ireland', *Nordic Irish Studies* 13:2 (2014), pp. 99–113; John Horne and Edward Madigan, eds., *Towards Commemoration: Ireland in War and Revolution 1912–1923* (Dublin, 2013); Taylor, *Heroes or Traitors*, pp. 3–4; Richard S. Greyson, 'Ireland's New Memory of the First World War: Forgotten Aspects of the Battles of Messines, June 1917', *British Journal of Military History* 1:1 (2014), pp. 48–65.

4. Peter Karsten, 'Irish Soldiers in the British Army, 1792–1922: Suborned or Subordinate?', *Journal of Social History* 17 (1983), pp. 31–64.

5. Karsten, 'Irish Soldiers in the British Army'; William Butler, *The Irish Amateur Military Tradition in the British Army, 1854–1992* (Manchester, 2016).

6. Con Costello, *A Most Delightful Station: The British Army on the Curragh of Kildare, Ireland, 1855–1922* (Cork, 1996).

7. See Thomas Bartlett and Keith Jeffery, *A Military History of Ireland* (Cambridge, 1996).

8. See Brian Bond, *The Victorian Army and the Staff College 1854–1914* (London, 1972); Halik Kochanski, 'Field Marshall Viscount Wolseley, a Reformer at the War Office', unpub. PhD thesis, King's College London (1996).

9. Lawrence Mcbride, *The Greening of Dublin Castle: The Transformation of Bureaucratic and Judicial Personnel in Ireland, 1892–1922* (Washington, DC, 1991).

10. See Fearghal McGarry, *The Rising: Ireland: Easter 1916* (Oxford, 2016).

11. Cf. István Deák, *Beyond Nationalism: A Social and Political History of the Habsburg Officer Corps, 1848–1918* (Oxford, 1990).

12. Barry Crosbie, *Irish Imperial Networks: Migration, Social Communication and Exchange in Nineteenth-Century India* (Cambridge, 2012), p. 96; Fergus Campbell, *The Irish Establishment, 1879–1914* (Oxford, 2009).

13. David Fitzpatrick, ed., *Ireland and the First World War* (Dublin, 1988); David Fitzpatrick, 'Unofficial Emissaries British Army Boxers and the Irish Free State', *Irish Historical Studies* 30 (1996), pp. 206–232; Crosbie, *Irish Imperial Networks* passim.

14. David French, *Military Identities: The Regimental System, the British Army, and the British People, c.1870–2000* (Oxford, 2005), passim.

15. Alvin Jackson, *Colonel Edward Saunderson: Land and Loyalty in Victorian Ireland* (Oxford, 1995); Thomas P. Dooley, *Irishmen or English Soldiers?*

The Times and World of a Southern Catholic Irishman (1876–1916) Enlisting in the British Army during the First World War (Liverpool, 1995); David George Boyce and Alan O'Day, eds., *The Making of Modern Irish History: Revisionism and the Revisionist Controversy* (Abingdon, 1996); David Fitzpatrick, *The Two Irelands 1912–1939* (Oxford, 1998). See also note 18 for recent interventions on this subject.

16. Gordon Craig, *The Politics of the Prussian Army, 1640–1945* (London, 2007); Elizabeth Muenger, *The British Military Dilemma in Ireland* (Lawrence, KA, 1991); Deák, *Beyond Nationalism*; Lawrence McBride, *The Greening of Dublin Castle* (Washington, DC, 1991).

17. Nicholas Perry, 'The Irish Landed Class and the British Army, 1850–1950', *War in History* 18 (2011), pp. 304–333; Jane Leonard, 'Survivors', in John Horne, *Our War: Ireland and the Great War* (Dublin, 2008); Peter Martin, 'Dulce et Decorum: Irish nobles in the Great War, 1914–19', in Adrian Gregory and Senia Pašeta, eds., *Ireland and the Great War: 'A War to Unite Us All'?* (Manchester, 2002); Steven O'Connor, *Irish Officers in the British Forces, 1922–45* (New York, 2014).

18. David N. Haire, 'In Aid of the Civil Power, 1868–90' in Lyons, F. S. L., and R. A. J. Hawkins, eds., *Ireland under the Union* (Oxford, 1980), p. 147.

19. Recent work in this area includes David Swift and Oliver Wilkinson, *Veterans of the First World War: Ex-Servicemen and Ex-Servicewomen in Post-War Britain and Ireland* (Abingdon, 2019); Seán Gannon, *The Irish Imperial Service: Policing Palestine and Administering the Empire, 1922–1966* (London, 2018); Joseph Clarke and John Horne, eds., *Militarized Cultural Encounters in the Long Nineteenth Century: Making War, Mapping Europe* (Basingstoke, 2018); Richard Grayson, *Dublin's Great Wars: The First World War, the Easter Rising, and the Irish Revolution* (Cambridge, 2018); Elizabeth Malcolm and Dianne Hall, *A New History of the Irish in Australia* (Sydney, 2018); Eugenio Biagini and Clare Daly, eds., *The Cambridge Social History of Modern Ireland* (Cambridge, 2017); John Crowley, Donal Ó Drisceoil, Mike Murphy, and John Borgonovo, eds., *Atlas of the Irish Revolution* (Cork, 2017); Enrico Dal Lago, Róisín Healy, and Gearóid Barry, eds., *1916 in Global Context* (Abingdon, 2017); Sharon Crozier-De Rosa, *Shame and the Anti-Feminist Backlash: Britain, Ireland, and Australia, 1890–1920* (Abingdon, 2017); Dominik Geppert, William Mulligan, and Andreas Rose, eds., *The Wars Before the Great War: Conflict and International Politics before the Outbreak of the Great War* (Cambridge, 2015); O'Connor, *Irish Officers*. New writing in this field continues to be produced and speaks to the currency of these questions. Forthcoming works include Conor Morrissey, *Protestant Nationalists in Ireland, 1900–1923* (Cambridge); Robert Lynch, *The Partition of Ireland*

(Cambridge); David Brundage, *Irish Nationalists in America: The Politics of Exile 1798–1998* (Oxford); Dan Milner, *The Unstoppable Irish: Songs and Integration of the New York Irish, 1783–1883* (Notre Dame); D. Durnin, *The Irish Medical Profession in the First World War* (Palgrave); Jennifer Redmond and Elaine Farrell, eds., *Irish Women in the First World War Era* (Routledge).

20. Nora Robertson, *Crowned Harp: Memories of the Last Years of the Crown in Ireland* (Dublin, 1960), p. 23.

CHAPTER 2

Defining an Irish Military Elite

If Irish national sentiment became respectable and was organised by respectable people, who would introduce sound principles into it, it would be a great power for good in our country.
—Viscount Powerscourt, Irish Guards, Lord Lieutenant of Wicklow, 1916

The British Army officer corps of 1870 was experiencing a period of institutional crisis. The upsets of the Indian Rebellion and the Crimean War had dealt a dual blow to the British imperial psyche, and senior military officers and politicians were engaged in an ongoing debate about the efficiency of the army, which called into question the role of elites and aristocrats as the natural leaders of society. Ireland, as the location of a significant amount of the British Army's garrison capacity and the source of up to a quarter of the army's manpower and one-fifth of its officers, could not avoid becoming embroiled in these debates.

The Cardwell reforms of the early 1870s, and the Childers reforms of the 1880s, respectively, brought an end to the 'purchase system', wherein officers were required to post a bounty in order to receive their commissions, and established territorially linked battalions, which localised the enlistment of soldiers to a greater degree than before.[1] In the elite regiments, both Irish officers and those from other parts of the United Kingdom regarded these reforms as a challenge to the fundamental ethos of the officer corps, striking at the heart of this traditionally aristocratic

© The Author(s) 2019
L. Sweeney, *Irish Military Elites, Nation and Empire, 1870–1925*,
https://doi.org/10.1007/978-3-030-19307-2_2

occupation. The reforms raised the spectre of 'democratisation', as the officer corps threatened to become accessible to a wider swathe of the middle class—a spectre which would haunt elite officers for decades.

At the same time, in the Irish context, territorialisation fuelled anxieties about disloyalty, which had just a few years prior contributed to a scare about Fenian 'infiltration' of the British Army.[2] The army in Ireland was therefore regarded by the military establishment as a potential frontline in the defence of the British Empire—a friendly neighbour, but one which nonetheless could allow imperial subversion, with potentially catastrophic consequences. Irish officers in the British Army existed with a foot on both sides of this imagined frontier, a situation which could be at turns convivial, uncomfortable, and even dangerous. In Ireland's revolutionary moment after the First World War, it could be deadly.

This book has three main aims: first, it argues that the British Army was not just a foreign imposition in Ireland, but rather a longstanding institution in Irish society, with deep interconnections to Irish people from all walks of life. Irish officers, therefore, played an important role as part of Ireland's social elite. Second, this book illustrates that these officers were drawn from a much wider social base than is usually assumed. This calls into question assumptions about Irish officers' actions and reactions to Irish nationalism, unionism, and the independence movement, as well as officers' self-perceptions as the functionaries of a system that consistently misunderstood the Irish context. Third, it charts the long decline in military officers' moral authority in Irish society, and explores the reasons underlying the curious continuity of the Irish officer tradition in the British and imperial armies, even after the independence of the twenty-six counties. In order to address these questions, it is first necessary to define, for the purposes of this study, what is meant by the term 'Irish officer'—an ostensibly simple term which conceals a great deal of political, cultural, and class ambiguity.

DEFINING MILITARY IRISHNESS

Careful navigation of historical terms is essential in defining an Irish military tradition, in order to make sense of nuanced and overlapping identities like 'Irishness', 'Britishness', 'imperialism', and 'Anglo-Irishness'. There have been various attempts at clarifying these subtle categories in other works, though it is a complex task as Irish officers are, by definition, awkwardly

juxtaposed between margin and metropolis, geographically and culturally.[3] A good example of this difficulty is encountered in the person of
Lord Kitchener, a man with Irish family connections who was born in
County Kerry, but who spent very little time there and who did not display much indication of possessing affective ties to Ireland. On the other
hand, there is Sir Garnet Wolseley, who (usually) did not identify himself
as Irish, but was closely connected to the country through family, lived
there extensively, and would appear objectively to be a Dubliner through
and through. Further problematising the issue are officers like General
Reginald Dyer, the notorious perpetrator of the 1919 Amritsar massacre,
a man described as having an Irish family (though, according to Nigel
Collett, this is disputed), who was educated in County Cork, but who
nonetheless was born, raised, and lived most of his life in the Punjab.[4] His
Irish identity was ascribed to him by others, and he does not evince a close
link to the country, though he was socialised into the officer corps in
Ireland. In order to navigate these shifting sands, I seek to enumerate the
common signifiers of a 'military Irish' identity, drawing together a number
of the influences that defined Irish officers' identity in the nineteenth century, including empire, ancestry and familial links, occupational identities,
social distinction, and socialisation.

The evolution of Ireland's multifaceted relationship to the British
Empire in the late nineteenth century is a central aspect of Irish military
identity. Officers constituted one of the major links between Irish society and the overseas empire; as Jill Bender observes, 'the archetypal
Irishman in the empire was a soldier'.[5] Their status as imperial practitioners, members of an elite network with first-hand experience of life in
the overseas empire, made them fairly unique in Irish society, which for
the most part interacted with the British Empire through the interme-
diaries of commodity imperialism and imperial reportage in books,
pamphlets, and newspapers.[6] While many studies of Ireland's relationship with the British Empire make reference to the role played by military officers, the way in which their outlook was formed by and
interacted with Irish society has not received extensive engagement.[7]
The unique position of Irish officers, predisposed them to view Irish
issues through a strategic imperialist prism. As popular nationalism won
over a widening section of Irish society, Irish officers found themselves
increasingly concerned with the status of Ireland within the empire
as a whole.

There have been attempts by historians to define the 'Irish soldier' in various contexts, such as Doherty and Truesdale's *Irish Winners of the Victoria Cross* and Anthony P. Quinn's *Wigs and Guns: Irish Barristers in the Great War*. Doherty and Truesdale's typology is as follows: 'if one or other of a VC's parents were Irish-born, then he is regarded as Irish. Those born in Ireland of non-Irish parents are not excluded from this book, but it is made clear that they were, perhaps, not as Irish as some.'[8] The question of methodology is a significant one, as any definition of 'the *Irish* officer' is bound to make certain assumptions about the perceived historical importance of nationality as a marker of identity. Doherty and Truesdale's approach seems too focused on geographical location, rather than self-identification; it appears to do the opposite of what it sets out to do, namely include those who were not, in one of many possible ways, culturally Irish, and exclude those who had Irish ancestry but lived overseas. The methodology adopted in this book places Wolseley within the category of Irish officer, and Kitchener and Dyer outside it, on the basis that what is important is a self-identification with 'Irishness' and a tangible link to the country. The officers examined for this study resided in Ireland for an extended period and had familial links to Ireland. It is not primarily concerned with sons of English, Welsh, or Scottish military families who may have been posted there for a short time with their regiment. Additionally, it was taken as an indicator of affinity if the officer had spent part of their career working or training in Ireland, and was thus exposed not only to the institutional identity of imperial Irishness, but also tied to the country and other officers through property, first-hand experience, intermarriage, and shared cultural signifiers.

Of course, the other essential criterion for the category 'Irish officer' is that the individual in question held a commission in the British Army or the various colonial forces of Britain's overseas empire. The length of service in the officer corps varied greatly, from over 60 years in the case of career imperial officers like Lord Roberts, to just a few short weeks for the temporary officers who met their end in the opening engagements of the First World War. Other officers joined for a short period before taking up other occupations, or inheriting the ownership of landed estates. Naval officers have been excluded, as the mechanisms of elite identity that operated in the Royal Navy were substantively different to those of army officers, tied more closely to personal patronage and operating on a much more mobile basis than army regiments; there were never 'Irish warships' in the same way there were 'Irish regiments'. Naval officers were not as visible in Irish society as army officers, who were physically present in Ireland's many garrison towns for periods of years.[9] There was a degree of overlap between the services, and certain families sent sons into both. The Royal Air Force, originating as it did from the Royal Flying Corps which was attached to the Army, is included, though naturally the number of officers thus added to the study is small. Considering the inherent interest of these individuals' stories, it seemed worthwhile to include them.

The framework employed herein is, of course, deliberately broad; when considering the complexities of group affinity and the contentious status of Irishness in this period, it is of great importance that the tendency towards reductionism and pre-definition is resisted, so that a picture of the mental boundaries of the Irish officer corps can be discerned which incorporates all of the dimensions of the Irish officer's experience.

Information was collected on Irish officers' religious affiliation, length of service, identity of potential patrons, commissioning route (whether through a military academy, the militia, or promotion from the ranks), education, club and political party memberships, socioeconomic background, and service history. Six hundred Irish officers as defined above were identified, and represent the major source base for this study. Archival and official records were examined for information on these men (and women within the Royal Army Medical Corps [RAMC] and Queen Alexandra's Imperial Military Nursing Service [QAIMNS], who also held Crown commissions).[10] Religious affiliation was identified for 561 officers, educational background for 334, and a detailed service history was found for 126 officers, who left behind letters, diaries, and memoirs detailing their experiences. The majority of officers identified saw service in the First World War, while the officers commissioned in the nineteenth century were more likely to have had lifelong service careers, spanning several decades.

While this approach identified a varied selection of Irish officers, it also mirrored the conclusion of prior studies in finding that there was a common background and set of experiences which was shared by the majority (but by no means all) of the officers, and therefore defined the 'typical' characteristics of an Irish officer. Throughout the period under consideration, the typical Irish officer had close family connections with the landed gentry. A plurality of officers belonged to the Church of Ireland, attended a major English public school, and then went on to the Royal Military College at Sandhurst. This contributed to a dominant mindset shared by officers and formed the cornerstone of their socialisation into the officer corps.

This is not to say, however, that this background was common to all officers. A significant minority of atypical Irish officers were also identified, including members of the old Catholic aristocracy, officers commissioned from the ranks, and middle-class officers who benefited from the army's halting, contentious moves towards professionalisation throughout this period. There was also a significant representation of Presbyterian officers, reflecting the importance of Ulster as a recruiting area, who were generally speaking drawn from similar elite backgrounds to Anglican officers. Officers came from all over Ireland, a reflection of the prominence of gentry officers, and often had been highly mobile before securing their commissions, with many having spent part of their childhood in the overseas empire, and receiving their education in England, Belfast, or Dublin.

One of the terms which is frequently employed when describing the social *milieu* of the Irish officer is 'Anglo-Irish'. This appellation, both self-applied and deployed by historians, denoted a section of Irish society whose boundaries shifted over time and according to the distinctions and prejudices of the speaker.[11] Generally, the label denoted a broadly defined social 'set' with familial, cultural, economic and/or educational ties to both Ireland and England. Some commentators conflate it with an Ulster-Scots elite, which broadens the definition significantly, while others draw a distinction between them.[12] The different definitions of 'Anglo-Irish' in the reminiscences of those who self-identified as such tended to extend across a broad swathe of the upper and middle class in Ireland, from the highest echelons of the Irish peerage and the circle of the Viceroy, through the minor gentry in various degrees of economic distress, and well into the professional, urban and suburban middle classes. It defies attempts at identifying the social origins of these men as anything other than an undifferentiated elite: in the words of Gann and Duignan, 'the peerage tended to shade off into the gentry, and the gentry to merge into the higher strata of the upper middle class.'[13] This is problematic, as the boundaries of the term appeared to shift in the period between 1870 and 1925.

By focusing on army officers in particular, this study intends to add contour and detail, and to supersede the use of this rather vague label. Nora Robertson, the daughter of an established military family with links to Fermoy, in her insightful and oft-quoted account of the world of the Irish rural officer expostulates extensively on the Anglo-Irish sense of identity: it took as its touchstones 'King, Country, religion, one's personal

safety, one's family's property and, above all, one's class'; she recalls nothing 'Irish but the scenery' about barrack life, with officers emerging from
the cocoon of the army only to visit 'large and bitterly cold country
houses'.[14] Robertson's evocation suggests similarities between the officer
corps and the gentry: both expressed identities which incorporated empire,
Britishness, Protestantism, social and economic status, the 'garrison mentality', elite memories of catastrophe relating to agrarian unrest, and concern over the advance of an Irish national consciousness. This description,
however, certainly overstates the isolation of the late-nineteenth century
army from Irish society, even in garrison towns where officers were physically separated from the rest of the community.

   A more middle-class picture of the Anglo-Irish, illustrating the wide
range of class striations the term has been used to cover, is encapsulated in
the reminiscences of Brian Inglis, a journalist who recalls the imperially
connected middle-class suburb of Malahide, during his childhood under
the Union:

> The houses were conventional and undistinguished ... Their owners, also
> conventional and undistinguished, were most of them business men, or in
> the professions ... loyal to their railway season tickets (Second Class: First
> was for the gentry, and Third for servants) ... A few retired Indian Army
> officers and colonial civil servants lived in our village, and several elderly
> widows and spinsters, each with some mild eccentricity ... it was, in fact,
> quite a typical English village ... in Ireland[15]

Many of the cultural signifiers of these two worlds were the same—
most notably military service, but also public school education, loyalty
to the Crown, and the Church of Ireland—though none of these, save
perhaps the English public school, were unique to what Harold Perkin
defines as 'the predominantly upper-class, major public school-educated
elite' that is denoted by the term Anglo-Irish.[16] The term conflates many
of the cultural signifiers of the Irish officer corps while not covering all
of its members; it draws cultural similarities between the landed gentry
and the urban middle class, and while certain commonalities did exist
between these groups, within the context of the Victorian officer corps
this was a rather significant distinction. Additionally, it elides the important position of Presbyterian and Catholic senior officers in the corps and
the minority experience of officers—those who were not public school-
educated, or indeed those few who rose from the ranks. There were

other, more subtle distinctions internally, as well: all officers, of any level, would have had experience of English barrack life and elite society almost as a matter of course during their careers, but a key distinction within the officer corps was not between England and Ireland but between the British home army and the colonial forces—the latter being regarded as somewhat down-at-heel by elite officers.

Even between officers from the Protestant urban middle class, there were mechanisms of social distinction operating between those with familial connectións to the gentry, and those without. Their professional networks and their social circles were different, manifested by the distinction of the in-group of the Viceregal Lodge 'set', or the differing social signifiers of leisure activities like hunting, golf, and club life, which altered based on the relative exclusivity of clubs and voluntary organisations.[17] The officer corps formed a major bridging link across these class distinctions and allowed those with less social capital, if they succeeded in their career ambitions, to circulate among the Irish landed elite.[18] As Robert Tobin has pointed out, these sub-groups taken together did not represent Ireland's Protestant population as a whole; there were also more 'low-key' Protestants, who defined their difference from more well-connected co-religionists by consistently pointing to their lack of English relations, that they did not attend an English public school, or serve in the British Army.[19] This was again par for the course in Victorian society more broadly: the middling ranks of society, modest farmers, artisans, and the like were neither so distressed as to enlist in the ranks, nor had the social capital to seek an officer's commission. It is useful to remember, therefore, that despite the ease of assuming religious difference denoted particular social, economic and political differences, this can leave significant grey areas in the study of Victorian Irish society.[20]

Given the problematic and overlapping levels of nuance in these pre-existing labels, this study proposes the term 'military Irishness' to encapsulate the totality of the social and cultural experience of Irish military officers in this period, recognising that it extends, to a greater or lesser degree, across the seemingly rigid boundaries of religion, culture, and class. The connections and qualities which dictated who got in and got on in the officer corps rested on a highly nuanced system of social distinction.

The Culture of the Victorian Officer Corps: Modernisation Versus Tradition

From the 1870s onwards, a ponderous and contentious process of modernisation and professionalisation took place within the army. Reform was long overdue, and in this period the effects of centralisation and expansion of the army were beginning to be felt. Before the Crimean War there was little interest among British officers in translating into English the didactic texts in use by other European armies—though the work of American, French and German military thinkers was certainly available to those few who took an interest.[21] In the 1870s, with the advocacy of reformers like the Irish General Garnet Wolseley, the army Staff College was beginning to convince senior military authorities of its usefulness as a tool for training effective and experienced officers, and starting to make up for aimless decades under a conservative War Office who saw no value in 'book learning'.[22] Correspondingly, the corpus of literature in the English language on strategic and tactical thought was expanding rapidly (Clausewitz was finally translated into English in 1873), and a more efficient organisational structure was being put in place.[23]

Commissions and promotions, while still influenced to a great extent by patronage, were no longer subject to purchase, which over time diminished the extent to which well-connected older officers could stand in the way of abler men.[24] Reform in the British Army was, however, predominantly reactive—it tended to evolve in knee-jerk responses to outside stimuli as opposed to innovating in a self-directed and planned manner. Despite the changes to the composition of the officer corps anticipated by planners, large-scale disruptions to the character, professional norms, and strategic thought of the officer corps were sluggish and much remained the same in the period after Cardwell's reforms. According to Brian Bond, the immediate effects of increased attendance at Sandhurst and the abolition of the purchase of commissions in 1871 were slight; the reforms instead evolved slowly over decades.[25] As late as 1899, there were still generals who blamed the ineffectiveness of the Staff College for the failures of the British Army in fighting the Boers.[26]

Such reforms as did take immediate effect in the British officer corps did so in response to innovations in the militaries of other great powers. The officer corps in all major militaries in Europe and also in the United States were, in the second half of the nineteenth century, reforming themselves into professional bodies, a process which has attracted sustained interest from historians to perhaps a greater degree than it has in the United Kingdom. In Austria-Hungary, this standardisation of the officer's experience was driven by social policy, as a necessary means of ensuring order in the complex web of disparate national identities and cultural allegiances in the Austrian Army.[27] Unofficial exclusion from elite regiments on the basis of insufficient wealth and lack of noble title, enforced by the necessity of supplementing one's pay with private income and attending numerous expensive social events, served to foster and maintain an exclusive and aristocratic identity in the officer corps.[28] A similar system operated in the aristocratic regiments of the British officer corps throughout the nineteenth century.[29] In the Russian Empire, a class divide emerged between elite metropolitan officers and their less well-connected counterparts in isolated, uneventful postings across the vast land area of the Empire. For the latter, opportunities for corruption, boredom, and continuing inefficiencies in the Russian command structure contributed to a situation where officers felt that they were above the law—they quite literally held the effective power of life and death over soldiers and civilians in their districts.[30] While British officers in colonial regiments were, at least in theory, bound to a more stringent legal accountability than their Russian counterparts, there is nonetheless a parallel here: the home army boasted prestigious and aristocratic Guards and cavalry regiments, while the Indian Army and other colonial forces developed a more middle-class character. In the metropolitan centres of both the Russian and British Empires, the experience mirrored that of European officer corps, as military elites sought to emulate the efficiency and professionalism of Prussian officers.[31]

In Britain, the Prussian officer corps was widely lauded, particularly after its success in the Franco-Prussian War, for its overbearing insistence on maintaining the 'character' of its officers, focusing on aristocratic values, Christian morality, and reactionary conservatism. As it was opened up to bourgeois career soldiers, it was expected that middle-class officers would 'raise' themselves to these values, instead of diversifying the corps; liberals and Jews were discriminated against particularly vehemently.[32] With the wake-up call of the Crimean War, it became apparent that a British Army which had remained organisationally stagnant since 1815, however '*magnifique*' it appeared at Balaklava, was untenable in the face of mid-nineteenth-century great power *guerre*.

The major unresolved issue which concerned both military and political establishments, however, was not the institutional character of the officer corps, but a lack of clear military policy, or indeed any single person to execute such a policy. While matters of war were delegated to a single cabinet minister in the second half of the century, this was a civilian post, and its authority was frequently curtailed by opposition from the Commander-in-Chief, who for most of this period was the highly traditionalist Duke of Cambridge. Proposals for a general staff on the Prussian model ran into opposition from prominent people in both the military and political hierarchies.[33]

In the later decades of the nineteenth-century British military leaders began taking reform more seriously, though it has been argued that the identity and character of the officer corps was not altered significantly by the reforms of the 1870s and 1880s.[34] In Ireland these moves towards reform produced a small demographic widening of the officer corps, while simultaneously constructing a system which privileged family connections overall in officer selection. A lack of professionalism remained a significant problem, and reformers constantly contrasted the British corps unfavourably with the Prussian all the way up to the twentieth century.[35] There was a telling difference, however, between the British officer corps and its continental rivals: questions of nationalist influence, which led to the development in many continental European armies of a specific nationality policy, have no parallel in the British Army. It was assumed the elite identity of imperial Britishness (often referred to, by officers of all four nations, as 'Englishness' in this period) precluded the necessity of developing such a policy.[36] Although, as we shall see, this assumption was sometimes questioned by British officers when faced with civil unrest in Ireland.

While Gordon Craig describes an informal system of coercion and influence which enforced and sustained the conservatism of the Prussian officer corps,[37] Hew Strachan describes the political affiliations of British officers as developing in response to the army's imperial role, *despite* the avowed apolitical nature of the officer corps.[38] However, this is not to say that individual officers had no agency in constructing the political identity of the wider officer corps. It is particularly important to examine the attitudes of individual officers in shaping this response, if we are to accurately describe the posture of the officer corps to developments in Ireland: Virginia Crossman contends that officers acting in support of the civil power in Ireland 'prefer[red] to deal with things from a military point of view, but [were] quite capable at the same time of taking in the political bearing of the situation'.[39] Thus officers ought to be viewed in their elite context as actors exercising a degree of moral authority in society, even though they were caught up in political and social ructions over identity which they only partially understood.

Despite the wide-ranging reforms which fundamentally altered the institutional structure of the army in the 1870s, the social identity of British officers remained more or less fixed, retaining their Napoleonic War-era overtones. An officer's foremost allegiance was to his regiment.[40] He retained a nonchalant, aristocratic disdain for grand strategic thought and expected a certain degree of independence—not for reasons of operational flexibility or more efficient tactical decision-making, but because he was expected to have the necessary strength of character to carry out his role steadily and reliably, without oversight.[41] This he was, for the most part, able to do, as long as he was fighting from a position of strength on open, colonial battlefields. When faced with the complexity and nuance of civil unrest and the struggles for national identity, however, the socialisation of the Irish officer placed him hopelessly out of his depth.

POLITICS, CLASS, AND IMPERIAL AUTHORITY

Prior work on the military in Irish society has identified the crucial importance of the imperial dimension in understanding the army's social role.[42] A side-effect of this has been the resurrection of the hoary question of Ireland's 'colonial' status, and whether it is possible that Ireland could have derived certain benefits from its position in the British Empire, and from the army that was the instrument of that empire. Some historians seek to steer a middle path through this persistent if rather unhelpful question, characterising nineteenth-century Ireland as simultaneously 'coloniser' and 'colonised'. From the perspective of the officer corps, Ireland's role was evidently more imperial than colonial: its elites were practitioners and beneficiaries of empire, and while they occasionally drew upon colonial language to make sense of Irish affairs, there was of course no racial distinction present in officers' relations with their countrymen—even among those who considered themselves more 'British' than 'Irish'.[43] The relations between the British officer corps and Irish society are better explained through a class than a colonial lens. Whatever the shortcomings of approaches seeking to 'colonialise' the Irish experience, however, they have had utility in raising the question of Ireland's place in the wider British Empire, and in privileging the importance of cultural factors in addressing questions that may be overlooked by approaches based on economic or political history.

By the nature of the deeply-held patriotic and national feeling engendered by practices of commemoration, their role as arbiters of institutional violence, and controversies surrounding the legitimacy of sacrifice on behalf of the state, militaries are a source of contention within societies. This is illustrated particularly poignantly by the continuing importance of highly emotive rituals surrounding the remembrance of the First World War in the United Kingdom, and increasingly in Ireland as well.[44] The centenary years have provoked not only new historical approaches to these issues, but also— as seen in popular exhibitions, television programmes, and state ceremonies in Britain and Ireland—a significant change in public attitudes. The vision of the military as a symbol and a tool of cooperation in Irish society pre-dated the First World War: the army's role in the nineteenth century as both a unifying and dividing influence in Irish society—a unifying force within the rural aristocracy,[45] a conduit for developing affinities between upper- and middle-class groups, and a barrier reinforcing difference between these groups and the urban and rural working class[46]—has been hinted at in prior studies.

In Bartlett and Jeffery's *A Military History of Ireland*, the army's role in Ireland is defined by the transition from a state of apolitical feeling among military commanders before 1880, to an alignment of interests between the military and the government in the increasingly militaristic period following the Second Boer War.[47] The reactions of military officers to their most active role in Ireland, that of aiding the civil power, appears to bear this out to an extent. During the land war and throughout the turbulent years of the 1880s, during which, according to Virginia Crossman, the army began to lose its veneer of political impartiality in Ireland, officers came to the aid of landlords at the request of the civil power, providing a public face of authority.[48] In 1872 and 1886, for example, officers and enlisted men were deployed in large numbers to quell rioting in Belfast, as they were in other places throughout the 1880s and 1990s.[49] These were consequential, large-scale deployments, but they attracted little comment at the time. Two similar occasions twenty years later illustrate the increasingly controversial political position of the officer corps: army officers manoeuvred out of the civil authorities' contentious and impolitic request for military support during the 1913 Dublin Lockout, and the possibility of large-scale deployment to Ulster in order to enforce Home Rule was the root cause of one of the most significant events in the history of British Army politics, the 1914 Curragh 'mutiny'.[50] Army officers' traditional mistrust of politicians, in this incident and others, was clearly a highly significant factor despite the 'politicisation' of the officer corps in this period.[51]

According to Lawrence McBride, the professionalisation of the civil service, which allowed for a larger segment of the middle class to enter the Irish elite, contributed to the changing political landscape in late nineteenth- and early twentieth-century Dublin.[52] In *The Irish Establishment*, Fergus Campbell notes a correlation between religion and political affiliation among members of the aristocracy in Ireland, with Catholic landowners more likely to identify with the Liberal or Home Rule parties; however, his analysis does not consider the officer corps, and thus the extent to which this was also true for the military.[53] On the one hand, officers were deeply interconnected with the aristocracy and for the most part retained an aristocratic mentality. On the other hand, however, the officer corps was becoming gradually 'democratised', opened to the middle class in the late Victorian and Edwardian periods, which may have induced a slight 'greening' effect.

There are tantalising hints that this might be the case: in the period preceding the First World War, some rank-and-file Irish soldiers certainly displayed nationalist sympathies;[54] and during the Great War, questions were posed about the wisdom of raising a brigade from the Irish Volunteers, and whether or not staffing it with Irish (and therefore, in the official mind, Catholic and Nationalist) officers would lead to a dangerous security risk.[55] We must, of course, be wary of assuming that religion or class maps neatly onto political persuasion, but nonetheless the relationship between professionalism and nationalism in the officer corps, and the extent to which a 'greening' took place, is an important consideration. The Army's allegiance to the Crown, and its close institutional links with the largely unionist landowning class in Ireland, provided potential obstacles and embarrassments for nationalist officers.

THE ARMY, IRISH OFFICERS, AND THE BRITISH EMPIRE

From the end of the Crimean War to the beginning of the twentieth century, the day-to-day concerns of the military lay not in the possibility of another war with a European great power, but with the more immediate imperative of keeping order in British colonies overseas. Imperial service was popular among officers for several reasons: it allowed them to trade a routine and unexciting existence in a home barracks for the excitement of the colonies; colonial warfare provided experience and prestige to an officer, above that of his counterparts on home service; colonial conflicts carried with them opportunities for rapid advancement; and the regiments of imperial forces, predominantly those of the Indian Army, provided better opportunities for pay and promotion to impoverished or non-aristocratic officers.[56] Michael Silvestri's important inquiry into colonial Irishness, *Ireland and India*, contextualises the longstanding popularity of imperial service, and argues that it contributed a great deal to Irish identity, particularly in Ulster, where Empire Day was 'redefined as a celebration of Protestantism and Unionism' around the turn of the twentieth century.[57]

A flavour of the Irish officer's life on colonial service can be gleaned from the war diary of Colonel Bryan Mahon for the year 1900, which takes us from January mornings at the Kildare Street Club in Dublin, to dining with Cape Town society in April en route to the frontlines of the Boer War. His time at the front was short, as he was wounded in combat in the same month and brought to the rear to convalesce. By September he had resumed light duties, disciplining drunken soldiers in the guard-room in a camp near Bloemfontein. Mahon visited headquarters to meet with fellow Irish commanders Lord Roberts and George White in October, and closed out the year in South Africa, recording that he had repaid unspecified debts to a fellow officer in December.[58]

As well as underlining the importance of socialisation to officers' lives, accounts like Mahon's reveal the unavoidable presence of colonial violence in the lives of Irish officers in the overseas empire. This was an intrinsic aspect of army officers' identity, underlying their attitudes to race and ethnicity, citizenship, culture, revolution, and social change—all of which, in turn, constitute aspects of identity. It is important to note, however, that colonial violence was highly contextual; attitudes and methods were not simply 'imported' back and forth between metropole and periphery. The highly visible militarism of imperial rule had a definite impact on all aspects of European society, but the use of violence as a method of rule cannot be extricated from its racial and colonial context.[59] As subsequent chapters will illustrate, the experience of differing conditions of colonial warfare—whether in the huge and elaborate organisational structure of the Indian Army, smaller forces engaged in frontier policing in the African interior, or full-scale warfare in South Africa—predisposed officers to view Irish issues in diverse ways. Additionally, officers on imperial service reacted differently to distant developments in Ireland than officers who were stationed in the country.

Throughout the nineteenth century and into the twentieth, Irishmen, predominantly but not exclusively from urban counties, made enthusiastic imperialists in colonial military and police units. Colonies and dependencies were where the real job of the British soldier was done—where campaigns were conducted, and where the army could take a more active role in administration.[60] It was considered anomalous and slightly deviant for an officer to take an active interest in the staff college or the War Office, though officers who did, such as the County Longford native Henry Wilson, could end up in positions of high command if they were shrewd.[61]

PLACING THE MILITARY IN IRISH SOCIETY

When sketching the contours of an Irish officer corps, of particular salience is the extent to which aristocratic officers' actions in 'aid to the civil power' operations—during riots and evictions from encumbered estates—can be conceived of as constituting a defence of their class interests. This is most clearly manifest in Irish officers' reactions to the Land War, which were characteristic of the attitudes of the military in general in late nineteenth-century Ireland. It was not generally regarded as a desirable or exciting posting: according to Muenger, 'for an officer, duty in Ireland was a three-year testimonial to the glories of leisure and the respectability of amateurism. As long as the country was quiet, an officer was surprisingly unhampered by official obligations.'[62] While officers with commercial or landed interests saw a benefit in remaining close to their property, especially during the tumult of the Land War, and Irish officers may have prioritised proximity to family, Ireland provided neither the opportunities for advancement and experience of the colonies nor the capability for social networking of the fashionable cavalry and guards regiments of London.[63] While this might suggest that a posting in Ireland was more desirable for officers of an Irish background, in fact officers from throughout the United Kingdom could be found in Irish regiments, and Irish officers often joined English, Welsh, Scottish, and Indian regiments.

Particularly in isolated garrison towns, the officer's mess was a centre for social gatherings and a focal point for high society. The memoirs of Nora Robertson recount many such occasions. She divides the officer corps in Ireland into four distinct categories based on class: the wealthiest and most established landowners would send their sons to a Guards regiment, the 10th Hussars or the Navy; the second-tier aristocracy officered rifle brigades, other cavalry regiments, artillery, and the Highland regiments; the third tier of 'less solvent country gentry' officered Irish regiments or the Indian Army; finally, the professional class with no claim to

land or title may have had the economic means to enter the most fashionable and expensive regiments, but did not have the social capital to interact with the aristocratic officers they found there.[64] As Michael McConville
notes, there is a commonality here: 'in all four of Mrs. Robertson's rows it
was taken almost for granted that the proper role in life for a young man
was as an officer in one of the British armed services.'[65] The social interrelations between the civilian and military elites in Ireland provided an
opportunity for the mutual reinforcement of status—officers were accepted
as social equals by Irish elites, while elite civilians sought connections with
the army as an outward display of affinity for Britishness, the empire and
the symbolic 'crowned harp' which the royal Irish regiments displayed
prominently in their insignia. In more pragmatic terms, one source points
out the importance of the officer corps in providing a supply of eligible
young single men to the diffuse and isolated world of rural Irish aristocracy.[66] Military service was a common bond among aristocratic Irish landlords; Fergus Campbell, in his study of *The Irish Establishment*, notes that
it was a common occurrence for the sons of aristocrats to join the army
instead of attending university, while waiting their turn to take over the
running of an estate. In 1881, over a third of the aristocrats in Ireland had
been army or naval officers.[67] However, as has been noted previously, the
primacy of the aristocratic officer was slowly but perceptibly diminishing
in the late nineteenth century, ceding ground to a new kind of military
officer of greater technical nous, but a lesser family pedigree.

The professional classes, both Unionist and Nationalist, had a slightly
different relationship with the officer corps than the aristocracy. Their
interest lay not only in advancement via the elite socialisation of the officer
corps, but also in the vocational aspect of a military career. They sought to
join the aforementioned majority of hereditary military families which
supplied the army with officers over multiple generations.[68] The primary
practical consideration for a middle-class man seeking a military career was
money—specifically, the lack of it.[69] While purchasing a commission was
no longer permitted after 1871, there were additional expenses to consider: for those without a public school education, passing the officer's
examinations required the services of a 'crammer' to provide a crash course
in the necessary academic and military subjects. If a commission was
awarded, a subaltern's pay did not stretch very far—it had increased little
throughout the nineteenth century, and in the 1890s amounted to considerably less than the average middle-class civilian Londoner's salary, and
certainly not enough to maintain a respectable household.[70] An average

London clerk received anywhere between £140 and £210 *per annum*, and could expect an annual raise of £10–20. Army subalterns, by contrast, received an income of less than £100, and less still if placed on the 'half pay' list (i.e. not on service), which was insufficient to cover their necessary expenses. Pay for an Indian Army captain, the highest in his bracket, amounted to around £1 11s. 5d. per day (Rs 563), which, after special expenses are deducted, is roughly comparable with a clerk's salary. Pay in the home army was about 20% lower than in the empire.[71]

However, the costs and benefits of a military career fluctuated over time, and additional social and cultural factors also played a role. David Fitzpatrick reminds us that 'the decision to become a soldier cannot easily be explained in terms of rational action.'[72] It is a relevant observation for the entirety of the period under consideration, as the economic incentives to pursue a military career were few. Due consideration must be given to the subjectivities of duty, masculinity, and identity which also undoubtedly played an important role. To a greater extent even than civilian service in the empire, the decision to enlist in the military required a particular commitment to ideas of duty, honour, imperialism, and an aristocratic vision of gentility. Officers made a trade-off between expense and prestige when expressing preference for a regiment. Local pride, family tradition, the opportunities provided by patronage, and territorial attachments were all powerful incentives to choosing a regiment—but other officers appeared to choose almost at random.[73]

While traditional accounts indicate that the majority of Irish officers originated from elite Anglo-Irish families, Elizabeth Muenger argues they were very far from 'monopolising' military careers, and the officer corps may in fact have contained more diversity than had previously been assumed—though she admits, the evidence for this remains 'fragmentary'.[74] Military life was certainly a comparatively popular career choice in Ireland: Peter Karsten has found that in the army of 1872, the ratio of Irish-born officers to English-born was 11 to 8.[75] Similar occupations were certainly not limited to the upper class or to Protestants: Irish Catholics constituted, on average, 19% of the Indian Civil Service between 1855 and 1913, and 30% of Royal Irish Constabulary (RIC) officers in the period between the 1830s and the 1920s.[76] To the civilian population, the army officer corps was a highly visible and meaningful signifier of imperial identity and of the aristocratic elite. According to C.B. Otley's 1966 study, *Militarism and the Social Affiliations of the British Elite*, though, the officer corps in Britain during the late nineteenth and early twentieth centuries was much less dominated by the landed aristocracy than is generally assumed—of his sample of 330 senior officers between 1870 and 1959, only one quarter were landed, while 39% came from military families and the majority came from minor gentry or professional family backgrounds. Despite this, Otley discerned clear linkages to the 'old ruling order'.[77]

By all accounts, the experience of an army officer in Ireland in the late nineteenth century was a largely pleasant one: daily military duties at a home posting in peacetime constituted little more than a morning's work: officers were expected to attend company orders at 10 am, and to discipline misbehaving soldiers, and in some regiments to partake in a bibulous lunch in the officers' mess. The afternoon was usually free for recreation. The social season, along with the horse racing, shooting, fishing, and sport officers were able to take part in during extended periods of 'hunting leave', gave an officer's existence the feel of a leisurely sojourn at a country house, rather than confinement to a barrack block.[78]

Other aspects of barrack life, however, were rather less savoury in the eyes of Victorian society. Ireland, as a particularly militarised part of the United Kingdom in the mid-nineteenth century, was subject to the Contagious Diseases Acts in the garrison areas of Cork, Queenstown, and the Curragh. These acts were the basis of the British Army's semi-official policy for the regulation of prostitution, and as such drew sharp criticisms from social reformers and early feminists in Ireland, and the Acts were eventually overturned following vigorous lobbying in 1883.[79] Attitudes to gender and sexuality in the British military remained highly restrictive; the army command set parameters for acceptable sexual activity as a method of social control, and as a tool to produce more effective soldiers following the upsets of the Crimean War, according to Elizabeth Malcolm.[80] On the Curragh camp, the 'wrens', local prostitutes who worked around the camp, largely served the enlisted soldiery; for an officer to openly consort with women other than his wife would have been a career-ending scandal—with a prostitute, grounds for total ostracism. However, what the degree of acceptable behaviour was under the officer corps' conspiracy of silence, it is difficult to say: Charles à Court Repington was drummed out of the service when it came to light that he was embroiled in the divorce case of Lord and Lady Garstin, although the unforgivable offense was not Repington's affair with Lady Garstin, but rather his continuation of the liaison after swearing to Henry Wilson, on his honour as an officer and gentleman, to break it off.[81]

On imperial service, in an environment of structural racial inequality, the social strictures surrounding prostitution were much looser, though in the late nineteenth century missionaries, reformers, and what Heather Streets has identified as the development of a culture of 'domesticity', were beginning to impose social boundaries.[82] On active campaigns, officers particularly were given the benefit of the doubt and assumed to have acted 'chivalrously' towards women. Oftentimes accusations of improper conduct, on the occasions they made it to a court martial, were simply dismissed out of hand.[83] Marriage too was highly regulated. The Curragh began constructing married quarters for officers and men in the late nineteenth century, but it was considered a general rule for officers pursuing marriage that captains could marry, but were dissuaded from doing so, whereas majors and more senior officers should be married.[84]

All of this suggests a deep importance for questions of gender in Victorian military life. The army sought to harness male sexuality to its own ends, while strictly policing the presence of women in military spaces. According to Verity McInnis, women's role in reinforcing codes of behaviour operated based on a ranked hierarchy, in much the same way that it did in civilian elite society.[85]

Barrack life insulated officers from the general population, and high-ranking officers, particularly staff officers who operated above the regimental level, had a different outlook to line officers. This is particularly manifest with officers who worked closely with the civilian administration, such as Colonel Alfred Turner, who was a district commissioner of the RIC in the 1880s. His position on the 'frontline' of the Land War, interacting directly with the people of his distressed district, afforded him a feeling of wisdom and moral superiority above both the rarefied functionaries of Dublin Castle *and* the insular, straightforward mentality of the line officer in his barracks, an attitude which is tangible in his memoirs.[86] This suggests a diversity of attitudes were present in the Irish officer corps. During active deployment, too, the attitude of the officer towards the task at hand appeared to vary, though in the words of one officer in the 1880s, 'At that time I, like most other people, only considered the effect and not the cause; the crimes were a plague to be eradicated by the most forcible means, but one thought little or not at all of the necessity of investigating the origin and cause of the offenses.'[87] While by no means the universal view, such testimonies suggest that officers with a more professional outlook may have been more insulated from the civilian population than others.

Irish officers were not blind to cultural forms of nationalism, nor were English officers in Ireland necessarily unsympathetic to the cultural and national aspirations of the Irish. Indeed, even officers regarded as blustering, dyed-in-the-wool imperialists by the nationalist press, such as Redvers Buller, displayed sympathy and even support for the oppressed in Irish society, and Alfred Turner, though a unionist himself, conceded in 1912 that opposition to home rule was to some degree fuelled by an unfair demonisation of Catholics.[88] Especially after the First World War, many Irish officers revised their earlier opinions of the national movement in light of its increasing popularity and successes. Unlike their English colleagues, though, they rarely underestimated the depth of national feeling among the population.

When it came to performing their duties, officers were naturally expected first and foremost to follow orders without question regardless of their personal opinions. While the few occasions when officers openly disobeyed orders are illuminating, it must not be overlooked that most of the time, in most places, military officers performed their role as instruments of the state, whether they liked it or not, reliably and without protest.

The interaction between officers and Irish elites was complex, administratively existing at arm's length but nonetheless reliant on interconnected networks of patronage and reputation. For example, the Lord Lieutenant could call on the services of at least one—and occasionally as many as twelve—military aides-de-camp, who tended to be younger aristocratic officers. There was a degree of autonomy accorded to officers in Ireland, as they reported to the War Office in London, and not the Dublin Castle administration. Attitudes towards breaches of military protocol in this period, particularly during flashpoints of public outrage, are intriguing indicators of continuity and change in this relationship: when questions of political sensitivity emerged in Ireland, the strictures of military discipline were often more honoured in the breach than the observance. During the land agitation of the 1880s, there were soul-searching debates surrounding the army's use of 'coercion', which were mirrored in later periods where parts of Ireland were placed under martial law, in 1916 and 1920–22. Serving militia and military officers also took an active part in drilling the Ulster Volunteer Force in 1913, a clear violation of King's Regulations, though no reprisals or courts martial were forthcoming in response.[89] The most spectacular breach of military protocol in this period was the Curragh incident of 1914, often referred to as a 'mutiny' in which aristocratic officers protested the prospect of visiting 'coercion' on Ulster unionists. For the most part, the War Office considered it impolitic to mete out punishments following the affair. By contrast, after the King's Own Scottish Borderers fired into a crowd in Dublin during the 1914 Howth gun running, questions were asked almost immediately and two of the commanding officers were dismissed.[90] Generally speaking, senior officers seem to have practiced a 'hands-off' approach to questions of Irish identity, and sought first and foremost to avoid embarrassment.

Against the intentions of the army brass, however, the officer corps was increasingly drawn into the contentious political battles over Home Rule from 1885 onwards, and by 1914 its politicisation was irreversible. The officer's role as a guardian of the status quo, supplemented, according to Alvin Jackson, by a moderate, conservative political posture of 'constructive unionism', degraded the politically disinterested position of the officer corps as nationalism and unionism became polarised mass movements, contesting the legitimacy of different forms of imagined Irishness. The development of armed militias drew officers further into the fray. The politicisation of the officer corps was regarded as disastrous by Irish officers, and precipitated the Curragh incident in 1914.

Hubert Gough, the Anglo-Irish cavalry officer who was at the centre of the Curragh affair, recorded the extent of the discussion about Home Rule and unionism in military circles, writing in his journal in the winter of 1913: 'I made no secret of my views. I however avoided saying anything in the Army which would tell against discipline, but at the same time officers in the Army were seriously uneasy & the Irish question was the subject of constant discussion.'[91] This was a unique development, and led to an increasing split between officers adopting a hardline Unionist position, and those more open to conciliation. Another prominent officer of half-Irish parentage (and Indian birth), Lord Kitchener, undoubtedly had a crucial effect on the army in Ireland—not least because of his efforts to encourage Irishmen, as well as other subjects, to enlist in huge numbers at the outset of the First World War.[92] This too was affected by the army's political crisis in Ireland.

During the First World War, particularly as the optimism of the recruitment of the 'first 100,000' drained away and the appalling loss of life began to sink in, motives for enlisting in the army become more complex. Irishmen enlisted not only for patriotic reasons but political ones as well, as the Unionist and Nationalist camps attempted to prove the worthiness of their cause through collective sacrifice.[93] The entire demography of the British Army was altered, from a small, decentralised force resistant to change, into a large-scale volunteer army, constituted not of professional soldiers but militarised civilians: labourers, bricklayers, shipbuilders, lawyers, students, and sportsmen.[94] The officer corps was no exception: commissions from the ranks increased, and Irish troop numbers swelled, as the attempt was made to raise three divisions from the island's inhabitants.[95] In the midst of war, Irish officers' placement at the centre of networks of imperial Irishness retained their importance, even within an officer corps of an unprecedented diversity. Clara Cullen's important study of the diaries of the socialite and military nurse Elsie Henry, for example, illustrates the convergence of the military, elite society, and empire which officers embodied.[96]

The 1916 Rising signalled a foundational upheaval for the officer corps and its role in Irish society. This undoubted turning point has led historians such as Dan Finlay to pose the question of whether 'the Easter Rising, and the way it was handled by the British Government, along with the forces it unleashed, left the War as merely an irrelevancy for [southern] Irish history?'[97] This question has since received a great deal of attention from historians, and it is becoming clear that the Great War and the Easter Rising can claim equal weight as turning points, for different segments of Irish society. The crises facing the officer corps, and the Irish elite in general, were deeply bound up in both, as is examined in subsequent chapters.

The situation that confronted Irish officers following the First World War was one of rapid and dizzying change. Officers faced a shrinking army, a political situation they did not understand, and—most disastrously of all—the prospect of active operations in their homeland. When General Nevil Macready arrived as the commander of British forces in Ireland during the crisis of 1920, he wrote that he was 'honestly flabbergasted at the administrative chaos that seems to reign here'.[98] As he wrote those words, he may or may not have remembered the occasion, seven years previously, when the Secretary of State for Ireland called him to Whitehall to ask his advice on the deployment of troops in aid of the civil power during the febrile and dangerous climate that prevailed in Ireland before the Great War, when 200,000 armed political militiamen marched in the streets, and the army command faced the very real threat of civil war. While this, too, was undoubtedly a moment of chaos for the Irish command, it was one in which Macready, and the rest of the officer corps securely placed within the Irish elite, felt much more in control than when faced with the uncertainties of the War of Independence.[99]

The period of martial law was a crucial one for the officer corps in Ireland. The aristocratic and landed officers found themselves on the frontlines of the conflict around the country. The wartime 'temporary gentlemen' who had joined the army from the volunteer movements became increasingly politicised and frustrated by the intransigence of politicians over the Home Rule question. Many, driven by economic necessity, re-joined the army; others found themselves engaged on operations in Ireland as part of the notorious Auxiliary Division of the Royal Irish Constabulary, a body of former officers which was responsible for some of the worst excesses during the War of Independence.[100]

The revolutionary period and its contestation over nationality precluded the British Army's impartiality in Ireland permanently, and this was due to its deep interconnections with Irish society. Hubert Gough reflected that because of his background 'it was many years before I could look on the Irish question without prejudice'.[101] The roots of this deep connection extended back into the nineteenth century: as noted by Hew Strachan, three of the most vocal and influential men directly subordinate to the Commander-in-Chief in this period were Irish: Garnet Wolseley, Frederick Roberts, and Henry Wilson.[102] Irish officers' connections to the affairs of their homeland can be read into their behaviour during the various incidents in Ireland when the military was called in to assist the civil power, which was increasingly contentious and politically charged. In Strachan's words, 'they were willing to split the army in their pursuit of Unionism ... to give their political objectives priority over their sense of professional soldiery.'[103] Clearly then, to some officers, the preservation of an intact Ireland, within the union and the empire, was an ideal held so deeply that they would jeopardise their careers for it.

After the Anglo-Irish treaty, the remnants of the military establishment in the south—in the form of its social clubs, its aristocratic members tied to the land, its retired veterans and their serving sons—retained symbolic and physical links to the British elite which did not reconcile themselves neatly with the narratives of the new Free State, or indeed of the partitioned North. In the face of the general resentment of the British military within the Free State following the excesses of the War of Independence, ex-soldiers were 'regarded with considerable suspicion' and as a group, their place in society became undefined and other.[104] Their experience was one of sharp changes, which concealed rather remarkable underlying similarities borne of the inheritance of six decades in which the Irish military elite enjoyed unparalleled social cachet and authority. In spite of all this, such men were not invisible: the British Legion continued openly and actively commemorating service in the British Army until the escalation of the Troubles in the 1960s.[105] How these remnants of the officer corps interacted with their still-serving counterparts in the North is particularly important, as their long-held and tight-knit institutional linkages attempted to weather the upheavals of partition and sectarianism. While their authority ebbed away with the making of two new Irelands in the 1920s, Irish officers' particular sense of identity, though distinctly diminished, persisted.

OUTLINING A NEW APPROACH TO IRELAND'S OFFICER CORPS

Historians of the late nineteenth century military have argued that elite officers remained a fundamentally reactionary force within the army, preserving a socially exclusive, aristocratic mentality and criticising the effectiveness of reform. This contributed to a well-defined institutional identity, which was permitted to sustain itself because of the extensive independence granted to line officers by their commanders, and difficulties in the chain of command and in military policymaking. The importance of regimental affinity, colonial service, and gentlemanly character all played a role in defining the identity of the British Army officer. On the other hand, this was an era of professionalisation, of the expansion and evolution of the officer corps, and of the development of a number of disparate Irish identities within it. The ways in which this tension between reaction and reform affected questions of class, society, nationality, and institutional identity, has yet to be drawn out adequately in an Irish context.

It is the central contention of this book that the army's failure to professionalise, and the adoption of a reactionary position by prominent military elites, contributed to undermine officers' moral authority in Ireland, and in turn facilitated the development of spaces where unionist and nationalist movements could position themselves as outlets for popular militarism in the general population. In reaction to these developments, the officer corps fell back on a sense of identity that emphasised Ireland's imperial connections; ironically, by resisting 'politicisation' in the army, officers retreated into a position which was becoming increasingly politically contentious. As the twentieth century progressed and the Irish revolution entered its critical stage, the actions of the officer corps irreparably diminished the moral authority of military elites and militarism in Irish society.

To carry forward the social history of Ireland in this period, then, a number of key questions must be addressed concerning the Irish officer class. The mechanism by which Irish officers were socialised into the corps is clearly of paramount importance, as is the placement of the officer corps within wider elite society. The demography of the officer corps has thus far been too narrowly assessed; throughout this book, therefore, the experiences of significant but overlooked components of the officer corps will be foregrounded, such as the small number of rankers who earned commissions in the pre-First World War period. A significant and disproportionate number of such officers were Irish, due to the role of institutions like the Royal Hibernian Military School in Phoenix Park. Also important to note are the handful of (former) British officers who chose to remain in the Free State after 1922. These personalities, embodied by the gentry TD and former officer Bryan Cooper, continued to play a key role in the social, political, and occasionally military life of the new state, but their stories have yet to be told within the historical context of the military imperial Irishman. Particularly interesting are the handful (one source counts five) of former British officers who gained commissions in the Free State Army—by all accounts an unlikely development.[106] The Irish military identity described in this chapter was complex and mutable, influenced by Victorian reform, Irish imperial affinities in the Edwardian period, the challenges of the Irish Revolution, and the curious cultural continuities which prevailed through the diverging Irish futures of the 1920s.

Notes

1. F. S. L. Lyons and R. A. J. Hawkins, eds., *Ireland under the Union: Varieties of Tension* (Oxford, 1980); Peter Karsten, 'Irish Soldiers in the British Army, 1792–1922: Suborned or Subordinate?' *Journal of Social History* 17:1 (1983); David Fitzpatrick, 'Militarism in Ireland, 1900–1922' in Bartlett, Thomas, and Keith Jeffery, eds., *A Military History of Ireland* (Cambridge, 1996).
2. A. J. Semple, 'The Fenian Infiltration of the British Army', *Journal for the Society for Army Historical Research* 52:211 (1974), pp. 133–160.

3. John Bew, *The Glory of Being Britons: Civic Unionism in Nineteenth-Century Belfast* (Dublin, 2009), p. 3; Terence de Vere White, *The Anglo-Irish* (London, 1972) passim.; Paul F. Power, 'The Anglo-Irish Problem: A Matter of Which Question', *Comparative Politics* 26 (1994) passim.; S. B. Cook, 'The Irish Raj: Social Origins and Careers of Irishmen in the Indian Civil Service, 1855–1914', *Journal of Social History* 20 (1987), p. 508; Jennifer Ridden, 'Making Good Citizens: National Identity, Religion and Liberalism among the Irish Elite c.1800–1850', unpublished PhD thesis, King's College London (1998), p. 14; Wendy Webster, *Englishness and Empire 1939–1965* (Oxford, 2005); Heather Streets, *Martial Races: The Military, Race and Masculinity in British Imperial Culture, 1857–1914* (Manchester, 2004), p. 158; Bubb, 'The Life of the Irish Soldier in India', pp. 779–780; Silvestri, *Ireland and India* passim.

4. According to Nigel Collett, the Irish connection of the Dyers, while it was identified by commentators at the time, was a misinterpretation, and the family actually had roots in Devon going back centuries. Reginald's parents' choice to send him to Midleton College was, according to Collett, 'inexplicable'. See Nigel Collett, *The Butcher of Amritsar: General Reginald Dyer* (London, 2007), pp. 1–16 passim.

5. Bender, 'Ireland and Empire', in Bourke, Richard and Ian McBride, eds., *The Princeton History of Modern Ireland* (Princeton, 2016), p. 347.

6. Simon J. Potter, *Newspapers and Empire in Ireland and Britain: Reporting the British Empire, c.1857–1921* (Dublin, 2004), p. 101.

7. The most extensive treatments of this topic so far are Michael Silvestri, *Ireland and India: Nationalism, Empire, and Memory* (Cambridge, 2009), and Kevin Kenny, *Ireland and the British Empire* (Oxford, 2004).

8. Richard Doherty and David Truesdale, *Irish Winners of the Victoria Cross* (Dublin, 2000), p. 11.

9. Oscar Gruzinsky, 'Career Patterns and Characteristics of British Naval Officers', *British Journal of Sociology* 26 (1975), passim. See also Aoife Bhreatnach's excellent compendium of Irish garrison towns, for reflections on the visibility of soldiers in Irish society: <www.irishgarrisontowns.com>.

10. For example, 253 students from the Queen's University Belfast Officer Training Corps memorial, including twenty-eight recipients of the Military Cross, are not included in the dataset of 595 as little information on socioeconomic background, or further detail concerning educational background, was available.

11. See Anonyous (William Cairnes), *Social Life in the British Army* (London, 1900), p. 168; Shane Leslie, *The Irish Tangle for English Readers* (London, 1946), pp. 150–151; F. P. Crozier, *The Men I Killed* (Belfast, 2002), p. 8; Steven O'Connor, *Irish Officers in the British Armed Forces* (London,

2014), p. 35; David Cannadine, *The Decline and Fall of the British Aristocracy* (London, 1996), pp. 269–271.

12. Catherine Nash, Bryonie Reid and Brian Graham, eds., *Partitioned Lives: The Irish Borderlands* (Farnham, 2013), p. 26; John Bew unpacks these distinctions in *The Glory of Being Britons: Civic Unionism in Nineteenth-Century Belfast* (Dublin, 2009), pp. 3–4.

13. Lewis H. Gann and Peter Duignan, *The Rulers of British Africa, 1870–1914* (London, 1978), p. 91.

14. Nora Robertson, *Crowned Harp* (Dublin, 1960), pp. 37–38. Her father, a Colonel, was of course not an aristocrat; but as a career officer, the rural gentry milieu was the world into which he was socialised.

15. Brian Inglis, *West Briton* (London, 1962), pp. 10–12.

16. Harold Perkin, *The Rise of Professional Society: England Since 1880* (London, 1989), p. 91.

17. An example of the networks of socialisation in clubland outside of Dublin can be found in Peter Hession, 'Mapping the Establishment in Edwardian Ireland' in Crowley, John, Donal Ó Drisceoil, Mike Murphy, and John Borgonovo, eds., *Atlas of the Irish Revolution* (Cork, 2017).

18. Robertson, *Crowned Harp*, p. 74; Inglis, *West Briton*, p. 33.

19. Homan Potterton, quoted in Robert Tobin, '"Tracing Again the Tiny Snail Track": Southern Protestant Memoir Since 1950', *The Yearbook of English Studies* 35 (2005), p. 178.

20. See Eugenio Biagini, 'The Protestant Minority in Southern Ireland', *Historical Journal* 55:4 (2012), pp. 1163–1164.

21. Samuel J. Watson, 'Professionalism, Social Attitudes, and Civil-Military Accountability in the United States Army Officer Corps, 1815–1846', unpublished PhD thesis, Rice University, 1996, p. 18.

22. Halik Kochanski, 'Field Marshall Viscount Wolseley: A Reformer at the War Office', unpublished PhD thesis, King's College London, 1996, pp. 240–241.

23. Brian Bond, *The Victorian Army and the Staff College 1854–1914* (London, 1972), pp. 124–126.

24. Brigadier A. E. C. Bredin, *A History of the Irish Soldier* (Belfast, 1987), p. 357.

25. Bond, *The Victorian Army*, pp. 117, 122–123.

26. David French, *Military Identities: The Regimental System, the British Army, and the British People, c.1870–2000* (Oxford, 2005), p. 146.

27. István Deák, *Beyond Nationalism: A Social and Political History of the Habsburg Officer Corps, 1848–1918* (Oxford, 1990), pp. 163–164.

28. Gunther E. Rothenberg, 'Nobility and Military Careers: The Hapsburg Officer Corps, 1740–1914', *Military Affairs* 40 (1976), p. 183.

29. Fergus Campbell, *The Irish Establishment, 1879–1914* (Oxford, 2009), p. 27.

30. John Bushnell, 'The Tsarist Officer Corps, 1881–1914: Customs, Duties, Inefficiency', *The American Historical Review* 86 (1981), pp. 757–759 passim; Gregory Vitarbo, 'Nationality Policy and the Russian Imperial Officer Corps, 1905–1914', *Slavic Review* 66 (2007), p. 694.

31. Peter Kenez, 'Russian Officer Corps before the Revolution: The Military Mind', *The Russian Review* 31 (1971), p. 231; J. E. O. Screen, 'Marshal Mannerheim: The Years of Preparation', *Slavonic and East European Review* 43 (1965), p. 296.

32. Gordon A. Craig, *The Politics of the Prussian Army, 1640–1945* (London, 2007), pp. 236–237.

33. Bond, *The Victorian Army*, pp. 146–147.

34. Elizabeth Muenger, *The British Military Dilemma in Ireland* (Lawrence, KS, 1991), p. 13.

35. French, *Military Identities*, p. 146.

36. See Wendy Webster, *Englishness and Empire* (Oxford, 2005).

37. Craig, *The Politics of the Prussian Army*, p. 236.

38. Hew Strachan, *The Politics of the British Army* (Oxford, 1997), pp. 74–75.

39. Virginia Crossman, 'The Army and Law and Order in the Nineteenth Century' in Bartlett, Thomas, and Keith Jeffery, eds., *A Military History of Ireland* (Cambridge, 1996), p. 376.

40. Strachan, *The Politics of the British Army*, p. 15.

41. French, *Military Identities*, p. 32; Robertson, *Crowned Harp*, p. 102.

42. Campbell, *The Irish Establishment*; Thomas P. Dooley, *Irishmen or English Soldiers? The Times and World of a Southern Catholic Irishman (1876–1916) Enlisting in the British Army during the First World War* (Liverpool, 1995); Keith Jeffery, ed., *An Irish Empire? Aspects of Ireland and the British Empire* (Manchester, 1996); John Horne, ed., *Our War: Ireland and the Great War* (Dublin, 2008).

43. Kevin Kenny, *Ireland and the British Empire* (Oxford, 2004), p. 93; Hiram Morgan, 'Empire Building: An Uncomfortable Irish Heritage', *Linen Hall Review* 10 (1993), pp. 8–11; for an opposing view, see Liam Kennedy, *Colonialism, Religion and Nationalism in Ireland* (Belfast, 1996); Stephen Howe, 'Questioning the (Bad) Question: "Was Ireland a Colony?"', *Irish Historical Studies* 36 (2008), pp. 138–152.

44. See Jane Leonard, 'The Twinge of Memory: Armistice Day and Remembrance Sunday in Dublin since 1919' in English, Richard, and Graham Walker, eds., *Unionism in Modern Ireland: New Perspectives on Politics and Culture* (Basingstoke, 1996), passim.

45. Robertson, *Crowned Harp*, p. 101.

46. Dooley, *Irishmen or English Soldiers?*, p. 12.

47. Crossman, 'The Army and Law and Order', p. 377; David Fitzpatrick, 'Militarism in Ireland, 1900–1922' in Bartlett and Jeffery, *A Military*

History of Ireland, p. 379; see also Michael Silvestri, *Ireland and India: Nationalism, Empire and Memory* (Cambridge, 2006), pp. 126, 147.

48. Fintan Cullen, 'Marketing National Sentiment: Lantern Slides of Evictions in Late Nineteenth Century Ireland', *History Workshop Journal* 54 (2002), p. 164.

49. Soldiers from the Highland Light Infantry and the West Surrey Regiment were involved in assisting the Constabulary in quelling the riots. Mark Radford, '"Closely Akin to Actual Warfare": The Belfast Riots of 1886 & the RIC', *History Ireland* 7 (1999), p. 29.

50. Lydia Redman, 'Industrial Conflict, Social Reform and Competition for Power under the Liberal Governments 1906–1914', unpublished PhD thesis, University of Cambridge, 2014, pp. 183–186.

51. Strachan, *The Politics of the British Army*, p. 74.

52. Lawrence McBride, *The Greening of Dublin Castle* (Washington, DC, 1991), p. 11.

53. Campbell, *The Irish Establishment*, p. 29.

54. Peter Verney, *The Micks: The Story of the Irish Guards* (London, 1970), p. 15.

55. Terence Denman, 'The Catholic Irish Soldier and the First World War: The "Racial Environment"', *Irish Historical Studies* 27 (1991), p. 358.

56. T. G. Fraser, 'Ireland and India' in Jeffery, Keith, ed., *An Irish Empire? Aspects of Ireland and the British Empire* (Manchester, 1996), p. 78.

57. Silvestri, *Ireland and India*, p. 125.

58. Diary of Bryan Mahon, 1900. Mahon Papers, NLI.

59. Volker Barth, ed., *Imperial Co-operation and Transfer, 1870–1930: Empires and Encounters* (London, 2015); Joseph Clarke and John Horne, eds., *Militarized Cultural Encounters in the Long Nineteenth Century: Making War, Mapping Europe* (Basingstoke, 2018); Dominik Geppert, William Mulligan, and Andreas Rose, eds., *The Wars Before the Great War: Conflict and International Politics Before the Outbreak of the Great War* (Cambridge, 2015); Laura Sjoberg and Sandra Via, eds., *Gender, War, and Militarism: Feminist Perspectives* (Santa Barbara, 2010); Robert Gerwarth and John Horne, eds., *War in Peace: Paramilitary Violence in Europe after the Great War* (Oxford, 2012); Jill Bender, *The 1857 Indian Uprising and the British Empire* (Cambridge, 2015); Richard Reid, *Frontiers of Violence in North-East Africa: Genealogies of Conflict Since 1800* (Oxford, 2011).

60. Strachan, *Politics*, p. 75.

61. Keith Jeffery, *Field Marshal Sir Henry Wilson: A Political Soldier* (Oxford, 2006), p. 20; Watson, 'Professionalism', p. 18. Wilson's career, it should be noted, also benefited greatly from his early involvement in the Anglo-Burmese War.

62. Muenger, *The British Military*, p. 24.
63. French, *Military Identities*, p. 50.
64. Robertson, *Crowned Harp*, p. 74.
65. Michael McConville, *Ascendency to Oblivion: The Story of the Anglo-Irish* (London, 1986), pp. 249–250.
66. Terence de Vere White, *The Anglo-Irish* (London, 1972), p. 168.
67. Campbell, *The Irish Establishment*, p. 27.
68. Fraser, 'Ireland and India', pp. 77–78.
69. Silvestri, *Ireland and India*, p. 80.
70. Muenger, *The British Military*, pp. 15–16.
71. Michael Heller, 'Work, Income and Stability: The Late Victorian and Edwardian London Male Clerk Revisited', *Business History* 50:3 (2008), pp. 256–257; Harold E. Raugh, *The Victorians at War, 1815–1914: An Encyclopaedia of British Military History* (Santa Barbara, 2004), p. 253.
72. David Fitzpatrick, 'The Logic of Collective Sacrifice: Ireland and the British Army, 1914–1918', *The Historical Journal* 38 (1995), p. 1017.
73. French, *Military Identities*, pp. 50–53.
74. Muenger, *The British Military*, pp. 18–19.
75. Peter Karsten, 'Irish Soldiers in the British Army, 1792–1922: Suborned or Subordinate?', *Journal of Social History* 17 (1983), p. 36.
76. James McConnell, 'John Redmond and Irish Catholic Loyalism', *English Historical Review* 75 (2010), p. 86.
77. Cited in Strachan, *Politics of the British Army*, p. 15. The three categories listed above are not mutually exclusive.
78. Muenger, *The British Military*, p. 25.
79. In India, the Cantonment Acts, passed in the same year (1864), provided for an even more overt system of official army brothels, staffed by Indian women. See Philippa Levine, *Gender and Empire* (Oxford, 2004); Anne McClintock, *Imperial Leather: Race, Gender, and Sexuality in the Colonial Context* (New York, 1995).
80. Elizabeth Malcolm, '"Troops of Largely Diseased Women": VD, the Contagious Diseases Acts, and Moral Policing in Late Nineteenth-Century Ireland', *Irish Economic and Social History* 26 (1999), pp. 1–14; See also Sjoberg and Via, *Gender, War, and Militarism*.
81. Jeffery, *Henry Wilson*, p. 51.
82. Heather Streets, *Martial Races: The Military, Race, and Masculinity in British Imperial Culture, 1857–1914* (Manchester, 2004); Ian F. W. Beckett, 'Women and Patronage in the Late Victorian Army', *History* 85:279 (2000), pp. 463–480; Katherine Lyttelton, 'The Memsahib in British India', *The New Review* magazine, 1892. Lyttelton Papers, Queen Mary University of London Library NL/38/18.

83. Stephen M. Miller, 'Duty or Crime? Acceptable Behaviour in the British Army in South Africa, 1899–1902', *Journal of British Studies* 49:2 (2010), pp. 311–331; Philippa Levine, 'Rereading the 1890s: Venerial Disease as "Constitutional Crisis" in Britain and British India', *Journal of Asian Studies* 55:3 (1996), p. 601.
84. See Con Costello, *A Most Delightful Station: The British Army on the Curragh of Kildare, Ireland 1855–1922* (Cork, 1996).
85. Verity G. McInnis, 'Indirect Agents of Empire: Army Officers' Wives in British India and the American West, 1830–1875', *Pacific Historical Review* 83:3 (2014), pp. 378–409.
86. Alfred Turner, *Sixty Years of a Soldier's Life* (London, 1912), pp. 222–223.
87. Muenger, *The British Military*, p. 39.
88. Turner, *Sixty Years*, p. 179.
89. Timothy Bowman, *Carson's Army: The Ulster Volunteer Force, 1910–22* (Manchester, 2007), p. 46.
90. Muenger, *The British Military*, pp. 113–114; John Ross of Bladensburg to Augustine Birrell, 19 August 1914, Balfour Papers, British Library.
91. Hubert Gough, quoted in Ian F. Beckett, *The Army and the Curragh Incident 1914* (London, 1986), p. 37.
92. Miles Dungan, *Irish Voices from the Great War* (Dublin, 1998), p. 85.
93. Fitzpatrick, 'The Logic of Collective Sacrifice', pp. 1027–1028.
94. Ibid, p. 1022; Tom Johnstone, *Orange, Green and Khaki: The Story of the Irish Regiments in the Great War, 1914–18* (Dublin, 1992), p. 89; Henry Hanna and Bryan Mahon, *The Pals at Suvla Bay: Being the Record of D Company of the 7th Royal Dublin Fusiliers* (London, 1917).
95. Dan Finlay, 'Outflanked by Easter Week: Death in the Flemish mud', *Books Ireland* 226 (1999), p. 311.
96. Clara Cullen, ed., *The World Upturning: Elsie Henry's Wartime Diaries, 1913–1919* (Sallins, 2013), p. 4.
97. Ibid. p. 311.
98. Nevil Macready, *Annals of an Active Life* (London, 1923), p. 82.
99. Ibid. p. 171.
100. A. D. Harvey, 'Who were the Auxiliaries?', *The Historical Journal* 35 (1992), p. 667; D. M. Leeson, *The Black and Tans* (Oxford, 2011), pp. 107–108.
101. Hubert Gough, *Soldiering On* (London, 1954), p. 23.
102. Strachan and others refer to these men as 'Anglo-Irish', though I explain elsewhere why this term is generally a vague and unhelpful one when examining the social history of the Irish officer corps.
103. Strachan, *Politics*, p. 115.

104. Ibid. p. 147.
105. Leonard, 'The Twinge of Memory', p. 100.
106. Robertson, *Crowned Harp*, p. 153; Jane Leonard, 'Survivors', in Horne, John, ed., *Our War: Ireland and the Great War* (Dublin, 2008), p. 219.

CHAPTER 3

'One Ought To Do What One Can for People in His Circ': Patronage and Affinity among Irish Military Elites

My dear Mayo,
I have been asked by Charles Clinton to send a letter of introduction to
you for Major George Forbes, in the India Service … a clever and
deserving officer.
—The Duke of Abercorn, 1871 (From an extensive dossier entitled
'Patronage'.)

While the purchase of commissions in the British Army was discontinued in 1871, access to the officer corps was still governed by privilege and the patronage of prominent figures. These institutional barriers, in turn, influenced the institutional character of the officer corps. The experience of Irish officers in the late nineteenth century was defined by two factors: the first was this patronage mechanism, which governed the selection and advancement of officers and defined what was possible within the officer corps.[1] The second was the large representation of Irish officers in this period—as pointed out by previous studies, these numbers were vastly disproportionate to the population of Ireland relative to Britain.[2] The British Army therefore constituted a major social phenomenon in late-nineteenth-century Ireland.

However, this did not necessarily make Irishness and the British officer mentality happy bedfellows; there was a lingering, unofficial proscription on

© The Author(s) 2019
L. Sweeney, *Irish Military Elites, Nation and Empire, 1870–1925*,
https://doi.org/10.1007/978-3-030-19307-2_3

Irishmen officering Irish regiments, which seemingly persisted well into the twentieth century and speaks to a tension between these two identities.[3] Irish officers' position as an interface between Ireland and the British Empire remains poorly understood: Jill Bender has identified a persistent lacuna in the Irish historical narrative around 'pro-imperial' society and the experience of Irish imperial practitioners.[4] This chapter is about the world of these Irish imperial practitioners—the mechanisms of social distinction that governed access and affinity within the spaces through which they moved, and the way they navigated an identity that was at once Irish and imperial.

This is not to say that Irishness was in any way hidden; for the officers serving under the high command, as, in turn, for the rankers serving under them, it was a matter of significance and frequent comment to be officered by an Irishman—perhaps for reasons of novelty as much as cultural affinity. To see Irish officers commanding Irish troops was virtually unheard of in the regular army before the Childers reforms of the 1880s, remarkable before the formation in 1900 of the (almost) wholly-native Irish Guards, and still problematic at the time of the formation of the three Irish Divisions during the First World War. Despite the problematic aspects of officers' Irishness, then, an expanding cohort of Irish officers was nonetheless able to successfully navigate the intricacies of access and advancement in the British officer corps.

Getting In

With the 1871 abolition of the purchase system, which had been in place since the seventeenth century, the most immediate and potentially the most expensive of the numerous economic barriers to entry to the officer corps was removed. However, the backlog of candidates seeking a commission by purchase was still so extensive that in 1872 an impecunious young man despaired, 'so many candidates under the late rule remained to be absorbed that there seemed little chance of the open competition's being established for me to avail myself of it.'[5] The two essential components for a successful career as a British officer were still wealth and patronage; but in the late nineteenth century it was theoretically possible to hold a commission in some regiments without an independent income, despite the generally low pay. Regiments were still socially stratified, with those higher up the order of precedence evincing greater prestige. These still required a significant independent income, in addition to the complexities of aristocratic socialisation, to enter successfully. There was also, however, a third imperative which arguably was gaining importance in the final decades of the nineteenth century—that of professionalism. The implicit assumption of the old Wellingtonian army, that aristocrats made ideal officers by dint of their upbringing and social station, was beginning to be challenged by the changing nature of officers' educational and professional requirements in technical branches like the artillery and medical corps, and debates over the utility of inculcating in line officers a more intellectual approach to problems of strategy and leadership.

However, if the object of the abolition of purchase was to professionalise the officer corps by broadening its demography and reducing the aristocratic monopoly, it can hardly be said to have succeeded. In various studies of the officer corps in this period, it is revealed that its demography changed only very gradually between the abolition of purchase and the outbreak of the First World War. For example, the proportion of major-generals from aristocratic backgrounds remained the same between 1875—when men at that level of their career would mostly have entered the service by purchase—and 1912, when they would all have been commissioned post-1871.[6] Between 1896 and 1900, 15–20% of Sandhurst candidates were titled or came from large landowning families, and around 13% came from middle-class families engaged in business. An increasing percentage were the sons of officers from the purchase period, who were by and large members of the minor gentry.[7] Thus, while the gradually widening access to the officer corps may have allowed officers from a professional background to rise to the top and influence policy, the social character of the corps, as expressed by the majority of its members, remained distinctively aristocratic. As we shall see in subsequent chapters, the professionalism of the corps remained a vexed question well into the twentieth century.

If we are to understand the internal relationships and affinities of Irish military officers in this period, the first question to ask is: what kind of man would be likely to choose a military career? Prior studies of the British Army in this period reveal that motivations were complex, though it appears that family pressures, lack of alternative opportunities, a sense of Imperial loyalty, and a desire to do important and adventurous work all figured into the decision.[8] Contrary to the predominant explanations put forth for increasing middle-class uptake to the officer corps in this period, the desire for economic or social advancement cannot provide the whole explanation: subalterns' pay throughout the late nineteenth and early twentieth centuries did not compare favourably to that of an entry-level professional post, and the social desirability and acceptability of affiliation to a certain regiment still operated very much along class lines.[9]

An independent income was still a requirement for a successful career as an officer. As late as 1900, 29 years after the abolition of purchase, the Irish infantry officer William Cairnes complained, 'An outcry has recently been raised against the expensive mode of life practically forced on all our officers, a mode of life which forbids the possibility of any young officer supporting himself on his pay.' By Cairnes' reckoning, a line officer's expenses ran to £150 in excess of his salary. An infantry captain, on 11s. 7d. per day, would thus require an independent income equivalent to almost three-quarters of his army pay.[10] Cavalry officers required an independent income of over £600.[11] Indeed, some historians have put the upper figure as high as £1000 in excess of salary.[12]

Cairnes was writing in 1900, but other sources reveal that similar conditions prevailed throughout the period—the *Freeman's Journal* in 1877 advanced the opinion that 'Not the least reform has been made in the cost of living in the army ... On the contrary, the messing expenses were greater than they ever were. In cavalry regiments they are a vulgar scandal ... wise parents of moderate means should think twice before permitting their sons to enter [the army].'[13] In the 1870s officers complained publicly about the expense incurred in 'cramming' for the new competitive examinations, not because of a resistance to the professionalisation of the corps *per se*, but because it was feared the proliferation of officers from middle-class professional families, who could afford to train their children to pass the examinations, could crowd out the well-connected though less financially endowed sons of established military families.[14] It was the rather economically distressed officers of the minor gentry, 'of gentle birth and small bank accounts', in the words of one officer, who most felt the strain.[15]

The socialisation of individuals into the elite networks of Irish society eased the way into the officer corps. In the line regiments, connections to military families and recommendations from the landed aristocracy practically guaranteed entry.[16] For the branches of service which necessitated technical, professional expertise, the route was rather more peripatetic. William Bent, a middle-class student who went up to Trinity College Dublin to read medicine in 1872, is an example of an officer from a professional background. He initially intended to exercise his family's network of contacts to inculcate himself into the precincts of Dublin's intellectual elite: his father gave him many letters of introduction, and he found the two most socially and professionally well-connected contacts to be most 'useful' to him: one, an 'already graduated' medical colleague 'hunting a fellowship; the other to Lady Wilde who ... had been a former friend of Father's ... the mother of ... the since notorious Oscar'.[17] His decision to pursue a military career was borne out of necessity, after finding himself unable to effectively exercise this network, as well as the prospect of poor performance at university. The centrality of figures like Lady Wilde to Bent's burgeoning professional network highlights the importance of elite women as gatekeepers in upper-class society, as well as arbiters of acceptability and behaviour. Nora Robertson, Lady Londonderry, Lady Roberts, and Lady Dunraven performed similar functions in the regimental societies presided over by their male family members.[18]

William Bent received helpful guidance and advice from his brother Jack, who was already at Woolwich training to become a Royal Engineers officer and proved a useful contact, offering reassurance and insider knowledge.[19] Bent, later to become an army surgeon, was not one of those aristocratic officers who drifted effortlessly into the corps, facilitated by a lifetime of networking and family tradition—though the toehold in the officer corps carved out by his brother was crucial in securing his commission. In choosing the officer corps over a medical career, he writes, 'whatever happens with a Commission once in my hand I have at least *something* under my fist ... surely it is better to take an inferior but present thing.'[20] His letters and recollections give the impression that his motivations for joining the army are opportunistic, and also evince a general feeling that middle-class officers could not advance socially to as great a degree within the officer corps, as without.

Hew Strachan has argued that the proliferation of middle-class officers in the late nineteenth century led to an increasing sense of professionalisation and a corresponding decline in the aristocratic character of the officer corps.[21] However, the pace of demographic change in the officer corps was slow. In Ireland, apart from the technical branches like the Engineers and Medical Corps favoured by the Bent brothers, the aristocratic character of the officer corps was retained, and its values remained those of the landed gentry and aristocracy. Looking at the different political and cultural touchstones of upper- and middle-class officers, one finds an upper class which, until the First World War, was politically and culturally incestuous, mixing nationalist and unionist, Protestant and Catholic, Ulster Scots,

Anglo-Irish, and old Gaelic gentry together; the common denominator was social status.[22] It was the middle-class officer, Catholic or Protestant, without social connections, thrust into this microcosm of aristocracy, who felt under pressure to 'play the game' and adopt the most conservative of cultural identifiers in order to gain acceptance. There was less opportunity overall as well, compared to the situation in Britain: after 1907 Ireland had only two university Officer Training Corps at Trinity and Queen's, a scant uptake of the initiative 'founded, in the words of Lord Haldane, in order "to get young men of the upper middle class" from "the Universities and big Public Schools" to train for Regular and Reserve commissions'.[23]

The social sphere of the officer corps was generally conservative, aristocratic, reactionary, and founded on the dual loyalties of Crown and empire—but despite this outwardly facing, British and imperial identity, there is evidence to suggest that a tangible sense of Irishness, both political and apolitical, also existed in some quarters. Some officers followed the example of Wellington and disavowed their Irishness outright. Others treated it as a badge among many other markers of identity, to be worn when it suited. Others still became increasingly active in Irish affairs, as JPs or members of parliament, as officers in the Irish or Ulster Volunteers, and as key members of the Gaelic Revival.[24]

If one considers the strong feeling of militarism pervading Irish society at the beginning of the twentieth century, and agrees with David Fitzpatrick and Michael Silvestri that such a feeling 'transcended political divisions in Ireland', then it certainly follows that the officer corps—the epitome of elite institutional militarism—could present a space where nationalist, unionist and imperialist rhetoric could be subsumed by resorting to common notions of honour, service, nobility, and masculinity.[25] The military clubs, unlike other clubs, could not prevent officers of good standing from joining based on religion or politics—indeed, membership was practically compulsory—and so their capacity for mixing together different facets of elite identity was greater than the politically and socially delineated environments of other gentlemen's and county clubs.[26] While such establishments (Fig. 3.1) have been seen as preventing social interaction between unionist and nationalist segments of the upper class, the diaries, letters, and commonplace books of Irish officers suggest that class affinity trumped political difference; after all, it would have been completely impracticable to shun every upper-class nationalist from elite society in the capital and the county towns, especially considering that some of them would invariably be familial relations.[27] At the same time, the customary proscription

Fig. 3.1 The Kildare Street Club, Dublin: a locus for officers' socialisation into the Irish elite. *Alamy*

on discussing such matters in polite society certainly facilitated these interactions.

There were a number of avenues available to those who wished to pursue a career as a British officer. The most desirable method for gaining admission to the officer corps was through attendance at the military academies at Woolwich, for the technical branches, and Sandhurst for the infantry and cavalry. In order to gain access to these academies, a public school education was virtually required, with several of the more military-focused schools such as Eton, Marlborough, and Wellington offering specialised 'army sides' (classes), teaching to the academies' entrance examination.[28] The examination, while broad, intensive and very long (passes in eight papers, including at least one language and one science subject were required), could be conquered by rote learning, and the services of a 'crammer' were often employed to this end.[29] While there were certainly places available for university men like Jack and William Bent at

Woolwich and the Army Medical School at Netley, this avenue for officers of a professional background was by and large restricted to the technical branches: the Engineers, Artillery, and Royal Army Medical Corps (RAMC). Additionally, the numbers taken on from the university examination were small. William Bent estimated that in his year, out of 500 university applicants, only 49 were accepted.[30] Sandhurst, on the other hand, continued to privilege a public school ethos of games, muscular Christianity, and the old school tie when selecting its cadets.[31]

In the late nineteenth century, questions were raised both in public and in private about the apparent shortage of Irish officers, particularly in Irish regiments. As one commentator wrote in 1888, with reference to the army reforms of that decade, 'If we are to have territorial linked battalions, why in all reason should there not be territorial officers to lead them … officers of Irish birth or extraction were few and far between in this regiment of Irish soldiers.'[32] The argument ran that this was an outdated and unfair proscription based on an unfounded assumption of disloyalty on the part of the Irish. In the Victorian period it was rare for large groups of Irish officers to be found in regiments considered Irish. In 1879 for example, the 94th Foot, which would be merged into the 88th (Connaught Rangers) only two years later, sent 706 enlisted men as reinforcements to the Zulu War, of whom 457 were Irish, or 65%. Accompanying them were twenty officers, fifteen of whom were English, one Scottish, and four Irish.[33] By 1891 the military establishment in Ireland was considering avenues by which the numbers of Irish officers could be increased. A report from that year on the two government schools for the sons of non-commissioned officers (NCOs) and enlisted men, the Royal Military Asylum in London and the Royal Hibernian Military School in Dublin, noted with approval that there were at that time twenty-nine serving commissioned officers who had been educated at the Royal Hibernian, more than twice the number from the Military Asylum, and recommended: 'if it be intended, in the interests of recruiting, to increase the number of soldiers' sons to be educated by the State, I think the increase ought to be to the Hibernian School.'[34] This is notable as an early example of army planners searching for non-traditional sources of 'officer material', particularly in Ireland.

If entry to Woolwich or Sandhurst proved impracticable, a would-be officer could always seek to attain a commission in a militia regiment. This was a reserve force which could not be compelled to fight overseas, but which in times of war would be assigned to garrison duties. Not being a frontline force, it was considerably easier to secure a commission therein, and considering its local nature, it would be both convenient and accessible to members of the aristocracy and gentry. Many notable officers, including Oliver Nugent, Bryan Mahon, and Henry Wilson, fell back on the militia after failing the Sandhurst entrance examinations. Militia regiments had a long history; in the late nineteenth century they were integrated into the regular army in intervals through successive reforms, and after 1881 each militia regiment was attached to a regular army regiment. Every year a limited number of militia officers could attempt to gain commissions in the regular army through a system of competitive examination. William Bent recalls taking the competitive examination in 1874, where his own cohort of university candidates was joined by the two other classes of applicant, militia officers and candidates for 'open competition'—the 'front door' to the militia's 'back door'.[35]

Finally, there was the opportunity of applying for a commission in imperial service, in which vacancies were generally more readily available than in the home army. Popular options were the Indian Army, and, in the case of there being a 'small war of Empire' ongoing, the various units of mounted infantry and border gendarmerie in Africa, such as the King's African Rifles. This was a very common route taken by Irish officers from minor gentry or middle-class backgrounds, and there are many examples of clergymen's sons entering the military this way.[36] Commentators frequently noted that the stereotypical officer in a colonial regiment was heavily in debt, and had transferred to the unit in search of a sustainable way of life.[37] Pay was better and cost of living much cheaper in India than it was in England or Ireland, with one officer recounting that almost everyone in his Regiment's mess could afford to keep a horse and take part in the requisite networking and bonding activities of British officers, such as riding and shooting, polo, tent-pegging, and pig sticking.[38] It was in the overseas empire that middle-class officers were thus socialised into the army elite.

For all the attractions and opportunities of colonial service, mechanisms of class stratification also operated in the overseas empire: commissions in British Army regiments were the most prestigious, followed by the Indian Army, and then on down to the other colonies, and this was mirrored in the social class of the officers in each force.[39] The Sudan was considered a respectable posting; the West African colonies, 'the white man's grave', less so.[40] Living expenses were minimal, as the necessities of life were provided for officers in the cantonment, so a stint of imperial service meant the opportunity to save some money for when the battalion rotated back to the United Kingdom for periods of home service or training. After performing some frontline service, many such officers attempted to secure a place in the Staff College, Camberley, in order to 'get on' in their careers. Overseas service of course also meant greater opportunities to see action, and to garner a good recommendation from one's commanding officer after the test of battle. The kinds of qualities looked for in an army officer can be seen in a typical letter of recommendation, such as that written by Col. James Dunlap for the County Clare landed officer Evelyn ffrench in 1902 or 1903: 'Mr. E. ffrench served in the column under my command in South Africa ... He was in charge of the scouts whom he organized: he was a most efficient scout officer, hardworking, energetic and capable, and a gallant leader ... he behaved with great gallantry and was badly wounded.'[41] Gallantry, self-reliance, and 'efficiency' were the common attributes valued by officers, the former two inculcated by socialisation, and the latter an indication of trust borne of professional collaboration.

It was most unusual for men who enlisted in the ranks to be given commissions in peacetime, and only slightly less so for them to be granted field commissions in wartime. Those who did manage to break into the officer corps generally found a berth outside the regimental system, in the Paymaster's corps or as a quartermaster.[42] The internal logic of the pre-First World War officer corps precluded any extensive advancement from the ranks; as one officer put it in 1900, 'men will follow a "gentleman" much more readily than they will an officer whose social position is not so well secured.'[43] This comment is interesting in itself, coming as it does from the son of an academic, in a family of brewers, who entered the officer corps through a Militia regiment—a typical late Victorian middle-class officer.[44] Of course, even to those who had the contacts to try for a commission, or to put in an application for a transfer to a more 'fashionable' regiment, the economic barriers to entry were still a serious consideration, as is evidenced by this letter from the Assistant Military Secretary (AMS) to the General Officer Commanding Belfast District: 'in the case of Lieut. Atkinson, 4th Bn. Royal Irish Rifles, who requests to be appointed to a Commission in the Cavalry ... His Lordship the Commander of the Forces desires you to be informed that before he can recommend the application it is necessary that it should be guaranteed that the gentleman in question will have sufficient means to live in a Cavalry Regiment.'[45]

The Assistant Military Secretary was one of the key arbiters of officers' bids to advance their careers through social networks. They not only counselled officers to reconsider their decision, as above, but also enquired after promising officers and sought recommendations from their superiors. In January 1893, the AMS wrote to the commander of the Dublin district: 'Please call on Lt. Colonel Johnston, Command. 1/Bt. Munster Fusiliers, to state if he can thoroughly recommend Capt. Congdon as a first rate officer in every respect as regards military efficiency tact & temper, as it is only the very best officers his Lordship the Commander of the Forces can recommend for this special service. Lt. Col. Johnston should report his opinion confidentially on this officer in the fullest terms—pro & con.'[46] Above all, then, the officer corps relied on personal reputation—one might say 'clubbability'—as the mark of a reliable officer.

During the second Boer War, the varying new challenges of waging war in South Africa meant that many irregular regiments such as the Frontier Light Horse took part in the fighting and attracted officers of many nationalities and backgrounds to their banners. In South Africa, as in the early stages of the First World War, the overwhelming response of men of the 'officer class' to the call of combat meant that many who sought commissions were compelled to enlist instead; those who owned horses and rode enthusiastically favoured the cavalry regiments, though, as recounted in the reminiscences of the Donegal gentry officer J.G.V. Hart, many were uneasy in mixing with people below their own social rank.[47] Anthony Bruce, in his account of the change from purchase to a supposedly merit-based system of commissions, asserts that 'a clear example of the way in which influence continued to play a role in the latter part of the century may be seen in the rapid promotion of those individuals known as "gentleman rankers". These were men of high social origin who, unable to succeed in the competitive examinations, enlisted in the ranks and then after a short period of service were awarded a commission.'[48] An example of such a man is recorded in the *Belfast News-Letter* in 1894—John D'Arcy Evans, of the Royal Irish Rifles, 'a smart, young Irish officer who rose from the ranks' in 1886, though who then had to wait eight years before attaining a Captain's rank.[49] According to the 1901 census, D'Arcy Evans, whose occupation was 'landed proprietor', had to wait until he was twenty for his commission—later than some of his peers, but not to the extent that his career prospects were greatly affected. The seaside house in which he resided alone at Clontarf and the servant he employed are evidence that D'Arcy Evans had access to an independent income. The phenomenon of 'gentlemen rankers' returned during the First World War, as a solution to the necessity of quickly inculcating discipline and knowledge of drill into new officers.[50]

The transition from a small professional army to a large volunteer force in 1914 meant a rapid expansion of the officer corps, vastly altering its social composition. In response to Kitchener's planned expansion of the army by 100,000 men to fight in the First World War, the pre-existing commissioning routes were overwhelmed by enthusiastic candidates. Applications for commissions for the duration (for the so-called temporary gentlemen) quickly exceeded the available vacancies in the officer corps. Priority was given to men who had expressed some interest and demonstrated a level of commitment to training before applying, such as membership of a volunteer unit, a university Officer Training Corps, or a territorial regiment. The pressures on young men in universities to do their bit during the war were immense. Shane Leslie and his colleagues at Cambridge felt the pull of duty, despite their generally nationalist sympathies. Though Leslie himself did not volunteer for service—apart from travelling to the Admiralty in 1914 'to offer my feeble services ... not needed though I rowed once'—Leslie was deeply involved with the Red Cross on the Western Front, and indeed was in Belgium when the German Army took Brussels, narrowly escaping capture on the last cross-channel ferry.[51] Leslie also attempted to volunteer for the Royal Army Medical Corps (RAMC). His family was touched by the high mortality of officers in the First World War: his brother Norman, who had been granted a commission in the Connaught Rangers, was killed less than two months after the outbreak of the war.[52]

While Leslie was later given a service medal for risking his life in France, he cannot be said to have been part of the officer corps as a cultural institution—though he is an important example of an elite cultural and political nationalist circulating among members of the Irish military establishment. Leslie was acquainted with several prominent military Irishmen, not least General Hubert Gough, whom he hosted at the Reform Club on at least one occasion.[53] The consequences of this closeness among politically opposed Irish elites will be examined further in Chap. 6.

Members of volunteer units, the Unionist and Nationalist political militias which attracted widespread support across Irish society in 1913–14, were generally reticent about joining the army. A significant minority preferred to remain in Ireland to 'defend' their respective traditions and homes from each other; it was down to politicians and prominent officers attached to the volunteers to induce men to enlist.[54] The expansion of the army also opened the officer corps further to Irishmen in 1914—according to John Redmond, in his preface to Bryan Cooper's divisional history, 90% of the officers in the 10th Division were Irishmen.[55] Given the increased competition for commissions in the period of the First World War, it became imperative for men seeking commissions in 'good' regiments to make use of their networks of patronage extensively, even if they only intended to keep their commission for the duration of the war. Military families were theoretically in the most favourable position as far as this was concerned, though military officers were not always enthusiastic for their sons to follow in their footsteps. Colonel Maurice Moore, for example, initially declined to use his influence to secure a commission for his son.[56] However, the fact that he and many other temporary officers from military families did later serve in prestigious regiments speaks to the continuing importance of systems of patronage, even after 1914.

Getting On

Once a commission had been secured, the newly minted subaltern had to turn his attention to making a go of his occupation, and in so doing he still relied heavily on his contacts and acquaintances. A successful army career in the late nineteenth century relied on the officer passing a set of defined thresholds; if he was unable to secure promotion after a set number of years (e.g. if a Major was unable to ascend to a Lieutenant-Colonelcy after five years), he would be forced to retire and be thrown into the relatively impecunious circumstances of living on his army pension, which, according to one officer, constituted exactly enough money to cover membership of a gentleman's club where the officer could snooze in an armchair and await death.[57] As the time towards this forced retirement ticked closer, officers exercised their networks of contacts, imploring commanding officers and other contacts for transfers or brevet promotions. An officer with good connections and the requisite seniority in his regiment would be able to avoid the armchair and continue to the next stage of his career. In this way the importance of networks and cliques was ingrained in the functioning of the late nineteenth-century army. Some military men, like Major Richard Studdert, were not so lucky. Invalided out of active service in the Royal Marine Artillery after an accident with a field gun, 'for many years Major Studdert's sole income was 8/- a day [his pension], together with occasional small fractions of Irish rentals'. However, Studdert once again fell foul of unforeseen circumstances, and 'in order to meet legal expenses entailed by the unsatisfactory state of Irish land property, he had to commute his half pay in the RM Artillery', receiving a lump sum in lieu of a daily pension. Despite support from his military family (his father was an admiral), Studdert remained in a state of financial distress for many years and was compelled to return to service as Adjutant of the City of London volunteers, a position with little chance of promotion compared to his promising early career as an artillery officer.[58] Clearly, alongside the prospect of death or debilitating injury, impoverishment was also a significant hazard for officers.

The best-known example of officers using social networks to advance their careers is the so called ring of officers surrounding the Irishman Garnet Wolseley, Gilbert, and Sullivan's inspiration for the Modern Major-General in 'The Pirates of Penzance'. Wolseley, and his fellow Irish field-marshal Frederick Roberts, both gathered around them a network of protégés, men of proven capacity whose services would be specifically requested by the field marshals during operations. The apogee of this particular brand of semi-official patronage was reached during the South African War, when the 'Roberts Ring' effectively took control of the running of the campaign. Of the members of the Roberts ring on the staff— Herbert Plumer, Archibald Hunter, Hector Macdonald, Redvers Buller, Robert Baden-Powell, Roberts himself, Earl Dundonald, Herbert Kitchener, Reginald Pole-Carew, Frederick Carrington, George White, and John French—a majority had Irish connections, and the senior staff, Roberts, White, and French, were themselves all Irish.

Plumer was the first CO of the 10th (Irish) Division, from 1903 to 1904, though the Division wasn't a major presence in the Army until the First World War. Hunter, MacDonald, and Dundonald were Scotsmen, with no Irish connection. Buller came from Devon, though had served in Ireland during the Land War. Baden-Powell had no connection to Ireland. Kitchener, though English with a deep connection to both mainland Europe and the Empire, was in fact born in Ireland to English parents who had recently acquired land there, though he did not live there for an extended period. Reginald Pole-Carew was also an Englishman, though like Plumer, he commanded a division (the 8th) in Ireland, as well as serving as a JP and marrying into the ancient family of the Butlers of Ormond. Between 1910 and 1916, he represented the Bodmin constituency as a Liberal Unionist. Carrington, likewise, was an Englishman, though immediately before joining Roberts' staff he commanded the Belfast district in 1899–1900. Thus, of the twelve individuals depicted, three, the senior commanders, were Irish, four were not Irish but spent a portion of their professional lives stationed there, four were English or Scotsmen with no Irish connection and one, Kitchener, was English though spent some of his childhood in Ireland.[59]

There is little evidence to suggest that the Irishness of commanders such as Wolseley or Roberts led them to favour other Irishmen in the selection of bright officers for addition to their staffs. Roberts in particular rarely mentions or remarks upon the Irishness of his officers in correspondence. The Boer War nonetheless evinced a disproportionate Irish contribution and was an incredibly significant event for imperial Ireland.[60] The ambivalence of high-ranking officers such as Wolseley to questions of Irishness is not to say that this facet of their personalities was unattractive to the Irishmen serving under them; indeed, then-Lieutenant Maurice Moore wrote of Wolseley's activities in Egypt in 1882 that 'Matters there look not too bright but Sir Garnet is an Irishman & doubtless he will put matters straight soon.'[61] On St. Patrick's Day, 1900, Irish officers serving in Rangoon sent a telegram to Lord Roberts reading, 'Irishmen in Burmah send St. Patrick's day greetings to Your Excellency and fellow countrymen of all ranks under your command.' In response, Roberts spoke for his countrymen: 'on behalf of all Irish soldiers here and myself I tender hearty thanks to brother Irishmen Rangoon.'[62] There was clearly a sense of apolitical, culturally based Irishness that was expressed and even encouraged among Irish officers, of which these are but two examples. As we shall see however, the increasing politicization of cultural forms of Irish nationalism in the Edwardian period would problematise officers' sense of Irish identity, and lead the officer corps into an institutional crisis.

The developing political situation in Ireland in the early twentieth century cast a shadow over the officer corps. Officers' loyalty was always expressed in relation to the Crown and to empire—not to Parliament or politicians. The interaction between this conception of loyalty and the development of political Unionism will be discussed in Chap. 4. While there certainly were a handful of nationalist Irish officers, the corps in general presented a moderate unionist attitude which other Irish people could find contentious: an officer visiting an Irish regiment in South Africa lamented the situation at a dinner hosted by the Mayor of Cape Town, the Irishman Thomas O'Reilly, having for some time congratulated myself on being seven thousand miles away from the strife of parties, I took my leave with a last recollection of seeing his Worship the Mayor with a glass of the wine of his country, 'Jameson' probably, in hand expiating in an eloquent brogue upon the manifold advantages to his native land of government by a system of Home Rule; a proposition fiercely combated by the Colonel.[63]

In the overseas empire, questions of nationality and Irishness were approached differently by Irish settlers, civilians, and military officers—but they were present and visible nonetheless. The effect that this attitude to nationalism had on Irish officers wanting to 'get on' in their careers manifested itself in the social pressure on officers to conform to the example of high-ranking unionist Irishmen such as Garnet Wolseley, Hubert Gough, George White, Edward Saunderson, and others. Elsie Henry, a member of Ireland's cultural and military elite circle, writes of a remarkable turn of events when Captain De Montmorencey, an aristocrat and Gaelic revivalist,

> was asked to resign from the Naval and Military Club on account of being a Nationalist. He refused, whereupon he was told that if he did not resign, his name would be struck off the list. He wrote to the King, as being the most important member of the Club, and pointed out the flagrant injustice.[64]

De Montmorencey, who retained his membership of the club, illustrates the (clearly contentious) feeling among some Irish officers that military service, Crown loyalty, and a sense of Irish nationalism were quite compatible. Henry tells us that, just over a week after the Naval and Military Club affair, 'He is leaving his work as a county inspector of NIVs [National Irish Volunteers] and has got a commission in the Dublin Fusiliers.'[65] Clearly, there was a space in the military elite, though a problematic and contentious one, for officers who saw no contradiction between loyalty to the King and support for Home Rule.

During the First World War, the hasty amalgamation of the Irish Divisions, particularly the 10th, which included locating and engaging suitable officers, gives something of an insight into what were considered to be desirable traits in an Irish officer. Irishmen in the reserves of the Indian Army were called up for service, as were certain district inspectors in the Royal Irish Constabulary. These men were considered reliable as they 'united to a knowledge of drill and musketry a valuable insight into the Irish character', according to Bryan Cooper.[66] This was the first time Irish officers in particular were sought out to command Irish troops. Additionally, the Officer Training Corps at Trinity College, a bastion both of Anglo-Irishness and of the professional classes, was expanded significantly.[67] Major Cooper describes the way in which the men of the IX Corps, which included the 10th (Irish) Division, received their commanding officer, Lt.-Gen. Stopford: 'We knew little of him, but we knew that he was an Irishman and were prepared to take him on trust.'[68] This is indicative of the usual incidental references to the Irishness of individual officers made by other commentators. Clearly, a kind of common identity was important enough to be present in these men's minds, and to be given voice to on occasion, but it was often alluded to with a breezy inconsequentiality. As a sense of identity it seemed to be less important than other considerations such as professional skill or gentility, but it was also revealing of the community of interest amongst Irishmen in the army, at a time when new lines of demarcation were being drawn across commonly-understood Irish identities.

The development of Irish volunteer regiments and their service during the Great War had a limited impact on the general character of the Irish in the British Army's officer corps. According to many historians the constitution of the officer corps returned with 'surprising rapidity' to its pre-war state.[69] The advancing pace of change in Ireland, as well as the avowedly temporary nature of the demographic widening during the Great War, meant that Irish officers were truly 'outflanked by Easter Week' in perhaps a more substantial sense than many other segments of Irish society, returning to a rapidly changing political situation at the end of the war in which their social position became undermined.[70] Additionally, the high mortality rate, which applied to line officers and enlisted men alike, and particularly to officers, meant that career officers were replaced over the years with short-service men who returned to civilian life after the war, if they survived.[71] A number of the political personalities of the newly partitioned Irish Free State and Northern Ireland had served in the British officer corps during the war, most notably members of the Free State Senate and the civil service of Northern Ireland.[72] Whether or not their short experience of life therein had an effect on later events, it is undoubtedly true that the connections, acquaintances, and friendships formed in the officer corps retained a great significance in civilian life.

GETTING OUT

For those officers who lived to see retirement, life after the officer corps could require the maintenance of a strong network of connections. The provision of patronage remained an important part of the relations between officers and men, and among former officers. Career officers exercised their networks, where they could, to gain appointments in elite civilian roles which gave them the power to dispense patronage: as educators (particularly in the Staff College), as members of the home administration, or as colonial administrators. Additionally, many officers (indeed, a majority before 1914) were also landowners, and their position in the local community—as the inhabitants of the big house, as resident magistrates, and sometimes as the commanders of militia or local Irish regiments—meant that many former officers and men applied to them when seeking to advance their position in life.[73]

There are surviving examples of patronage between military colleagues which may be taken as indicative of the general situation. One such example is a letter of September 1893 from Major E.S.E. Childers, Assistant Military Secretary, to William Wheeler, a prominent Dublin surgeon and former officer of the Army Medical Corps. Childers writes, 'If you have a vacancy for a man will you bear in mind Patrick Donohoe, about whom Lord Wolseley is trying to do what he can. He was very unfortunate in (through no fault of his) losing an appointment at the Custom House … another man was by some mistake given his berth. So we are trying to get some work for him.'[74] Here we see how networks were important not only in order to advance one's own career, but also to fulfil the obligations of an officer and gentleman to those perceived to be less fortunate; an example of the very strongly felt sense of 'noblesse oblige' in the officer corps, which took the rural aristocracy as its predominant point of cultural reference. Major-General William Hickie, for instance, a man who spent the majority of his military career in Ireland and led the 16th (Irish) Division during the First World War, worked after the war with the British Legion to fund a furniture factory to employ Irish veterans.[75]

Irish officers attempted to keep in touch with their regimental networks. One example is the colonial officer Lt. Col. J.G. Hart, a Donegal landowner from a long military tradition who sought to track down his transatlantic comrades. A.S. Barchard, a brother officer, wrote to Hart saying, 'I hear very little of the Regt. now—there are a few of the old lot left and I don't know who will succeed Bliss in command. Pomeroy has only a few months to do ... and that will be the last of the WIR [West India Regiment] Officers to command.'[76] Hart was a frequent correspondent who did what he could for his former colleagues. His papers intimate that he was in some financial difficulty after the end of the First World War, and he relied on the reciprocity of his military network in seeking a solution. When a matter came up in front of the courts concerning his investments, he wrote to his solicitor and asked whether he might work with an old army comrade, Major Lipsett, on the case. Hart's letter perfectly encapsulates the sense of obligation and affinity shared by Irish army officers in the period: 'I should like to have Lipsett as he has often done much for us in France & Italy & I think one ought to do what one can for people in his circ. apart from which he has the reputation of being a good lawyer.'[77] Which of the intersecting qualities which formed the bond between Hart and Lipsett led to this show of consideration, it is impossible to say; nonetheless, in his demeanour there can be detected perhaps the interconnected affinities of a shared Irishness (both men came from Co. Donegal), a sense of shared hardship and tribulation (it was only a year previously that General Louis Lipsett, a relation, became the last British general of the war to be killed), and a strong sense of occupational affinity which, together, defined the cultural landscape of the Irish officer.

The situation was further complicated by economic considerations. Peacetime pay for officers, particularly those of the post-1871 generation who could not look forward to the reimbursement of their commission payment, was quite low compared to the middle-class professions, and there was accordingly a very immediate pressure for retired officers to make a living—particularly if they had to provide for sons who were beginning a career in the services themselves. Temporary officers, who had become accustomed to combat pay during the First World War, were openly resentful at returning to a much lower rate of pay and an undistinguished civilian life after the war.[78] Officers who persisted in the army often went on the half-pay list in order to seek out more lucrative employment in other branches of government, most notably in the Royal Irish Constabulary.

Irish officers' career paths demonstrate the importance of connections to the British Empire, as well as Ireland. Service in the officer corps was an avowedly imperial endeavour; arguably, that was one of its major attractions. Michael Silvestri argues that the Anglo-Boer War should be seen as a turning point in the history of Ireland's relationship to empire, not only because of the great number of Irish who took an active part, but also because this was the point when Irish unionists (and, by some accounts, the majority of Irish society) began to see themselves as 'Imperial Irishmen', couching their imagined Irish future in the language and ideals of the British imperial project.[79] For Irish officers, this connection was strengthened by the economic imperatives which linked them to the overseas empire. One publicly prominent Irish officer, Charles Vane-Tempest Stewart, the Marquess of Londonderry, writing in 1917, couches the nationalist movement (which he opposed) in an explicitly imperial context:

> Let me say that there is no difference between the loyal Nationalist programme and the Sinn Féin programme, the distinction lies in the attitudes of those two sections towards the Empire as explained by their leaders. Redmond so far as he expresses a definite view at all, claims that the feelings of benevolence which he undoubtedly entertains towards England and the Empire will ensure that separation will not be the result of the policy. Sinn Féin frankly states that the policy is intended to lead to complete separation ... the suggestion of Ireland as a separate national political and fiscal unit has never received support in the Colonies and must present a strategic danger[80]

In order to understand the linkages which constituted Irishmen's involvement in the elite institution of the officer corps, it is important to keep in mind that these connections were fostered first and foremost by a sense of shared social class—an affinity between gentlemen. Secondary to this was a sense of shared struggle, borne of surviving the 'trial by fire' of active service. Third was the increasing sense of regard in the twentieth century between officers as fellow professionals, even though this conflicted with a still-important aristocratic ethos. In his study of the aftermath of the First World War in Britain, Martin Petter makes the case that, by 1914, the professionalisation of the officer corps had advanced to the extent that the pre-existing officer corps regarded themselves as 'professionals' and the new short-service volunteer officers as 'amateurs'; a complete reversal from the pre-1871 officer corps, in which, as Strachan notes, the 'presumption that aristocrats and gentry cannot by definition be professionals—a presumption with which somehow the British army, but no other army, is saddled'—was predominant.[81]

Despite the imposition of competitive examinations and moves towards 'professionalisation', patronage persisted as a method of constructing and defending the elite position of officers in Irish society. Even as the officer corps in the late nineteenth century gradually incorporated a wider class profile and an increasing diversity of opinions, the social environment was still defined by the rules of the traditional upper classes. Once access to the officer corps was secured, however, the benefits of elite socialisation became available to those who met the predetermined criteria, and performed the correct rituals of social distinction. By embodying these rules and traditions, the Irish military tradition solidified its position in Victorian Irish society, and by the end of the nineteenth century, Irishmen came to dominate the senior echelons of the officer corps.

NOTES

1. See Edward Spiers, *The Army and Society, 1815–1914* (London, 1980), pp. 4–7.
2. David Omissi and Andrew Thompson, eds., *The Impact of the South African War* (Basingstoke, 2002), pp. 278–279; David Fitzpatrick, 'Militarism in Ireland, 1900–1922' in Bartlett, Thomas, and Keith Jeffery, eds., *A Military History of Ireland* (Cambridge, 1996), p. 383.
3. Some historians, such as Peter Karsten, argue that a proscription on Irish officers was not widespread, although he presents little evidence of this. Other approaches to Irish officers include David Cannadine, *The Decline and Fall of the British Aristocracy* (London, 1990), p. 268; Timothy Bowman and Mark Connelly, *The Edwardian Army: Recruiting, Training and Deploying the British Army 1902–1914* (Oxford, 2012), pp. 11–13; Donal Lowry, ' "The World's No Bigger than a Kraal": The South African War and International Opinion in the First Age of "Globalization", in Omissi, David, and Andrew Thompson, eds., *The Impact of the South African War* (Basingstoke, 2002), pp. 278–281.
4. Jill Bender, 'Ireland and Empire', in Bourke, Richard, and Ian McBride, eds., *The Princeton History of Modern Ireland* (Princeton, 2016), pp. 356–357.
5. William Bent, 'Fifty Years of a Former Day', unpublished memoir, n.d., Manuscripts and Archives Research Library, Trinity College Dublin.
6. Anthony Bruce, *The Purchase System in the British Army, 1660–1871* (London, 1980), p. 158. There would be no Major-Generals from the pre-1871 period in 1912 as if the officer had failed to secure promotion after a set number of years he would be forced to retire.
7. Ibid. p. 157.
8. Fergus Campbell, *The Irish Establishment, 1879–1914* (Oxford, 2009), p. 27.
9. Michael Heller, 'Work, Income and Stability: The Late Victorian and Edwardian London Male Clerk Revisited', *Business History* 50 (2008),

p. 257; Thomas E. Jordan, 'Queen Victoria's Irish Soldiers: Quality of Life and Social Origins of the Thin "Green" Line', *Social Indicators Research* 57 (2002), p. 85.

10. Harold E. Raugh, *The Victorians at War, 1815–1914: An Encyclopaedia of British Military History* (Santa Barbara, 2004), pp. 248–249.

11. Anonymous (William Cairnes), *Social Life in the British Army* (London, 1900), pp. xi–xii.

12. Anthony Bruce, *The Purchase System in the British Army, 1660–1871* (London, 1980), p. 160.

13. *Freeman's Journal*, 9 October 1877.

14. *Pall Mall Gazette*, 18 September 1874.

15. Horace Wyndham, quoted in Steven O'Connor, *Irish Officers in the British Forces* (London, 2014), p. 165.

16. Peter Karsten, 'Irish Soldiers in the British Army: Suborned or Subordinate?', *Journal of Social History* 17 (1983), p. 35; Halik Kochanski, 'Field Marshall Viscount Wolseley, a Reformer at the War Office', unpub. PhD thesis, King's College London (1996), p. 16; Alexander Bubb, 'The Life of the Irish soldier in India: Representations and Self-Representations, 1857–1922', *Modern Asian Studies* 46:4 (2012), p. 808; Oscar Grusky, 'Career Patterns and Characteristics of British Naval Officers', *The British Journal of Sociology* 26 (1975), pp. 39–40; Robert Given to Lord Mayo, 22 May 1869. Mayo Papers, British Library; George Atkins to Lord Dufferin, 1 July 1898. Papers of the 1st Marquess of Dufferin, PRONI.

17. Bent, 'Fifty Years'.

18. Diane Urquhart, *The Ladies of Londonderry: Women and Political Patronage* (London, 2007); Ian F. W. Beckett, 'Women and Patronage in the Late Victorian Army', *History* 85:279 (2000), pp. 463–480; Matthew Potter, '"The Most Perfect Specimen of Civilised Nature": The Shannon Estuary Group—Elite Theory and Practice', in O'Neill, Ciaran, ed., *Irish Elites in the Nineteenth Century* (Dublin, 2013).

19. William Bent to father, 13 June 1874, TCD.

20. William Bent to father, 22 February 1873, TCD.

21. Hew Strachan, *The Politics of the British Army* (Oxford, 1997), p. 15.

22. See, for example, Karsten, 'Suborned', pp. 35–36; Fergus Campbell, 'Who Ruled Ireland? The Irish Administration, 1879–1914', *The Historical Journal* 50 (2007), p. 639.

23. C. B. Otley, 'Militarism and Militarization in the Public Schools, 1900–1972', *British Journal of Sociology* 29 (1978), p. 330.

24. See, for example, Clara Cullen, ed., *The World Upturning: Elsie Henry's Wartime Diaries, 1913–1919* (Sallins, 2013), p. 40.

25. Silvestri, *Ireland and India*, p. 126.

26. Barbara Black, *A Room of His Own: A Literary-Cultural Study of Victorian Clubland* (Athens, OH, 2012), pp. 149–151; R. B. McDowell, *Land and Learning: Two Irish Clubs* (Dublin, 1993), pp. 34–35; Maj-Gen. Louis C. Jackson, *History of the United Service Club* (London, 1937), p. 122.
27. Campbell, 'Who Ruled Ireland', p. 33.
28. A. H. H. Maclean, *Public Schools and the War in South Africa, 1899–1902* (London, 1903), pp. 6–7.
29. C. B. Otley, 'Militarism and Militarisation in the Public Schools, 1900–1972', *British Journal of Sociology* 29 (1978), p. 328.
30. William Bent to father, 13 June 1874. Manuscripts and Archives Research Library, TCD.
31. Hubert Gough, *Soldiering On* (London, 1954), p. 15; John M. Mackenzie, *Propaganda and Empire: The Manipulation of British Public Opinion, 1860–1960* (Manchester, 1985), p. 181; Jeffery, *Henry Wilson*, p. 4.
32. *Belfast News-Letter*, 6 June 1888.
33. *The Standard*, 14 February 1879.
34. Military Secretary, Horse Guards, 'Report on Military Schools', 1891, Miscellaneous Letters rel. Army Matters, 1891–1894, National Library of Ireland.
35. William Bent to Father, 13 June 1874, TCD.
36. Spiers, *The Army and Society*, pp. 8, 11.
37. *Freeman's Journal*, 16 November 1877; L. H. Gann and Peter Duignan, *The Rulers of British Africa, 1870–1914* (London, 1978), p. 183; Robertson, *Crowned Harp*, p. 74; Captain Kemmis to Father, Delhi, 26 November 1913. Kemmis Papers, LUL.
38. Captain Roly Grimshaw, *Indian Cavalry Officer 1914–15* (Tunbridge Wells, 1986), p. 10; Alexander Godley, *The Life of an Irish Soldier: Reminiscences of General Sir Alexander Godley* (London, 1939), pp. 123–124.
39. Captain Kemmis to Father, Simla, 30 October 1913. Kemmis Papers, LUL.
40. Anthony Kirk-Greene, *Symbol of Authority: The British District Officer in Africa* (London, 2006) pp. 19–20; Gann and Duignan, *The Rulers of British Africa*, p. 171; F. P. Crozier, *Five Years Hard* (London, 1932), p. 44.
41. J. Dunlap, Letter of Recommendation for Evelyn ffrench, n.d., Evelyn ffrench Papers, NLI.
42. Bowman and Connelly, *The Edwardian Army*, p. 29.
43. Cairnes, *Social Life in the British Army*, p. xvi.
44. Roger T. Stearn, 'Cairnes, William Elliot (1862–1902)', *Oxford Dictionary of National Biography* (OUP, 2004, online edn. 2006).

45. Major Asst. Military Secretary to General Officer Commanding Belfast District, 24 December 1892, NLI.
46. Major Asst. Military Secretary to General Officer Commanding Dublin District, 20 January 1893, NLI.
47. J. G. V. Hart, 'Reminiscences of a Rolling Stone', Hart Papers, PRONI.
48. Bruce, *The Purchase System*, pp. 164–165.
49. *Belfast News-Letter*, 17 May 1894.
50. Letter from Capt. W. B. Rennie, HQ 16th Division, Mallow, n.d. (1914). Moore Papers, NLI.
51. Shane Leslie's Diary, 3–21 August, 1914, Shane Leslie Papers, NLI.
52. Shane Leslie's Diary, August–October 1914. Shane Leslie Papers, NLI.
53. Ibid. 20 December 1920.
54. Maurice Moore, account of the Howth gun-running and aftermath, 1914. Moore Papers, NLI.
55. Bryan Cooper, *The Tenth (Irish) Division in Gallipoli* (Dublin 1993), p. 13.
56. Toby Moore to Col. Maurice Moore, 30 May 1915, Moore Papers, NLI.
57. Maurice Moore to his mother, 16 October 1882, Moore Papers, NLI.
58. 'Information rel. to Major Richard Augustine Fitzgerald Studdert, RMA', n.d., Studdert Papers, NLI.
59. Stephen Badsey, 'Plumer, Herbert Chares Onslow, first Viscount Plumer (1857–1932)', DNB (OUP, 2004, online edn. 2011); Roger T. Stearn, 'Hunter, Sir Archibald (1856–1936)', DNB (OUP 2004); Roger T. Stearn, 'Macdonald, Sir Hector Archibald (1853–1903)', DNB (OUP, 2004, online edn. 2011); Ian F. W. Beckett, 'Buller, Sir Redvers Henry (1839–1908)', DNB (OUP 204, online edn. 2008); Allen Warren, 'Powell, Robert Stephenson Smyth Baden-, First Baron Baden-Powell (1857–1941)', DNB (OUP 2004, online edn. 2008); Brian Robson, 'Roberts, Frederick Sleigh, first Earl Roberts (1832–1914)', DNB (OUP 2004, online edn. 2011); Roger T. Stearn, 'Cochrane, Douglas Mackinnon Baillie Hamilton, Twelfth Earl of Dundonald (1852–1935)', DNB (OUP, 2004, online edn. 2006); Keith Nelson, 'Kitchener, Horatio Herbert, Earl Kitchener of Khartoum (1850–1916)', DNB (OUP 2004, online edn. 2011); 'Lt.-Gen. Sir Reginald Pole-Carew', thepeerage.com (2013), <http://thepeerage.com/p3867.htm#i38665>; C. V. Owen, 'Carrington, Sir Frederick (1844–1913)', DNB (OUP, 2004, online edn. 2006); F. B. Maurice, 'White, Sir George Stuart (1835–1912)', DNB (OUP, 2004, online edn. 2011); Ian F. W. Beckett, 'French, John Denton Pinkstone, first Earl of Ypres (1852–1925)', DNB (OUP, 2004, online edn. 2011).
60. David Omissi and Andrew Thompson, eds., *The Impact of the South African War* (Basingstoke, 2002), pp. 278–279.
61. Maurice Moore to Mother, 14 September 1882, Moore Papers, NLI.

62. *Belfast News-Letter*, 10 April 1900.
63. *Belfast News-Letter*, 6 June 1888.
64. Cullen, *The World Upturning*, p. 40.
65. Ibid. p. 64.
66. Bryan Cooper, *The Tenth (Irish) Division in Gallipoli* (Dublin, 1993), p. 23.
67. Ibid. p. 23.
68. Ibid. p. 44.
69. Martin Petter, '"Temporary Gentlemen" in the Aftermath of the Great War: Rank, Status and the Ex-officer Problem', *Historical Journal* 37 (1994), pp. 128–129.
70. Dan Finlay, 'Outflanked by Easter Week: Death in the Flemish Mud', *Books Ireland* 226 (1999), Passim.
71. Peter Martin, '*Dulce et Decorum*: Irish Nobles and the Great War 1914–19' in Gregory, Adrian, and Senia Pašeta, eds., *Ireland and the Great War 'A war to unite us all'?* (Manchester, 2002), p. 41.
72. Paul Bew, Peter Gibbon, and Henry Patterson, *Northern Ireland 1921/2001: Political Forces and Social Classes* (London, 2002), p. 28.
73. Examples of diverse requests for patronage can be found in the Mayo Papers, Cambridge University Library; The papers of the 1st Marquess of Dufferin, PRONI; Lord Roberts Papers, British Library; Doneraile Papers, NLI; Kitchener Papers, TNA.
74. E. S. E. Childers to William Wheeler, September 1893, Miscellaneous Letters Rel. Army Matters, 1891–94, NLI.
75. Jason R. Myers, *The Great War and Memory in Irish Culture, 1918–2010* (Palo Alto, 2013), p. 51.
76. A. S. Barchard to Col. G. J. V. Hart, 14 January 1923, Hart Papers, PRONI.
77. J. G. Hart to Cousin, 10 October 1919, Hart Papers, PRONI.
78. Taylor, *Heroes or Traitors?*, p. 111; Petter, 'Temporary Gentlemen', pp. 131–132.
79. Kurt Bowen, *Protestants in a Catholic State: Ireland's Privileged Minority* (Dublin, 1983), p. 34; Silvestri, *Ireland and India*, p. 125.
80. Charles Vane-Tempest to Mother, 27 November 1917, Vane-Tempest Papers, PRONI.
81. Petter, 'Temporary Gentlemen', p. 140; Strachan, *The Politics of the British Army*, p. 14.

CHAPTER 4

Ireland's Imperial Moment: Wolseley and Roberts in Command

*6 November: The Duke [of Cambridge] furious because I have
recommended Brackenbury to be Depty. Adjt. Genrl. He forgets I strive
to employ only the best men and don't care whether they be My Lord
Tom Noddy or Mr. Jones as long as I believe them to be the best men for
the Public Service.*

*28 December: He [Brackenbury] is of quarrelsome overbearing
temperament ... Indeed, I have looked upon him as 'not quite a
Gentleman'. Neither has he the tact of the educated & experienced
Gentleman.*
—Diary of Garnet Wolseley, 1884

William Francis Butler was a young Irish lieutenant from a minor landowning family of daily-declining prospects. Unable to muster the considerable personal wealth required to support an ambitious, career-focused officer, there appeared but few options open to Butler in the army, and he was considering resigning his commission—'selling out' for his bounty payment. Every other avenue he attempted was closed to him, and advancement by merit as opposed to wealth was an uncertain prospect in an army still lumbered with the purchase system, the abolition of which was still a year away. His last hope was Colonel Garnet Wolseley, a fellow Irishman who was quickly establishing himself as one of the army's rising stars. In 1870 he dispatched a terse yet effective request for patronage to Wolseley, who was organising an expedition into the Canadian wilderness, in the form of a four-word

© The Author(s) 2019
L. Sweeney, *Irish Military Elites, Nation and Empire, 1870–1925*,
https://doi.org/10.1007/978-3-030-19307-2_4

telegram: 'Remember Butler, 69th Regiment.'[1] The telegram served its purpose: Wolseley, who had met Butler two years earlier and remembered being impressed by the young officer, invited him onto his staff and thereby into the fraternity of officers who would later become known as the Wolseley Ring. The officers who ventured into the wilds of Manitoba with Wolseley in 1870 to combat the Red River rebellion, including Butler, would go on to become some of the most successful and influential senior officers of the late-Victorian army. Wolseley himself would continue to rise through the ranks, becoming Commander-in-Chief in Ireland in 1890.

On the Northwest Frontier of British India, a world away from Manitoba, an undistinguished middle-aged scion of a County Antrim aristocratic family, Major George Stuart White, caught the eye of another of the prominent imperial Irishmen of the age, Frederick Roberts, in 1879. They formed a professional and personal friendship, and White benefited greatly from the patronage and promotion that came with existing within the orbit of Roberts's brightly-shining star. By 1893 White had risen to become Roberts's replacement as Commander-in-Chief in India.[2] He, and other members of Roberts's own 'ring' of officers, would also attain great prominence in the British Army, particularly in the period of the second Boer War. These are but two examples among many of the potential benefits of seeking the patronage of these two rival Irish officers in the late nineteenth century, and in taking advantage of staff appointments under their command in India, Africa, and Ireland.

This chapter concerns the careers of Wolseley and Roberts, and the way that their pre-eminence in the late-Victorian officer corps influenced questions of imperial Irishness, professionalism, and patronage. The two men were quite similar in background: not only were they both Irishmen who would become the most successful soldiers of their era, they were also of similar age, and were both the products of military families—Roberts was born in Cawnpore to the Commander of the Bengal European Regiment in 1832,[3] and Wolseley in Dublin in 1833 to a retired Major of the Borderers. They both had Irish mothers. Their differences, as will become clear, were in their socialisation into the officer corps and their sense of Irishness. They were awarded their commissions along with a cohort of Irishmen who would become particularly successful senior officers, though none would garner quite their level of acclaim. The creation of Wolseley's and Roberts's 'rings' of officers would have an instrumental effect, directing the trajectory of the officer corps of the British imperial armies right up until the outbreak of the First World War. As successive

Commanders-in-Chief in Ireland in the 1890s, they were also important influences on other Irish officers in their interaction with the politics and society of Ireland in the late nineteenth century. The Irish officers who benefited from Wolseley's and Roberts's patronage are exemplary of the interaction between Irishness and imperial soldiering in the late nineteenth century. Their visions were crucial in taking an officer corps which, at the time of their commissioning, was 'near its nadir in terms of efficiency and competency' and, eventually, in transforming its chequered record of defeats and inefficiency into one reflecting a more professional and effective imperial force.[4] The officer corps began the twentieth century on the way to a victory in South Africa that would precipitate a raucous spirit of imperial triumphalism in Britain and Ireland, with Roberts and his staff at the helm.

This transformation was not straightforward. The officer corps continued to rely on decentralised networks of trust and regimental affinity, rightly viewed by many officers as a major strength of the British system. Wolseley's vision of professionalism and his relationships with his staff officers will be discussed in this context, as will his complex relationship with Irishness. This will be contrasted with the other Irish officers in the 'ring'. Wolseley's sense of identity will be examined in relation to his stint as Commander-in-Chief in Ireland from 1890 to 1895, a period which has thus far attracted little attention from his biographers.

After 1895, the position of Commander-in-Chief in Ireland was handed over to Lord Roberts, just returned from India. The two men presented a striking contrast: Roberts appeared to wear his Irishness much more easily, in ways which are telling of differing attitudes to social placement, public profile, and sense of identity. Roberts's time as Commander-in-Chief in Ireland was cut short by 'black week', a string of British defeats in the opening phase of the South African War which threw the army into a crisis of command and necessitated Roberts' return to frontline service. His cult of heroism grew as the old officer once again went to defend the empire. The Boer War was the point at which the British Army reached a saturation point of prominent Irish officers, with the effect of producing an enthusiastic 'imperial moment' in Ireland.

An examination of Roberts, Wolseley, and the Irish officers who received their patronage reveals that military Irishness, though only a single point in a constellation of imperial Irish identities, and of less salience to officers' lives than questions of social distinction or patronage, was nonetheless an important and often remarked-upon feature of identity among officers in the overseas empire. The vexed question of the professionalisation of the officer corps had a heavy Irish element due to the influence of Wolseley and Roberts, and Irish military families were, more by inertia than intention, major beneficiaries of the resulting changes.

PROFESSIONALISM AND MILITARY IRISHNESS: ROBERTS' GENERATION

Frederick Sleigh Roberts was commissioned into the East India Company Army in 1851. Roberts sought specifically to enter the Royal Bengal Artillery, attracted by the unit's solid reputation, and by the 'smart turnout and picturesque uniforms' of the artillery officers.[5] While opportunities for advancement came less frequently in the artillery than in line regiments due to its specialised nature, Roberts was drawn towards the Royal Bengals for the increased likelihood of active service, and potentially for its professionalism and its popularity with Irishmen.[6] He found more commonalities with his fellow officers than shared Irishness: the defining features of Roberts's early life, his stints at Eton and Sandhurst, were shared by a large proportion of officers.[7] Indeed, at the end of the nineteenth century, the officer corps contained a greater number of products of the Eton-Sandhurst combination than those of any other educational background, and this was not a new occurrence.[8] As Hew Strachan and others have noted, this affinity of brother officers was reproduced from generation to generation, giving the officer corps 'the features of a hereditary class'.[9] Tim Travers's enquiry into the structure of the officer corps suggests that 'there was a strong tendency to perpetuate the way in which senior army officers, the aristocracy and the royal family seemed to "own" the later Victorian army'.[10] Getting on successfully as a senior officer, then, necessitated the acceptance of this tightly-knit 'old school' of officers.

Roberts, however, spent the majority of his career prior to the 1890s in India, at some remove from the aristocratic milieu of Chelsea Barracks and Horse Guards Parade. In India Roberts encountered a number of officers who found themselves on the subcontinent for reasons of economic necessity. Life in the home regiments was notoriously expensive, particularly in the regiments near the top of the order of precedence; for example, a Guards officer received just £70 per year more than an officer in a line regiment, while the living expenses at the Guards' Club in London were at least £240 per year.[11] A Guards captain, even if he took no leave, could not count on earning much more than that in a year, at 13s. 6d. *per diem*. Officers of the Indian Army, by contrast, could live the privileged life of the colonial master—the high pay, low costs, servants, and aristocratic pretensions enjoyed by most Europeans in India.[12] Before the Indian Rebellion, the East India Company armies were in constant need of officers and men, and officers lacking connections or wealth flocked to meet this demand. With the advent of direct rule in 1858, the demand for officers and gentlemen in the Indian Army did not abate.

Indian Army officers were not all from socially disadvantageous backgrounds; even individuals from large landowning families such as George Stuart White were enticed by the inexpensive, active life of the cantonment. However, as social networks scholars such as Gruzinsky and Razzell contend, the demographics of the Indian service were markedly different to those of the home army.[13] The extreme barriers to entry of the aristocratic home regiments had no parallel in the Indian Army. The constant expeditions to the Northwest Frontier also provided ample opportunities for officers to distinguish themselves—or indeed, to disgrace themselves—providing some scope for advancement by merit. Roberts thus had at his disposal a group of ambitious and (relatively) diverse officers from whom to construct a coterie of talented individuals.

Garnet Wolseley, on the other hand, while having an old and famous family name, did not have the opportunity to go to Eton or Sandhurst. In his autobiography, Wolseley's pride in his ancestry is clear to see, when he discusses the link between his bloodline and that of the Wolseley baronets of Stafford, 'one of the very few that could trace its direct descent in the male line from ancestors who had lived before "the [Norman] Conquest" on lands still held by us, their descendants.'[14] A century of life in Ireland, following the professions of politics and soldiering, had not brought Wolseley's branch of the family wealth or prestige, however. While the General's later success would enable him to mix with the officers of the home armies who did conform to the elite stereotype, Garnet Wolseley began his career by following the path of other impecunious officers to India, after being granted a commission without purchase by the Duke of Wellington in 1852, in recognition of his father's military service.[15] On his way, he was first posted to a depot in Chatham, which, according to his memoirs, was 'over-crowded with boy recruits, chiefly obtained from Ireland, and of ensigns of all ages waiting for conveyance to India … nine out of ten of us were very poor, and looked forward to an Indian career where high pay enabled the infantry officer to live without assistance from home'.[16] He recalled,

> The great bulk of men who then usually went to India were socially not of a high order. Of course, though very poor, many were the sons of old officers of good families, whose poverty compelled their sons to serve in India … But the great bulk of those I met at Chatham, and afterwards in India and Burmah, at that time, struck me, I remember, as wanting in good breeding, and all seemed badly educated.[17]

Throughout his life, Wolseley continually came up against the barrier of impecuniousness, and was frustrated that economic necessity rather than prestige directed his decisions on which appointments to pursue.[18] When he became a distinguished officer, he surrounded himself with officers of the aristocratic and gentry type. Wolseley dispensed a great deal of patronage and favour, occasionally with some reservations, to this class of officers.[19] Such patronage appeared to Wolseley to be an expected part of his job, and an established facet of the Victorian officer corps, to the extent that he remarked in 1890, 'I open my eyes in astonishment whenever anyone halts in their success to thank me for anything in more than the most perfunctory manner for having pushed them on, and possibly made their whole career for them.'[20]

The most readily apparent common thread running through the officers of both Roberts's and Wolseley's rings was that the majority came from established military families. The continuing importance of contacts and the patronage of senior officers in the late nineteenth century, along with the aforementioned affinity borne of a shared background, contributed to a system which privileged the selection of such men. Though they were economically distressed, their one avenue for the maintenance of their social position was military service, and it was this occupation that they, by and large, encouraged their sons to take up. Over time, this had a cumulative effect, increasing the proportion of the sons of military families in the officer corps. Among the officers examined for this study, under one-third of those commissioned in the 1850s came from military families. By the first decade of the twentieth century, this had increased to around half of all Irish officers.

Roberts and Wolseley were not the only bright and ambitious Irish officers to have been granted commissions in the 1850s: Sir George

Pomeroy Pomeroy-Colley, a polymath officer from Kildare and darling of the Staff College, reputed to be the most intelligent officer of his day, passed out of Sandhurst first in his class in 1852;[21] George Stuart White, later to be Roberts' protégé, was commissioned in the Inniskilling Fusiliers in 1853; William Godfrey Dunham Massy, Tipperary landowner, Trinity College graduate and colleague of Lord Roberts, was gazetted in 1854; though he died young, Robert Home, commissioned in 1856, was described by Wolseley as 'one of the most remarkable men I have ever known … An able, daring and imaginative Irishman';[22] Thomas Kelly-Kenny, later to serve with Roberts in South Africa, embarked as a young ensign in 1858 for 20 years' service in Asia; and John Charles Ardagh, a talented engineer and country gentleman, later an important member of the Wolseley ring, was commissioned in 1859. All of these men (save the aforementioned Home), among others, became general officers and were highly decorated for their service. The reasons for this steady accumulation of talented and successful Irishmen in the officer corps are varied. Ireland was still economically and demographically exhausted after the Great Famine, and the minor gentry was hit by the resultant economic collapse. This may have driven more Irish officers into the Indian Army, seeking to secure a livelihood. The heroic narratives of old Irish officers who served with the Duke of Wellington (who also had connections to the East India Company) may have had a complementary effect on recruitment, according to Chris Bayly.[23]

R.G.L. von Zugbach, C.B. Otley, and Edward Spiers have examined the British officer corps as a social network, in order to understand the processes of socialisation and reproduction that sustained its character.[24] Von Zugbach's survey of the twentieth-century officer corps set out to challenge the view of the officer corps as 'a monolithic institution, characterised by highly centralised bureaucratic structures', drawing out evidence of institutional and class influences.[25] All three studies highlight the importance of public schools in the socialisation of British officers, tracing the connections between old boys and appointments to staff positions and regimental commands. They identify the late nineteenth and early twentieth century as the high point of school-military interconnection.[26] Spiers seeks to overcome the shortcomings of approaches focusing solely on cadets from Woolwich and Sandhurst by attempting to uncover other routes to entry, and address the question of the apparent expansion of middle-class access to the officer corps in this period—this too foregrounds the importance of schools as locations of officer socialisation.[27] The focus on the English public school in these studies seems to imply that the influence of Ireland and Irishness on officer socialisation was minimal; however, we have seen how efforts to reduce the economic burden on officers in the mid-nineteenth century benefited the sons of Irish military families predominantly, and they constituted an increasing proportion of the corps in the late nineteenth century. While many Irish officers were products of the English public schools, others like Butler and Kelly-Kenny were not; networks of patronage remained important, particularly under the leadership of officers like Wolseley and Roberts.

In Harold Perkin's study of the development and expansion of professional society in late nineteenth and early twentieth century England, it is argued that this period saw a transition in the mode of economic life from an industrial society, where the acquisition of merit was based on entrepreneurship and competition, to a professional society which valued training and the possession of qualifications as benchmarks for assessing expertise. Preceding this shift from an 'industrial' society run by entrepreneurs to a 'professional' society run by bureaucrats and professionals, and providing evidence for the change, is a shift in the methods by which individuals entered the social elite. Thus, in the later nineteenth century, Perkin argues, there was a proliferation of professional elites, who 'live by persuasion and propaganda, claiming that their particular service is indispensable … [following the pre-industrial example of] generals like Marlborough and Wellington … [who] were able to buy land and try to found a family'.[28] This is echoed in McBride's 'greening' thesis, which, alongside a widening of Irish political opinion, also identifies a shift in the class composition of civil servants in Ireland coinciding with the institution of competitive examinations for positions, contributing to a broadening of access. According to McBride, the acceptance of a civil service position was looked upon by this new batch of professionals as an 'opportunity', rather than a 'duty'.[29] Both Perkin and McBride do not extend their analysis to the army, however.

Catriona Kennedy and Matthew McCormack, in their study of the mid-nineteenth century military, contend that the army provides an exception to Perkin's thesis, due to 'its particular structures of admittance and emphasis on practical experience over technical expertise', though they note that a 'dialogue' between histories of the military and those of professions can be helpful.[30] This approach to the Victorian officer corps invites the question of whether the role of the rings of officers surrounding Wolseley and Roberts can be seen as evidence of the adoption of professional norms and practices in the army, or whether they represent the army's 'particular structures of admittance', relying on the same old imperatives of elite connections, wealth, and status. On the one hand, there is evidence that the political establishment viewed senior military officers as the possessors of indispensable and specific knowledge, and noted their contributions to debates on public order and imperial defence. This can be discerned in the dialogues between the army command at the Royal Hospital, Kilmainham, and the civilian functionaries at Dublin Castle, during periods of unrest.[31] On the other hand, soldiers who resented political 'interference' could be seen as truculent and elitist.

Hew Strachan contends that Wolseley instilled in his officers his own 'contempt for parliamentary government', a highly adversarial position which can be read into his accounts of the Gordon Relief Expedition, concealed behind an appearance of disinterest and an almost technocratic impulse to remain above the political fray.[32] Wolseley displayed an exasperation with politicians who lacked military experience making decisions about imperial defence. This speaks to his increasing awareness of the role of senior officers in offering invaluable professional insights that were beyond the ken of outsiders. However, attempts at reform, by Wolseley and other officers, were increasingly frustrated by a growing tendency to conflate professionalisation with politicisation by conservative opinion within the officer corps.

As commanders, Roberts and Wolseley enthusiastically encouraged a professional outlook by adopting updated manuals of practice for various branches of service: Wolseley wrote *The Soldier's Pocket-Book*, a field reference guide for officers and enlisted men, and Roberts endorsed a number of field manuals in the period of the South African War. These were widely distributed and favourably received by what Wolseley called the 'young school' in the officer corps, who were keen to adopt a more comprehensive training regime.[33] However, there was neither a major demographic shift in the socio-economic backgrounds of army officers nor was there any enthusiasm from the Commander-in-Chief, the Duke of Cambridge, to countenance any attempt at army reform, despite numerous attempts from the civilian side of the War Office to enact such changes.[34] Professionalisation thus remained a highly contentious issue.

Several historians have made studies of the Roberts and Wolseley rings, though the effect that their Irishness and other social characteristics had on the shape of the wider officer corps has not been examined in detail. The rings are generally seen as indicative of wider professionalising trends in the British Army of the post-Crimean War period, while Jeremy Black cites them as evidence of the continuing importance of patronage.[35] In his study of the structure of the officer corps, on the other hand, Tim Travers characterises the rings of officers as an artefact of an old-fashioned 'personal' officer corps, with colonial cults of personality standing in the way of a more modern, centralised army.[36] Hew Strachan contends that the existence of these concatenations of officers suggests a finely-honed political awareness on the part of the officers involved, and that the associated intrigues and factional struggles—both within the ring and with exterior officers—developed in them an ability and willingness to utilise political leverage for their own ends.[37] Strachan even makes a link between this politicisation and the Curragh incident, in which former members of the Wolseley and Roberts rings took part.[38] Historians generally agree that late-Victorian officers were savvy negotiators of a world defined by patronage and connections, and that they were conscious of their political role, even if they did not specifically describe it as such. Officers' 'political' imaginations, however, were confined by their positionality; the Curragh incident and later challenges to the Irish military elite were increasingly enunciated in a mode that was exterior to the bounded political horizons of the nineteenth-century officer.[39] The late-Victorian officer corps was thus an organisation laden with contradictions: conscious of the necessity for reform, but hidebound by its aristocratic heritage; highly successful in its campaigns, but constantly agonising over its lack of technological or methodological advancement; increasingly meritocratic, but nonetheless dominated by a very specific socio-economic group, that of the 'less solvent country gentry' with the familial and social connections to open the way to an officer career.[40]

Leigh Maxwell's *The Ashanti Ring* charts the development of the Wolseley ring through the campaigns of the war against the Asante (Fig. 4.1) in present-day Ghana in 1870–82. Maxwell points out Wolseley's diverse mixture of Irish companions and defines the contours of their internal relationships within the Wolseley Ring. The differing backgrounds of the wealthy Hugh McCalmont, the impecunious William Butler, and the 'intellectually minded' George Pomeroy Pomeroy-Colley, are described, as are the implications of their changing relationship with Wolseley: Butler's inability to work in a team eventually drove a wedge between them, but Pomeroy-Colley's enquiring mind and professional mentality captured Wolseley's interest.[41] It is important to note, however, that there were also many Englishmen and Scotsmen in the Wolseley and

Fig. 4.1   Sir Garnet Wolseley with officers of the Wolseley Ring during the Ashanti Campaign, 1874. *Alamy*

Roberts Rings, and that the prominence of Irishmen is probably due more to the disproportionate representation of Irishmen in the army, than to some kind of explicit favouritism on the part of Wolseley or Roberts. While not necessarily representing the most important touchstone of their self-perceptions, the factors of shared background and organisational mentality were nonetheless of great significance to these officers, as we shall see in the next section. In prior studies of the institutional character of the British officer corps, there is a sense that professionalisation and patronage are somehow incompatible; however, the examples of Wolseley and Roberts demonstrate that, far from this being the case, it was the relationship between these two factors that defined the character and identity of the late-Victorian officer corps.

WOLSELEY AND IRISHNESS

The case of Garnet Wolseley presents an interesting insight into the mentality of the Victorian officer, as in his letters and diaries he could not help but pass commentary on the political and social aspects of his experience

of soldiering. His political outlook was broadly Tory, although he harboured a deep disdain for politicians of all stripes and for the democratic
process in general, and appeared at times to advocate a form of neo-
Cromwellian military dictatorship: in particular, his impatience with
responses to social unrest in Ireland, and his exasperation with what he
took to be the dread influence of 'socialism' in political life, provoked
Wolseley to write to his wife in 1890, 'In the end the men of talk will give
way to the men of action, and the politician will black the boots of some
successful cavalry colonel. A new Cromwell will clear the country of frothy
talkers.'[42] Much is made of this letter in defining Wolseley's political outlook and his willingness to engage with politicians, though Halik Kochanski
urges: 'This should not be interpreted as a demonstration of Caesarist
tendencies on Wolseley's behalf, but more as a cry of desperation from a
man who could see how the British Army could be improved yet found his
efforts thwarted by party political requirements.'[43] Indeed, petulant but
ultimately toothless outbursts of this sort by officers would become
increasingly common by the turn of the century. They belied a frosty but
essentially stable relationship between the officer corps and the British
state: while in the colonies it could be as brutal as any other European
army, in its relations with the home government it was one of the more
politically moderate European officer corps of the era.[44]

Surely, Wolseley never made any move to make his 'Caesarist' fantasy a
reality, but his distaste for the exigencies of the democratic process and the
necessity for ponderous deliberation and oversight by elected officials is
well documented elsewhere, and mentioned frequently in his diaries. In
the preface to the *Soldier's Pocket-Book*, Wolseley's frustration with the
government's lack of enthusiasm for professionalisation is tangible when
he alludes to 'economical motives' standing in the way of the publication
of the book, and the prevalence of military texts by 'men who have never
seen a shot fired in anger', while in the second edition he notes with satisfaction that 'the necessity for military education is being recognised every
day more and more'.[45] Wolseley thus realised the importance of pressing
his case with politicians: in 1893, he wrote to the then-Secretary of State
for War, Henry Campbell-Bannerman, in support of his 'young school',
who 'want to make the Army a real profession, in which the best men,
made by their own exertions, rise to the top, as do lawyers, doctors, civil
engineers, &c.'—as clear a declaration of his policy position as he ever
made.[46] However, Wolseley's constant disagreements with the Duke of
Cambridge—the embodiment in Wolseley's mind of the 'old school'—

and his willingness to air his grievances publicly, gave him the reputation of being politically unpredictable.[47] He proved to be a less effective Commander-in-Chief than an active service officer, unable to navigate the factional landscape of the War Office. Neville Lyttelton, a member of Wolseley's ring, remarked that his appointment as C-in-C 'came some ten years too late', implying that Wolseley had lost some of the boldness and effectiveness that characterised his campaigning days.[48]

His attitude towards Ireland was complex and contradictory, informed by his family history, class, social circle, and profession. Little is known about Wolseley's early life save what he himself recounts in his autobiography, which is heavily if not exclusively relied upon by his biographers. Wolseley's maternal grandfather, he wrote, was 'a typical spendthrift Irish landlord', a class which Wolseley had little time for: his letters often evoke the image of a rack-renting, parochial, inconsequential squireen, whose life is constantly in danger from Fenian assassins.[49] By contrast, his father, 'a poor major in a marching regiment' (the King's Own Scottish Borderers) who on retirement rented Golden Bridge House in Co. Dublin from his father-in-law, was remembered by Wolseley as a man of charity and sympathy.[50] It is not a great leap to suggest that, to Wolseley's mind, Irish gentlemen were only of any use if they pursued a military career. From the beginning of his career to his deathbed regret that he would not die gloriously in combat, the army was Wolseley's muse.[51] He was animated by the belief that 'war with all its horrors exercises a healthy influence on all classes of society'.[52] This was to become the majority view among Irish officers in the Edwardian period.

Wolseley's private correspondence suggests a certain self-consciousness about, and antipathy to, his Irish background. His letters when stationed in Ireland suggest very little affinity with the country or its people. Of Dublin he wrote, 'I feel as if this place was entirely a foreign town, and I seem surprised to hear its people speak English, even though it be with a strong accent.'[53] He was more at ease with aspects of martial Irishness: Wolseley records, for example, that he was deeply touched to be invested as a Knight of St. Patrick.[54] He attributes his affinity for soldiering with Irishness too, noting the apparent credulousness and bravery of the Irish in his diary: 'when I was a young man, if any General had [appealed to my heroism] it would have made every nerve in my body tingle … But then I was always very impressionable which I owe to my Irish education and early Irish surroundings.'[55]

While Wolseley's antipathy towards his Irish background was evidently based on a sense of inferiority about his family's early poverty and his lack of elite schooling, the land agitation of the early 1880s especially alienated him. Wolseley wrote to his wife from Cairo in 1882, intimating that, were he to return to Dublin, he ran the risk of assassination: 'I believe I am to have a sword presented to me here by the people of Cairo, and I see some talk of the Irish people giving me one also. I hope I may not have to go there to receive it if the rumour is true.'[56] In his diary of the Gordon relief campaign, Wolseley writes of an assassinated fellow officer, 'I wish he had died in battle in place of being murdered like an Irish landlord by a cowardly skulking reptile such as this country and Ireland produce in large numbers.'[57] Wolseley seemingly harboured an extreme form of the siege mentality evinced by some landlords during the Land War, reinforced by the attitude of Lady Wolseley, who according to her husband was 'strongly prejudiced against everything on this side of St. George's Channel'.[58] It was an attitude that remained with him for the rest of his life.

The extent to which Wolseley felt a commonality with his fellow Irish officers is unclear. In common with most people in the Victorian Empire, Wolseley used the general term 'English' and 'Englishman' to refer to those, himself included, from all parts of the United Kingdom.[59] For those without an advanced national consciousness, this carried no particular political connotation. This is not to say that he never employed the term 'Irish'; it is much in evidence in his writings, used in both a positive and a negative context. In describing his fellow officers, for example, he records in his diary a disagreement with '[t]hat *blathering*, inaccurate Irishman Frazer who is Wood's Chief Staff Officer'.[60] He also described one Colonel Collingwood as possessing 'all the faults & all the vulgarity of the Irish squireen without the manly character that poor Paddy is sometimes remarkable for'.[61] However, he noted with approval the 'gallant Irishman', Lieutenant, later General, Magrath and his 'coolness and indifference to bullets', and remarked, 'I am proud of being still the friend of so brave a soldier.'[62] This complex view of Ireland and the Irish shares many similarities with the popular perceptions on display in the contemporary press, which have been expounded upon at length by Roy Foster and others.[63] It is encapsulated in Wolseley's remarks on visiting a country house, when he complains that 'you can imagine what an Irish establishment this is!' but notes with approval, 'But the welcome is Irish also—sincere, hearty and warm.'[64]

However, when Wolseley employs Irish terminology in discussing enlisted men, it is usually meant to disparage. As a junior officer, Wolseley had a run-in with the men of the Royal Irish Regiment, who refused to follow his orders on parade: 'seeing that I was very young and ignorant of my drill, [they] thought they would, in their Hibernian fashion, bamboozle and perhaps terrify me.'[65] Meeting a battalion of Royal Irish in later life, he described them as 'a very *varmint*-looking lot all truly Irish in appearance'.[66] Puzzlingly, Wolseley's frequent othering of lower-class Irish soldiers even edged into an orientalising of their Irishness: in his autobiography, he wrote, 'how necessary it is that Irish soldiers should have Irish officers over them, who understand their curiously Eastern character, and who are consequently better able to deal with them than strangers can.'[67] According to Peter Karsten, when he commanded an Irish regiment, Wolseley sought to enquire 'whether [a prospective officer] is an Irishman, or has property in Ireland, and what are his connections with Ireland and with this [regiment]'.[68] Here is a clear expression of Irish affinity, and a sense of some intangible quality that set Irish officers apart from others—however reluctant Wolseley was to associate himself with it.

Wolseley's ambiguous relationship with Irishness manifests itself less, if at all, in the other officers of the Wolseley ring. This suggests that it was a problem unique to Wolseley, and Irishness was either less important or less problematic to those under him. Colonel William Butler, for example, freely inhabited his Irish identity; General Henry Brackenbury remarked that, as an Irish Catholic, Butler criticised the historian J.A. Froude for his writing on religion and civilisation, as 'in the woes of Ireland they had a subject of deep common interest to both'—clearly, once again, discussion (and championing) of Irish affairs was an important component of military Irishness.[69] Unlike the majority of his fellow officers, Butler also harboured constitutional nationalist sympathies and regarded Parnell as 'the greatest leader of his time'.[70] Wolseley remarked frequently on Butler's pronounced Irish accent in his letters during the Gordon relief expedition, presumably in contrast to the absence of his own—being educated by the Jesuits, Butler never cultivated an English public school accent, nor, clearly, did he ever feel the need to.[71] Undoubtedly to his fellow officers he possessed a quintessentially Irish identity, but as his interactions with Wolseley and others illustrate, it was one of many such identities. In his autobiography he takes issue with Wolseley's stereotyping of the Irish as emotional, overly 'sympathetic', and lacking in Protestant moral fibre, contending that 'human nature has no reason to be ashamed of [sympathy]. Nor is the sentiment of sympathy, even when it is misdirected [i.e. towards distressed tenants on unproductive estates], peculiar to the people of Ireland.'[72] Butler's Catholicism, of course, makes him an atypical case.[73]

Officers from other traditions and backgrounds, such as Colonel Edward Saunderson, General Hubert Gough or Colonel Oliver Nugent, also retained a deep affinity for Ireland, and the animating strength of their Irishness is evidenced by their later controversial support for armed volunteer movements.[74] These connections were undoubtedly strengthened by the bonds of land and family: an incentive to return to Ireland on retirement, particularly in the form of property, was a powerful pull against the enticing possibility of settling in London, with its clubland, the War Office, or, for really successful officers, the House of Lords. Officers with broad nationalist sympathies like Butler settled in Ireland for political reasons, but this was a rare occurrence.[75] A wide spectrum of military Irishness was thus manifest in the Wolseley ring, and the prominence of Wolseley and Roberts as successive Commanders-in-Chief in Ireland played an important role in the relationship between the army and Irish society.

WOLSELEY AND ROBERTS ASCENDANT: COMMANDERS-IN-CHIEF, 1890–1902

Garnet Wolseley became Commander-in-Chief in Ireland in 1890 (Fig. 4.2), and in moving to Dublin that year, re-acquainted himself with the city of his birth and early maturity, becoming a master in a local chapter of Freemasons among other honours. He had little positive to say about the city: 'I loath the idea more and more of going to Dublin. The squalor of the people, the wet climate, etc., make the notion more and more repulsive.'[76] His previous experiences had not endeared the city to him: of his time as a subaltern in the 1850s he reminisced, 'Dublin was a dreary quarter for a man like me who could not afford to hunt, and whose wounded leg prevented him from dancing. Its fragrant river, its quays lined with decaying houses, its squalid streets, made it an undesirable place of residence.'[77] Wolseley found the provincial garrison towns of Ireland even less to his liking. Of Fermoy, he wrote, 'a remarkably clean town for Ireland. At least, the *place* where the hotel is situated is trim and tidy, and unlike this dirty Paddyland.'[78] However, Wolseley found the city of Belfast much more amenable: 'there is more activity here at dawn than at noon in any other Irish city … This town is so entirely different from Dublin that it is difficult to realise one is still in Ireland.'[79] This had been a common senti-

Fig. 4.2   Wolseley as Commander-in-Chief, Ireland, with his staff, 1896. *Courtesy of the National Library of Ireland*

ment of those visiting Ireland for decades, echoed by other colonial personalities like Rudyard Kipling on his visits to the city, and illustrates Wolseley's intention to distance himself from the social and cultural milieu of his early background.[80] His characterisation of Ireland in general as 'foreign' is interesting in the light of Lady Wolseley's comment that her husband feels it '[his] duty as a Briton to hate the foreigners'.[81] The Irish soldiers he commanded, for their part, regarded him highly, and the 'varmint' Royal Irish Regiment raised a subscription to install a memorial plaque in St. Patrick's Cathedral following his death.

Ireland was, of course, a home command, with a number of regimental depots established in towns and cities throughout the country. However, Wolseley's letters suggest that, to him, service in Ireland had some of the characteristics of an overseas posting:

It is curious to find these troops of cavalry, with sixty or seventy big Englishmen and a couple of English officers, living in a filthy little village or town as if they were in a foreign country. They all seem to like these detachments, which is still more curious.[82]

While the sentiment Wolseley describes is not unusual for officers, the majority of whom seemed to find the country by turns congenial and dull, very few save Wolseley himself seemed to regard service in Ireland as 'foreign'.[83] Wolseley's exasperation in dealing with the Irish civil establishment is also manifest in his letters:

> What an amusingly, provokingly, inconsequent people these Irish are: untidy and unpunctual beyond measure. The proverbial Irishman always wants a place under government, and as soon as he gets one, he wants to leave it with a good pension, and do nothing the rest of his life.[84]

The contrast between Wolseley's and Roberts's attitudes towards Ireland is sharply illustrated in the replacement of the former by the latter as Commander-in-Chief in Ireland in 1895. Unlike Wolseley, Roberts appears to have found it 'a congenial post' and was welcomed with an enthusiasm that he graciously reciprocated.[85] Roberts's tenure was successful in earning the approval of both nationalist and unionist opinion, who regarded him as an exemplary manifestation of Victorian military virtue.[86] Returning from India after almost 40 years' glittering service defending the frontiers of the empire, Roberts was immensely popular in the United Kingdom, and this enthusiasm was reflected in Ireland in the four years he spent there as Commander in Chief.[87] As far as his social life went, Roberts eased back into the activities he had enjoyed in the 1850s almost as if no time had passed, including riding to hounds with the gentlemen of Meath and Kildare.[88] The opportunities of life in Ireland clearly appealed to Roberts more than they had to Wolseley. Roberts was an enthusiastic public presence in Ireland, a course of action which he pursued partially in order to fill the days: he wrote to Lord Lansdowne that after coordinating the military affairs of a land as large and complex as India, he considered that there was 'not enough real work' in the Irish Command.[89] Like Wolseley, Roberts cultivated a close relationship with the press, notably with Charles Bell, H.A. Gwynne, and J.L. Garvin, influential Irish newspaperman of humble origins who also counted such officers as Hubert Gough as friends and allies.[90] In 1897 Roberts was invested into the Order of Saint Patrick, though at the time the Irish press were more preoccupied with the publication of his memoirs, which provoked a great deal of public interest. The Irish military establishment also remembered 'dear, wise, sagacious Roberts' fondly—the Earl Dunraven held that no other officer had such a deep understanding of Ireland and the empire, and lamented, 'would that his advice [on the professionalisation of the army] had been taken; but alas! It fell on deaf ears.'[91] Even Roberts, the establishment darling, was too tenacious a moderniser for some.

Given the differing attitudes of the two Commanders-in-Chief to their Irish background, it is curious that Garnet Wolseley is memorialised in grand style in St. Patrick's Cathedral, Dublin (albeit not so grandly as he is on Horse Guards Parade), while Frederick Roberts has been claimed by Eton College, and is the subject of a large memorial there. This is telling of the importance of class in defining belonging; Wolseley's impecunious Irish background led to an enduring association with Ireland, even though he viewed himself in a wider imperial context. Roberts, on the other hand, socialised into the elite and equipped with the skills to navigate the military establishment with ease, could enthusiastically take up the Irish command confident that his Irishness would not bury the imperial focus of his career.[92] Perhaps we can read into Wolseley's attitudes to Ireland a sense that, no matter how far distant he travelled from the land of his birth, it was always too close for comfort.

Much has been made by historians of the rivalry between Wolseley and Roberts, and the way in which it eventually came to a head after the debacle at Colenso in 1899, when Roberts was impelled out of retirement in Ireland to command the armies in South Africa following a series of calamitous defeats at the hands of the Boers. the appointment of Roberts 'meant victory of his "ring" over the Wolseley "ring"', according to Andre Wessels.[93] However, in the twenty preceding years, their correspondence was at least courteous, if terse and infrequent. It has been suggested that the perception of a rivalry between the two commanders encouraged bright, ambitious officers to seek to associate with them and serve on their staffs.[94] In actuality they only clashed over professional reforms: until they came to a disagreement over the implementation of short service, the two men inhabited their separate spheres having little to do with one another. Their differences were, however, significant, encapsulating their backgrounds, their vision for the officer corps, and—crucially—their sense of Irishness.

Roberts appeared to resist mentioning nationality in the assessments of his officers, preferring to keep to descriptions of operational ability. His evaluation of two Irish officers, taken from the voluminous collection of Roberts' correspondence, is typical: 'Kelly Kenny seems to me to be nervous and over cautious ... French has hitherto done well and I hope he will justify his position as commandant of the cavalry.'[95] In either of these situations, Wolseley might have mentioned the Irishness of these men when describing their characters, but Roberts does not. This might be due partly to the different composition of Roberts's and Wolseley's rings. The diaries and papers of some of Roberts's stalwart officers, such as George White, give the impression of a level-headedness, professionalism and focus which makes a rather jarring contrast from Wolseley's adventurous, risk-taking, youthful officers. White's diary for 1886, for example, lists tasks and meetings accurately and neatly, and hardly misses a day; only once does he show the effects of the stress and tedium of active service in India, when he writes, 'Eight months more. Can I stand it?'[96] White's 1893 letter to a colleague encapsulates his mindset perfectly as Roberts' successor as C-in-C in India: 'You ask me how I like my new command. It is full of interest but the work is too constant a grind ... I hope as long as I hold it to be of some use.'[97] The contrast with the effusive Butler is striking: Butler's account of the Manitoba expedition alongside Wolseley reads like a swashbuckling adventure novel.[98] Despite this professional outlook, White also expressed an intense belief in the imperial project, telling a fellow officer embarking on active service that he would look back on it as '*the* event of your life & will rejoice that you got so successfully through it'.[99] White also appears to have shared the Victorian officer's standard mistrust of politicians, particularly the Military Secretary: he wrote in 1896, 'there is a tendency to let the [Army] Council drift to the Mily. Dept. and our army would then become a political one.'[100]

White kept a collection of newspaper cuttings, which illustrate the public activities and the degree of popularity afforded a distinguished Indian officer in the confidence of Lord Roberts. White was celebrated by the mercantile elites of various Ulster towns, and was lionised by the global membership of the Orange Order, as many of his fellow northern officers were.[101] It was his association with the popular Roberts, even comparatively late in his career, that occasioned this rise to prominence. Roberts himself was an Orangeman, while Wolseley was not, and the two commanders were also prominent Freemasons, but neither of these connections appears to have influenced their selection of officers particularly—perhaps this is unsurprising, in light of their often-vocalised concerns about the army becoming 'political'.

Although it is by no means as extensively studied as Wolseley's ring, Lord Roberts also assembled a group of trusted officers, originating in the Afghan campaign of 1878. As well as the aforementioned White, Roberts succeeded in enticing Colonel George Pomeroy Pomeroy-Colley of the Wolseley ring to act as his military secretary. More permanent members of Roberts' ring included Hugh Gough, VC, a cavalryman from a Tipperary military family, and Jack Sherston, Roberts' nephew and fellow Old Etonian—evidence of Roberts' attitudes toward nepotism, a manifestation of his socialisation in the military elite.[102] Enjoying a less than cordial relationship with Roberts after the Afghan War was Lieutenant-Colonel William Godfrey Dunham Massy, who felt aggrieved at what he perceived as Roberts's scapegoating of him for the reversals of late 1879 in the Chardeh Valley.[103] The majority of Roberts' ring was constituted of non-Irishmen, including James 'Jemmy' Hills, Sir Donald Stewart and Ian Hamilton—Scotsmen—and Reginald 'Poley' Pole-Carew, Neville Chamberlain and Sir George 'Prettyboy' Pretyman, all English.[104] Many of these officers came to India because of lack of opportunity elsewhere; indeed, it was this which brought them into Roberts' orbit: Ian Hamilton wrote in his memoirs that 'had I gone to the Staff College I should probably have gravitated towards the Wolseley Ring!'[105] These associations endured throughout Roberts' career in India, and his inner circle changed little even after he entered the high command.[106] Indeed, on his triumphant arrival in London in 1895, many of the same faces congregated to welcome him back to the imperial metropolis.[107]

In South Africa, another prominent Irish officer was admitted to Roberts' close circle of protégés—Henry Hughes Wilson. The son of a County Longford landowner who entered the officer corps through the militia backdoor, Wilson found his way to the Staff College and thence into the circle of Lord Roberts. The laurels he won in South Africa smoothed his way to the War Office, where his enthusiastic pursuit of unionist politics earned him a reputation as a 'political soldier' and a troublemaker.[108] Unlike Roberts, he could be tactless and dismissive in person which did not endear him to his colleagues.[109] His unceasing promotion of Irish issues from the centre of the British military establishment in London, particularly his opposition to Home Rule, played a part in drawing the officer corps into a political crisis in Ireland in 1914, as we shall see in the next chapter.

Wilson, while certainly a close ally of Roberts, appears Wolseleyesque in certain particulars: like Roberts he comfortably and effortlessly inhabited his Irishness in his senior position, though like Wolseley, his political troubles at the War Office made him unpopular with the 'old school' of the military establishment. He was involved in a number of indiscretions and scandals even with other officers of Roberts's ring, though he found him-self drawn to Roberts as a leader and earned his friendship.[110] He was not the only one.

Roberts embodied the popular image of the Victorian Irish officer: like Kitchener in a later decade, Roberts's distinctive image as the 'little general' was extensively reproduced and his face on posters was as recog-nisable to the public as Kitchener's. '"A cute, little, jobbing showman" in Wolseley's opinion, the dapper "Bobs" became the national saviour' for his role in the Boer War, according to Piers Brendon's account of popular British imperialism (Fig. 4.3).[111] But the appeal of these two men may not have been as different as Wolseley assumed. According to Gifford Lewis, 'the Anglo-Irish in the British Army were eccentrics; their high spirits, dash and impulsive overriding of the regular "right thing" made them sometimes anathema, although always curiosities, to the stolid British officer.'[112] This characterisation could apply to many Irish officers, both Anglo-Irish and others. High spirits and dash were, after all, long-held virtues of the officer corps, and eccentricity, while not a particularly military virtue, could be considered a luxury of the social elite. The quality of 'overriding the regular "right thing"' as we have seen, belies not simply a playful subversion of the strictures of military identity, but suggests that Wolseley and Roberts were uniquely placed, through a concatenation of class and identity, to be effective profession-alisers of the officer corps.

The Second Boer War secured the careers of many Irish senior offi-cers, the beneficiaries of the patronage of Wolseley, Roberts, and other prominent soldiers of their generation. Being the high water-mark of Irish saturation in the high echelons of the British Army, the Second Boer War also provoked an unprecedented sense of popular imperialism and political militarism in Ireland, which, we shall later see, fed into the proliferation of armed militia groups and placed the officer corps into a central—and fatal—position in Irish politics.[113] For these reasons, the period of the South African War is crucial for military Irishness. Edward Spiers has pointed out that there were more senior officers of Irish back-ground in the army in 1899 than at any other time between the Crimean War and the First World War. According to Spiers's data, 21% of colonels in the army in 1899 were Irish, while Irish generals made up 16% of the total. This is contrasted with Scotland, which at the time had a slightly larger population, which produced 12% of colonels, while Scottish gen-erals also comprised 12% of the total.[114] The conflict led to the formation

Fig. 4.3   Ireland's imperial moment: jubilant crowds waving Irish symbols greet Lord and Lady Roberts outside Buckingham Palace on his return from South Africa. Supplement to *The Sphere* newspaper, 12 January 1901. *Alamy*

of the Irish Guards as recognition of the contribution of Irishmen to imperial victory, and an unprecedented proliferation of war memorials and commemorative memorabilia in Ireland and elsewhere. Around the country, gentry families endowed Church of Ireland windows, plaques, and tablets memorialising fallen sons and brothers, while in the centre of Dublin, a commemorative arch to the Dublin Fusiliers was erected on the corner of Stephen's Green. This was Ireland's imperial moment.

As previously noted, the socio-economic makeup of the British officer corps saw a minimal change in the period preceding the First World War, contrary to the expectations of reformers that the abolition of purchase would lead to a rapid broadening of officers' backgrounds.[115] The major change in the relations between officers in this period, therefore, was the development of Wolseley's and Roberts's circle of officers, which has been seen by historians as a professionalising influence, a kind of embryonic general staff, which anticipated the necessity of army modernisation in 1914. The Roberts and Wolseley rings in the Victorian army illustrate that, while identity was important to Irishmen in the officer corps, the presence of Irishmen in senior positions did not present any particular advantage, and may, due to the self-consciousness and prejudice of Garnet Wolseley, have presented a slight disadvantage, to the advancement of other Irish officers. Irish commanders' role in the Irish saturation of the officer corps during the Boer War was much less significant than the aforementioned demographic trends—class and social distinction—as the factors delimiting the boundaries of the officer corps.

Socialisation, more than social advancement, was thus the driving force behind the increasing prevalence of Irish military families in the officer corps. Wolseley and Roberts both benefited from, and facilitated, the growth of this trend. The measures by which officers were primarily judged were gallantry, dash, steadiness, and 'character'—the signifiers of Victorian elite masculinity. These were by no means objective measures, of course, and approval of officers for active service positions ultimately lay with the local commander and the Commander-in-Chief. While Irish officers could traverse the empire and encounter countrymen from similar backgrounds, there was also the congeniality of home service drawing them to Ireland. Hew Strachan notes that while the existence of Wolseley's and Roberts's rings of imperial officers constitutes evidence of the political awareness and engagement of the late-Victorian officer corps, it was in Ireland that the fruits of faction ripened and fell, and the politicisation of the army reached its fullest expression.[116] The way in which, as Strachan contends, 'a century of continuous influences' led to a crisis of officer identity taking place in Ireland in 1914—the Curragh incident—is the subject of the next chapter.[117] Wolseley, Roberts, and their attitudes to professionalisation and identity were important influences in explaining why this crisis took place in Ireland, as opposed to elsewhere. The experiences of Irish officers constituted two sides of a coin: the first was the overseas empire; the other was the military establishment at home, and its connection to the landed interest.

NOTES

1. W. F. Butler, Sir William Butler: An Autobiography (London, 1911), pp. 111–112; Leigh Maxwell, The Ashanti Ring: Sir Garnet Wolseley's Campaigns 1870–1882 (London, 1985), p. 232.
2. F. B. Maurice, 'White, Sir George Stuart (1835–1912)', DNB.
3. Cawnpore was, until the mid-1830s, administered as part of the Bengal Presidency. The Bengal European Regiment eventually became part of the Royal Munster Fusiliers during the Childers reforms in 1881.
4. Halik Kochanski, Sir Garnet Wolseley: Victorian Hero (London, 1999), p. 3.
5. Byron Farwell, Eminent Victorian Soldiers (London, 1986), p. 149.
6. Ibid.
7. Even though Roberts did not complete his studies at Eton, his association with the school persisted throughout his life. See David James, Lord Roberts (London, 1954), p. 7.
8. A. H. H. Maclean, Public Schools and the War in South Africa, 1899–1902 (London, 1903), p. 86.
9. Hew Strachan. The Politics of the British Army (Oxford, 2005), p. 15; Robinson, Bryan Cooper, p. 44.
10. Tim Travers, 'The Hidden Army: Structural Problems in the British Officer Corps, 1900–1918', Journal of Contemporary History 17 (1982), pp. 524–525.
11. Anonymous (William Cairnes), Social Life in the British Army (London, 1900), pp. 19–20. For a more in-depth discussion of officers' rates of pay and living costs, see Chap. 2.
12. Ibid. p. 74; Steven Patterson, The Cult of Imperial Honor in British India (New York, 2009), pp. 89–91. There was a strict racial hierarchy inherent in the social structure of British India; while most Europeans enjoyed a privileged lifestyle, 'Anglo-Indians' of mixed parentage faced structural discrimination and were largely excluded from the precincts of European society. Elite Indians themselves, apart from royalty, were also systematically excluded until concessions to the movement for Indian independence began to manifest themselves in the 1930s.
13. Oscar Gruzinsky, 'Career Patterns and Characteristics of British Naval Officers', British Journal of Sociology 26 (1975), pp. 35 36; P. E. Razzell,

'Social Origins of Officers in the Indian and British Home Army: 1758–1962', *British Journal of Sociology* 14 (1963), pp. 249–255.

14. Garnet Wolseley, *The Story of a Soldier's Life* (London, 1903), p. 1.
15. Halik Kochanski, *Sir Garnet Wolseley: Victorian Hero* (London, 1999), p. 3.
16. Garnet Wolseley, *The Story of a Soldier's Life* (London, 1903), p. 8.
17. Ibid. p. 10.
18. Halik Kochanski, 'Field Marshall Viscount Wolseley, a Reformer at the War Office', unpub. PhD thesis, King's College London (1996), p. 16.
19. Garnet Wolseley to Lady Wolseley, 16 April 1875, in Arthur, George, ed., *The Letters of Lord and Lady Wolseley* (London, 1922), p. 23; Garnet Wolseley to Lady Wolsey, 20 September 1884, in Ibid. p. 121; Garnet Wolseley to Lady Wolseley, 18 January 1905, in Ibid. p. 423.
20. Garnet Wolseley to Lady Wolseley, 18 October 1890, in Arthur, *Letters of Lord and Lady Wolseley*, pp. 270–271.
21. Colley's downfall at Majuba during the First Boer War would serve as ammunition for those officers of the 'old school' who saw little utility in a professionalised officer corps. Colley's death in 1881 on Majuba Hill was not the only tragedy endured by the family; thirty-one years later Colley's nephew, Edward, was killed in the sinking of the RMS *Titanic*.
22. Wolseley, *The Story of a Soldier's Life*, p. 282.
23. C. A. Bayly, 'Ireland, India and the Empire: 1780–1914', *Transactions of the Royal Historical Society* 10 (2000), p. 389.
24. R. G. L. von Zugbach, *Power and Prestige in the British Army* (Aldershot, 1988); C. B. Otley, 'Militarism and Militarisation in the Public Schools, 1900–1972', *British Journal of Sociology* 29 (1978), pp. 321–339; Spiers, *The Army and Society*, p. 6.
25. Von Zugbach, p. 1.
26. Otley, 'Militarism', p. 332.
27. Spiers, *The Army and Society*, p. 6.
28. Harold Perkin, *The Rise of Professional Society: England Since 1880* (London, 1989), p. 6.
29. Lawrence McBride, *The Greening of Dublin Castle* (Washington, DC, 1991), pp. 2–3.
30. Catriona Kennedy and Matthew McCormack, *Soldering in Britain and Ireland* (New York, 2013), p. 10.
31. McBride, p. 281; Garnet Wolseley to Sir H. Ponsonby, Royal Hospital, Kilmainham, 13 June 1893, in Arthur, *Letters of Lord and Lady Wolseley*, p. 304.
32. Strachan, *The Politics of the British Army*, p. 101; Adrian Preston, *In Relief of Gordon: Lord Wolseley's Campaign Journal of the Gordon Relief Expedition, 1884–1885* (London, 1967), p. 141.

33. Wolseley quoted in Kochanski, 'Viscount Wolseley', p. 123.
34. Ibid. p. 110; Strachan, *The Politics of the British Army*, p. 111.
35. Jeremy Black, *A Military History of Britain* (London, 2006), p. 92.
36. Tim Travers, 'The Hidden Army: Structural Problems in the British Officer Corps, 1900–1918', *Journal of Contemporary History* 17 (1982), p. 525.
37. Strachan, *The Politics of the British Army*, p. 103.
38. Ibid. p. 7; Arthur Paget, the Commander-in-Chief at the time of the Curragh incident, had served in the Ashanti War with Wolseley, while the 5th Lancers, the regiment which played the major role in the incident, had served under Wolseley in Egypt, and Roberts in India and South Africa.
39. See Chaps. 6 and 7 for an extensive discussion of this shift in the Irish political landscape.
40. Robertson, *Crowned Harp*, p. 74.
41. Leigh Maxwell, *The Ashanti Ring: Sir Garnet Wolseley's Campaigns 1870– 1882* (London, 1985), pp. 232–233.
42. Lord Wolseley to Lady Wolseley, 1 November 1890, in Arthur, *Letters of Lord and Lady Wolseley*, p. 272.
43. Kochanski, 'Viscount Wolseley', p. 29.
44. Cf. Rothenberg, 'The Habsburg Officer Corps'; Vitarbo, 'The Russian Imperial Officer Corps'; Screen, 'Marshal Mannerheim'; Tim Wilson, 'Ghost Provinces, Mislaid Minorities: The Experience of Southern Ireland and Prussian Poland Compared', *Irish Studies in International Affairs* 13 (2002), p. 80.
45. Garnet Wolseley, preface to *The Soldier's Pocket-Book for Field Service* (London, 1871), pp. iii–v.
46. Ibid. p. 123.
47. Kochanski, *Sir Garnet Wolseley*, p. 121.
48. Kochanski, 'Viscount Wolseley', p. 179.
49. Wolseley, *Story of a Soldier's Life*, p. 6; Wolseley to Lady Wolseley, Pietermaritzburg, 18 February 1880, in Arthur, pp. 59–60; Preston, *Wolseley's Campaign Journal* (London, 1967), pp. 86–87.
50. Wolseley, *Story of a Soldier's Life*, p. 5; Kochanski, 'A Reformer at the War Office', p. 16.
51. Ian F. W. Beckett, 'Wolseley, Garnet Joseph, First Viscount Wolseley (1833–1913)', *DNB*; Halik Kochanski, *Sir Garnet Wolseley: Victorian Hero* (London, 1999), p. 4.
52. Wolseley, *Story of a Soldier's Life*, p. 20.
53. Garnet Wolseley to Lady Wolseley, 2 October 1890, in Arthur, *The Letters of Lord and Lady Wolseley*, p. 268.
54. Wolseley to Spencer, Cairo, 6 June 1885, in Arthur, p. 83.

55. Preston, *Wolseley's Campaign Journal*, p. 77.
56. Garnet Wolseley to Lady Wolseley, 28 September 1882, in Arthur, George, ed., *The Letters of Lord and Lady Wolseley 1870–1911* (London, 1922), p. 83.
57. Preston, *Wolseley's Campaign Journal*, pp. 56–57.
58. Garnet Wolseley to Lady Wolseley, 5 June 1895, in Arthur, *The Letters of Lord and Lady Wolseley*, p. 333.
59. Preston, *Wolseley's Campaign Journal*, p. 77.
60. Ibid. p. 35.
61. Adrian Preston, ed., *The South African Journal of Sir Garnet Wolseley, 1879–1880* (Cape Town, 1973), p. 74.
62. Wolseley, *Story of a Soldier's Life*, p. 69.
63. For an examination of the loaded nature of the term 'Irish' in Victorian popular culture, see Roy Foster, *Paddy and Mr. Punch: Connections in Irish and English History* (London, 1995).
64. Lord Wolseley to Lady Wolseley, 15 September 1896, in Arthur, *Letters of Lord and Lady Wolseley*, p. 354.
65. Ibid. p. 30.
66. Preston, *Wolseley's Campaign Journal*, p. 18.
67. Wolseley, *Story of a Soldier's Life*, p. 35.
68. Karsten, 'Suborned', pp. 35–36.
69. William F. Butler, *Sir William Butler: An Autobiography* (London, 1911), p. 183; Lennox Robinson, *Bryan Cooper* (London, 1931), p. 45.
70. Butler, *Autobiography*, p. 351.
71. Garnet Wolseley to Lady Wolseley, 24 April 1884, in Arthur, *The Letters of Lord and Lady Wolseley*, p. 116; Garnet Wolseley to Lady Wolseley, 5 November 1884, in Ibid. p. 128; Garnet Wolseley to Lady Wolseley, 17 March 1885, in Ibid. p. 207.
72. Butler, *Autobiography*, p. 13.
73. Throughout the period, an estimated 15–20% of Irish officers were Catholic. See David Fitzpatrick, 'Militarism in Ireland, 1900–1922' in Bartlett, Thomas, and Keith Jeffery, eds., *A Military History of Ireland* (Cambridge, 1996), p. 380.
74. Timothy Bowman, *Carson's Army: The Ulster Volunteer Force 1910–22* (Manchester, 2007), p. 57.
75. Edward McCourt, *Remember Butler: The Story of Sir William Butler* (London, 1967), p. 254.
76. Lord Wolseley to Lady Wolseley, 22 August 1890, in Arthur, *Letters of Lord and Lady Wolseley*, p. 266.
77. Wolseley, *Story of a Soldier's Life*, p. 81.
78. Lord Wolseley to Lady Wolseley, 17 May 1891, in Arthur, *Letters of Lord and Lady Wolseley*, p. 282.

79. Lord Wolseley to Lady Wolseley, 30 June 1894, in Arthur, *Letters of Lord and Lady Wolseley*, p. 317.
80. Cf. Andrew Lycett, *Kipling Abroad: Traffics and Discoveries from Burma to Brazil* (London, 2010), p. 167.
81. Lady Wolseley to Lord Wolseley, 2 August 1893, in Arthur, *Letters of Lord and Lady Wolseley*, p. 313.
82. Lord Wolseley to Lady Wolseley, 18 October 1890, in Arthur, *Letters of Lord and Lady Wolseley*, p. 271.
83. Bowman and Connelly, *The Edwardian Army*, p. 9; Crossman, 'The Army and Law and Order', p. 358; Dan Harvey and Gerry White, *The Barracks: A History of Victoria/Collins Barracks, Cork* (Cork, 1997), p. 38.
84. Lord Wolseley to Lady Wolseley, 16 October 1890, in Arthur, *Letters of Lord and Lady Wolseley*, p. 270.
85. Brian Robson, ed., *Roberts in India: The Military Papers of Field Marshal Lord Roberts 1876–1893* (Stroud, 1993), p. 448.
86. John M. Mackenzie, *Propaganda and Empire: The Manipulation of British Public Opinion, 1880–1960* (Manchester, 1986), p. 181.
87. *Freeman's Journal*, 2 October 1895; *Freeman's Journal*, 5 September 1896; *Belfast News-Letter*, 3 September 1896.
88. David James, *Lord Roberts* (London, 1954), p. 251.
89. Ibid. p. 260.
90. Bowman and Connelly, *The Edwardian Army*, p. 173; John O. Stubbs, 'Garvin, James Louis (1868–1947)', *DNB* (OUP 2004, online edn. 2011); Heather Streets, *Martial Races: The Military, Race and Masculinity in British Culture, 1857–1914* (Manchester, 2004), p. 131.
91. Windham Wyndham-Quin, 4th Earl Dunraven, *Past Times and Pastimes*, vol. 1 (1921), p. 178.
92. Obituaries of Roberts reported that he was 'simply worshipped' particularly by Indian troops. *The Times*, 17 November 1914; *The Times*, 18 November 1914; *Illustrated London News*, 21 November 1914.
93. Andre Wessels, *Lord Roberts and the War in South Africa 1899–1902* (Stroud, 2000), p. 11.
94. Brian Robson, Introduction to *Roberts in India: The Military Papers of Field Marshal Lord Roberts 1876–1893* (Stroud, 1993), p. xix.
95. Roberts to Lord Lansdowne, 29 January 1900, in Wessels, *Roberts and the War in South Africa*, p. 47. Thomas Kelly-Kenny was a County Clare landowner and JP; John French was a landed officer with a deep family connection to Wexford.
96. Sir George Stuart White's private diary for 1886, BL Mss Eur F108/119.
97. White to Gipps, 8 August 1893. White Papers, British Library.
98. William Butler, *The Great Lone Land* (London, 1872).

99. White to General Sir Robert Low, Simla, 30 August 1895. White Papers, British Library.
100. White to Lockhart, Calcutta, 1 March 1896. White Papers, British Library.
101. See Philip Ollerenshaw, 'Businessmen and the Development of Ulster Unionism', *Journal of Imperial and Commonwealth History* 28 (2000), pp. 35–64.
102. James, *Lord Roberts*, pp. 83–84.
103. Ibid. p 142.
104. Chamberlain, no relation to the prime minister who shared his name, was on Roberts' staff in India, and came from a military family with strong ties to the East India Company army. Following his retirement in 1901, he was appointed commissioner of the Royal Irish Constabulary, and was later forced to resign over his handling of police intelligence in the aftermath of the 1916 Rising.
105. Hamilton quoted in Kochanski, 'Viscount Wolseley', p. 25.
106. James, *Lord Roberts*, p. 182.
107. Ibid. p. 237.
108. Keith Jeffery, *Henry Wilson: Political Soldier* (Oxford, 2006), p. 107.
109. Mark Coulter, 'Field-Marshal Sir Henry Wilson: Imperial Soldier, Political Failure', *History Ireland* 13 (2005), pp. 26–27.
110. Jeffery, *Henry Wilson*, pp. 110, 114.
111. Piers Brendon, *The Decline and Fall of the British Empire, 1781–1997* (London, 2007), p. 219.
112. Gifford Lewis, *Somerville and Ross: The World of the Irish RM* (New York, 1985), p. 162.
113. Keith Surridge, '"You Soldiers Are What We Call Pro-Boer": The Military Critique of the South African War, 1899–1902', *History Ireland* 8 (2000), p. 29; Peter Donaldson, *Remembering the South African War* (Liverpool, 2013), pp. 140–143; Andrew Porter, 'The South African War and the Historians', *African Affairs* 99 (2000), pp. 634–635.
114. Spiers, *The Army and Society*, p. 297. Scotland's population in the 1901 census was just under 4.5 million, while Ireland's was 4.4 million.
115. Anthony Bruce, *The Purchase System in the British Army, 1660–1871* (London, 1980), pp. 157–158.
116. Strachan, *The Politics of the British Army*, pp. 103–112 passim.
117. Ibid. pp. 111–112.

CHAPTER 5

Aid to the Civil Power: The Military Establishment, the Land War, and the Home Rule Crisis, 1879–1914

I am a landlord, a Protestant, and a Unionist. I hold to my class, my creed, and my political faith.
—4th Earl Dunraven, 1907

The plurality of Irish military officers who were members of the landowning class, such as the Earl Dunraven, is indicative of the prominent social role played by the military establishment in Ireland. In the late nineteenth century, the class characteristics of the officer corps changed very little.[1] Dunraven, a large landowner with his elite English education, Sandhurst training, service history in aristocratic regiments, and elite institutional connections to the Kildare Street Club, Royal Yacht Squadron, and both the Liberal and Conservative political establishments, was a figure at ease within the aristocratic *milieu* of the Victorian officer corps.[2] However, all of these signifiers of identity would face a 'perfect storm' which challenged officers' elite position from the start of the Land War in 1879 until the Curragh incident in 1914, bound up in declining landlord power, the professionalisation of the military command, and the fracturing of the elite political consensus in Ireland. The previously uncontroversial, even centrist political position of 'constructive unionism' espoused by the military establishment gradually lost ground to adversarial mass movements divided on the issue of Irish Home Rule. The gravity of these challenges can be discerned in the reactions of Irish officers to the successive social and political crises which wracked Ireland in this period.

© The Author(s) 2019
L. Sweeney, *Irish Military Elites, Nation and Empire, 1870–1925*,
https://doi.org/10.1007/978-3-030-19307-2_5

103

A recurring observation about Irish elites in this period is that there was very little about them that was 'Irish'; however, officers' Irishness played a central role in their responses to the escalation of sectarian politics in 1912–14. There is an implication in other writing on the subject that Irish soldiers' class difference, or imperial affinity, isolated them from questions of Ireland's future: 'Ireland was far too much a place which [military and aristocratic] people *used* rather than lived in ... nor was it much different with Irish families whose sons had to make their careers abroad', in the words Terence de Vere White.[3] In a similar vein, Peter Verney's regimental biography of the Irish Guards contends that military life attenuated soldiers' concerns about Irish affairs: 'it was not that they did not deeply feel the unrest in their native country—it was just that they were above it; once in uniform they felt and owed allegiance to a higher cause.'[4] This perspective, arrived at in hindsight, glosses over the deep interconnections between the army and society in late-Victorian Ireland.

A key apprehension of officers was 'politicisation'; the feeling that the army's ability to operate effectively was being curtailed, by the politically motivated actions of politicians and the War Office, was a major factor leading to the Curragh crisis of summer 1914. The military's traditional allegiance to the crown, not parliament, turned the question of political influence into a battle for the soul of the army. In Ireland, as mass mobilisation and social unrest crystallised around the Home Rule issue, and armed unionist and nationalist militias emerged in 1912–14, the army's internal disputes over authority were mapped onto the increasingly fraught political situation. Ironically, officers' instinct to resist political influence in the army now threatened to draw it into an Irish civil war.

The spectres of 'politicisation' and 'democratisation' of the officer corps were often enunciated by elite Irish officers. The perceived 'political' influence on the War Office was a major sticking point for officers in the early twentieth century, though the relationship with the administration in Ireland was generally more congenial. While there was a functional separation between the military and civilian administrations in Ireland, there was a certain amount of crossover between the two: the Viceroy, more often than not, had a military background, military officers were sometimes appointed to positions in the civil administration and police, and landowning resident magistrates often had military connections. It was certainly not unheard of for military officers to enthusiastically give voice to their opinions regarding civil policy, particularly with regard to policing and to the appointment of senior officials.[5] Irish officers were a particularly important facet of life in the precincts of the rural gentry and aristocracy in the decades dubbed by David Cannadine 'the twilight of the Ascendency', and like the landed interest they found their elite position becoming increasingly precarious in Ireland.[6]

While officers found themselves in Ireland primarily for occupational reasons, they were not completely lacking in agency when transferring from posting to posting; those young officers who, fresh from Sandhurst, expressed an interest in Irish regiments clearly had an Irish affinity, and oftentimes a familial connection to Ireland. It was also not unknown for senior officers to request specific junior officers to serve under them, a feature of military life which increased the strength and importance of social networks. It was in this way that Colonel Henry Brackenbury found himself with a position in the Irish civil administration in 1882, and how he in turn attracted Major Alfred Turner to Dublin as his aide-de-camp.[7] It is also possible, however, that an officer would be ambivalent about his designated regiment, and it is worth noting that regiments, both at home and abroad, were moved frequently between stations—though a line regiment's enlisted men always originated from the same locality.[8] Professional incentives to take an Irish posting were low: officers were encouraged and expected to apply for colonial postings, and ambitious early-career officers seeking promotion were better served by going on campaign or attending the Staff College. That said, the army lists for regiments stationed in the Irish military area record many aristocratic officers alongside those with more common surnames.[9]

IRISH OFFICERS, RURAL LIFE, AND THE LANDED INTEREST

The lives of Irish military officers were defined by a number of common features. Nora Robertson, the daughter of an infantry colonel, produced a valuable and incisive memoir about life in the barrack town of Fermoy in the late nineteenth century. The regiment divided its time between the Northwest Frontier of India and County Cork, and Robertson gives a rich description of a world onto itself, in which 'the barracks dominated my outlook'.[10] Histories of Irish barracks in the period relate similar themes in towns and cities of various sizes and locations, which reveal interconnections between the military and the town: local tradesmen and suppliers were sometimes (though not always) employed to provide goods and services, and to undertake repairs and expansions to barracks; local labourers were needed by the remount and ordinance departments to work at stables and firing ranges; civilians shared their places of worship (Catholic and Protestant) with the military; local pubs were popular with the soldiers, and reciprocally, civilians with military connections were permitted to socialise in the camp; and, there was an officially tolerated, semi-sanctioned system of prostitution, which was particularly in evidence at the Curragh, the largest military station in the United Kingdom at the time.

Con Costello, in his extensive history of the Curragh camp, relates that even after the camp was abandoned by the British in 1922, the soldiers' legacy remained due to a large number of marriages between military personnel and local women in nearby towns like Kildare and Newbridge, providing further proof of a close interrelation between soldiers and civilians in such localities.[11] Unions with local women were also common in the officer corps, with minor gentry and professional families seeking an alliance with a military officer as an avenue for social advancement.[12] Histories of other barracks in Ireland, like Victoria (Collins) Barracks in Cork, illustrate identical interactions at work all over the country.[13] We should not, however, dismiss Nora Robertson's characterisation of barrack life as insular out of hand; despite these variegated connections, there were still very important institutional, cultural, and physical barriers between the internal world of the army barracks and the civilian world beyond. The built environment of the barracks was designed to be reproduced on the same design anywhere around the world—the officers of Tipperary barracks remarked on its similarity to a station in Hong Kong—and as a mental and physical space it encouraged detachment and disinterest on the part of the soldiers to local issues.[14] Officers were meant to be apolitical; the institution of geographically tied regiments in the 1880s did not make a difference to officer selection, as they were expected to remain aloof from local difficulties.[15] In the words of Hubert Gough, one of the officers serving at the Curragh in this period, and later a key player in the 1914 'mutiny', 'None of us cavalry soldiers were much interested in Irish politics, as far as we were aware, the people apart from the professional politicians were not much interested either.'[16] As we shall see, his actions in 1914 suggest that he experienced a subsequent change of heart.

What comes across most strongly in Robertson's account is the extent of social interaction which took place between officers and local gentry.

An Irish posting was variously described as 'congenial', 'boring', 'pleasant' for sports though containing only a small 'society set'. The Earl of Dunraven issued the following appraisal of life in the country, when seeking to explain why so many Irish strove to leave: 'It is said that Irish life is so deadly monotonous, is so lacking in all the allurements of modern civilization, and so devoid of all the pleasures gained by social intercourse … in a new environment [the Irish] may [hope to] find life more varied and attractive.'[17] Even as a County Limerick aristocrat deeply involved in the land issue, the defining aspect of Dunraven's world was its monotony. Officers who enjoyed rural pursuits, particularly hunting and horse racing, were well catered for. Those who chose to dwell on negative aspects of life in Ireland—its remoteness, its poverty, and its cold, wet climate—were less disposed to look favourably on their time there.

Officers often interacted with local gentry and aristocracy, and thus remained appraised of the local and national political situation, however disinterested they may have appeared.[18] While women and politics may have remained taboo subjects for discussion in the officer's mess, in civilian company they seemed to become the primary diversions of the officer class. Politics in particular was unavoidable in the 1880s, when Childers' proposals to reform the regimental system and institute a period of short service, and the very public disagreements on the subject between Roberts and Wolseley, were a constant subject of discussion in the press. The imperial situation, too, was a source of interest and debate: Nora Robertson recalls a dinner party with officers, where a beautiful young lady, the daughter of Colonel Thomas Gonne, unrelentingly took to task a young Indian Army captain for Britain's imperial record in the country. This was, of course, Maud Gonne, who would go on to become a prominent Irish nationalist, supporter of the Boer republics and campaigner for the Land League. Colonel Gonne, a cavalry officer, was himself active in commanding troops to protect process-servers in evictions in the west of Ireland, a further illustration of the differing generational outlooks which could be discerned among elites at this time.[19]

Robertson's writings serve as a salutary reminder that the world of the Irish officer corps was not confined solely to men—women at all levels of the social scale, from the aristocratic circles of Lady Londonderry, to the aesthetic Dublin society of Elsie Henry, to the imperial interconnections of Nora Robertson—played a crucial role in the social interaction that arbitrated respectability within the military elite.[20] This was true of imperial service, as much as home service. Officers' wives operated within a prescribed role, which mirrored the role of the colonial civilian's 'service wife' charged with the maintenance of the intimate colonial frontier.[21] Wives sometimes acted as proxies for their husbands, occasionally adopting military styles of dress and even taking on their husband's rank, according to Verity McInnis.[22] On the home front, from the wives of enlisted men, introduced onto military camps from the mid-nineteenth century, to the agency seized by officers' wives in the drawing room, to the social arbiters of the peerage and the Dublin Castle establishment (Lady Arnold-Forster is an indicative example), officers' good relations with the Irish social elite required navigating familial and female spaces, as much as it did the masculine environs of the gentleman's club and the officers' mess.

After the relatively calm 1870s, the 1880s was a turbulent decade for Irish officers. As land agitation threatened to erode the economic basis of their lifestyle, members of the landed class felt under siege in their own country. Constitutional nationalism and the development of a 'Hibernicised' professional elite gradually began to shift the focus away from British linkages as marks of distinction.[23] This coincided with the spread of religious sectarianism as an inextricable component of Irish political life, cutting new divisions across the Anglo-Irish as well as other social groups. The rudest shock of all came in the spring of 1882 when, in Phoenix Park, just steps from the Viceregal Lodge, the Chief Secretary of Ireland and his Permanent Undersecretary were murdered by the Invincibles. Suddenly, it seemed, nowhere was safe. Alvin Jackson recounts that it was this event, and the concomitant 'threat of anarchy, and not the early and generally pacific land agitation' which precipitated the deep divisions of the next 40 years between nationalists and Unionists, fracturing the political consensus and germinating a future crisis for the Irish officer corps.[24] Irish officers, most prominently and vocally Lord Wolseley, were appalled.[25] The previous chief secretary, William Forster, summarised the feeling of the Irish establishment, saying simply, 'things are as bad as they can be.'[26] However shocking the isolated incidents of urban violence were, and however localised and varying was the severity of the land agitation in the countryside, this ought not detract from the fact that the Land War was the major consideration of the political class, the landed interest, and the military establishment in Ireland in the early 1880s.[27]

'A STRONG DETACHMENT OF REDCOATS THOROUGHLY COWS THE MOST ... MUTINOUS LOCALITY': THE MILITARY ESTABLISHMENT AND THE LAND WAR

The Land War, the period of agrarian unrest in the early 1880s surrounding the eviction of tenants from encumbered Irish estates, came as a severe blow to rural Irish officers, particularly those who could be said to constitute Victorian Ireland's equestrian class: suddenly, their lives and livelihoods came into collision with their soldiering careers.

The role of the military had always included the stipulation of providing assistance to the civil power when necessary, but in 1880 the Chief Secretary of Ireland considered it necessary to reinforce the military presence and expand the role of the military in the face of the increasing threat posed by land agitation.[28] Playing a crucial role in this increased presence were the cavalry regiments. Throughout the nineteenth century, cavalry officers were the cream of the military elite, although by the Edwardian period their elevated position had become somewhat precarious. In 1910, Horace Wyndham complained that the cavalry corps had been stocked with the arriviste sons of 'wealthy tradesmen ... it is practically impossible to keep the expenses within the limits which may be met by men of gentle birth and small bank accounts.'[29] Captain William Armstrong, of County Tipperary, was one such gentleman. In his letters home he complained about the mounting cost of living in the cavalry regiments.[30] This invasion of the sacred precincts of the cavalry by moneyed but socially undistinguished officers seemed particularly odious in the context of cavalry officers' position within the declining landed interest in Ireland. The hussar and dragoon officers of landed families who were deployed to assist with evictions were in a very real sense fighting to preserve their livelihoods: according to Fergus Campbell, the rent revisions of the 1880s and 1890s had led to an average reduction in landlord incomes from rent of 38%.[31]

Amid the social whirlwind of race meetings, hunt balls, and staff rides that typified home service in Ireland, however, the military were only occasionally called upon in aid of the civil power: to keep order at polling places, to suppress rioting, and to protect constables and process-servers during evictions.[32] There was a significant amount of resentment from some of the officers who were called upon to do jobs which, it was felt, should have fallen fully within the purview of the police. Frank Percy

Crozier, later a prominent Irish officer himself, recalled that 'Her Majesty's Army, in the bad days, carried out a difficult and thankless task with their customary courtesy and good humour and my father ... used to tell me of the pathetic scenes he used to witness while accompanying the Royal Irish Constabulary (RIC) to evictions.'[33] Those with a more in-depth understanding of such operations, however, were generally in favour of employing the military. According to one officer,

> Many people decry the use of troops to aid the civil power, but probably such people have no experience of the great difficulties and responsibilities of those who are charged with this unpleasant duty. The presence of the military has the most salutary effect even upon the most unruly spirits, who would not shirk a tussle with the police. I had a free hand as to requisitioning troops ... I was often asked why I did so often in cases when the police would have sufficed. My invariable reply was that I would not have any resistance or bloodshed.[34]

The cavalry was favoured for such action, due to the perceived crowd-calming and deterrent effects of their warhorses.[35] The attractiveness of having trained, steady soldiers standing against sometimes violent mobs was underlined following incidents such as in Sligo in 1881, where during evictions on the ffrench estate, Royal Irish Constabulary constables panicked and fired into the crowd.[36]

The socialisation of cavalry officers meant that their sympathies lay with the landlord class, and this may have increased the authorities' confidence in their abilities during the Land War. In his memoirs, the 4th Earl of Dunraven, as a young officer in the Life Guards in London, recalled having to return to his country house during periods of agrarian unrest, and that he was called upon in his capacity as an officer to inspect the local constabulary barracks and report on their suitability. Even though he had no idea what he was supposed to be inspecting, he recounts, the presence of an officer reassured the RIC men.[37] In addition to cavalry, a deployment of soldiers to a trouble spot would often employ foot troops of the Royal Engineers and the Royal Garrison Artillery, whose horses and carronades were useful for hauling equipment.

The presence of soldiers at evictions and rallies led to scuffles between rioters and officers which are illustrative of the interrelations between the officer corps and the rural labouring class in general. A typical account of such a scuffle in the 1880s involved a column of Hussars who were deployed to Scariff to keep the peace. The townspeople, unaccustomed to the sight of flamboyantly attired soldiers parading through their village, formed a boisterous crowd and one bystander 'out of curiosity' grabbed at the bit of an officer's horse. The affronted officer, who according to his commander had a 'peppery' temperament, struck the man and called him a 'damned ugly fellow'. A riot ensued, and it was only the quick thinking of the police commissioner and the coolness of the other officers, in extricating themselves from the situation in an orderly manner, that avoided a bloodbath.[38]

Officers were thus occasionally at pains to keep their men under control—Michael Davitt's assessment of Colonel Turner's attempts to control his men was one of 'more pity than contempt'—suggesting that, from the point of view of the campaigning crowds, the soldiers appeared to be uncontrollable.[39] A serious breach of discipline occurred in 1888 at a Land League meeting in Ennis, which was attended by a large detachment of hussars. According to Turner, who was once again in command of the column, 'the worst thing that happened was that a hussar broke out of the ranks, drew his sword and rode amok into the archway, where he cut at the tall hat of Mr. Hill, the correspondent of the Irish "Times"'. When brought under control and asked to explain himself, the hussar said he had assumed the man was a nationalist MP, on account of his dress.[40] In precarious moments like this, it was the role of officers to prevent a situation from developing: 'the breaking away from the ranks of the hussar and the use of their batons by the police of another county were unjustifiable, but they both occurred in the twinkling of an eye and were stopped as soon as possible by the officer.'[41] The 'outrageous' behaviour of the hussars and constables, particularly in targeting a journalist, ensured that the incident received a great deal of coverage in the *Times*, *Freeman's Journal* and other newspapers. The Secretary of State for War was called upon in Parliament to explain how this breach of discipline took place, and maintained that it was unclear whether 'the Hussar who left his post was the man who wounded Mr. Hill. It further appears that this Hussar had been ordered by his officer to return to his post before Colonel Turner had intervened.'[42] It transpired that other irregularities had taken place on the day; Turner recalled that, as his hussars were following Michael Davitt and a procession of supporters through the town, they passed an Artillery Militia barracks and were 'greeted by a shower of stones by the militiamen. I myself, the trumpeter and one or two troopers were struck, but not hurt, and we took no notice.'[43] However, tensions were evidently higher than Turner admits, as observers later reported that the soldiers were in a state of excitement and there was a debate over whether their singing of 'Rule, Britannia' was calculated to inflame the crowd, or whether it was intended to steady and reassure their own men.[44] In any event, when the hussars were once again pelted with stones by members of the crowd at the nationalist rally, it was too much for the one hussar who broke ranks. The crowd was contained in a yard surrounded by hussars and police, and soldiers were engaged in arresting the stone-throwers, which may have added to the tension. Following the hussar's charge, Turner ordered the constables to 'go inside and arrest all there', and in the subsequent enquiry there was much debate as to whether or not this constituted an authorisation of the police baton-charge that then took place, leading to a large number of casualties.[45] Of particular concern was the question of why hussars were then ordered into a crowd that was already being pacified by baton-wielding constables, whether they drew their swords on their own initiative or were ordered to by Turner, and whether they were 'slashing left and right' as Parnell characterised it, or 'using the flats of their swords' as Balfour argued, when the matter came up for discussion in the House of Commons.[46]

There are a number of intriguing aspects to this incident. First, it illustrates the potential for tension between militia soldiers and hussars indicated by the throwing of stones, which, though an isolated incident, gives an indication of both the class and social differences of the various army corps, and of the aforementioned feeling of some officers that they were operating among a hostile and unpredictable populace. Second, it illustrates the extent of the tension between Irish officers and the people whom they were intended to pacify; in the aftermath of the incident the Irish Parliamentary Party politician T.M. Healy commented upon this tension in Parliament, and reiterated the generally accepted position that military officers should strive to stay out of politics, despite the evident impossibility of this in the context of aid to the civil power operations:

the Army was very popular in Ireland, and, undoubtedly the people liked the soldiers, who gave them very little trouble. There were, however, English and Irish regiments, and he was sorry to see, in this morning's newspapers, that there had been a row between English and Irish regiments. Once you began this sort of thing you did not know where it would end, and it was a characteristic of Irishmen that whenever they thought an insult was offered to their country, were it even so far as the North Pole, it was felt and resented by the Irish race always. *Officers then should not begin to lead off the chorus …* In all these matters, whether it was Ennis or Mitchelstown, they should grant an inquiry and let the people see that justice was absolutely impartial, and that whether the malefactor was Colonel Turner or John Smith, he would be liable to equal punishment.[47]

The subsequent enquiry, in which Colonel Turner was grilled about his actions at Ennis, also illustrates the limitations on the power of the officer corps to coerce the population, and the tensions between the military and political establishments which manifested themselves during the Land War. The antipathy of officers for politicians could well be understood when, after being ordered to pacify a turbulent locality, their explanation of their method is met with the riposte of William O'Brien, that 'Colonel Turner's story, I submit to this House, is an insult to common sense. It is the story of a man who is driven to the wall for an excuse, or a man who … like every Irish official, imagines that no excuse is too preposterous to go down with the men who are ruling Ireland.'[48]

The reorganisation of the regimental system under the Childers Reforms in 1881 meant that regimental identity became identified with a specific recruiting area to a much greater degree than previously. While under the old system, some officially 'Scottish' or 'English' regiments became popular with Irishmen and vice-versa, there was now an official system of geographical designations attached to regiments. From this period, it became much easier to avoid potential divisions of loyalty by, for example, using Scottish instead of Irish troops in aid to the civil power operations in Ireland.[49] This did, on occasion, lead to resentment, however: in 1887, two English regiments stationed at Athlone, the Berkshires, and the Border Regiment, 'marched from the barracks in a body to Irishtown, in the Westmeath division of the town, and, without the slightest provocation, commenced wrecking houses', according to a report in the *Irish Times.* This led to a confrontation in which 'a number of artisans, armed with stout cudgels', set to driving the soldiers off, while the police 'were powerless to cope with the riot while it lasted'. Once again, blame accrued to the officers, 'for not confining the men to barracks'.[50]

Officers, of course, were not assigned to territorially linked regiments, and could express a preference for their regimental affiliation. Immediately after the implementation of the reforms, there was a period of transition in the Irish regiments. The Connaught Rangers, well-known in military circles as the most 'Irish' of the Irish regiments, found itself in the curious and singular position of possessing a predominantly Irish officer corps, and a predominantly non-Irish contingent of enlisted men. According to the *Freeman's Journal*, 'A considerable number of the officers of the 2nd Connaught Rangers are Irishmen, but I believe that the great majority of the men are English. Hence the gushing anxiety of the authorities to send them to Tipperary' to take part in aid to the civil power duties.[51] The Connaught Rangers would remain stationed in Ireland through the worst years of unrest, not leaving their home station again until 1887. It is intriguing that, while military planners were clearly apprehensive about the reaction of Irish enlisted men towards civil power operations in Ireland, these concerns did not extend to Irish officers. Clearly, the contentious position of Irish nationality in the British official mind had a class dimension, which excluded Irish officers by dint of their socialisation into the officer corps. Across the late nineteenth and early twentieth century, the potential for divided loyalties among Irish soldiers was consistently overstated, while, at the same time, its effect on the Irish officer corps was misunderstood by politicians and senior commanders.

The Royal Irish Constabulary, too, was closely linked with the military command; it was not uncommon for army officers to undertake a spell of half pay in order to take up a position in the RIC. In the entire period under consideration, in fact, there was only a single inspector general, Andrew Reed, who did not have a military background, and it was his unfortunate duty to occupy the post during the Belfast riots of 1886. Several well-known and successful military officers were closely associated with the RIC, including John French, Bernard Montgomery and Redvers Buller of the Wolseley Ring. French, later to become a well-known First World War general, served alongside RIC officers in the Captain Boycott incident (examined below). Montgomery was involved in counter-insurgency operations in Co. Cork during the War of Independence, and his brother Hugh, an intelligence officer, was killed in 1920 by the IRA, on Bloody Sunday. Buller served as District Commissioner for Kerry and Clare in the 1880s and often directed Irish officers in evictions.

Another officer assisting Buller, who in 1886 was 'struggling with considerable difficulties to carry out my task in maintaining law and order in the south-west and west of Ireland' was the aforementioned Alfred Turner, a half-Irish officer who saw 'brute force' employed to pacify the countryside first-hand (Fig. 5.1). He observed that it was effective in restoring order only temporarily, and then only at the price of fanning a smouldering discontent among the populace.[52] According to Turner's testimony, Buller's work in the west of Ireland was carried out as fairly as possible under the circumstances: with 'the appointment of Sir Redvers Buller ... certain classes in Ireland, as opposed to the masses ... thought that Clare

Fig. 5.1 Evictions at the Vandeleur Estate, Kilrush, Co Clare. 120 Constables of the Royal Irish Constabulary, supported by 50 troopers of the 3rd Hussars, 70 men of the Sherwood Foresters, and 50 of the Berkshire Regiment, were deployed to evict 114 tenants from the estate. Colonel Alfred Turner is pictured, second from left. *Courtesy of the National Library of Ireland*

and Kerry would soon be dragooned into abject submission by military procedure and brute force … the tenants had come to learn that, if he was not their friend, he was no partial or one-sided official who had come to oppress them.'[53] Buller proved to be a man unafraid to express his opinion, that 'the law in Ireland was made for the rich and not for the poor', much to the chagrin of his superiors, Turner recounts.[54] Buller was constantly at loggerheads with a political authority who seemingly had little understanding of affairs on the ground. In a letter to Lord Carnarvon in 1887, he wrote

> There is a state of things in Ireland which never occurred before and was not dreamed of when you were Viceroy. A series of slum houses are carefully and thoroughly fortified and defended by desperate women with boiling water, hot lime, gaff hooks etc. etc. Each house is a small fort, and each house has to be taken out by the military … in the face of any number of military opinions I acted on my own military responsibility that to take 31 strongly fortified houses … (not half a dozen cottages as you say) without the use of some such explosive is not and cannot be made 'an affair of hours'—In this general subject I have only to say: i. that there was an overwhelming force, as evidenced by the fact that no resistance was attempted by the mob, ii. that the seize of 31 houses was carried through with extreme decision precision and rapidity- iii. that every one who resisted the law was arrested on the spot. iv. that the 47 persons so arrested were brought to trial the day the evictions were completed. v. that public opinion is not yet prepared for the use of explosives in this sort of resistance … I am merely following what I take to be the path of duty.[55]

Regardless of the moral convictions of the officers involved in evictions, their duties often necessitated a significant show of force. In May, 1887, Buller and Turner were given the task of carrying out evictions on the Bodyke estate: 'I was directed to proceed with "full military precautions", reporting constantly to Dublin Castle', including the deployment of three officers and one hundred men of the Welsh Fusiliers.[56] Despite the tense situation, 'the conduct of the troops and the police was excellent throughout … A cordon of infantry surrounded the houses one after the other, and prevented the large crowds of people … [from] interfering with the sheriff. In this the military rendered the most invaluable assistance and prevented rioting.'[57] Other accounts of the proceedings at Bodyke were not so positive; in Dublin, the Chief Secretary was concerned about the 'terrible collision between police and people' during the evictions, and according to a report by Lady Arnold-Forster, five people had been need-lessly killed as a result of the military's actions.[58]

Other accounts of evictions and military activities in Ireland at the time centred on something of a *cause celebre*: the treatment of Captain Boycott by the tenants of Lord Erne, and the eventual relief of his farm at Lough Mask by a work battalion of Orangemen. The first 'boycott', so-named, in history, was recorded by an English journalist, Bernard Becker, who was travelling through the west of Ireland as a correspondent for *The Daily News* reporting on distressed agrarian districts. Even in places where sol-diers were not present, the imprint of military men in leading roles in the RIC is tangible in his account: constables are characterised as 'soldiers in all but name'.[59] As the boycott against Captain Boycott developed, the nearby towns of Ballinrobe and Claremorris were swamped with hundreds of soldiers, shoring up the local police presence, commanded by Colonel Bedingfield of the Royal Artillery, and Major Coghill of the 19th Hussars, a member of a Co. Cork military family of distinction. In Ballinrobe alone, Becker estimated in November 1880, there were 750 soldiers making ready to break the boycott.[60] The efficacy of the policy of deploying over-whelming military force at Lough Mask and elsewhere, as enunciated by Buller and other officers, clearly impressed Becker:

> A small force, insufficient to overawe the countryside, only provokes the resistance it is unable to overcome, but a strong detachment of redcoats thoroughly cows the adventurous spirits of the most mutinous localities. What threatened at one moment to become a civil war in Mayo was put down without the loss of a drop of blood by an imposing military force.[61]

At the level of the rank and file, the RIC provided the same attractions to non-elites as imperial military or civil service offered to the subjects of this study: the work was difficult, dangerous and badly paid, but it was steady, and there were opportunities for advancement and the promise of a pension at the end of it.[62] For the most part, relations between the RIC and the military were amicable, though certain military officers felt that camps and patrols in rural Ireland were a waste of their time.[63] John Ross of Bladensburg, an officer from a distinguished Irish military family who would later become a senior officer in the Dublin Metropolitan Police, grumbled in 1882 that the military were 'considered to be police escorts', and generally facilitated, rather than usurped, the duties of the police.[64]

Colonel JH Dopping recorded harmonious civil-military cooperation at evictions in 1887. According to his testimony of the Gweedore evictions, subscriptions were received from grateful landlords by the Anti-Plan of Campaign Association, which helped to coordinate these responses. Subscribers included the Earl of Courtown, Lord Castletown, Major Somerset Maxwell and Major HL Barton.[65] The cooperation of local RMs, the Constabulary, the government and the military was essential in effecting evictions. This is underlined in the journals of Lady Florence Arnold-Forster, in 1880–81, the niece of Chief Secretary William Edward Forster. Lady Arnold-Forster recounted that 'the arrival of the 1st Coldstream Guards in Dublin is the only act of the present Govt which has given satisfaction to elegant society here'.[66] While no serious comparison can be made between the condition of Ireland at the time and the battlefields of South Africa, the Sudan or the Northwest Frontier, the Guards officers approached their assignment in Ireland with the same zeal: Lady Florence notes slightly incredulously in 1881 that '300 of the Coldstreams, and 100 of the Scots Guards are to go off as a flying column somewhere; the officers seem much pleased, and say this is really serious work, they will have bottles thrown at them etc. etc.'[67] They were on their way to New Pallas, where once again the overwhelming presence of the military served to dissuade a hostile crowd from attacking the local constables, supported by cavalry and Royal Artillery. Bernard Becker, who witnessed the operation, wrote 'Everybody knew that there was no chance of a row, and that the very presence of all the Queen's horses and all the Queen's men would make it certain that a blank would be drawn … Pallas was evidently taken by surprise, for any movement on a western Irish town before nine in the morning may be taken as a night attack.'[68] By 5 June, 'the G[uard]s had come back from New Pallas much impressed with the villainous faces of the men, the beauty of the women, and the wonderful influence of the priests.'[69]

Another young officer, later to find distinction as a war correspondent for *The Times*, who took part in evictions was Charles à Court Repington, whose memories of his time stationed in Ireland have proven a valuable source and appear in many historical works on the period. While stationed at Oughterard in 1881–82, Repington commanded a detachment of troops tasked with putting down an agrarian riot. Taking the initiative, Repington was able to diffuse the situation by ambushing and capturing the local leader of the rebellious tenantry: '"All quite illegal," he later happily admitted to Raymond Marker, "but we inspired such a funk that …

outrages ceased."'[70] Repington illustrates here the degree of autonomy granted officers in the carrying out of such operations, and hints at the mundanity of the vast majority of the military's involvement in the Land War. In those few moments when tensions bubbled and military force was required to restore order, however, the officer's role on the 'front lines' of the Land War was evident. Lady Florence reminds us that there was a degree of hysteria in all this reporting, too: 'As for the way in which people talk of Ireland ... one would think that we had been living in a barbarous country infested with brigands and assassins, and on the verge of civil war—I can quite believe that if we had gathered all our impressions of the state of things from the London papers instead of from the facts in Ireland we should have been.'[71]

Another source of useful information about the attitudes of elites during the Land War is the fourth Earl of Dunraven, Windham Wyndham-Quin. His manor house, at Adare outside Limerick, was located in an area of high land agitation—in 1881 a detachment of guardsmen was dispatched to Limerick to supplement the police presence.[72] The Wyndham-Quins themselves were considered conscientious landlords, however, and suffered little from unrest.[73] This military and political dynasty was at the peak of their influence and prestige in the late-nineteenth and early twentieth century, and practically every male member of the family served in the army with distinction, after attending the Royal Military College, Sandhurst. Wyndham-Quin would later take a key political role in the settlement of the Irish land question at the conference preceding the 1903 Wyndham Land Act (named for George Wyndham, no relation), which required the exercise of Wyndham-Quin's extensive network of civilian and military elites. Among the other officers present at the Land Conference Committee in 1902–03 were Colonel Hutcheson-Poë, scion of a longstanding military family, Colonel Nugent Everard, one of Wolseley's favourites, and Lieut. Gen. William Massy, a well-known war hero.[74] He was also congratulated by fellow military officers for his success in chairing the proceedings, receiving letters of encouragement from the de Montmorencys and Colonel Hanford.[75] Many though not all of these landowning officers shared Wyndham-Quin's political convictions, and the fact that they were decorated military men was a significant and frequently remarked-upon feature of the conference.[76]

During the years of the Land War, the presence and severity of violence differed vastly between localities.[77] Bernard Becker contrasted the coercion by the military at Ballinrobe with the situation at the estate of Richard

Stacpoole in County Clare: 'There is none of the pomp and circumstance of open war. There is not a soldier or policeman on the premises.'[78] Naturally, the generally low intensity of the Land War did nothing to calm the panic and apprehension of the landlord class: 'To a person unconnected with the landed interest in Ireland it is at first a little difficult to understand the almost insane terror of nearly all persons endowed with property.'[79] In this context of elite hysteria, the military can be said generally to have acted with some restraint, even proportionality.

The old order, centred on the landlord interest, was unmistakeably in financial and social decline, not least as a result of the 1903 Land Act.[80] The military, however, still played a key role in the lives and identity of the rural gentry, and this was never more manifest than when Irish officers had to defend their class interests with the sword during the Land War. By 1910, following the Land Acts and the continuing work of the Land Commission, agrarian unrest had died down and the cause of Home Rule had become the most pressing political issue, debated by urban, well-connected, cross-class mass movements.[81] Though the land issue had declined in importance, the mental environment which military officers inhabited was still steeped in the values and customs of the rural aristocracy and gentry. According to Virginia Crossman, 'The deeper the military was sucked into the political morass of the land war and the plan of campaign the more difficult it was to preserve the impartial image on which army personnel so prided themselves.'[82] Though the Plan of Campaign had the explicit backing of the Irish Parliamentary Party, the actions of the army were not regarded by officers as being a 'political' issue—even with hussars charging about attacking supposed Nationalist MPs. The political situation was accelerating beyond the ability of the hidebound and old-fashioned identity of the officer corps to keep pace; unlike during the land issue, the officer corps was not of one mind concerning Home Rule. The 'politicisation' of the corps, as it was unavoidably confronted with challenges to its identity, social position, and moral authority in Ireland, was to be the unwelcome result.

HOME RULE AGITATION: 'AKIN TO ACTUAL WARFARE' OR 'RELATIVE CALM'?

While the threat of agrarian outrages rumbled on at a low level throughout the period of evictions, the Home Rule question had the potential to explode into a serious breach of the peace for short bursts at a time. This

was a particularly dangerous problem in large towns and cities, and it contributed to the most extreme disruptions of law and order in Belfast. While
rioting was a fairly regular occurrence in Victorian Belfast, the most severe
flareup occurred in 1886, following the defeat of the first Home Rule Bill
in Parliament, and necessitated the deployment of troops. Sectarian rioting between gangs of Catholic and Protestant shipyard workers developed
into a melee with police lasting for months, punctuated by periods of relative calm. The rioting was so severe and widespread that extra constables
from the south of Ireland had to be brought in to augment the force
already present in the city. This fanned the flames of sectarian violence, as
it was widely believed that these Catholic constables would discriminate
against Protestant workers, and would throw off the carefully maintained
balance of Catholic and Protestant officers in the city's units of the Royal
Irish Constabulary.[83] The army was deployed in a limited supporting role,
including soldiers of the Highland Light Infantry and the Queen's (West
Surrey) Regiment. Matters came to a head when rioters descended on the
RIC barracks on the Shankill Road, and the panicked officers fired indis-
criminately into the crowd, against orders. The situation quickly deterio-
rated into chaos.

As RIC reinforcements continued to pour into Belfast, the General
Officer Commanding the Belfast district, Major-General Montgomery
Moore, recommended the withdrawal of all constables from the Shankill,
which had by this point become totally lawless. As Mark Radford explains,
'the *de facto* abrogation of police responsibility to the military was ... a
controversial move'[84] The 'steadiness' of the military in the face of riot
conditions as opposed to the panic of the Constabulary was once again in
evidence here. During the riots, policemen shot and killed over 30 civilians, most of them innocent bystanders, before receiving any authorisation
to use lethal force. The military units, though deployed in a support role,
fared much better, and held their nerve even after the mortal wounding of
a private of the West Surrey Regiment by rioters.

Radford contends that this was a turning point for the RIC, who had
become too dependent on the carbine rather than the truncheon as the
correct tool of civil policing. Inspector-general Andrew Reed's policy 'that
if it was necessary to fire on rioters the army should be the only ones to do
so', led to a re-evaluation in policing practices throughout Ireland in the
late nineteenth century.[85] In the context of the present crisis, however,
both Reed and Montgomery Moore agreed that the police should remain
armed unless 'the banditti in Belfast give up their rifles permanently'.[86]

The comparison of unionist rioters with Italian brigands is revealing of official attitudes to these upsets: the evocation of the extreme violence with which the Italian state was contemporaneously suppressing unrest suggests that the British official mind considered these riots to be a fundamental threat to state security. According to Gareth Jenkins, street violence was conceived in this case not only as a reflection of sectarian strife, but 'a form of "social protest" directed against community and national elites'.[87] In other words, these riots amounted to a political challenge to the status quo, fanned by discontentment with the government's Irish policy. It was a taste of things to come in the polarising political environment of the early twentieth century. The potentially disastrous social implications of this drove home the necessity of handling such unrest without recourse to shooting, and fed into the army's reluctance to involve itself in future security operations. The necessity of falling back upon the army to maintain order in 1885, based in part on apprehensions about the perceived sectarianism of the RIC, would have the consequence of eroding the army's popular perception as a neutral or impartial actor. This would not be the last time this hard lesson was forgotten on the streets of Belfast.[88]

Belfast experienced another riot during the second Home Rule crisis in the 1890s. The changes in policing policy in the intervening decade meant that the military was not involved in this disturbance. This was a significant difference from the situation in previous decades. During the Dublin police strike of 1882, for example, soldiers stepped into policing roles as special constables. The crisis placed such demands on the army that officers complained that the strike had occasioned the cancellation of a society ball.[89]

From the 1890s onwards, the army was called upon in fewer instances to assist the constabulary. As a direct result of the handling of the 1886 Belfast riots, it was argued that the needs and standards of policing were changing in Ireland, and it was no longer necessary to arm constables with carbines and revolvers—indeed, in the course of day-to-day activities, firearms were rarely carried. While military deployments against the public in Ireland thus became less common, the use of soldiers retained its coercive capability due to the discipline of the army. Rioters knew that, if ordered to, soldiers would fire into a crowd, and were less susceptible to intimidation than policemen; soldiers' detachment from the communities they pacified meant there were no social penalties for their actions. In the words of one witness at a military deployment to aid a beleaguered local RIC force, '[the people] were already completely cowed by the sudden appearance of the military from two quarters at once. By no means wanting in keenness of perception, they knew that, if ordered to do so, the soldiers will fire "at" them, and not vaguely, after the manner of the police.'[90]

Despite the army generally resenting the thankless task of aiding the civil power, officers considered their men well able to carry these duties out: when the prospect of unrest in Belfast emerged in 1912, Lady Londonderry heard that officers 'thought 4 Batt Infantry & 2 Regts Cavalry would be sent to Belfast ... [The Cheshire Regiment] were very popular with the Belfast people with whom they played football during the last 2 years. People here [Dublin] incline to think that there will be now no trouble; but a few recognise what an inflammable element there is in Belfast.'[91] When soldiers were deployed in numbers to quell a dock-worker's strike in July 1912, a much greater emphasis was placed on the limited role of the army, and there was considerable apprehension about inflaming sectarian tensions. A memorandum from the Irish Command urged, 'The general policy to be followed is that the soldiers are not police, nor are they ... to take any party or political sides.'[92] The army acted once again with restraint in the event, though the question of legality was ever-present. The Commander of XV Brigade, Count Gleichen, who directed the operation, castigated the RIC for what he took to be dereliction of duty: 'we are called out illegally ... under any circumstances which admit of being dealt with a force less menacing than a military force ... the Police will not—they say cannot—deal with [the rioters] ... I beg to protest strongly against this attitude on the part of the civilian authorities.'[93]

The more coercive side of the military presence can be demonstrated in the three instances in the early twentieth century in which troops were called out to combat a major breach of the peace. Two of these were non-sectarian strike-breaking actions, suggesting that troops particularly avoided violence during politically sensitive Home Rule unrest while using harsher methods to deal with strikes. In 1907, troops fired on rioters in the Falls Road, in 1912 they assisted police in the aforementioned strike in Belfast (another occasion in which elements of the police attempted to strike), and in 1914, in the incident which provoked the greatest outrage, troops killed civilians on Bachelor's Walk in Dublin, following the landing of guns at Howth by the Irish Volunteers.[94]

The reporting of these events in the press reveals, however, that sectarian tensions were on the rise, particularly in Belfast, and the army could not avoid being drawn into the fray. According to Michael de Nie, the reportage was highly partisan: 'a solid majority of liberal newspapers dismissed the various declarations of Orangemen, loyalists and their English allies as blather and bluff, a position they and the party maintained until Ireland stood on the brink of civil war in 1914. Few if any conservative journalists predicted armed resistance in the late spring of 1886.'[95] Of the 1898 riots, the *Freeman's Journal* editorialised 'there was more violence in last week's unrestrained savagery in Belfast than in the whole National agitation for the last twenty years, which was made the pretext for passing Coercion Act after Coercion Act ... there is one law for the Nationalist and another for the Orangeman.'[96] Of the 1907 riots, *The Times* wrote 'With regard to the cause of these deplorable disturbances in the Nationalist quarter of the city, it is unquestionable that the inflammatory street speeches of the past few weeks have contributed ... the attack on the police and military ... was absolutely unprovoked. The better-class Nationalists deeply deplore the unhappy outbreak.'[97] Increasingly, these incidents were characterised as 'Nationalist' or 'Orange'. Already in the 1890s, nationalists were beginning to feel that the military was discriminately targeting them, a feeling perhaps not helped by the alignment of Unionism with 'imperial nationality' by the leader of the Unionist party, Colonel Edward Saunderson.[98]

As the differing reactions to military violence in the era of Home Rule illustrate, the political landscape was shifting. The paternalistic 'constructive Unionism' of the landlords was giving way to a partisan mass movement. According to Alvin Jackson, the moderate patriotism which was the political centreline of the officer class, as embodied by Saunderson, was an evolution of ancient principles: 'to a very great extent the Unionism which he defined in the 1880s was merely a modification of several antique political principles, and in particular, the Whiggery and evangelicalism of the late eighteenth century.'[99] By the twentieth century, however, unionism was evolving into a mass movement. Less than a decade after rioting in Belfast, the potential use of troops to 'coerce Ulster' was drawing unfavourable comment from within the military establishment. An anonymous letter from an Irish officer in the *Morning Post* gave voice to these concerns:

> With reference to the correspondence that has taken place between the duke of Norfolk and Colonel Saunderson, may I venture through your columns to suggest to my countrymen that in their opposition to Mr. Gladstone's bill for the destruction of Ireland it would be well to totally eschew the religious aspect of the question ... we may rely on the best and most noble of our Roman Catholic fellow countrymen joining us ... at present the men of the

Irish Constabulary are discontented; they have not forgotten Mr. Dillon's threats; and quite half, if not a larger proportion of them, are averse to Home Rule … although the Army may remain in Ireland, I feel sure the officers will never order their men to fire on those who are cheering for England's Queen, and only claiming their right to remain under her Government and Parliament. At present there does not appear to be any necessity for Irishmen to prepare to use force; at the proper time, if it ever comes, there will be plenty of willing hands prepared to oppose the laws or orders of a Home Rule Government.[100]

The mass nature of the political movements which came to fruition with the establishment of volunteer militias in 1912–14 left officers in a condition of uncertainty—what had previously been a relatively uncontroversial defence of loyal institutions was becoming the central political question of the day.

The military's role as an aid to the civil power evolved and responded to events as the situation required. They acted as a stop-gap when the RIC and the Dublin Metropolitan Police proved unable to keep the peace. Officers were willing, when ordered, to perform this role, however much they may have disagreed with it in private. Military loyalty to the crown, calculated since the Wars of the Three Kingdoms to ensure political neutrality, ironically drew the officer corps into the orbit of mass Unionist politics, leading to increasing resentment and resistance from Irish nationalist society. The cachet garnered by Unionism in the person of sympathetic Irish officers was welcomed enthusiastically by James Craig, who, in 1913 reported, 'I tell you this, that a day does not pass that I do not get—to put it at a really low average—half a dozen letters from British officers asking to be enrolled.'[101] The political neutrality of the British Army in Ireland was permanently compromised. The army had weathered the storm of agrarian outrage and urban rioting in the late nineteenth and early twentieth century, as well as the reading of two Home Rule Bills; but the intersection of politics and professionalism that came to a head in 1914 in the context of the third Home Rule Bill would subject the army in Ireland to its greatest test.

POLITICS, PROFESSIONALISM, AND IDENTITY: THE CURRAGH INCIDENT, 1914

This chapter begins with the Earl Dunraven's succinct summary of the characteristics of his Irishness: his conception of martial Irish identity was defined first and foremost by class.[102] According to David Cannadine and

Corelli Barnett, Irish officers were still 'the nearest thing Britain ever possessed to the Prussian *Junker* class'.[103] It appears, however, that this elitist
view was gradually changing in the pre-First World War period, particularly, according to Bowman and Connelly, as a result of the Curragh incident: 'While a snob like General William Nicholson could voice concern
about those risen from the ranks … other senior officers were concerned
at the narrow social basis of the officer corps. Lieutenant General Sir Ian
Hamilton … returned to this theme after the Curragh Incident, when he
felt that public opinion might be more sympathetic to reform.'[104] This is
a salutary reminder that the history of the officer corps is one of clinging
to traditional practices which, in the wake of some crisis of confidence,
are re-assessed: the Gordon Expedition, the 'black week' of the Boer War,
and the Curragh incident all occasioned a great deal of soul-searching
from senior officers. It is in this historical context that we consider how a
temporary breakdown in discipline stemming from a miscommunication
could have shaken confidence in the officer corps so significantly.

    In 1914, the officer corps in Ireland was developing an expanding
political role, as individual officers became increasingly involved in the
Home Rule issue. Military officers on both sides of the Home Rule debate
were breaking King's Regulations by becoming enthusiastically and publicly involved in the Irish Volunteers and the Ulster Volunteer
Force (UVF).[105] Indeed, as Brigadier-General Hubert Gough went about
his business at the Curragh camp, he would have been able to see, beyond
the firing ranges, the local Irish Volunteer chapter drilling on the plain
under the direction of a serving British soldier—a situation inconceivable
two years earlier.[106] Considering the pro-union stance that was increasingly vocally adopted by a number of senior Irish officers, and into which
the army in Ireland was falling into *de facto* alignment, this turn of events
would have seemed an intolerable affront and a possible danger to public
order. The concatenation of a crisis in military authority, and the proliferation of popular paramilitary groups in civilian society, contributed to the
Curragh crisis, when 61 serving officers resigned in protest at proposals to
mobilise against Ulster Volunteers opposing the Home Rule Bill. A further
exacerbating factor was the feeling among Irish officers that their superiors
in London did not grasp the seriousness of the situation: the dispatch to
Ireland of General Nevil Macready to coordinate the response to the
Home Rule backlash, on the basis of his prior experience with riot policing
and aid to the civil power work in Wales, led to accusations that they were

treating officers' legitimate, disinterested resistance to Home Rule 'like a Pontypool coal strike', in the words of John French.[107] The Curragh Incident was not simply an internal matter; its ultimate importance to the British officer corps lay in its wide coverage in the press, which had been endlessly fascinated by the imperial military since the mid-nineteenth century.[108] *The Times'* military correspondent Charles à Court Repington wrote in July 1913 of his fears that the Ulster crisis would bring questions of the military's politicisation to head, and gave his opinion of what the press' editorial policy ought to be:

> I have no doubt that our line ought to be to deprecate in the strongest manner any inconsiderate and hasty action on the part of officers in the Army. We can sympathise with them, share their indignation, and throw the onus of any trouble upon the government. But we should, I think, in a temperate but firm manner, hold up the maintenance of discipline as the first duty of the corps of officers, and even suggest that disciplinary measures will have to be taken against any who desire to retire for the purpose of aiding Ulster in resisting the law. We *dare not* admit politics to the Army, and I think that you should make a special appeal to regimental feeling and invite senior officers to set an example and to repress ... any conversations and tendencies which might lead the younger hot heads astray.[109]

Repington characterised the Ulster Volunteer Force as 'a democratic army', in order to dismiss critical claims that it was based on 'the old Ascendency trying to regain their power'.[110] Hubert Gough, the main player in the crisis, kept in close contact with Howell Arthur Gwynne of the pro-military *Morning Post* throughout the incident, in order to dictate the reception of events in the press.[111] According to Costello, 'some observers saw the stance taken by the officers as a reflection of the "socialised and isolated" class to which they belonged, or the influence of the Anglo-Irish officers. General Gough was greeted as a hero by the Irish Times'—though many also saw the incident as dangerous proof that the government had lost control of the army.[112] The Curragh crisis was viewed as a confirmation by all sides of their own political positions: it was simultaneously a principled stance against a coercive government, and the subjugation of the democratic process to the caprices of a cabal of reactionaries: 'few events managed to polarize press reportage and comment so violently ... with fanfares from the Unionist press ... and howls of outrage from the Liberal and Labour papers.'[113]

The background of the crisis was the increasing politicisation of the army; the changing nature, over three decades, of the military's role in aid of the civil power, the decline of the landed interest and the rise of social, economic and political challenges to the elite consensus. The precipitating moment, however, came down to a miscommunication between Arthur Paget and Hubert Gough about the nature of the military response to the rise of armed volunteer movements, particularly in Ulster. Despite Gough's undeniable role in exacerbating the crisis, Paget was, according to the generally unfavourable impressions of his fellow officers, something of a fantasist, an officer too long in a staff position and over-excited by the prospect of active service. He also displayed a poor understanding of the Irish situation.

On 20 August, Paget was in Dublin to deliver his ultimatum to the senior officers—the government and the War Office in London being under the impression that a Unionist insurrection was likely to break out, officers were to make preparations for active operations in Ulster. Those Irish officers with a familial connection to Ulster would be allowed to 'disappear' for the duration of the operation. This proviso was greeted with puzzlement by the officers; Hubert Gough, in particular, made clear his intense dissatisfaction with this vague promise. In briefing the Curragh officers, Paget greatly overstated the potential role of the military in aiding the civil power in Ulster: he gave the impression to the bemused officers that active operations were anticipated in short order in Ulster, and that the Royal Navy was already steaming north to provide support.[114] It is possible that he did not appreciate the importance of the developing connections between Irish officers and political Unionists. In any case, the Curragh officers reacted strongly to his characterisation of a potential deployment as 'active operations', and were told that officers with homes in Ulster would be allowed to 'disappear', whereas those from other parts of Ireland or Britain were to obey their orders or be dismissed.[115] It seems likely that this was meant merely rhetorically by Paget, but the Curragh officers interpreted it as a choice given to them between following orders and resigning, and over half the officers on the Curragh duly threatened resignation, with the vigorous encouragement of Gough and to the evident delight of Henry Wilson, the strongly pro-Unionist Director of Military Operations at the War Office.[116] It was clear at this point that Paget had bungled badly, and had unwittingly instituted a dangerous precedent whereby officers could effectively pick and choose as a body which orders they wished to follow, and which they did not.

The 'mutiny' came to an end when a delegation of Curragh officers was summoned to the War Office, and received a guarantee in writing that there was no intention on the part of the government to use the army to coerce Ulster. Gough attempted also to secure a guarantee that the army would never be used to enforce Home Rule on Ulster, but this was repudiated by the War Office as blatantly unconstitutional.[117] In the end, the officers returned to their posts, the Home Rule Bill was passed, and rather more pressing martial matters occupied the attention of officers for the next four years. The matter appeared settled—although, of course, the gathering political unrest which precipitated the Curragh crisis was not going away.

Outside of the Curragh, the officer corps tended to give the resigning officers their full support. Captain Bryan Cooper, then in a reserve regiment, tendered his own resignation in solidarity, and later defended the Curragh officers' actions.[118] It is interesting to note that the officers who resigned were predominantly from socially exclusive regiments (Table 5.1), suggesting that this was a revolt by the wealthiest and most well-connected of officers—the guardians of the Irish officer establishment. Amongst the more professional corps, the response was muted.

Enlisted men at the Curragh were generally supportive of the mutineers, also. The wife of one non-commissioned officer wrote: 'it is one of the finest things they could have done ... all our men say they would have been shott [sic] first than take arms against Ulster.'[119] Other Irish regiments, however, were ambivalent; for example, according to Verney, 'the Curragh Incident might never have happened for all the interest the Irish Guards showed.'[120] Major-General W.P. Pultney, CO of the 6th Division in Cork, was asked about the potential for the incident at the Curragh to spread to his station. This was his reply:

Table 5.1 Regimental affiliations of Curragh mutineers

Brigade officers	2	3rd Signal Troop	1
3rd Hussars	19	4th Field Troop	0
16th Lancers	16	Royal Horse Artillery	8
15th Lancers	18		

Source: Ian F.W. Beckett, *The Army and the Curragh Incident* (London, 1986)

My opinion of the general state of feeling in the 6th Division as regards Ulster, is as follows:

1. They can be relied on to support law and order.
2. They would not enforce Home Rule on an actively reluctant Ulster.
3. There is little chance of this feeling altering unless HM the King proclaims the Ulster Volunteers as rebels
4. In fact, the troops move for the king.[121]

Pultney's characterisation neatly sums up the general stance of the officer corps as regards the Curragh incident. Although not involved, as an officer in Ireland he stood with his colleagues, in a way that the Irish Guards, stationed in London, did not have to worry about or engage with. Henry Wilson, also in London, was a controversial character in the eyes of Irish officers. Nora Robertson characterises him thus:

> Most fateful of all individuals was Sir Henry Wilson in the key position as Director of Military Operations. Wilson had the Ulster *idée fixe* and was a man who liked operating from behind the scenes. He was hand in glove with Carson and Bonar Law and, although in an official position, made it a habit to give and take official secrets from the War Office to the Ulster leaders.[122]

F.P. Crozier called Henry Wilson 'the greatest political soldier of our day and probably the worst CIGS [Chief of the Imperial General Staff] that has ever been ... At times a "playboy", at times an actor, he was never a good soldier.'[123] Clearly, this peculiar Irish staff officer cut little ice with the traditionalists in the officer corps. Crozier's vitriolic reminiscences of the affair make this clear: 'the lamentable case of Sir Henry Wilson almost turns me into a reactionary jingo, yearning for the days of the old Duke of Cambridge, and "purchase."'[124] Wilson was a product of the Roberts ring, a new man—both moderniser and consummate 'political soldier'. His actions, and those of the officers on the Curragh, reveal the extent to which the political neutrality of the officer corps had been compromised in Ireland by 1914.

Many of the officers involved afterwards professed that, had Lieut.-Col. Paget not given them the choice (as he was technically unauthorised to do in the first place) between following orders and resigning their commissions, they would have followed orders without reservation.[125] One wonders whether this would have indeed been the case. While the military had enforced order upon the people of Ulster before, becoming involved in major riots in 1886, 1912, and 1907 with a degree of grumbling but no major problems, the situation had changed dramatically now that the UVF counted a membership of over 100,000 armed and drilled men.[126] There had been a political sea-change over Home Rule.[127] Unlike in 1886, in 1914 the implementation of Home Rule was a very immediate prospect. A civil war between organised and armed *franc-tireurs* of the Ulster Volunteer Force and the army was an unsavoury proposition, particularly for the many officers who sympathised with the UVF. The Curragh incident demonstrated the potential for desertions, and officers harboured severe reservations about making war on members of their own class.

The prospect of brother officers fighting against each other in the event of such a collision was very real. Timothy Bowman has calculated that 'the UVF had, at one time or another, just over 130 former or serving British Army officers serving in its units', including Viscount Acheson, Colonel Oliver Nugent, Viscount Northland, and Captain Basil Brooke.[128] Frank Crozier recalled being persuaded over lunch by Lord Londonderry to join the fight for Ulster in 1912; 'the upshot of the lunch ... was that in a few months' time I found myself in Belfast training a Special Service Section.'[129] Thus, through the institutional links of the officer corps and the social milieu of the Irish elite, officers found themselves on opposing sides of a deepening political divide.

Henry Wilson was an intransigent unionist, but he was also a reformer from the Roberts ring. The distaste many officers held for him as a 'political soldier' was due to the apprehension that professionalisation implied politicisation—the distasteful position of officers being in thrall to politicians, even those of a Unionist stripe, and of losing their operational autonomy. Other, more traditionalist, less vocal officers with connections to Ulster Unionism who did not rock the boat quite as much evinced much less comment and appear to have been a common feature of the officer corps at this time.[130] Dunraven was one officer who opposed professionalisation, arguing that officers' elite 'character' would be eroded by the development of an attendant 'democratisation':

that every knapsack holds a possible [marshal's] baton is a fine ideal, and the democratisation of the army has a plausible sound ... [but] soldiers are not above the ordinary prejudices incidental to average human nature, and a strong, though, perhaps, an unwarrantable, dislike exists generally among human beings to being 'bossed' by their social peers. Men do not like being ordered about by one who is, as they would say, 'no better than themselves.'

From this weakness, which shows itself in every walk of life, soldiers are not exempt … a Company or Squadron would yield more ready obedience to the youngest subaltern than to the oldest non-commissioned officer. Tradition dies hard and after all it is not so very long ago that men went into action led by the country gentlemen who raised the corps and who were looked up to as natural leaders of the yeomen, tenants and peasants of which is was composed.[131]

By 1914 there was a tangible sense that the landed interest by which officers set their store was in decline.[132] The change that had taken place was not one of the officers' own making; the myth of 'the apolitical army' had blinded them.[133] To be a military officer in the age of professionalisation meant the abdication of the right to act according to one's convictions, as aristocrats: it meant being subjugated to the interests of the state. The Curragh incident was an implicit revolt against the role of the military officer in modern, democratic society, a petulant and futile attempt to reclaim the nostalgic virtues of aristocracy, and a rejection of the professional officer and his mentality. Crozier's repudiation of Henry Wilson, like that of Nora Robertson, persisted despite his support for the Curragh mutineers. They resented his meddling as detrimental to the identity and historical role of the officer corps, and its particular definition of loyalty— to 'my class, my creed, and my political faith', in the words of the Earl of Dunraven. Professionalisation destabilised the old-fashioned mentality of the officer corps, and the Curragh crisis was the reaction.

Harold Perkin and others paint the late nineteenth and early twentieth century as an 'age' of professionalisation, in which the power of traditional elites began to give way in the face of an increasingly complex social structure that relied on highly trained specialists to function.[134] In this context, the British Army actually appeared to change very little: according to Bowman and Connelly, 'It is very difficult to agree with Tim Travers' view that the Edwardian period saw growing professionalism over the late-Victorian period. The officer corps continued to be drawn from a tiny section of society and the requirement that officers had to be able to support themselves financially meant that selection processes were far from rigorous.'[135] Thus, considering the vehement opposition to the professionalising tendency within the officer corps, and the association of professional reforms with imperial 'decline', politicisation, and 'coercion' in Ulster, we might conclude that events in Ireland not only revealed a deep political crisis at the heart of the officer corps but also represented a robust and reactionary challenge to professionalisation in general.[136]

Officers found it easy, for the most part, to align with Unionism: not only was it enunciated by many of their natural allies in the political establishment, but after 1900 it increasingly inhabited a pro-imperial position designed to appeal to the jingoistic spirit engendered by the Boer War.[137] It appealed to officers who, as a result of internal issues in the officer corps, were railing against the 'decline' of the empire. It is curious, therefore, that there were officers who were opposed to this trend: Dunraven recalls being introduced to Edward Carson by their mutual friend, Lord Londonderry, 'one of the best Viceroys that Ireland has had', and refers to their politicking as 'the seductive poison of the extreme Northern Unionism. I don't know what I, with my Home Rule and Fair Trade tendencies, was doing in that very pleasant gallery.'[138] The escalation of the political situation, which came to a head during the Curragh crisis, was a dislocating experience for the officer corps and opened a rift within their establishment. The institutional identities, dynastic connections, and imperial affinities which were their reference points in society all appeared to become unmoored at once.[139]

The Home Rule issue had a profound effect on the identity and outlook of Irish officers, and it is easy to overlook its significance considering the Curragh incident was shortly followed by the horrors of the First World War, and the Irish revolutionary period. However, in order to understand officers' reactions to these crucial events, it is important to note the political and professional challenges which faced the officer corps in 1914. The changing social role of officers from the Land War to the Curragh incident reveals a divided military establishment facing a potential civil war in Ireland, and inhabiting an increasingly reactionary position in Irish society.

Notes

1. See Timothy Bowman and Mark Connelly, *The Edwardian Army: Recruiting, Training, and Deploying the British Army, 1902–1914* (Oxford, 2012).
2. Loughlin Sweeney, 'The British Army Officer Corps in Irish Society, 1870–1920s', unpub. PhD thesis, University of Cambridge (2017).
3. Terence De Vere White, *The Anglo-Irish* (London, 1972), p. 170.
4. Peter Verney, *The Micks: The Story of the Irish Guards* (London, 1970), p. 15.
5. Lawrence McBride, *The Greening of Dublin Castle* (Washington, DC, 1991), p. 281.

6. David Cannadine, *The Decline and Fall of the British Aristocracy* (London, 1996), p. 269.

7. Alfred Turner, *Sixty Years of a Soldier's Life* (London, 1912), p. 54.

8. Jeremy Black, *A Military History of Britain* (London, 2006), p. 86.

9. To take an example at random, the list for 1913 includes a 32-year-old Earl of Pembroke as a captain and ADC to General Arthur Paget on the general staff in Dublin.

10. Nora Robertson, *Crowned Harp: Memories of the Last Years of the Crown in Ireland* (Dublin, 1960), p. 38.

11. Ibid. p. 24; Con Costello, *A Most Delightful Station: The British Army on the Curragh of Kildare, Ireland, 1855–1922* (Dublin, 1996), p. 119.

12. Costello, *A Most Delightful Station*, p. 176.

13. See Dan Harvey and Gerry White, *The Barracks: History of Victoria/ Collins Barracks, Cork* (Cork, 1997).

14. Walter S. O'Shea, *A Short History of Tipperary Military Barracks*, (Cashel, 1998).

15. See Harvey and White, *History of Collins Barracks* for a discussion of disciplinary problems relating to regimental rivalries.

16. Hubert Gough, quoted in Costello, *A Most Delightful Station*, p. 265.

17. Earl Dunraven, *The Outlook in Ireland: The Case for Devolution and Conciliation* (Dublin, 1907), p. 13.

18. Robertson, *Crowned Harp*, p. 102.

19. Costello, *A Most Delightful Station*, p. 182; For a discussion of generational change in the revolutionary period, see R. F. Foster, *Vivid Faces: The Revolutionary Generation in Ireland, 1890–1923* (London, 2014).

20. See Clara Cullen, *The World Upturning: Elsie Henry's Wartime Diaries, 1913–1919* (Sallins, 2013) passim.; Diane Urquhart, *The Ladies of Londonderry: Women and Political Patronage* (London, 2007) passim.; Ciaran O'Neill, introduction to *Irish Elites in the Nineteenth Century* (Dublin, 2013), p. 22.

21. Ian F. Beckett, 'Women and Patronage in the Late Victorian Army', *History* 85:279 (2000), p. 465; Alison Blunt, 'Imperial Geographies of Home: British Domesticity in India, 1886–1925', *Transactions of the Institute of British Geographers* 24:4 (1999), pp. 421–440.

22. Verity G. McInnis, 'Indirect Agents of Empire: Army Officers' Wives in British India and the American West, 1830–1875', *Pacific Historical Review* 83:3 (2014), pp. 378–409.

23. Alvin Jackson, *Colonel Edward Saunderson: Land and Loyalty in Victorian Ireland* (Oxford, 1995), p. 48; Virginia Crossman, 'The Army and Law and Order in the Nineteenth Century' in Bartlett, Thomas, and Keith Jeffery, eds., *A Military History of Ireland* (Cambridge, 1996), p. 360.

24. Jackson, *Edward Saunderson*, p. 48.

25. See pp. 81–82. Wolseley corresponded at length with his family and colleagues about the incident.
26. T. W. Moody, Richard Hawkins and Margaret Moody, eds., *Florence Arnold-Forster's Irish Journal*, (Oxford, 1988), p. 160.
27. See S. B. Cook, 'The Irish Raj: Social Origins and Careers of Irishmen in the Indian Civil Service, 1855–1914', *Journal of Social History* 20 (1987), p. 507.
28. Moody, Hawkins, and Moody, *Arnold-Forster*, pp. 6–10 passim.
29. Wyndham, quoted in Bowman and Connelly, *The Edwardian Army*, p. 165.
30. Armstrong to his mother, Rawalpindi, 13 October 1910. Armstrong papers, LUL.
31. Fergus Campbell, 'Irish Popular Politics and the Making of the Wyndham Land Act, 1901–1903', *Historical Journal* 45 (2002), p. 758.
32. Crossman, 'The Army and Law and Order', pp. 358–359; David N. Haire, 'In Aid of the Civil Power 1868–90' in Lyons, F. S. L., and R. A. J. Hawkins, eds., *Ireland Under the Union: Varieties of Tension* (Oxford, 1980), p. 115.
33. F. P. Crozier, *Ireland For Ever*, (London, 1930), p. 46.
34. Turner, *Sixty Years*, p. 230.
35. Crossman, 'The Army and Law and Order', p. 359.
36. Moody, Hawkins, and Moody, *Arnold-Forster*, pp. 110–111.
37. Dunraven, *Past Times*, p. 23.
38. Turner, *Sixty Years*, p. 222.
39. *Irish Times*, 13 June 1887.
40. Turner, *Sixty Years*, p. 241.
41. Ibid. p. 242.
42. Hansard, 26 April 1888, vol. 325 c596.
43. Turner, *Sixty Years*, p. 240.
44. Hansard, 12 April 1888, vol. 324 c1102.
45. *Freeman's Journal*, 21 April 1888.
46. Hansard, 12 April 1888, vol. 324 c1080.
47. Hansard, 12 April 1888, vol. 324 c1103. Emphasis mine. At Mitchelstown, Co. Cork, police had fired into a crowd the previous year during a no rent demonstration.
48. Hansard, 12 April 1888, vol. 324 c1082.
49. Ewen A. Cameron, 'Internal Policing and Public Order, c.1797–1900', in Spiers, Edward M., Jeremy A. Crang and Matthew J. Strickland, eds., *A Military History of Scotland* (Edinburgh, 2012), p. 441.
50. *Irish Times*, 13 June 1887.
51. 'Military Intelligence', *Freeman's Journal*, 10 April 1882.
52. Turner, *Sixty Years*, pp. 177–178.

53. Ibid. pp. 194–195.
54. Ibid. p. 196.
55. Buller to Carnarvon, 19 June 1887. Carnarvon Papers, British Library.
56. Turner, *Sixty Years*, pp. 210–211.
57. Ibid. p. 219.
58. Moody, Hawkins, and Moody, *Arnold-Forster*, p. 165; *Irish Times*, 13 June 1887.
59. Bernard Becker, *Disturbed Ireland: Being the Letters Written during the Winter of 1880–81* (London, 1881), p. 120.
60. Ibid. p. 123.
61. Ibid. pp. 200–201.
62. Fergus Campbell, 'The Social Composition of the Senior Officers of the Royal Irish Constabulary', *Irish Historical Studies* 36 (2009), pp. 24–27.
63. Haire, 'In Aid of the Civil Power', p. 115.
64. Ross of Bladensburg, quoted in Crossman, 'The Army and Law and Order', p. 372. Ross was the descendant of Major-General Robert Ross, the victor of the Battle of Bladensburg in the War of 1812, and the man who ordered the burning of the White House in 1814.
65. Property Defence Association, Castletown Papers, NLI.
66. Moody, Hawkins, and Moody, *Arnold-Forster*, 9 December 1880, p. 34.
67. Ibid. p 165.
68. Becker, *Disturbed Ireland*, pp. 202–203.
69. Moody, Hawkins, and Moody, *Arnold-Forster*, pp. 168–169.
70. A. J. A. Morris, introduction to *The Letters of Lieutenant Colonel Charles a Court Repington CMG Military Correspondent of* The Times *1903–1918* (Army Records Society, 1999), pp. 3–4.
71. Moody, Hawkins, and Moody, *Arnold-Forster*, p. 180.
72. Ibid. p. 275.
73. Illustrated in a Memorial to Earl Dunraven from 21 Tenants, 20 December 1883, Dunraven Mss, Limerick University Library.
74. Dunraven, 'The Crisis in Ireland', pp. 33–34.
75. Letter to Earl Dunraven, 21 February 1903, Dunraven Mss, Limerick University Library; *Hart's Army List*, 1885, p. 161; David Grant, <theauxiliaries.com>; 'Major Hervey Guy Francis Edward de Montmorencey, Royal Dublin Fusiliers', TNA WO 339/19202. Colonel Hanford was probably John Compton Hanford, who attained his majority at the same time as Lord French and served with Wolseley in the Gordon Relief Campaign. The de Montmorenceys were a family of the Irish peerage with a number of serving military officers in the late nineteenth century. Hervey de Montmorencey, a decorated veteran of the Boer War, would go on to join the Irish Volunteers before the First World War, and later worked for British Army intelligence during the War of Independence.

76. "The Land Conference", *Leinster Express*, 27 December 1902. Two-thirds of the report on the conference is taken up with the recounting of the involved officers' military adventures.
77. Cook, 'The Irish Raj', p. 507.
78. Becker, *Disturbed Ireland*, p. 153.
79. Ibid. p. 274.
80. Cannadine, *Decline and Fall*, p. 173.
81. Paul Bew, *Conflict and Conciliation in Ireland 1890–1910. Parnellites and Radical Agrarians* (Oxford, 1987), p. 203.
82. Crossman, 'The Army and Law and Order', pp. 377–378.
83. Mark Radford, '"Closely Akin to Actual Warfare": The Belfast Riots of 1886 & the RIC', *History Ireland* 7 (1999), p. 27.
84. Ibid. p. 30.
85. David M. Anderson and David Killingray, eds., *Policing the Empire: Government, Authority and Control, 1830–1940* (Manchester, 1991), p. 4; Mark Radford, 'Andrew Reed (1837–1914): A Very Civil Policeman', *History Ireland* 13 (2005), p. 33.
86. Mark Radford, 'Andrew Reed (1837–1914): A Very Civil Policeman', *History Ireland* 13 (2005), p. 34.
87. Gareth Jenkins, 'Nationalism and Sectarian Violence in Liverpool and Belfast, 1880s–1920s', *International Labour and Working Class History* 78 (2010), p. 164.
88. Andrew Sanders and Ian S. Wood, *Times of Troubles: Britain's War in Northern Ireland* (Edinburgh, 2012); Edward Burke, *An Army of Tribes: British Army Cohesion, Deviancy, and Murder in Northern Ireland* (Liverpool, 2018), p. 333; A. C. Hepburn, 'The Belfast Riots of 1935', *Social* History 15:1 (1990), pp. 91–93.
89. Turner, *Sixty Years*, pp. 64–65.
90. Becker, *Disturbed Ireland*, p. 205.
91. J. Mulcahy to Lady Londonderry, 2 February 1912. Hart papers, PRONI.
92. Irish Command memorandum, 20 July 1912. CO 904 Dublin Castle records, TNA.
93. Report on Aid to the Civil Power, Brigadier Commanding XV Brigade, 26 July 1912. CO 904 Dublin Castle records, TNA.
94. Maurice Moore, account of the Howth gun-running. Moore papers, NLI; Pádraig Yeates, *A City in Wartime: Dublin 1914–18* (Dublin, 2011), p. 26.
95. De Nie, Michael, 'Ulster Will Fight? The British press and Ulster, 1885–1886', *New Hibernia Review/Iris Éireanneach Nua* 12 (2008), p. 34.
96. *Freeman's Journal*, 14 June 1898.
97. *The Times*, 14 August 1907.

98. David W. Miller, *Queen's Rebels: Ulster Loyalism in Historical Perspective* (Dublin, 2007), pp. 109–110.
99. Jackson, *Edward Saunderson*, p. 19.
100. *Morning Post*, 24 March 1893.
101. Craig, quoted in Paul Bew, *Ideology and the Ulster Question: Ulster Unionism and Irish Nationalism, 1912–1916* (Oxford, 1994), p. 94.
102. Earl Dunraven, *The Crisis in Ireland: An account of the present condition of Ireland and suggestions towards reform* (Dublin, 1905), p. 237. Dunraven papers, LUL.
103. Barnett quoted in Cannadine, *Decline and Fall*, p. 269.
104. Bowman and Connelly, *The Edwardian Army*, p. 31. William Nicholson, like Wolseley, had not been to a public school and correspondingly adopted a rather overstated sense of aristocratic distinction when he achieved prominence as a member of the Roberts ring.
105. Timothy Bowman, *Carson's Army: The Ulster Volunteer Force, 1910–22* (Manchester, 2007), p. 46.
106. Costello, *A Most Delightful Station*, p. 274. Michael Smyth, Bureau of Military History WS 1531, p. 1. The Volunteers were instructed by Cpl. William Jones, Connaught Rangers, until he embarked for the Western Front in August 1914. Clearly, this was not the end of his nationalist activities however, as he was arrested in Ireland under the Defence of the Realm Act in October, 1915.
107. George H. Cassar, *The Tragedy of Sir John French* (Newark, 1985), p. 75.
108. See Simon J. Potter, ed., *Newspapers and Empire in Ireland and Britain: Reporting the British Empire, c.1857–1921* (Dublin, 2004).
109. Repington to Robinson, Hampstead, 3 July 1913, in Morris, *Letters of Lt Col Repington*, pp. 208–209.
110. Bowman, *Carson's Army*, p. 45.
111. Bowman and Connelly, *The Edwardian Army*, p. 171.
112. Costello, *A Most Delightful Station*, p. 270.
113. Bowman and Connelly, *The Edwardian Army*, pp. 170–171.
114. Keith Jeffery, *Field Marshal Sir Henry Wilson: A Political Soldier* (Oxford, 2006), p. 117; Brig-Gen. Hubert Gough to Brig-Gen. Johnnie Gough, Curragh, 3 April 1914, in Ian F. Beckett, *The Army and The Curragh Incident, 1914* (London, 1986), p. 356.
115. Gough, *Soldiering On*, p. 99.
116. Jeffery, *Henry Wilson*, p. 116.
117. Ibid. p. 120.
118. Robinson, *Bryan Cooper*, pp. 76–77.
119. Costello, *A Most Delightful Station*, p. 271.
120. Verney, *The Micks*, p. 15.

121. W. P. Pultney, 19 April 1914, quoted in Harvey and White, *History of Collins Barracks*, p. 45.
122. Robertson, *Crowned Harp*, p. 104.
123. Crozier, *Ireland For Ever*, p. 68.
124. Ibid., p. 103.
125. Gough, *Soldiering On*, p. 99.
126. P. Bew, *Conflict and Conciliation*, p. 4.
127. Jenkins, 'Sectarian Violence', p. 164.
128. Bowman, *Carson's Army*, pp. 57–58.
129. Crozier, *Ireland For Ever*, p. 48.
130. Paul Bew, *Ideology and the Ulster Question: Ulster Unionism and Irish Nationalism, 1912–1916* (Oxford, 1994); Miller, *Queen's Rebels*; F. P. Crozier, *The Men I Killed* (n.p., 1937), p. 56.
131. Earl of Dunraven, *No Army, No Empire*, n.d. (c.1902), pp. 33–34, LUL.
132. Cannadine, *Decline and Fall*, p. 269; Patrick Cosgrove, 'Irish Landlords and the Wyndham Land Act, 1903' in Dooley, Terence, and Christopher Ridgeway, eds., *The Irish Country House: Its Past, Present and Future* (Dublin, 2011), pp. 93–95.
133. Strachan, *The Politics of the British Army*, pp. 7–8.
134. Harold Perkin, *The Rise of Professional Society: England Since 1880* (London, 1989).
135. Bowman and Connelly, *The Edwardian Army*, p. 39.
136. Brendan Clifford, introduction to Crozier, *The Men I Killed*, p. 17.
137. Mackenzie, *Propaganda and Empire* passim.; David Omissi and Andrew Thompson, eds., *The Impact of the South African War* (Basingstoke, 2002), pp. 278–279.
138. Dunraven, *Pastimes*, p. 192.
139. Cannadine, *Decline and Fall*, p. 268.

CHAPTER 6

Status Quo Ante Bellum: The Irish Military Establishment, 1914

Sir Matthew Nathan came, his one great puzzle-query is, 'Who is going to be the ruling class in Ireland?' under Home Rule.
—Diary of Elsie Henry, 12 December 1914

We have seen in previous chapters that the Irish officer corps possessed certain institutional characteristics that governed its relationship with the rest of the elite establishment in Ireland and with society as a whole, and which allowed for the formation of important links with the global British Empire. While the events of 1870–1914 precipitated significant changes in the officer corps, the overall picture was one of social and cultural continuity, and its demography changed only very gradually. The period of war and revolution, 1914–22, has generally been considered more momentous and disruptive by historians.[1] The following chapters will test this contention by examining how the officers in Ireland's elite establishment sought to exercise moral authority in a period of shifting political realities.

From the point of view of officers looking back on the Great War and the Irish revolution, the centrality of the war appeared to be self-evident. It was the catastrophic event that occasioned the decline in the fortunes of their class, and the end of their monopoly on an avowedly imperial sense of Irish identity. Independence itself appeared to be merely an epilogue. This viewpoint is bound up with a narrative of the 'lost generation' which accompanied the disproportionately high death rate among the sons of

© The Author(s) 2019
L. Sweeney, *Irish Military Elites, Nation and Empire, 1870–1925*,
https://doi.org/10.1007/978-3-030-19307-2_6

the landed gentry, the inheritance of the land cut down in the flower of youth as inexperienced subalterns in no man's land.[2] The response of the landed class to the call for recruits was indeed enthusiastic, and was welcomed by the army: until 1916 it was possible for a gentleman to be directly commissioned without undergoing any cadet training.[3] While the death rate among young Irish officers was certainly high, the 'lost generation' narrative has received some critical engagement by Peter Martin, who has problematised some of its underlying assumptions; he provides a nuanced picture of this narrative backed up with important evidence, including a much-needed quantification of what constituted 'disproportionately high rates of death', and addressing the 'noticeable absence of hard evidence about the activities of the Irish upper classes during the war'.[4] There was a need to explain away the decline of an Anglo-Irish establishment that had grossly miscalculated the historical conditions in which it found itself; it was unable to effectively exercise its power and influence to weather the storms of war and revolution. Christopher Moore-Bick has recently written about how this narrative emerged from Edwardian notions of social and imperial decline: the war was imagined as 'a "blood sacrifice"' that would purify the nation 'of the vestiges of *fin de siècle* decadence and produce a regenerate manhood'.[5] It was a source of comfort, Martin argues, for Irish officers to conceive of their very apparent social decline after the war in the context of a noble sacrifice for crown and empire.[6]

In order to assess this narrative of decline and loss surrounding the First World War, it is necessary to examine the state of the Irish military establishment before the deluge. The institutions and characteristics of the Irish military elite will be examined in the context of Campbell, Cohan, and Radford's analyses of the civil authorities in Ireland.[7] Previous chapters have already discussed the processes of elite socialisation governing access to the officer corps, and have revealed the particular importance of class networks. The effect of this socialisation on the fractious political context in Ireland will be assessed, with particular emphasis on officers of non-traditional backgrounds who have been overlooked in other studies. This chapter will then question whether the armed volunteer movements can be conceived of as 'counter-elites' in the contested space of Irish martial identity, providing alternatives for middle-class Irishmen without the social capital to advance as a military officer. The implications of this for elite officers who were themselves involved in the volunteer movements will also be considered. The contested identities

of martial Irishness before the First World War reveal a military establishment that was already in decline, compromised by the battle over Irish
nationality.

COUNTER-ELITE CHALLENGES TO THE IRISH MILITARY ESTABLISHMENT

Any elite establishment is constructed and maintained by social and cultural mechanisms of elite reproduction. Working in the vein of the elite
theorists Gaetano Mosca, Vilfredo Pareto, and John Kautsky, A.S. Cohan's
study of 50 years of post-independence southern Irish elites reveals a striking lack of demographic continuity in the professional officer corps, and
the marginalisation in general of military men from the political process:
neither the 'old guard' with their connections to land and the professions,
nor the 'counter-elite' that replaced them and fought the Civil War, were
the people who built the new State.[8] Military identities, in all their forms,
became marginalised in the new Ireland in favour of democratic
civic norms.[9]

In the same elite-theory framework, John Hutchinson and Tom Garvin
propose that the rise of Irish constitutional nationalism can also be interpreted as the result of a frustrated counter-elite (in this case, educated
middle-class Catholics) adopting a disruptive political position in order to
challenge an ossified and decadent elite structure. This argument underlies
Fergus Campbell's monograph on *The Irish Establishment*, and Ciaran
O'Neill's counterpoising study of Irish elites.[10] This counter-elite, too,
ultimately lost its relevance, as constitutional nationalism declined in popularity following the Redmondite split in the volunteer movement in
1914, the Rising of 1916, and the anti-conscription campaign in 1917–
18, all of which contributed to the popularity of Sinn Féin.[11]

Although the impress of the military on the Irish landed interest runs
through Campbell's work, he does not deal specifically with Irish officers as
a component of the Irish establishment. Considering the importance of
patronage, schooling, class, and increasing professionalism that Campbell
identifies for other elites, it is a curious omission.[12] The officer corps, aside
from being a central component (Fig. 6.1) of early-twentieth century Irish
society, was defined by these self-same factors, and correspondingly was not
immune from the rise of nationalist counter-elites. Hutchinson maintains
that elite nationalism emerged as a result of 'exclusion operating at the
higher levels of almost all spheres of Irish society ... [and] "over-competi-

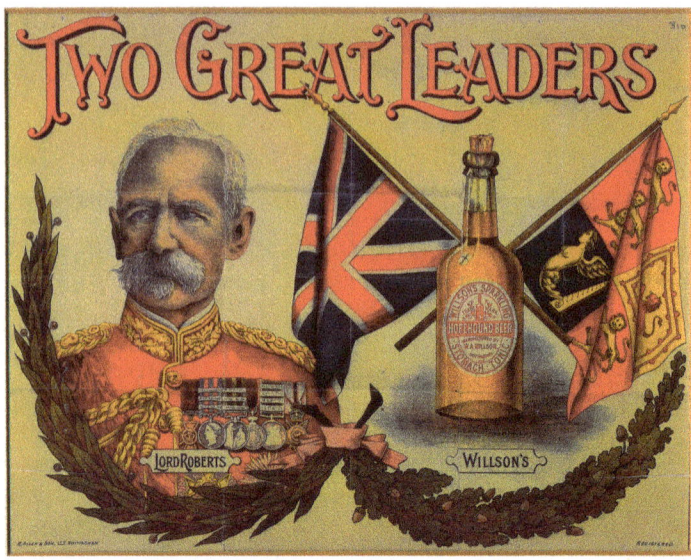

Fig. 6.1 Military Irishness as imperial celebrity: Lord Roberts and other popular officers' likenesses were used to produce collectible merchandise and to market products, as in this turn-of-the-century advertisement. *Alamy*

tion" of lower-middle-class Catholics'.[13] He points to the Curragh crisis and the rise of the volunteer movements in Ireland as evidence that 'the ability of the state to monopolize the legitimate use of violence … was already withering' in the years before the First World War.[14] It is not a huge leap to see how these dual factors converge on the Irish military establishment.

The limited scope for middle-class penetration of the officer corps, due to the latter's continuing association with the landed interest and its pre-occupation with preserving an aristocratic character, constituted a case of blocked mobility. This led to its marginalisation in the post-1922 state, in which the demography of the new Irish officer corps had barely any similarity to its predecessor.[15] However, this new counter-elite military establishment was also *itself* marginalised after 1923, and never had the social influence or centrality of the old, pre-independence officer corps.[16] This puts it at odds with other elite groups in Ireland: while the civil administration, business, medical, legal, and academic establishments of the pre-independence period managed to survive in some form in the Free State, and retained their role in elite society, the multiple military traditions present in Ireland in the 1920s—the Free State Army, the Irish Republican Army (IRA), and the British Army—were all marginalised under the new regime. This is despite the aforementioned centrality of the army to Irish society in the pre-independence period. There were a great number of prospective officers in 1920s Ireland, as there always had been—but these surplus officers were not competing for the limited spaces in the National Army's officer corps. There was a painfully evident demand for the skills of professional officers during the 1922–23 Civil War, which the new army found itself unable to procure.[17] The majority of prospective Irish officers continued to look to the British Empire, and did not consider the new Irish army to be 'the "real" army'.[18] There are many examples in the interwar period of non-belligerent countries in which the military retained its social importance, such as Switzerland, Austria, or Afghanistan, but Ireland presents a rather different example of a society in which the military establishment migrated dramatically from the mainstream to the margin after the First World War.

In other places in the British Empire, and in other European states formed post-First World War, there was a degree of continuity between the officer corps of the old and new regimes. In the successor states of the Austro-Hungarian Empire, for example, despite the nationalist ructions surrounding the collapse of the empire, the centrality of the officer corps to the elite structures of the new states was retained.[19] In Russia, Tsarist officers persisted in the Red Army until the purges of the 1930s.[20] In India and Pakistan, the high command of the army were products of the British officer corps and the Sandhurst system until the 1970s.[21] In Northern Ireland, too, military men played a significant role in the civil and political elite.[22] The Irish Free State, however, continued to dispatch its officer class to the British and Indian armies. Historians have dismissed this problem by speaking of the 'departure of the British army from Ireland', but, as we know, southern independence did not stop thousands of Irishmen from travelling to Britain to enlist or to take the King's commission.[23] For the first time since the end of the proscription on Catholics serving in the British Army in 1793, a considerable slice of Ireland's fighting strength was once again deployed in the service of another sovereign state. Considering the high saturation of Irishmen in the British Army, the idea of its 'departure' cannot be reconciled with the continuing commitment of significant numbers of Irish people to that army.

Ironically, the British Army's close social—and by extension, political—links to Irish society in 1914–22 contributed to the alienation of Ireland's indigenous officer corps. The Curragh crisis revealed officers' apprehensions about a 'democratic' rot setting in and poisoning the character of the army, and reinforced what they took to be their primary function: preserving the integrity of the empire, for idealistic reasons as much as access to the opportunities for soldiering that it provided.[24] Both Irish and non-Irish officers couched their support for the Union in imperial terms, and throughout the Home Rule crisis, Irish officers declaimed with ever more frantic cadence the potentially apocalyptic repercussions of a possible rebellion in Ulster. According to Timothy McMahon, 'one need only pay attention to the rhetoric of British Tories and Irish unionists to recognize that the spectre of "the breakup of the Empire" loomed large in their imaginations as they opposed Home Rule.'[25] Hew Strachan points to the spectre of imperial collapse as one of the factors leading to the Curragh mutiny.[26] While this sense of Ireland's links to the British Empire becoming imperilled was not new, the prospect of over 100,000 Ulstermen rising in revolt added a frantic urgency to the rhetoric, and accordingly it was taken much more seriously.[27] Charles Vane-Tempest, with his connections to the social and political elite, couched his efforts to conciliate with the nationalists during the Great War in imperial terms, arguing that, as the prospect of Irish independence 'has never received support in the colonies', its inevitable implementation after the war carried with it 'strategic danger', and the potential for counter-elite discord throughout the empire.[28]

It was Henry Wilson who, characteristically, came straight to the point in 1921 when he wrote simply, 'If we lose Ireland we have lost the Empire.'[29] The spectre of Home Rule leading to both imperial collapse and the marginalisation of the officer corps in Ireland can be read into this, and Wilson and others repeatedly expressed the central importance of officers in retaining Ireland's imperial links.[30] Following the First World War, however, the European political landscape had altered dramatically, and Ireland was no exception. In the context of a 'crisis of empire', some officers, including Dunraven and French, found themselves inhabiting a political position that looked suspiciously like moderate Home Rule, in an attempt to mount a relevant challenge to the Sinn Féin position.[31] While this seems like a monumental shift, the landed officers of Dunraven's circle were actually discussing the repercussions of dominion status for Ireland as early as 1907.[32] There were other officers, too, like Bryan Cooper and the Earl of Mayo, who evinced more openness toward conciliation than hardliners like Wilson. To examine this split in the officer corps, we must discern its political and social boundaries and the degree of atypicality that was acceptable in the corps of 1914.

Military Institutions and Irish Society in 1914

While the military establishment in Ireland was preoccupied in the years before the First World War by the Home Rule issue, certain officers were eagerly anticipating the possibility of conflict on the Continent: Sir John French, when appointed CIGS in 1912, announced his intention to get the British Army 'ready for war'.[33] General F.P. Crozier recalls in his memoirs 'the inevitable breakfast salutation of Lord Charles Beresford, R.N., since 1911: "Good-morning all; one day nearer to the German war!"'[34] However, according to Edward Spiers, such pronouncements 'evoked little interest in the press and Parliament. A civil war in Ulster still seemed more imminent than a major war in Europe', even after the murder of Archduke Ferdinand.[35]

For Irish officers in the overseas empire, life continued apace, without much sign that a global war was in the offing. In a faraway Indian cantonment, Captain William Kemmis was preparing to return to his family home in Ballinacor, County Wicklow for a long-awaited period of leave after four years in India. The privilege of seeing home was a rare one: in a letter to his parents, he predicted that 'the Regt should be home about 1919 not earlier'.[36] His leave was cut short after only a few short days, and much to his surprise his regiment of dragoons was mobilised in August for the Western Front. Kemmis did indeed serve with his regiment until 1919— but it was the calamitous Indian sacrifices at Neuve-Chapelle, rather than the pleasant sporting life of the United Provinces that awaited him as he left Ballinacor, brimming with confidence and a spirit of adventure.

How, one wonders, was the Irish officer corps in 1914 able to retain a façade of normality and confidence, swan-like, while under the surface thrashing about with rumours of civil war and apprehensions of imperial decline, right up until the outbreak of war? Key to its sense of security was the seeming strength of its traditional institutions. In the aftermath of the Curragh incident, and Hubert Gough and Henry Wilson could claim a victory for unionist officers and the elite institutions of the traditional officer establishment.[37] Evincing particular robustness in 1914 was the venerable Kildare Street Club, the predominant locus of interaction between military officers and the Irish landed interest. Indeed, the proportion of club members with a military connection had been rising since 1860—evidence of the enduring connection between the officer corps and the army, particularly as many of the 1860 members were still there in 1914![38]

R.B. McDowell, the historian of the Kildare Street and University Clubs, found the number of military members to be 'a remarkable feature of the club': in 1914 'over 230 members were serving or retired army officers and five others were members of the Royal Navy or Marines, the total amounting to just over one third of membership (34.8 per cent)'. This doesn't include the 103 members with connections to yeomanry, militia and territorial regiments, which brings half the membership of the club into the circle of the Irish military establishment.[39] This is particularly remarkable considering the members of other elite groups viewed access to the Kildare Street Club as a much more difficult attainment. For example, only a quarter of the civil servants studied by Fergus Campbell managed to gain membership to the Kildare Street, and, according to McDowell, only 'about a dozen' senior civil servants were members in 1914.[40] The gentility of the civil service was not a known quantity, as its increasing professional and meritocratic character admitted potentially 'unclubbable' sorts (such as Liberals) to high office.[41] An officer and gentleman, by contrast, could more easily attain the acceptance of the current members, his eligibility requirement—gentility—being tied to his profession. It is also striking, and most likely indicative of the close association between the landed interest and the British Army, that there were so many more army officers than naval officers in the Club. In Dublin and London officers could retreat into the United Service Club, a centre for officer socialisation particularly for older officers, and there were also the county clubs which drew members from a wider range of professions and the clergy as well as local gentry, and represented a wider cross-section of rural middle-class propriety, but these too were, in garrison areas at least, packed with serving and retired officers.[42]

The importance of affiliation to an elite school was mentioned in Chap. 3 as an important step in officer socialisation. This is borne out in the Irish officers examined here as well as in the primary sources. William Cairnes' anonymous study of the officer corps in 1900 and Maclean's survey of public schools' contributions to the Boer War are two contemporary studies which highlight the extent to which officers were drawn from these institutions. Cairnes finds that of the officers he examined, half were public-school educated, and a full quarter of the total were Old Etonians.[43] As aforementioned, this was a function of the institutional character of the officer corps and the increasing provision for military education in such schools as Eton, Harrow, Wellington, and Charterhouse. By 1900, 68% of public schools had instituted a preparatory programme encouraging a military career.[44] Certainly, in the reminiscences of Irish Old Etonian officers, encounters with former schoolmates are frequently recounted, in transit to and from the colonies, in cantonments, colony clubs, and officers' messes. 2nd Lieutenant William Armstrong of the 10th Royal Hussars, from Thurles, mentioned such meetings often in his letters home.[45] The War, it seems, did not dilute this network much: at Port Said in June 1915, Armstrong writes that not only was the first person he met an old school-friend, but that he went on to rendezvous with other childhood acquaintances from the school serving in such diverse circumstances as in Somalia with the native infantry, and at the Dardanelles in an Australian regiment.[46]

Of the officers who have been examined in this study, who served between 1870 and 1925, information on school attendance is available for 334 individuals. Drawing a sample of 125 from this group, 50 attended a major public school, 40% of the total.[47] However, if we include the proportion of officers who were educated in a military school, an elite school in Ireland or a less prestigious school with heavy similarities to the public school system is much higher—84% or 106 officers.[48] Of the 50 public school-educated officers, 13 attended Eton, 26% of all public-school educated officers, but only 10% of the total. This is less than the proportion William Cairnes identified for the United Kingdom as a whole, and this discrepancy is likely due to the multiplicity of educational routes taken by Irish officers. It also suggests a somewhat broader picture of the demographics of the Irish military establishment—both gentry and middle-class officers were educated at elite Irish schools, and the majority of Catholic officers were educated in Ireland at schools such as Clongowes Wood, Belvedere, or St. Stanislaus. There is also a significant tradition of service among the pupils of the prominent English Catholic school, Stonyhurst, which included a number of Irish officers in this period such as Maurice Dease, the recipient of the first Victoria Cross of the Great War.

Senior officers defended the system of elite socialisation because they considered it to work; in the invective pamphlet 'No Army, No Empire', the Earl Dunraven recounts the justifications for continuing to draw officer candidates exclusively from the traditional 'ruling class':

[The army has] been exceptionally well led by officers who, in addition to the courage and endurance shared by all, are animated by a keen sense of what is due not only to their military but *also to their social position*. I do not for a moment suggest that commissions should not be granted to men who show great ability and power of command in the ranks, but such cases are rare, and I do maintain that if democratising means officering the Army largely by promotion from the ranks it would be a fatal mistake.[49]

Other officers mirrored this sentiment uncritically. Hubert Gough, in the opening pages of his memoirs, feels it is necessary to make explicit his views on the importance of the 'old school tie' network.[50] Similarly, General Crozier recalled, 'the old Regular officer seldom thought at all. If he did it was in terms of flags and old school ties, of family history and regimental honour.'[51] A.H.H. Maclean, who examined the prevalence of public school-educated officers in the Boer War, summarised the argument thus: the British officer is, on the one hand,

uneducated, he is 'stupid'. Hence our many 'mishaps'. He was brought up on games. He is over-addicted to polo. He does not read military history … He does very well against savage or coloured races, but pitted against white men, he breaks down. More officers of the studious type are needed. The right sort cannot be got from the public schools. Look at Kitchener!

On the other hand … He is very adaptable. Give him full play and he is no fool. Games at school teach discipline. Outdoor sports keep a man in good condition. Roberts says polo is excellent training for cavalry officers. There can be too much 'book larnin' … The British officer of the present type is, and the mere student would not be, a fine leader of men … Look at Roberts![52]

It is interesting that Maclean's idea of an exemplary public school-educated officer is Lord Roberts, considering he only attended Eton for a few years and did not complete his education there. Clearly, it was socialisation, rather than particular skills training, that marked the pedigree of the public school officer according to Maclean. There were those minority voices who questioned the received wisdom of this 'noblesse oblige' formulation of officer recruitment. Francis Vane, a half-Irish aristocrat, was regarded as holding rather eccentric views on the issue of recruiting and training:

We must first find out what is required of the British officer … A liberal education is necessary … In the army it is becoming slowly realised that proficiency in polo, hunting, and golf, though not to be despised as accomplishments, cannot be reckoned as sufficient substitutes for a knowledge in tactics, strategy, and even general education ... I fear our system hardly encourages this.[53]

According to Vane, there was at least a suggestion that officers were beginning to wake up to the question of professional training. However, he was also frustrated that the army 'is never treated as [a profession]' and the two major reasons for this were clear: first, '[t]he fact that either the officer is not paid enough to enable him to live or his surroundings cause him to expend more than his pay is, I believe the chief cause of amateurism in the army'.[54] And second, 'an officer is not a soldier, but strictly a gentleman who condescends to lead his men in war ... He is mess-ridden ... There he meets the same class he has always met.'[55]

From 1908, this state of affairs was altered by the introduction of a formalised system of Officer Training Corps (OTCs) at schools and universities intended to expand, in a limited and controlled way, the scope of officer intake by making it more attractive to educated young men.[56] However, the extent to which this made a difference to the character of the corps before the huge catalysing influence of the First World War was limited; on the one hand, such men were usually already possessed of the gentlemanly ethos which dominated the officer corps, and on the other, the intake from this source was relatively limited before August 1914. Trinity College Dublin, for example, had 14 reserved spaces for officers before the War, and an OTC numbering around 400 cadets.[57] By 1915, the OTC contained 57% of the remaining student body—those who had not yet gone to the front—and an estimated 69% of members who were already fighting had been granted commissions.[58] These men were 'mainly from Protestant upper middle class families, with business and professional connections. There were also some Roman Catholics who had been educated in exclusive schools.'[59] The War, therefore, significantly increased the percentage of officers with some form of university education, which was only 14% in 1914. Timothy Bowman and Mark Connelly have examined the intake of officers from 1902 to 1914 by method of commissioning and find that, for Irish regiments, the percentage entering from universities was 5.5%. In the 4th Royal Irish Dragoon Guards, 2nd Royal Irish Rifles, and 1st Leinster Regiment, there were only three (5%), two (4.7%), and five (6.7%) officers commissioned from universities, respectively. By comparison, in the same period the 1st Buffs (East Kent Regiment) only commissioned two (3%) university-educated officers, so this pattern was not restricted to Ireland. Still, there was enough space for university-educated officers in the army that a total of seventy-four were commissioned throughout the United Kingdom in 1913.[60] In addition to the few university men commissioned into the line regiments, there were also the medical corps and chaplaincy—and to a lesser extent the engineers and artillery—which were more accustomed to recruiting officers from the universities. Trinity College alone sent 993 medics to the First World War, and their disproportionate contribution to the Indian Medical Service extended back to the mid-nineteenth century.[61]

There was also space for officers of non-elite backgrounds, though it is worth reiterating the absolute minority that such officers represented in the face of the overwhelming predominance of the public school-plus-Sandhurst background. In the case of the Irish military establishment, an intriguing and thus far overlooked manifestation of the extent to which this marginal space was opening up around the turn of the century can be found in the Royal Hibernian Military School (RHMS), an institution for the education of the sons (and, in some years, daughters) of enlisted soldiers in Phoenix Park. Orphaned children of enlisted men could receive a prestigious education here free of charge. This was a non-elite school operating as a charity, with roots extending back to the eighteenth century, and a vast majority of its pupils enlisted in the British Army after completing their schooling. Initially the school was open to boys from all parts of the United Kingdom, though from the 1890s steps were taken to ensure the 'Irish character' of the student body, and boys from Irish families were preferred for entry.[62] Throughout the nineteenth century, there was a considerable waiting list for a place at the school, and this level of demand suggests a Hibernian education was considered a prestigious and valuable asset for a young soldier-to-be. While many of the boys who enlisted were able to attain promotions to NCO and warrant officer positions, there were also those few who were able to become commissioned officers, which suggests a thus-far overlooked possibility of advancement for military families into the officer class over the course of several generations. That this opportunity was accorded disproportionately to Irish military families, due to the prominence of the Hibernian School, is worthy of mention and of further enquiry.

Soldiers known as Old Hibernians had a very close connection to the institutions of the Irish military establishment; not only was the patron of the school often a respected Irish officer like Sir Garnet Wolseley, the school was also visited by the British monarch on several occasions. In

1896, there were 1083 Old Hibernians in the Army, and of these, 27 held a commissioned rank, a commissioning rate of 2.5%.[63] In 1914, according to the calculations of Howard Clarke, there were 57 commissioned Old Hibernians out of a total of 1061, or 5.4% commissioned officers.[64] This may not seem like a great deal, but compared to Timothy Bowman's aforementioned estimation that, overall, only around 1% of officers were commissioned from the ranks (the officers in this study suggest a similar figure), these percentages seem very significant indeed. Edward Spiers has found that, out of the total number of officers, the percentage commissioned from the ranks was 3.2% for 1901–05 (117 officers) and 2.2% for 1906–10 (64 officers). Given these small numbers, the Royal Hibernian Military School undoubtedly loomed large as far as commissions from the ranks were concerned.[65] The outbreak of the First World War would allow a comparatively large number of Old Hibernians to rise to officer rank. This example serves to illustrate an important point about the boundaries of the officer corps in Ireland. In the institutions associated with the Irish military establishment, there were spaces like that created by the Hibernian school, allowing for very specific avenues of entry into the officer corps for those of non-elite backgrounds.

An example of such an officer can be found in the pages of *Hibernia,* the school's alumni magazine. F.R. Logan, of the 1st Lancashire Fusiliers, detailed his service history in a letter to the school's Commandant, with the hope that it would inspire current pupils to follow in his footsteps:

> it was always my ambition to rise in the ranks and be a credit to the old School, and having attained the rank of Captain at 30 years of age, I flatter myself that I am not doing badly... At 18 years of age I joined the ranks and was appointed Lance-Corporal ... within six months I was promoted to full Corporal ... In 1906 our 3rd and 4th Battalions were broken up and then came a regular slump in promotions at home, so I decided to get abroad, and was transferred to the 1st Battalion in India. It turned out to be quite a wise move, because within a month of my arrival I was appointed Lance-Sergeant ... [and] selected to attend the Musketry and Machine Gun course ... Again I proved myself a Hibernian, coming out top ... my Colonel promised me the first vacancy for promotion ... In September, 1914, I was promoted to Colour-Sergeant, and four months later to Company Sergeant Major. In March, 1915 we sailed for the Dardanelles ... In the first stage of the landings I received a bullet through the left shoulder and was later taken off to Malta, where I was informed I had been promoted to 2nd Lieutenant for services rendered in the Field. I really felt then that I had done some-

thing for the School. Two months later ... I took command of a company and was appointed Captain ... I would be delighted to meet or hear from any Old Hibernian boy.[66]

Logan's account clearly illustrates a man who is career-minded and seeking out ways to distinguish himself, and it is interesting that he associates this drive with his training in the Hibernian School. As for his commission, however, it is impossible to deny that the First World War came at an opportune time. It is likely that he would otherwise have remained at the rank of Company Sergeant Major, like many of his old schoolfriends, for several years. Unlike many of his fellow commissioned rankers, however, Logan was able to secure further promotion and apply himself as an effective officer, thus avoiding the fate of the 'dead end' appointment of Lieutenant and Quartermaster, a usual reward for NCOs who had won laurels in the field.[67]

Religion

When historians examine non-elite entry into the Irish ruling class in the late nineteenth and early twentieth century, they often utilise rising levels of Catholic involvement as an indication.[68] Spiers, Wilson, and Silvestri's examinations of military Irishness analyse religious difference as a category, although perhaps the centrality of religious motivations (ahead of other possible motivations) for serving in the army is somewhat overstated.[69] Jordan, Kennedy, and McBride go even further, assuming that Catholic involvement in the professions or officer corps is *prima facie* evidence for non-elite participation, Kennedy even claiming that the officer corps 'positions Catholicism outside Protestant Britishness'.[70]

While it is relatively easy to find evidence for the religious denomination of a particular individual, and indeed religious identity was utilised as shorthand for an entire range of social, economic, and political signifiers at the time, this approach is rather problematic. The officer corps was, indeed, largely a Protestant institution and, according to David Fitzpatrick, only 14% of officers were Catholic (Catholic officers in this study make up a similar percentage); however, this minority was not homogeneous.[71] There were a number of different and distinct groups of Catholic officers in the pre-war corps of 1914. The first were members of the Catholic gentry and aristocracy—such officers as William Butler, Edward Bellingham, and Maurice Dease all belonged to established landed families. The second were from Catholic families whose social cachet was rising, and had found a way into the officer corps despite not conforming to the typical background. Some were from families who had recently established themselves in new country houses, like William Hickie and Edward Bulfin, both sons of Catholic families which had become prominent in the 1860s and 1870s, who went on to become generals during the First World War. Others came from more middle-class backgrounds, like Brigadier-General Joseph Aloysius Byrne, later Inspector-General of the RIC, who was the son of a physician from Derry. Others still came from lower-middle class families with a service background, like Captain F.H. Mahony, whose father was an army bandmaster, and Colonel Edmond Cotter, son of a sergeant in the Buffs.[72] There were also those, like Winston Dugan, son of a school inspector from Parsonstown, King's County (Birr, Co. Offaly) who came from non-elite Protestant families, and thrived in the officer corps.[73] Thus, while religious affiliation can develop a rough outline of the demography of the officer corps, it cannot be assumed to act as a cipher for demographic change, or indeed evidence of a 'greening' of elite institutions, without losing a degree of nuance.

Out of the 561 Irish officers in this study for whom religious affiliation is known, 83 were Catholics—14.8%. The overall percentages could, however, be subject to selection bias; around two-thirds of the officers' religious affiliations were discerned by examining war memorials from churches, a mainly Protestant tradition, and the number of memorials displaying Church of Ireland parishioners accordingly far outstrips those for Catholics. Still, that David Fitzpatrick and Nicholas Perry identify a similar percentage of Catholics in the army of this period—14% and 15% respectively—suggests that this figure may be taken as generally accurate.[74] Of the Irish Catholic officers, it is estimated that over half were members of the aristocracy or landed gentry (i.e. with an entry in Burke's *Peerage* or *Gentry*), and the rest were from non-elite backgrounds.[75] The extent to which these non-elites had inculcated themselves into the officer corps of 1914 is fundamental to understanding the relationship between the military establishment and the political volunteer militias.

POLITICS AND BLOCKED MOBILITY

The state of the Irish military establishment as seen from the point of view of senior officers in 1914 can be ascertained with reference to a memorandum circulated by the Army Council on 4 July of that year.

At the present time two opposing forces, with approximately a total strength of 200,000 men, are being systematically and deliberately raised, trained and equipped and organised on a military basis in Ireland … if, unfortunately, these two large forces should come into conflict, a situation may arise which may require the whole of our available forces at home to deal with.

It is a manifestation of both the seriousness with which senior officers regarded the Home Rule crisis, and a warning about how civil war in Ireland could potentially leave the overseas empire vulnerable:

As we have not been informed what policy the Government proposes to adopt in the event of such a conflict, it is not possible for us to estimate the number of troops which might be required to restore order … it might be necessary to … involve general mobilisation, placing Special Reserve troops in the ports, and assembling the Local and Central Forces … we should be quite incapable of meeting our obligations abroad, and in this connection India and Egypt must be specially borne in mind … whilst certain countries in Europe may take this opportunity of creating trouble … We trust you will not think that in putting this forward we are making any attempt to interfere in a political question.[76]

The memorandum makes no mention, however, of questions of morale or 'political' interference contributing to a split in the officer corps, simply the unknowable number of troops required to keep order. In hindsight, it is certain that there was indeed a social and political shift taking place in the officer corps in 1914. Tim Travers identifies the period immediately preceding the First World War as the nadir of the officer corps' obsessive sense of self-interest, amateurism, and class snobbery; echoing the general theme of historians of elite professionalisation, he argues that the convergence and conflict of two ideals, 'the traditional, gentlemanly, amateur ideal and the technical, functionally competent, professional ideal—produced an awkward transition period for the officer corps'.[77] However contentious the prospect of professional reforms continued to be in 1914, it nevertheless appears that space was emerging for a widening social and cultural base in the officer corps: either in the increasing opportunities for non-gentry military families represented by the Royal Hibernian Military School, or the growing acceptance of university men with the advent of the Officer Training Corps. However, this widening took place within the bounds of the traditional values and identity of the British army. Opponents of professional reforms realised that professionalisation by definition involved diluting the class composition of the officer corps—it required accepting members of the 'professional class'. Successful career advancement for officers was still tied to very specific and rigid preconditions and ideals of gentility and imperial loyalty. The long waiting lists for a place at the RHMS, and the popularity of OTCs at Irish universities suggest that officer status was considered highly desirable among certain sections of society exterior to the gentry, though successive studies of the officer corps' demography demonstrate that the dominance of the landed class did not yield much to this demand.[78]

If the entrenched class composition of the officer corps did frustrate the ambitions of middle-class Irishmen who sought commissions, then their natural destination in 1914 would have been the volunteer movements—the Ulster Volunteer Force and the Irish National Volunteers. According to Marnie Hay, the volunteer movements can be interpreted as a display of masculinity and a manifestation of national vigour, in the vein of Edwardian popular militarism, as well as a political project.[79] They constituted the Irish component of an increasing militarisation of the political process that was taking root throughout Europe in 1914, and accordingly attracted many Irish officers to their ranks. From a class perspective, these bodies appeared to provide an outlet for blocked social mobility and a space for the performance of martial Irishness for the middle class.

While the Ulster Volunteer Force found sympathy with large numbers of the officer class (Fig. 6.2),[80] the Irish Volunteers tended to draw candidates for officer status from the classes just beneath that at which a commission in the British Army was feasible: the urban middle class and the middling farming families.[81] It was this demographic from which most of the eventual Sinn Féin leadership would emerge, and indeed from which the Free State Army's officers were drawn.[82] J.R. White, a Captain in the Irish Volunteers, wrote in August 1914 that 'there is quite a large percentage of smart, intelligent young fellows of some education' interested in officering in the Volunteers. However, he was less complementary about the quality of British Army officers who were involved in raising the force: 'The old soldiers and militia men ... were 95 per cent. of them quite unfit for the task of training a volunteer force.'[83] An insight into the blocked mobility thesis can be attained by examining the social origins and mentalities of the British Army officers who were drawn to these formations, and the associated vision they held for the socialisation of martial virtues.

In the Ulster Volunteers, there was, among members from the Ulster landowning class, a manifestation of the same kind of paternalism associ-

Fig. 6.2 Sir Edward Carson inspects members of the Ulster Volunteer Force. The UVF was commanded by General Sir George Richardson, who was recommended by Lord Roberts personally. He was one of many members of the military elite who were drawn to Unionism and the volunteering movement. *Courtesy of the National Library of Ireland*

ated with the Militia regiments of the pre-Childers Reforms British Army: landlords like Oliver Nugent, Basil Brooke, and Lord Farnham took up leadership positions in the Volunteer movement and sought to provide a didactic martial example and an opportunity for patronage for their tenants. There were also professional soldiers and politicians, not least James Craig, who himself had military experience, who were active in organising the Ulster Volunteer Force. The wide appeal among members of the military establishment for this mass manifestation of armed loyalism is illustrated in the strange case of Captain Wilfrid Spender, an English artillery officer on staff duty in India, who, in a seeming anticipation of the Curragh 'mutineers', announced in 1912 his intention to resign his commission in protest should Ulster be coerced into accepting the Home Rule Bill. Needless to say, his superiors in Simla were deeply puzzled by this spontaneous outburst, and their refusal and punishment of Spender were the cause of a minor scandal in military circles—an odd augury of the troubles to come in the following years. When Spender's plight became known, James Craig and Edward Carson offered him their wholehearted support (though they remained at arm's length until Spender actually retired), and eventually after a very messy departure from the army, including a disciplinary hearing, a number of awkward meetings with senior officers, several instances of 'passing over' for promotion, and a flurry of general paperwork across two continents, Captain Spender found a welcome home after retirement as an instructor for the Ulster Volunteer Force in 1919. As Spender recorded in his statement on resignation from the army,

> The Home Rule agitation was then [1912] very much in the public mind, and when an old Army comrade of mine asked whether I would sign the English form of the covenant ... I gladly did so. I became so interested in this question, more especially in regard to the strategic importance that I attributed to the [situation] ... that I decided to become a [Unionist] candidate for the British Parliament.

Exactly what drew Spender eventually to the Ulster Volunteers, aside from the strategic imperative of preserving the Union, is something of a mystery. He stayed with the cause of Ulster loyalism the rest of his life. During the First World War he wrote, as he followed the actions of the Ulster Division, 'I felt I would rather be an Ulsterman than anything in the world.'[84] His potentially mutinous declaration was regarded very seriously by his superiors:

> When I took up a new appointment on the staff on the Indian frontier I informed my new General of the fact that I had signed the Ulster Covenant, and that it would be my intention to retire from the army if any attempt should be made to place Northern Ireland forcibly under a Dublin Parliament without her consent ... Some months later a telegram was received from the War Office intimating that I was to return to revert to [*sic*] regimental duty forthwith and on no account to state the reasons for this censure ... I then heard from General Franklin that he was arranging for me to have an interview with the Secretary of State for War ... Colonel Seely began it on the most friendly and flattering terms, and I was just on the point of leaving the room when he interjected, 'Of course you understand that there is to be no more nonsense in regard to this Ulster question.' I then told him that I did not feel that I could withdraw from the undertaking

... and he thereupon lost his temper and said that I did not appear to realise the seriousness of the position.

It was decided to make an example of Spender, lest others follow suit. John French was in favour of throwing him out of the army, though in the event Spender found it quite difficult to leave:

> I got a letter informing me that I was to return to India forthwith to regimental duty, and that all future leave would be cancelled, and that there could be no question of my getting any Staff appointment. Feeling that my military prospects were at an end I asked for permission to retire.[85]

It took him another year to finally be allowed to leave the army, and take up a position with the UVF. While Spender was most certainly an exception—or, perhaps, an exaggeration—of the general rule in the military establishment, his example does illustrate both the association between military loyalty and unionist loyalism, and the generally panicked response of the military brass to the prospect of political interference in the officer corps. It is an intriguing juxtaposition with the more conciliatory tone grudgingly adopted in the case of the 61 officers at the Curragh two years later.

According to Timothy Bowman, there were over 130 serving or former British military officers associated with the Ulster Volunteers in this period.[86] The officer corps of the UVF appeared to be constituted of both the landed gentry and a similar middling professional class to that which provided officers to the Irish Volunteers. Reflecting the more industrialised and urban character of the North, there was also a strong representation from young urban professionals and industrialists, including the formation of a rival unionist militia, the Young Citizen Volunteers, in Belfast, 'a self-conscious "class corps" ... composed largely of young business men ... a very large number' of whom 'subsequently obtained commissions' during the First World War.[87] A similar corps was also formed in Dublin. James Craig's own war service was, according to the Patrick Buckland's biography, a key formative experience. As a Captain in the Royal Irish Rifles, he was 'increasingly angry at the way in which he and his men suffered from the ineptitude and arrogance of senior regular army officers'.[88] The shared experience of many Ulster military officers who opposed Home Rule as comrades fighting side by side in the Boer War is notable, from the grandfatherly figure of Edward Saunderson, to Oliver

Nugent, F.P. Crozier, and many others. Crozier's account of his time with the UVF illustrates that, beyond a general and unsophisticated political position of vague loyalism, some officers simply applied themselves to the task of raising a fighting force without troubling themselves overmuch about the political consequences: 'before I had been twenty-four hours in Belfast I realized that the position was serious and complicated. Luckily for me, however, my task was that of the soldier and as such I was able to keep the aim in view.'[89] Crozier also offered a possible explanation of why this compartmentalisation was so easy even for serving officers who knew they may have been transgressing against King's Regulations: 'in Ulster the volunteer movement had the blessing of the Army, the Navy, the Police, the Protestant churches, the ruling class and "gentry"; in the south the volunteering was opposed by the same forces.'[90]

There was little cognitive dissonance in British officers supporting a popular martial movement intent on preserving the integrity of the Union and proclaiming loyalty to the King; not so the Irish Volunteers, whose avowed intention to defend the cause of Home Rule—by force of arms if necessary—was anathema to the aristocratic British officer's identity and spoke to a 'fraying of the pro-Union consensus'.[91] It is interesting, therefore, that many of the officers who associated themselves with the Irish Volunteers came from non-traditional backgrounds. Noteworthy among them was Colonel Edmond Cotter, a retired officer of the Royal Engineers who had been commissioned from the ranks, and who took a key role along with Bryan Mahon and George Berkeley in organising the military aspect of the movement, all at his own expense. Bulmer Hobson recalled that 'He told us he had just enough money to last for about three months. He proposed to work for us in any capacity we liked until his money was done and then he intended to go home. He was a delightful old man, a man of first-rate ability ... [he] would not be a charge on the movement in any way.'[92]

It is remarkable that there does not appear to be any particular characteristic which links the members of the Irish military establishment who were involved with the Irish Volunteers. As was also the case with the UVF, many had experience of action in the Boer War—Captain Jack White attributed his conversion to revolutionary socialism to his experiences of the coercion visited on the Boers in that conflict, as an officer in the 1st Gordon Highlanders.[93] Erskine Childers, though not a regular officer before the First World War, was linked to the Irish military establishment due to his high-profile account of service with the City of London

Volunteers in the Boer War. The senior military advisers to the Irish Volunteers, Cotter and Mahon, had both been Colonels in the British Army. One of the most vocal supporters of the nationalist Volunteers was Captain George Berkeley, a minor County Cork landowner who provided the bulk of the military instruction to the Volunteer movement. His letters give some insight into the reception such officers had from the military establishment in general. In July 1914, Berkeley was dispatched to Belfast in order to stabilise the nationalist movement in the face of the tense situation. He wrote to Nevil Macready in July 1914, pledging the Irish Volunteers as an auxiliary local force for keeping order in the face of a possible unionist uprising:

> the town is in a serious state of some tension, and there are reports of a proposed attack on the Catholic district in order to raise a riot on a serious scale ... Without giving credence to reports, it is self-evident that there is some important demonstration in progress on the Unionist side. The town is filled with English Conservative journalists ... Therefore I felt it my duty yesterday to call upon both the Police and upon Count Gleichen and offer any assistance that I and my men can give towards preserving order.[94]

It seems that a number of officers (with the notable exception of Cotter) were in favour of what would become Redmond's position, and would lead to a split in the movement in 1914: that of using the volunteer movements as a unifying force for national defence. Officers imagined a situation in which the volunteers could work in concert with the Army, apparently with little difficulty. There appeared to be a feeling that professionalism would carry the volunteer movements through their tremulous formative experiences and make them into a competent citizen's army—the exact opposite view to the old guard of the army officer corps.

Another remarkable military officer associated with the volunteer movements was Edward John Moreton Drax Plunkett, 18th Baron Dunsany. His background and the basis of his political faith were typical: as a landlord, his allegiance lay with unionism first and foremost. A guardsman who once again saw active service in the Boer War, he ran guns for the UVF and was an associate of F.P. Crozier. His uncle was Horace Plunkett, the sometime Unionist MP. Despite being what Patrick Maume describes as an 'intransigent Unionist', Dunsany briefly supported the National Volunteers on the occasion of Redmond's pledge to come together against the common enemy in the First World War. Other officers reacted with incomprehension and suspicion at his temporary switching of allegiance: in the eyes of General Crozier and others, 'he had come under suspicion from army officers, who had assumed that his fantasies [novels; Dunsany was also a published author] were nationalist allegories.'[95] Dunsany illustrates most clearly how officers' agendas and intentions as regards these formations were based on the promotion of martial values, rather than a particular political solution to the Home Rule question. There was a surprising willingness to conciliate: a particular shade of moderate cultural nationalism could and did sit comfortably with the conservative ethos of the officer corps, and was professed by a number of Irish officers. When the Volunteers split over Redmond's call to the colours, Dunsany and many other moderate officers, began to distance themselves from the movement. The tone-deafness with which the officer corps engaged with the Volunteers, particularly those drawn increasingly to the independence movement, is illustrated by an episode in 1914, when Dunsany attempted to present a bemused Volunteer detachment with a Union Flag during a parade.

It is difficult to imagine that the likes of Jack White, the son of one of the empire's most celebrated Irish field marshals, or Lord Dunsany, an atypical Irish officer but a typical Irish landlord, ever considered themselves locked out of social advancement in the officer corps; however, what is clear is their abiding sense of alienation from that group, particularly—and spectacularly—in the case of Jack White, whose anti-imperialism and socialist ideals made him a highly atypical officer. It is possible to conceive their support for the volunteers as a mild form of rebellion against the strictures of the officer corps.

While these aristocratic officers did not in themselves constitute a counter-elite, the men whom they led and who would eventually go on to constitute the military establishment of the new states after partition can certainly be so conceived. These British Army officers represent, in their involvement with the Irish Volunteers, the clearest path of continuity between the pre- and post-1922 southern Irish military establishment; senior officers in the Free State Army like Michael Brennan, appointed Army Chief of Staff in 1931, or Major-General Hugo McNeill, shared a common experience in the Volunteer movement with their predecessors, Mahon, Cotter, White, Berkeley, Crosbie, and others.[96] It must be pointed out however that this was a limited inheritance; very few British Army officers were associated with the Irish Volunteers, and those Volunteers who went on to become Free State officers were also a very low proportion of the total.[97] Once again, what is exceptional about the Irish military establishment is its very limited continuity between pre- and post-1922 southern Ireland. Had the political situation in 1914 played out differently this may not have been the case, as the experience of Northern Ireland indicates: the officer corps retained its importance in the North until the mid-twentieth century, and indeed, many UVF supporters found themselves in senior posts in the Northern Irish government after 1922, including Wilfrid Spender. Therefore, the 1912–22 period was not the 'end of an era' for the Northern Irish military establishment, in the same way as it was in the south.[98]

As far as landed officers were concerned, the volunteer movements might have occupied much the same position as other manifestations of national and cultural identity, like the Orange Order or the Ancient Order of Hibernians. Such organisations as these—which, it is worth remembering, had enthusiastic Irish membership throughout the overseas empire—also drew the interest of Irish officers.[99] Edward Saunderson, Basil Brooke, and many others were enthusiastic Orangemen. For less socially prominent officers, however, the volunteer movements represented a space for the projection of a martial vision and the exercise of influence denied to them within the hidebound pre-war military establishment. What appears to draw these officers together is a general rejection of doctrinal authority in military policy, and an unwillingness to conform, beyond a basic minimum set of ritualistic observances, to an uncritical officer mentality and the evidently-undermined pretension to political neutrality described by Hew Strachan.[100]

The distinction is encapsulated in the writings of Dunraven, who very neatly summarises Irish officers' sense of nationality as they attempted to navigate the political complexities of 1914:

> The various ideals of Nationalists may, I think, be thus fairly described:—(1) independence, in the form of an Irish Republic; (2) Dualism; (3) Repeal, and restoration of the *status quo ante*. To none of these ideals can I assent, so I suppose I cannot count myself a Nationalist, though firm in the living faith that the people of Ireland are a nation. Home Rule is so often used as an alternative expression for Nationalism, that I am precluded from calling myself a Home Ruler, although I advocate what I believe to be Home Rule.[101]

The multivariate conceptions of military Irishness at play within the officer establishment were enunciated from a different premise to those of political nationalism. They took as their starting point not any of the 'various ideals' aforementioned, but from the dual conceptions of, first, the positive effect of martial virtues on the life of the nation, and second, a rarely-enunciated but oft-alluded to 'living faith that the people of Ireland are a nation'. Clearly, Irish officers could conceive of the Irish as a culturally distinct, nation—though on both sides of the political divide, they did not necessarily follow these ideals to the conclusion of others, that nationhood implied self-determination and independence. Within these mental boundaries, Irish officers saw their place as attempting to direct the martial development of volunteer movements, and apply the ideals of the officer class to wider society.

Hardly any of them, however, would subjugate the necessity for imperial defence to the promotion of nationalism, and as it became clearer that there was a split in the nationalist camp about this very issue, most officers deserted the movement. As Hervey de Montmorencey wrote to Captain Berkeley in the early days of the War, 'personally I am sick of playing soldiers in this awful crisis. Why can't the volunteers Orange and Nationalist alike enlist in K's army? Let us give a free-passage to Germany all the pro-Germans: who would be made to fight by the Kaiser or gelded.'[102] The following day, Captain de Montmorencey re-affirmed the essential point that the British officer identity overruled national sympathies:

> I am utterly sick of the Volunt'rs: they have excellent spirit and might make good soldiers under British officers, but they have no officers, are a useless mob and submit to a contemptible crew of leaders ... it is better to be a Captain in the British Army than a Field Marshal in the Irish Vols.[103]

The officer corps found themselves at the intersection of the dual factors of national upheaval and armed struggle in the year 1914, the tail end of the period called by one historian 'the end of "the Indian summer for the old order"'.[104] It certainly cannot have seemed that way to Irish officers. The rush to war at the end of 1914 saved the army from an institutional, as well as a political crisis: according to Nicholas Perry's study of the Irish landed class in the officer corps, the expansion of temporary wartime commissioning in 1914–18 conceals a decline in commissions of Irish career officers in 1910–19 overall.[105] The Irish military establishment was confounded by its class composition, compromised by its politics, and crowding out potential sources of new officers—but at the same time, spaces were being opened for the professionalisation and social widening of the officer corps, and individual Irish officers were experimenting with conciliation and an apolitical sense of Irish nationality. The officer corps would have to return to these themes in the period of Irish independence, this time in the aftermath of the Great War.

NOTES

1. Senia Pašeta, Before the Revolution: Nationalism, Social Change and Ireland's Catholic Elite, 1879–1922 (Cork, 1999), pp. 153–154.
2. Nicholas Perry, 'The Irish Landed Class and the British Army, 1850–1950', War in History 18 (2011), pp. 328–329; Peter Martin, 'Dulce et Decorum: Irish Nobles in the Great War 1914–19' in Gregory, Adrian, and Senia Pašeta, eds. Ireland and the Great War: 'A War to Unite Us All'? (Manchester, 2002), p. 41; Martin Petter, '"Temporary Gentlemen" in the Aftermath of the Great War: Rank, Status and the Ex-officer Problem', Historical Journal 37 (1994), p. 131; Paul Taylor, Heroes or Traitors? Experiences of Southern Irish Soldiers Returning from the Great War 1919–1939 (Manchester, 2015), p. 245.
3. Anthony P. Quinn, Wigs and Guns: Irish Barristers in the Great War (Dublin, 2006), p. 47.
4. Martin, 'Irish Nobles and the Great War', p. 28.
5. Christopher Moore-Bick, 'The Development of the Junior British Infantry Officer on the Western Front, 1914–18', PhD thesis, University of Cambridge (2005), p. 41; see also J. G. Darwin, 'The Fear of Falling: British Politics and Imperial Decline since 1900', Transactions of the Royal Historical Society 36 (1986), pp. 27–43.
6. Martin, 'Dulce et Decorum', p. 28.
7. A. S. Cohan, The Irish Political Elite (Dublin, 1972); Mark Radford, The Policing of Belfast 1870–1914 (London, 2015).
8. Cohan, The Irish Political Elite, p. 36.
9. The minor role of officer elites in the Blueshirts, as the political expression of the military establishment, illustrates this point further; see Mike Cronin, 'The Socio-economic Background and Membership of the Blueshirt Movement, 1932–5', Irish Historical Studies 29 (1994), pp. 242–243.
10. Ciaran O'Neill, Irish Elites in the Nineteenth Century (Dublin, 2013), p. 17.
11. Daithí Ó Corráin, 'A Most Public-Spirited and Unselfish Man: The Career and Contribution of Colonel Maurice Moore, 1854–1939', Studia Hibernica 40 (2014).
12. Fergus Campbell, The Irish Establishment, 1879–1914 (Oxford, 2009), pp. 27–30.

13. John Hutchinson, 'The Irish Revival, Elite Competition and the First World War' in O'Neill, Ciaran, ed., *Irish Elites in the Nineteenth Century* (Dublin, 2013), p. 270.
14. Ibid. p. 272.
15. Jane Leonard, 'The Twinge of Memory: Armistice Day and Remembrance Sunday in Dublin since 1919' in English, Richard, and Graham Walker, eds., *Unionism in Modern Ireland: New Perspectives on Politics and Culture* (Basingstoke, 1996), p. 101; Dan Finlay, 'Outflanked by Easter Week: Death in the Flemish Mud', *Books Ireland* 226 (1999), p. 312.
16. The only exception being the political cachet accorded the 'men of 1916'. See John Regan, 'Southern Irish Nationalism as a Historical Problem', *Historical Journal* 50:1 (2007), pp. 206–212.
17. Con Costello, *A Most Delightful Station: The British Army on the Curragh of Kildare, Ireland, 1855–1922* (Cork, 1996), p. 347; David Fitzpatrick, 'Unofficial Emissaries: British Army Boxers in the Irish Free State', *Irish Historical Studies* 30 (1996), p. 213.
18. Jane Leonard, 'Survivors', in Horne, John, *Our War: Ireland and the Great War* (Dublin, 2008), p. 219; Brian Inglis, *West Briton* (London, 1962), p. 59
19. István Deák, *Beyond Nationalism: The Habsburg Officer Corps* (Oxford, 1990), p. 203.
20. An indicative example was the talented young Marshal Tukhachevsky, a First World War veteran who was purged as Stalin regarded him as a potential opponent.
21. Pradeep P. Barua, *Gentlemen of the Raj: The Indian Army Officer Corps, 1917–1949* (London, 2003); Maj. Gen Partap Narain, *Subedar to Field Marshal* (Delhi, 1999).
22. Paul Bew, Peter Gibbon and Henry Patterson, *Northern Ireland 1921/2001: Political Forces and Social Classes* (London, 2002), p. 27.
23. See Steven O'Connor, *Irish Officers in the British Forces, 1922–1945* (London, 2014) passim.
24. Clifford, introduction to Crozier, *The Men I Killed*, p. 17; Andrew Thompson, *The Empire Strikes Back? The Impact of Imperialism on Britain from the Mid-Nineteenth Century* (Harlow, 2005), p. 130.
25. Timothy McMahon, 'A New Role for Irish Anglicans in the Later Nineteenth Century: The HCMS and Imperial Opportunity' in O'Neill, Ciaran, ed., *Irish Elites in the Nineteenth Century* (Dublin, 2013), p. 222; 'The Crisis in Ulster', *The Times*, 17 January 1914; '120,000 Anti-Home Rule Volunteers: A Rapidly-growing Force', *Illustrated London News*, 14 March 1914; 'The Liberal Press and Ulster', *The Times*, 20 April 1914.
26. Hew Strachan, *The Politics of the British Army* (Oxford, 1997), p. 116.

27. Paul Bew, *Ideology and the Ulster Question: Ulster Unionism and Irish Nationalism, 1912–1916* (Oxford, 1994), p. 29; David W. Miller, *Queen's Rebels: Ulster Loyalism in Historical Perspective* (Dublin, 2007), p. 118.

28. Charles Vane-Tempest to his mother, Kildare Street Club, 27 November 1917. Charles Vane-Tempest letters, PRONI.

29. Wilson quoted in Kevin Kenny, *Ireland and the British Empire* (Oxford, 2004), p. 91.

30. Keith Jeffery, *The British Army and the Crisis of Empire, 1918–22* (Manchester, 1984), p. 78.

31. 'The Officers' Petition', *Freeman's Journal*, 11 March 1919; see also Jeffery, *Crisis of Empire* passim.

32. Earl Dunraven, *The Outlook in Ireland: The Case for Devolution and Conciliation* (1907), passim.

33. Jeffery, *Henry Wilson*, p. 102.

34. F. P. Crozier, *A Brass Hat in No Man's Land* (Belfast, 1932), p. 27.

35. Edward Spiers, *The Army and Society 1815–1914* (London, 1980), p. 288.

36. Capt. William Kemmis to Lt. Col. Henry Kemmis, 12 March 1914. Armstrong Papers, LUL.

37. Richard Holmes, *The Little Field Marshal: The Life of Sir John French* (London, 2004), p. 194.

38. R. B. McDowell, *Land and Learning: Two Irish Clubs* (Dublin, 1993) p. 86.

39. Ibid., pp. 86–87.

40. Fergus Campbell, 'Who Ruled Ireland? The Irish Administration, 1879–1914', *THJ* 50:3 (2007), p. 632; McDowell, *Land and Learning*, p. 87.

41. McDowell, *Land and Learning*, p. 88. Liberals had not been admitted to the club with regularity since the 1880s.

42. Robertson, *Crowned Harp*, p. 76; Major General Louis C. Jackson, *History of the United Service Club* (London, 1937), p. 92.

43. Maclean, *Public Schools*, p. 14.

44. C. B. Otley, 'Militarism and Militarization in the Public Schools, 1900–1972', *British Journal of Sociology* 29 (1978), p. 324.

45. William Armstrong to his mother, en route to Pindi, September 1910. Armstrong Papers, LUL.

46. William Armstrong to his mother, Port Said, June 1915. Armstrong Papers, LUL.

47. The figure for the group as a whole is 47%, or 158 officers out of 334. It was felt that, due to the increased visibility of officers from elite schools in the primary evidence, the dataset probably over-stated the percentage of such officers; hence, a random sample was taken to attempt to ameliorate this.

48. Many of the remaining officers either attended day schools or were educated by private tutors.

49. Earl Dunraven, "No Army No Empire", n.d. (c.1902), LUL. Emphasis mine.
50. Hubert Gough, *Soldiering On* (London, 1954), p. 15.
51. F. P. Crozier, *The Men I Killed* (1937), p. 144.
52. A. H. H. Maclean, *Public Schools and the War in South Africa, 1899–1902* (London, 1903), pp. 6–7.
53. Capt. Sir Francis Vane of Hutton, Bart., *On Certain Fundamentals: Being Essays on Current Politics* (London, 1909), p. 69.
54. Ibid. p. 71.
55. Ibid. p. 74.
56. Otley, 'Militarism', p. 330.
57. Roger Willoughby, *A Military History of the University of Dublin and its Officers Training Corps 1910–1922* (Dublin: Medal Society of Ireland, 1983), pp. 2, 9.
58. Laura Dooney, 'Trinity College and the War' in Fitzpatrick, David, ed., *Ireland and the First World War* (Dublin, 1988), pp. 43–45.
59. Anthony P. Quinn, *Wigs and Guns: Irish Barristers in the Great War* (Dublin, 2006), p. 45.
60. Timothy Bowman and Mark Connelly, *The Edwardian Army: Recruiting, Training, and Deploying the British Army, 1902–1914* (Oxford, 2012), pp. 12–13.
61. Tomás Irish, *Trinity in War and Revolution 1912–1923* (Dublin, 2015), pp. 80–81; Christopher Shepard, '"I Have a Notion of Going Off to India": Colonel Alexander Porter and Irish Recruitment to the Indian Medical Service, 1855–96', *Irish Economic and Social History* 41 (2014), pp. 36–52.
62. 'Empire Day', *Hibernia: Quarterly Magazine of the Royal Hibernian Military School,* July 1914, p. 2. British Library.
63. Howard R. Clarke, *A New History of the Royal Hibernian Military School (1765–1924) Phoenix Park, Dublin* (Cleveland, Yorks., 2011), p. 436.
64. Ibid. p. 457.
65. Spiers, *The Army and Society*, p. 4.
66. *Hibernia*, vol. 4, no. 20 (October, 1916), p. 30.
67. Bowman and Connelly, p. 13; French, *Military Identities*, p. 32.
68. See, for example, Thomas E. Jordan, 'Queen Victoria's Irish Soldiers: Quality of Life and Social Origins of the Thin "Green" Line', *Social Indicators Research* 57:1 (2002), p. 85; Spiers, *The Army and Society*, p. 298; Caitriona Kennedy and Matthew McCormack, eds., *Soldiering in Britain and Ireland, 1750–1850* (Basingstoke, 2013), pp. 37–38; Michael Sivestri, *Ireland and India: Nationalism, Empire and Memory* (Cambridge, 2009), p. 182; Tim Wilson, 'Ghost Provinces, Mislaid Minorities: The Experience of Southern Ireland and Prussian Poland

Compared, 1918–23', *Irish Studies in International Affairs* 13 (2002), pp. 67–70; McBride, *The Greening of Dublin Castle* passim.

69. Silvestri, *Ireland and India*, p. 80.
70. Kennedy and McCormack, *Soldiering*, p. 38.
71. David Fitzpatrick, 'Protestant Depopulation and the Irish Revolution', *Irish Historical Studies* 38 (2013), p. 647.
72. *Hibernia*, January 1915.
73. P. A. Howell, 'Dugan, Sir Winston Joseph', *Australian Dictionary of Biography* (Manchester, 1996).
74. Perry, 'The Irish Landed Class', p. 322.
75. Random sample of 30 Catholic officers.
76. Memorandum by the Military Members of the Army Council on the Military Situation in Ireland, 4 July 1914, in Ian Beckett, *The Army and the Curragh Incident 1914* (London, 1986), pp. 379–380.
77. Tim Travers, 'The Hidden Army: Structural Problems in the British Officer Corps, 1900–1918', *Journal of Contemporary History* 17:3 (1982), p. 525.
78. Fitzpatrick, 'Collective Sacrifice', p. 1027; Spiers, *Army and Society*, p. 4; Peter Karsten, 'Irish Soldiers in the British Army, 1792–1922: Suborned or Subordinate?', *Journal of Social History* 17 (1983), p. 34.
79. Marnie Hay, 'Moulding the Future: Na Fianna Éireann and its Members, 1909–1923', *Studies: An Irish Quarterly Review* 100:400 (2011), p. 441; see also Sarah Benton, 'Women Disarmed', pp. 151–153.
80. Bew, *Ideology and the Ulster Question*, p. 94.
81. Peter Hart, 'The Social Structure of the Irish Republican Army, 1916–1923', *THJ* 42 (1999), pp. 200–201.
82. Karsten, 'Suborned', p. 33.
83. J. R. White, Irish Volunteers Handbill, 17 August 1914. Berkeley Papers, CCA.
84. Spender quoted in Paul Bew, *Ireland: The Politics of Enmity 1789–2006* (Oxford, 2007), p. 382.
85. Wilfrid Spender, 'Statement of Circumstances Leading Up to Sir Wilfrid Spender's Retirement from the Army in 1915', 1943. PRONI. As the Ulster Covenant referred to 'men of Ulster', separate documents were prepared for women and non-Ulstermen. Spender signed the English Covenant, though as we shall see his connections with other Unionist officers led him to settle in Ulster after the War.
86. Timothy Bowman, *Carson's Army: The Ulster Volunteer Force, 1910–22* (Manchester, 2007), p. 57.
87. Ibid., pp. 52–53.
88. Patrick Buckland, *James Craig Lord Craigavon* (Dublin, 1980), p. 7.
89. Crozier, *The Men I Killed*, p. 49.

90. Ibid. p. 56.
91. John Bew, 'Ireland under the Union, 1801–1922' in Bourke and McBride, *Princeton History of Modern Ireland*, p. 100.
92. Bulmer Hobson, BMH Witness Statement WS0050, p. 11.
93. Fearghal McGarry, 'White, James Robert ("Jack")', DIB.
94. Berkeley to Macready, Belfast, 24 July 1914, Berkeley Papers, CCA. Count Gleichen was a British aristocrat who commanded the 15th Infantry Division in Belfast during the Home Rule crisis.
95. Patrick Maume, 'Plunkett, Edward John Moreton Drax', Dictionary of Irish Biography.
96. Hay, 'Moulding the Future', p. 449.
97. Ibid. p. 449.
98. Michael McConville, *Ascendency to Oblivion: The Story of the Anglo-Irish* (London, 1986), p. 262.
99. Donald MacRaild, 'Wherever Orange is Worn: Orangeism and Irish Migration in the 19th and Early 20th Centuries', *Canadian Journal of Irish Studies* 28:29 (2002).
100. Strachan, *Politics of the British Army*, pp. 115–116.
101. Dunraven, *The Outlook in Ireland*, p. 170.
102. De Montmorencey to Berkeley, 13 September 1914, Berkeley Papers, CCA.
103. De Montmorencey to Berkeley, 14 September 1914, Berkeley Papers, CCA.
104. Costello, *A Most Delightful Station*, p. 263.
105. Perry, 'The Irish Landed Class', p. 41.

CHAPTER 7

Irish Officers in the Great War

There is a shortage of Irish. You idlers are deserting your country ...
You think to get your rights by refusing to do your duty. That is not the
way. Do your duty and claim your rights.
—4th Earl of Dunraven, 1917

As Lord Dunraven correctly pointed out, in one of his many publications
on the state of the army in Ireland, by 1917 the recruiting effort was running into difficulty.[1] Recruitment had been declining year on year from its
peak in September 1914, but the dearth of volunteers by 1917 was making the institution of conscription a much more likely prospect. Despite
declining recruitment figures throughout the United Kingdom, to commentators in Ireland the apparent rise in support for nationalism, the outrage at the executions of the 1916 rebels, the war-weariness of the Irish
regiments, and the virulent opposition to conscription were convincing
evidence that low recruitment was an Irish problem.[2]
The picture was very different in the autumn of 1914, when the outbreak of war occasioned great public enthusiasm and scores of Irishmen
applied for service. Among them were thousands of men eager to take up
commissions as temporary officers. The initial enthusiasm did not abate
quickly, and a substantial backlog of officer candidates presented itself.
Many solutions were proposed by military planners: the expansion of officers' training corps, the formalisation of training regimes; even the formation of battalions of enlisted 'candidates for commissions', from whom

© The Author(s) 2019
L. Sweeney, *Irish Military Elites, Nation and Empire, 1870–1925,*
https://Doi.org/10.1007/978-3-030-19307-2_7

would be drawn new officers, as and when they were required.[3] Once again, the officer corps found itself at the centre of the changing relationship between the British state and the Irish people.

This chapter will examine how the conditions of total war influenced the relationship between the army and the Irish society. The First World War saw the largest demographic change in the history of the British officer corps to that point, with a significant increase in commissions from the ranks and the recruitment of wartime officers from a widening swathe of the middle class—the so-called temporary gentlemen.[4] The demand for new officers necessitated a much more professional ethos in the officer corps and called into question the long-held narratives of gentility and aristocratic character which, as we have seen, had been integral to the officer corps in the nineteenth century.

The response of all sections of Irish society to the outbreak of war was enthusiastic, and multiple narratives of martial Irishness influenced recruiting. These were implicit in the foundation of the new Irish Divisions, solely Irish forces which proved surprisingly contentious among sections of the senior military establishment. The importance of national identity was not diminished by the outbreak of the war, and the first section of this chapter will examine new sources concerning the reactions of Irish officers to questions of identity in the wartime context.

Second, this chapter examines the experience of the many imperial Irish who served with the Indian Army, an often overlooked aspect of the First World War, and how they conceived of questions of nationality and loyalty in the context of the British Empire. The reactions of these officers to questions of Indian self-determination are illuminating in the context of the Irish officer corps' persistent and deeply held belief in the importance of imperial security and the imperative of preserving Ireland's link with the empire. Unlike some of their compatriots in the civilian administration, Irish officers tended to be more than usually opposed to Irish (or, for that matter, Indian) self-determination.

The third section examines the unprecedented opportunities opened up during the Great War for the advancement of officers from non-traditional backgrounds, and the effect of these 'temporary gentlemen' on new training regimes. Once again, new research will be mobilised to bring to light this little-examined subset of Irish officers. Many of these new opportunities required the acquisition of specialist knowledge, such as in the Royal Flying Corps, where the potential for fame and glory was married to an even greater risk of injury and death. After the war, the social base of the officer corps once again narrowed to its pre-war character, and only very few officers of non-traditional background remained in the officer corps.

The fourth section examines the reactions of Irish officers to the Easter Rising, particularly those present in Dublin at the time who answered the challenging conditions of active service in their homeland. Their reactions to the Rising were more complex and nuanced than those of officers serving overseas, and remarkably, some officers quite rapidly revised their opinions of the rebels in the light of subsequent political developments. The characterisation by Bartlett and Jeffery of the Easter Rising as an attempt to lay claim to the inheritance of an Irish military tradition which had been dominated by the British Army, will be assessed in relation to Irish officers' accounts of Ireland and Irishness throughout the years of the Great War.

In August of 1914, Irish people all around the world rushed to war. The outbreak of hostilities is popularly remembered to have taken place at Mons, with the engagement between the British Expeditionary Force and the German Army. This battle resulted in the posthumous award of the Great War's first Victoria Cross to Lieutenant Maurice James Dease of County Westmeath.[5] However, the first engagement of the war in fact took place in the West African colonies when an over-enthusiastic captain of the West African Frontier Force (WAFF) decided, on his own initiative, to invade German Togoland on 9 August, capturing the strategically important wireless station at Kamina and cutting off Germany's communications with its African colonies.[6] The WAFF, as was typical for colonial military forces, had its fair share of Irishmen as officers, including, in the early stages of his career, the aforementioned Frank P. Crozier, later to gain notoriety as the commander of the Auxiliary Division of the Royal Irish Constabulary during the War of Independence. The King's African Rifles, who were engaged in fighting in German East Africa in the longest campaign of the War, also had a large number of Irish officers, including Johnnie Gough, brother of Hubert of Curragh incident fame, and Colonel Richard Pope Hennessy, a Catholic officer from County Cork. This serves as a reminder of the imperial and global nature of the First World War and the importance of an imperial mentality to the self-identification and outlook of the officer corps in this period.

The mainstream of political and strategic thought in the Irish military establishment greeted the outbreak of war with a sense of relief, regarding it as eliminating, or at least postponing, the possibility of civil war in

Ireland.[7] However, as the Irish at home and in the empire prepared for war, it became clear that questions of Irish nationality and imperial allegiance had not gone away.

MOBILISATION: IRISH OFFICERS AND IMPERIAL ALLEGIANCE

The latest historical work on Irish recruitment in the First World War reveals the existence of a cross-denominational identity of militaristic Irishness, illustrated by the enthusiastic support of the war effort by the members of both major volunteer movements.[8] The militarism which had divided Irish society, it was posited, might also bring it back together if it was properly directed: according to Shane Leslie, 'When Redmond offered Ireland's sword, a unique opportunity had arrived for unison. This could have been found in Lord Roberts. Curiously enough he was considered as a leader for both Northern and Southern contingents taking the field.'[9] For his part, Roberts, who at the time was both Honorary Colonel of the Irish Guards and a senior member of the imperial general staff, was eager to avoid too close an association with either volunteer division. Some quarters of the Irish Volunteers resisted wartime conciliation, already regarding the war effort, and Roberts in particular, with suspicion: in August, the Volunteers in south Derry marched against being 'turned into militiamen to be generalled by Roberts or Kitchener'.[10] This anti-recruitment challenge to elite Irish militarism was dismissed by the military establishment, and many elite officers, including Lords Headfort, Monteagle, and Fingall, praised Redmond's call to make the Volunteers available for war duty.[11]

It was proposed that Ireland's contribution to the war effort should be three divisions, the 10th (Irish), 16th (Irish), and 36th (Ulster). Redmond attempted, unsuccessfully, to persuade Lord Kitchener to accept the enlistment of the Irish National Volunteers *en masse*. They would form an 'Irish Brigade', cloaked in the romantic imagery of the Wild Geese and drawing on signifiers of Irish identity (Fig. 7.1). According to Trevor Royle, this proposal was completely unacceptable to Kitchener, who neither trusted the Irish Volunteers, nor considered them worthy soldier material. Despite attempts by Irish officers to come to an agreement, Kitchener was implacable: 'Each time senior Irish officers put forward compromise plans, such as confining the force to ex-soldiers, these were stonewalled by officials and politicians who feared that disaffected Irishmen would join up only to turn their guns against

Fig. 7.1 'The Real
Irish Spirit', recruiting
poster, 1914. Appeals to
Irish nationality were
heavily utilised in the
recruiting effort, even as
senior officers remained
wary of Irish disloyalty
in the army. *Alamy*

the British … [Redmond's] offer was curtly refused by Kitchener who
regarded the National Volunteers as rebels in sheep's clothing.'[12] Indeed,
Kitchener seemed dead set against the idea of purely Irish regiments to
the last: Shane Leslie recorded as late as 1915 that 'Kitchener told
Redmond he would prefer no Irish regiments at all except to stiffen up
the English'.[13] Kitchener's reticence was curious; Home Rulers and cultural nationalists, as we have seen, were generally pro-imperial before the
War, and many had loyally served for years in the Irish regiments as
enlisted men and as officers—and senior officers wrote to Kitchener raising these points.[14] Kitchener was no stranger to serving with Irish officers and owned property in Ireland, which makes his extreme view
concerning the loyalty of Irish recruits even more puzzling. Kitchener's
attitude can only be explained as a manifestation of the officer corps' lack
of confidence following the escalation of the Irish question in 1913–14.

Ironically, Kitchener's suspicions had a detrimental effect on Irish recruitment.[15] Eventually, the Volunteers were incorporated, despite his severe misgivings, into the service battalions of the 16th Division, while the Ulster Volunteer Force (UVF) constituted the majority of the 36th.

Those who supported and assisted the Volunteers, likewise, were not united in their enthusiasm for John Redmond's scheme of mobilisation. Colonel Maurice Moore received a report from another nationalist officer George Berkeley, who was in the North to meet with local Volunteer movements there, and noted that there was a common apprehension both among the Nationalists and among the Ulster Volunteers that the call to enlistment would leave their communities vulnerable to sectarian violence from the other side.[16] Lord Ardee (later Lord Meath), an aristocratic Irish officer who was generally in favour of mobilising the Volunteers for imperial defence, added the caveat that the only way in which the Volunteers could retain their Irish character if mobilised was to ensure they were led by Irish officers—this was an old problem, resurrected by senior officers' sudden wariness concerning Irish soldiers, which now stood a chance of finally being addressed.[17]

Bryan Mahon and John Redmond, and their family members who took commissions in 1914, were adamant that the war would demonstrate not only Ireland's willingness to remain an enthusiastic imperial nation, but also that through Irish valour and martial prowess, they could make the argument that Ireland was fit for self-determination.[18] Even in 1917, as the battle for home rule was slowly killing him, John Redmond was still convinced that the path to Home Rule lay in military service to the empire, writing in support of the 10th (Irish) Division that

> it was the first definitely Irish Division that ever existed in the British army. Irish Divisions and Irish Brigades played a great part in history in the past, but they were Divisions and Brigades, not in the service of England, but in the service of France and other European countries and America. The creation of the 10th (Irish) Division, therefore, marks a turning point in the history of the relations between Ireland and the Empire.[19]

A not insignificant segment of the population, it appeared, agreed with Redmond, as the tens of thousands of Irishmen who answered the call to arms attest. Conceiving of war service as a test of Irish masculinity and valour was the common narrative inducing UVF and National Volunteer leaders to support enlistment.[20]

The motivations of Irish officers thus rested on a number of different allegiances: variously, the Union, the Crown, national identity, and empire. For Irish officers, the British Empire represented not only an economic good for Ireland, but the advance of Western civilisation itself; Ireland's close involvement within it was a necessary prerequisite if its internal issues stood any chance of being resolved.[21] The concept of a 'blood sacrifice' in the Great War as a way to unify the nation and demonstrate its loyalty and self-reliance had parallels in other parts of the empire: in the Canadian, Australian and New Zealander cases, the sense of the Great War as bonding the nation by blood is still an integral part of the national narrative.[22] For Ulster, an analogy can be drawn between the role of the Ulster Division on the Somme and the Australia and New Zealand Army Corps (ANZACs) at Suvla Bay, the former constituting the blood sacrifice which consolidated the loyalist Ulster 'nation' and contributed to its formation as an 'imagined community'.[23] In the south, of course, this sacrificial moment was embodied by those Irish Volunteers and other allied groups who died in Dublin during the Rising, occluding for nearly a century the memory of the many thousands of their fellow Volunteers who were at that time dying alongside the Ulster Orangemen at the Somme—and indeed who had fought and died alongside ANZAC forces at Suvla Bay the previous year.

The initial response to the call for recruits to the rank-and-file was less enthusiastic than expected: according to Peter Simkins, the 6th Leinster Regiment had to poach 600 men from Bristol in order to make up its numbers, while even the venerable Inniskilling Fusiliers were still almost 500 men short of their full complement in early 1915, having never reached full strength since the start of the war.[24] Kitchener was, despite his dismissive attitude towards the National Volunteers, frustrated at what he saw as the Irish refusing to do their bit. Nonetheless, 40,000 Irishmen enlisted in 1914, a contribution overshadowed, according to General Godley, by a regrettable lack of understanding and trust on the part of general officers.[25]

Another contentious factor was the man chosen to command the 16th (Irish) Division, Lieutenant-General Lawrence Parsons, who, though an Irish officer himself, had 'served in India for most of his career, and he gave great offence by appointing Ulster Protestants to senior posts and blocking the way of Catholics, including Redmond's son', even after Redmond had sent Kitchener a list of eligible Catholic officers in an attempt to alleviate this increasingly uncomfortable situation.[26] Parsons inhabited a complex position: as an old regimental officer steeped in the traditions and ethos of the Connaught Rangers, the discrimination against Catholic nationalists he displayed was rather out of character, and, like Kitchener's attitude, it once again illustrates the depth of feeling that had developed over the Home Rule issue in the months before the war. His treatment by his brother officers for even associating with the 'other side' of the issue is highly indicative: his daughter recalled 'my father passed through the Ulster divisional lines, to inspect his Northern Catholic Brigade, without being saluted by a single Ulster officer though he was wearing his full rig-out. This was his lesson for being a renegade, commanding Papists.'[27]

Thus, the political context of mobilisation in 1914 complicated and diminished martial Irishness' historical strength: its cross-denominational appeal. As in previous eras, the apprehension of senior military commanders overestimated the potential for Irish dissent to subvert the army and led to unnecessary tension and the alienation of moderate nationalists.

Irish officers like Maurice Moore, the most vocal of the pro-nationalist and pro-Volunteer officers, complained that Ireland was being disproportionately singled out for raising Kitchener's 'first 100,000' new army recruits:

> If we come now to the new Army, we find that for 100,000 men the proportionate quota from Ireland would be 9,509 recruits. The Division required from Ireland by the War Office is 20,000. This would be well over the proportion for 200,000 men, but Lord Kitchener intends this purely Irish Division of 18,000 or 20,000 to be the Irish contribution to his first army of 100,000. This seems to be a calculation based on 'Irish Generosity' ... It is not only, as we are told, the passing of the Home Rule Bill ... that will solve the military difficulty of Ireland. It is the organization of an Irish Army, trained on its own soil, with its national character recognised. Nothing less than this will prevent 'disappointment'.[28]

There was one section of army recruitment in Ireland, however, which exceeded demand greatly: that of candidates for commissions. There was a widespread feeling of entitlement among the well-heeled young men of Dublin when the call went out, and they flocked to join the Dublin University Officer Training Corps (OTC) in the hopes of securing a commission.[29] According to Francis Laird, an alumnus of Trinity College, Dublin and First World War officer, 'The headquarters of the OTC in Trinity College was an inspiring sight in those days, surrounded by a crowd of young undergraduates anxious to get their commissions and be off before the war was over.'[30] Maurice Moore's son, a student at the University of London, asked his father to secure him 'a position in the Irish Guards', not least because 'it is not very pleasant to be asked why one hasn't joined, by every body one meets'.[31]

The enthusiastic response to the call for temporary officers concealed a decline in the commissioning of Irish officers since 1900.[32] In the run-up to the war, Kitchener was anticipating an officer shortage, writing to retired or half-pay officers, inviting them to return to the colours, and detaining Indian Army officers on leave in the hope of persuading them to transfer to the home army.[33] After the declaration of war, recruiting offices and Officer Training Corps were inundated with thousands of applications from prospective officers. Candidates coming forward for commissions in Ireland quickly outstripped demand. Parsons, at the headquarters of the 16th, sought competent Irish officers for his politically sensitive division, and to that end, disseminated the following letter:

> Lieut. Gen. Sir Lawrence Parsons, Commanding 16th Division, wishes it to be known that applications for temporary Commissions in the junior ranks of the units of the 16th Division exceed the available vacancies many times over. It is therefore inevitable that for the present a fraction only of these applications can be successful.
>
> Candidates are strongly encouraged to enlist in the 7th Battalion, the Leinster Regiment in the 47th Brigade, stationed at Fermoy, where there is every reason to hope they will find many comrades, association with whom will prove congenial to themselves.
>
> Candidates can enlist at the nearest recruiting office, and presentation of this letter to the Recruiting Officer will ensure ... they will be posted to a Company composed of Candidates for Commissions under Major the Earl of Fingall, *in which they will be associated with many of their own class.* They will there, while waiting to be gazetted, be fitting themselves for commissions.
>
> Candidates who show their keenness to fit themselves for the position of officers ... instead of wasting their time waiting, will, in as many cases as possible, be recommended for commissions.
>
> In filling up the many vacancies, which will inevitably occur as time goes on, General Parsons will invariably look first to this source of supply.[34]

Gavin Hughes takes Parsons' concentration on Irish officers as evidence of a stubborn nationalist position, though it is more likely that Parsons was committed to raising a professional and efficient corps using the manpower he had available.[35] What is striking here is the evident attempt at reassuring potential officer candidates that no loss of social status would be implied if they were to enlist in the ranks, and that doing so would put them at the head of the queue for future vacancies. The very many officer candidates who sought to join prestigious regiments at the outbreak of the war suggests that the old system of regimental social gradations was still important—indeed, potentially more important, as this valuable symbol of status now appeared, fleetingly, to be within reach of middle-class Irishmen willing to prove themselves.[36] At the same time, senior officers, who sought a practical solution and did not want to dissuade potential recruits who were desperately needed, continued to express the message that candidates who were proactive and enlisted to learn the skills of soldiering would be favourably regarded for future promotion.

These companies of 'gentleman rankers', alongside the well-known First World War image of the 'temporary gentleman' wartime commissioned officer, seem to suggest that the ad hoc nature of commissioning and recruiting in the early stages of the war led to a significant disruption in the social structure of the army. However, it appears that, at least at the outset, army recruiters tended as much as possible to revert to their tried and trusted supply of wartime officers, the university and public school Officers Training Corps. Indeed, Simkins contends that in this first stage of wartime officer recruiting, the contribution of the OTCs was so significant that 'there was no sudden or radical change in the social composition of the officer corps during the first year of the war, unlike that of the rank and file. Indeed, in the early months it was often difficult for a man without OTC training or a public school background to become an officer.'[37] A War Office report from mid-1915 lamented the dearth of middle-class volunteers for the front from the population of the United Kingdom as a whole, noting: 'The upper and working classes have responded well but the middle classes and the farmer class have been rather backward.'[38] This was due to the over-subscribed Irish officer corps, as aforementioned for the 16th Division in particular. It is also a continuation of the general commissioning pattern of the nineteenth century—quite simply, positions were filled by traditional means first, and only then did recruiters look to the 'temporary gentlemen'.[39] By the time a systematic officer training regime was instituted in early 1916, 3700 Irish temporary officers had been commissioned.[40] Considering that, at the outbreak of the war, there were only 12,738 regular officers in total in the army, this was certainly a significant slice of the officer corps.[41] However, it was only after the tried and trusted sources of officer material were exhausted that the army widened its scope, and developed a professionally focussed training regime to socialise the new intake.

Just because 'traditional' officers were first to the fight does not mean there was no change among this segment of the officer corps. As we have seen, in previous conflicts and in peacetime, a high proportion of officers were Old Etonians. The image of the stalwart Etonian officer was a trope of imperial propagandists like the famous war artist Elizabeth Thompson Butler.[42] For the first eight months of the Great War, however, of the 20,577 men with OTC training who were commissioned, only 350 came from Eton, fewer than from Wellington, Charterhouse or Marlborough, other well-represented officer schools.[43] The total number of Old Etonian officers, however, was inflated by their high representation amongst pre-war career officers. Out of a sample of 125 Irish officers, a mere 8% of First World War officers were Old Etonians. Again, this is a smaller percentage than in the entire period from 1871 to 1922.

The officers on Eton's roll of honour from Irish regiments (which, it must be reiterated, does not particularly make them Irish, and so should be taken more as an indication than a total count of Irish officers) numbered just 149 out of the roll of 5650 Old Etonians who served in virtually every branch of service—a negligible proportion in relation to the over 1500 officers from Trinity College Dublin.[44] 1157 Etonians lost their lives in the war, a horrific sum in comparison to Belvedere College's 68, or the 41 officers from the Royal Hibernian Military School, and a comparable rate to the 463 Trinity men who were killed.[45] In addition to the 149 Etonians aforementioned were schoolmates who were most certainly Irish, but did not serve in Irish regiments, such as Captain Macmurrough Kavanagh, Lieutenant H.S. Keating, Colonel W.H. Wyndham-Quin, the Earl of Minto, and the Marquess of Londonderry (Table 7.1).

The Eton College roll of honour is also indicative of the continuing cleavage in the officer corps between the aristocratic elite regiments and the technical branches of service: of the entire product of the school, the roll of honour yields only 27 RAMC officers, and the same number of chaplains, as compared to 77 Irish Guards officers—themselves hardly a majority amongst the very many Etonians in all of the elite regiments.

Edward Spiers has noted that from the late nineteenth century, the percentage of aristocratic officers in the British officer corps as a whole was declining, while the percentage of gentry officers and those from professional backgrounds was correspondingly rising—and by 1914 the percent-

Table 7.1   Old Etonians serving in Irish regiments, 1914–19

Irish Guards	77	Inniskilling Fusiliers	7
Inniskilling Dragoons	12	Munster Fusiliers	2
Royal Irish Rifles	14	Royal Irish Fusiliers	6
Dublin Fusiliers	4	North Irish Horse	8
Leinster Regiment	2	South Irish Horse	6
Royal Irish Regt.	5	Irish Cavalry Depot	1
Connaught Rangers	5		

Source: Edward Littleton Vaughan, List of Etonians who fought in the Great War, 1914–19 (Old Etonians serving in other regiments also spent some of the war attached to one or more Irish regiments. The table does not count individual soldiers more than once and as far as possible locates officers in their original regiment.)

age of officers from professional backgrounds (including the clergy) had exceeded that of officers from military families.[46] The bulk of this change took place in the Edwardian period, which saw both increasing professionalisation and a reduction in the officer corps' numbers overall. As we have seen, this increasing diversity was not distributed evenly throughout the officer corps—there was a 'flight' to the elite regiments by aristocratic officers seeking to entrench their social position.[47] What did not change in this period was the extremely low proportion of officers from the working- and lower-middle classes—including those commissioned from the ranks—who were still considered unsuited to command.

It was the high casualty rate for officers—on the front line as well as, contrary to popular belief, in the higher echelons—that led to the proliferation of temporary gentlemen. Of the 109 Irish aristocrats who took part in the fighting as First World War officers, 29 were killed—over a quarter.[48] This above-average casualty rate was unlike anything encountered before and necessitated the temporary widening of the corps to a degree that was unprecedented. In previous conflicts, as we have noted, commissions from the ranks were not unheard of but generally tended to originate from the tried and tested pool of veteran non-commissioned officers, particularly sergeants-major. The casualty rate quickly outstripped this source of officers too, leading to a uniquely diverse officer corps, albeit constituted of temporary commissions for the duration of the war only. A more diverse officer corps did not reappear until the second half of the twentieth century.[49] These non-traditional officers will be examined in greater detail in section three. First, India, the impecunious officer's 'haven', will be examined.

IRISH OFFICERS IN THE INDIAN ARMY

The Indian Army played a crucial role in the First World War which tends to be forgotten in narratives focussed on the Western Front. India committed 1.4 million soldiers to the fighting across the world—in Africa, east Asia, Europe, and Mesopotamia. As noted in earlier chapters, the Indian Army was a popular destination for two varieties of Irish officers: the impecunious gentry subaltern, seeking an affordable life and the distinction and patronage which could be gained from active service on the Northwest Frontier; and the professional, middle-class officer who, particularly in the Engineers, Artillery or Medical Service, could find an occupation utilising his technical skills without any of the barriers of social class and expense that typified life in the home service. There had long been a heavy Irish presence in India; when Lord Roberts departed after an illustrious career as Commander-in-Chief, the *Times of India* remarked, 'thus an Irish Commander-in-Chief [George White] succeeds an Irish Commander-in-Chief, just as an Irish Viceroy [Lord Lansdowne] succeeded an Irish Viceroy [Lord Dufferin].'[50] Further down the social scale, the Indian Medical Service was dominated by Irishmen, and the Irish were also disproportionately represented in the army and civil service.[51]

The Indian Army was a large, professionalised organisation. Compared to the African colonies, India had by 1914 acquired a civilised character in the eyes of officers. F.P. Crozier unfavourably compared this with his preferred posting of Nigeria, as evincing 'the handicaps of civilisation … ice, white women, and competition in frocks and frills'.[52] Generally, the hierarchy of social cachet ran from the relatively rarefied heights of home service, to India, and thence to Kenya, the Sudan, and on down to the feverish, uncomfortable and often-brutalising postings of the so-called white man's grave in West Africa—the place where many impecunious Irish officers, notably Wolseley, cut their teeth.[53] While the domestic situation in India before the First World War may have caused some commentators to draw superficial comparisons with Ireland, particularly on the subject of Home Rule, even officers with sympathy for Irish nationalism had little time for its Indian counterpart.[54] As one Irish officer, an aristocratic and enthusiastically imperialistic client of Roberts, bluntly expressed:

Home Rule in Ireland … is nothing to this Home Rule for India agitation … I had always been rather keen [on the cause of] giving the Indian man [a] chance. But when they start this talk of clearing the British out of India then

I stiffen up my back and feel inclined to say alright come on and do your d-dest [*sic*].[55]

Colonial civilians, administrators, and civil servants, notably the Irishmen Roger Casement, Alfred Webb, and Maurice Collis, were more conciliatory towards Indian nationalism, but as a rule officers distrusted it in all its forms.[56]

Given the wider social base of the Indian Army (gentry officers complained of the harsh accents of their more proletarian comrades as 'half-castes … drop[ping] their "H"s'), and the fact that most Irishmen in the Raj were already occupied in the army or in some other form of government service, and therefore not likely to be able to seek temporary officer status, one might expect to see little change in the social structure among Irish officers of the Indian Army.[57] In the colonial context the mechanisms of social demarcation were inflected not only by class difference, but by colour. Imperial Irishmen had the privilege of inhabiting a protean space wherein they could be at once Irish, English, and British, as and when the situation required it.[58] Indian soldiers did not have this luxury.

The advent of King's Commissioned Indian Officers (KCIOs), Indian officers commissioned on an equal footing with their European colleagues (as opposed to those holding a Viceroy's commission, the most senior of whom were still subordinate to the most junior white subaltern), was a major upheaval in the ethos and identity of the officer elite during the First World War. As with the apprehension that greeted the widening of the officer corps in Britain, and the arguments over the incorporation of the Irish volunteer militias, in practice the implementation of 'Indianisation' produced little social upheaval and the small number of KCIOs assimilated into the officer corps with little difficulty.[59] The reasons for this are the same as for the other social changes wrought on the officer corps by the war: first, KCIOs were selected from experienced and trusted non-commissioned officers who were already well socialised into army life; and second, the type of person who expressed an interest in becoming a KCIO tended to be rather conservative and dedicated to the ethos and outlook of the British officer in the first place. Much like the situation surrounding Irish commissioning in 1914, fears of Indian nationalist fifth-columnists were consistently overstated, stoked by the increasing popularity of nationalist politics. Many of the KCIOs were in fact drawn from the gentry families of the Princely States, the indigenous landowning elite who were generally beneficiaries of British rule in India.[60] The rhetoric of 'martial races' which had been popularised in the late nineteenth century added another, racialised layer to the socialisation of Indian soldiers. Frederick Roberts and George White imbibed it to the degree that it informed their official recruiting policy as Commanders-in-Chief.[61]

The method by which KCIOs were commissioned illustrates the officer corps' conservative institutional mindset: Charles à Court Repington, the disgraced former officer turned war correspondent, wrote:

> the class which we wish to attract is the ruling class of India ... so that the Indian Army may be reinforced by the scions of the greatest families, and by those most fitted by character and family ... It might also be required that the Indian cadet should be educated at a school such as the Mayo College and Ajmer, where the training is more or less on the lines of an English public school.[62]

Thus, as late as 1917, the importance of a public school education was still deeply ingrained into ideas of officer socialisation. Repington recommended that Indian cadets should not come to Sandhurst, as they 'would be likely to fall into bad ways and to consort for want of companionship with Indians over here who are disaffected'.[63] Nonetheless he felt, in the spirit of the 'blood sacrifice', that Indianisation was justified as 'this great war ... has shown up the patriotism and loyalty of India as a whole in a favourable light. India has been quiet during three years of war'.[64] As we have seen, the same premises underlay Irish recruiting; evidently, some Irish officers viewed Indian issues as a cypher for their anxieties about Ireland.[65]

General O'Moore Creagh, the son of a County Clare military family who had been an officer in the Indian Army since 1870, was enthusiastic about the appointment of Indian officers and entertained them in London during the First World War.[66] The Irish officers on Indian service generally greeted the Indian officers cordially, and Roberts in particular had been campaigning for the appointment of Indians to the status of full British officers for years.[67] On the subject of nationalism, however, they found no common ground. Indeed, anecdotal evidence from Irish officers' correspondence suggests that soldering in India might particularly have predisposed officers to be more intolerant of Home Rule and Irish nationalism than otherwise: when officers made comparisons between India and Ireland, they did so with an eye to their concern about imperial disintegration, rather than in the spirit of transnational anti-imperial solidarity.[68]

Indeed, if there were commonalities in the approaches of Indian Army officers to resolving the turbulent state of the two countries, it was an enthusiasm for the early and frequent application of 'Rule .303'.[69] Captain William Kemmis was an Irish officer from a Co. Wicklow minor gentry family. Outwardly, he appeared to inhabit the breezy life of the typical gentry officer, but his experiences of colonial control in India brutalized him. He was given to violent outbursts against the local populace, borne of the frustrations of imperial service, the arrogance of the elite officer, and the pressures of a racist colonial system. Kemmis' letters reveal a side of the officer corps which is often concealed in surviving letters and memoirs; the violence and cruelty of the colonizer, which lurked behind an officer's mask of gentility, is expressed in shocking and explicit detail in his correspondence. Kemmis was stationed in Hera in 1914, from where he fulminated that 'a nigger doesn't understand kindness he only understands force & if you don't use it he only despises you and makes you are weak … I know if we kill a few of them there will be peace in Hera for some time but the papers will make a silly row over it all the same.'[70] He goes on to recount how he authorised the indiscriminate murder of civilians by his men, in reprisal for an assault on a European. Two years later, his reaction to the distant Easter Rising was also uncompromising: 'They seem to be acting at last in Ireland if only they would *shoot* de Valera etc. it should be alright.'[71] As this source indicates, the casual brutality of the soldiers in India went far beyond anything that took place in Ireland. Officers who were present in Ireland tended to evince greater sympathy towards the rebels, having to face the immediacy of the event, compared to Irish officers abroad who reacted to the Rising in a context of colonial violence.

Also present among Irish Indian Army officers was a paternalistic attitude towards their men. Roly Grimshaw, an Irish cavalry officer who commanded Indian lancers on the Western Front, recalled defending his Viceroy's Officers on a troop train in 1914: 'I nearly had a row with the RAMC major in charge, as he wanted to turn my Indian officers out of a first class carriage for his warrant officers. Typical of the attitude towards Indians.'[72] Colonial officers illustrate the importance of place and context in shaping officers' outlooks. Experience of colonial overlordship shaped the identity of the imperial Irishman and could create a sense of loyalty to Indian colleagues in a prejudiced European society. It could, on the other side, produce an acrimonious resentment between colonial officers and the subject population. The racial widening of the officer corps was generally considered by officers to be a positive change, despite the vehement opposition of some. The small-scale Indianisation of the First World War proved a success, even featuring an Indian Battalion Commander, Rana Jodha Jang Bhadur, the first nonwhite line officer in the army to command European officers. This he was able to do without difficulty and, indeed, with distinction.[73]

In the early days of the War, senior officers looked to the Indian Army to quickly provide trained soldiers to the places they were most needed.[74] Many Irish officers who commanded in India, like William Armstrong, Roly Grimshaw, and Alexander Godley, thus found themselves alongside hundreds of thousands of their fellow countrymen fighting in Europe. Officers who were not earmarked for the Western Front and who fought in colonial theatres resented their distance from the 'main event' in Europe, but this should not diminish the historical importance of these global aspects of the First World War. In Egypt, Tanzania, Namibia, Greece, New Guinea, throughout the Ottoman Empire, and in many other places, the First World War wrought scars across the physical and social landscape much deeper than those inflicted on the nations of Western Europe. Irish officers' presence across these distant battlefields underline the extent to which the Great War was an imperial war.

COMMISSIONED FROM THE RANKS: CLASS IN THE IRISH OFFICER CORPS

After the initial rush to commission men from the OTCs in public schools and universities, the army then looked to the traditional source of replacement officers due to attrition: experienced non-commissioned officers who had spent many years in the ranks and were inured to military discipline and culture, if not to the more genteel aspects of life in the officers' mess. We have seen in previous chapters how these men were usually given fairly socially isolated appointments in the quartermaster corps or similar, though they were occasionally appointed as line officers and were equipped with the professionalism required to do well. The annuals of the Royal Hibernian Military School provide a selection of Irish ranker officers, affording an insight into the commissioning of this group as the war went on: the 1914 issue of *Hibernia* reveals that of the old boys who were serving in the army, two were known to be officers, and the majority were enlisted men. The magazine contained frequent appeals to old boys to write in and tell them about their experiences at war and to encourage their colleagues to do the same. A roll of honour was produced in every edition tracking those Old Hibernians who had been wounded or made the ultimate sacrifice. This gives a small insight into the increasing or decreasing frequency of commissions as the war continued. In 1914, 11 Old Hibernians who had been commissioned that year were killed. By April 1915, this number had increased to 13. In the whole of 1915, 18 of the wounded Old Hibernians had been commissioned, bringing the total to 32. In 1916, the bloodiest year of the war, only three newly commissioned Old Hibernians were killed. The final figure at the end of 1918 was 41 officers killed, of whom at least 38 had been commissioned from the ranks during the war.[75]

This suggests that commissions from this group were at their most frequent in 1914–15 and diminished as the war went on. This may have been due to the appalling casualty rate among officers in the same manner that career officers were depleted at the beginning of the war, but the relatively low overall level of casualties among Old Hibernians—considering, as a correspondent to their magazine pointed out, 'there must be thousands of Old Boys fighting in different parts of the globe'—suggests that this is not the whole explanation.[76] Approximately 90 pupils left the school each year, almost all of them Irish and highly likely to enlist in the army: socialised in a military school setting, and mainly the orphaned sons of soldiers, it was recorded that in peacetime around five-sixths of Old Hibernians enlisted in the army. That only 41 of the officers who came from this background were killed suggests that many dozens may have survived the war.[77]

The dangerous, if glory-laden, new world of aerial combat offered opportunities for exceptional Irish ranker officers. Thomas Falcon Hazell, who enlisted in the South Irish Horse at the start of the war and rapidly gained a commission before the year was out, transferred to the Royal Flying Corps and became one of the most celebrated flying aces of the war. In 1919 he was offered a permanent commission and commanded RAF squadrons until his retirement in 1927.[78] The RFC was a possible route for officers seeking to keep their commissions after the war, as the technical training and battlefield experience gained flying in the war gave them rare and desirable new skills and made them irreplaceable—at the cost of a casualty rate that was far higher than even that of Irish aristocrats (30% compared to 27%).[79]

In the more established service branches, ranker officers who retained their commissions after the war had more traditional backgrounds and would not have been particularly unusual in the line regiments of the pre-

1914 officer corps—men like Eric Dorman-Smith, whose father, a self-made man, had purchased an estate and given his son a traditional gentry upbringing, education, and socialisation.[80]

After February 1916, a more coherent system of officer training was put into place as temporary officers of non-traditional background were increasingly commissioned. This put an end to direct commissioning from the ranks, and might account for the falling off in the commissions of Old Hibernians after this point as well.[81] In Ireland, many elite Catholic and Protestant schools had a strong tradition of military service, and their rolls of honour document the many Irish officers who were killed during the war. An indicative example is Clongowes Wood College. Their roll of honour records not only those Clongownians who gave their lives in the First World War, but also those who died fighting for Irish independence and on both sides of the Irish Civil War. Others, like Blackrock College, traced a pro-British tendency giving way to a pro-rebel tendency among its remaining students as the war went on.[82] It is worth noting that, following the establishment of the Irish Free State, elite schools, both Catholic and Protestant, managed to retain their prominent role in Irish society, even if the officer corps they previously supplied did not.[83]

The only third-level institutions with an officer training corps in Ireland were Trinity College Dublin, which as aforementioned was a long-standing centre for imperial professional training, and Queen's University Belfast, which had split from the National University of Ireland in 1908. A great deal of Irish officers also passed through the Royal College of Surgeons and Inns of Court Officers' Training Corps, the latter called 'one of the best schools of instruction that the Empire possesses'. In the Irish context this marked a class but not much of a religious change in corps demography. Candidates from a middle-class professional background, without gentry connections, became admitted in large numbers for the first time.[84] Anthony P. Quinn has studied the contribution of Irish lawyers to the war effort extensively and emphasizes the importance of the Inns of Court OTC in attracting 'men of university and public school class, and particularly those of sporting and outdoor experience … Membership was also open to non-lawyers of suitable backgrounds such as 2nd Lt. John Samuel Carrothers, a past pupil of Portora Royal School, a Land Commission clerk.'[85] Quinn finds that, in this specific sample of professional men, the general demographic trends previously established also applied: it was by and large the technical branches that were the domain of the middle class, containing very few from either the gentry or the working class. Likewise, Trinity College's OTC, though it began from the outbreak of the war to admit non-college members, preferred and catered for candidates with technical and professional skills predominantly (Table 7.2).

An account of the nature of officer training for enlisted men as it existed in the second half of the war can be found in the reminiscences of John Clarke MacDermott, a man who subsequent to the war found great success as a lawyer and judge in Northern Ireland. In late 1916, as an enlisted man, he was admitted for officer training through the auspices of the Queen's University OTC. The other two men he knew are indicative of the social origins of candidates who utilised this route to a commission: 'Frank W. Watson whom I had known for years and who had been at Campbell [College] with me, and Alec McCurry whose father was a senior official of the Belfast Banking Co. Ltd.'[86] After preliminary (and indeed perfunctory) training at the OTC, candidates were passed to a second training programme. 'If we passed we would be posted to a cadet battalion for four months and if we passed there we would receive our commissions. But until then we remained on trial … With a little more imagination it could have been made a most interesting course.'[87] On completion of the course MacDermott was commissioned into the Machine Gun Corps and served until the end of the war. Interestingly, MacDermott notes that at the time he was passing through the OTC, in late 1916, 'the officers were, for the most part, members of the university staff', suggesting that Queen's University employed a number of army officers with some amount of experience, continuing the trend which was set in motion with the establishment of the OTCs in 1908, of increasing the numbers of officers from a university background.[88]

Table 7.2   Trinity College OTC candidates in British and Commonwealth forces, 1914–18

RAMC	933	R. G. Artillery	105
Army Service Corps	186	R. F. Artillery	102
Royal Engineers	173	RAF	70
Dublin Fusiliers	149	Indian Army	81
Royal Irish Rifles	82	African forces	21
Inniskilling Fusiliers	77	Canadian regts.	30
Munster Fusiliers	53	Australian regts.	31
Connaught Rangers	47	NZ regts.	5

Source: Tomás Irish, Trinity College in War and Revolution (Dublin, 2015), *p. 94*

Another social and institutional change in the imperial officer corps that gained ground in the First World War was the large-scale inculcation of women into the active military sphere, through the Red Cross and Queen Alexandra's Imperial Military Nursing Service (QAIMNS), initially founded in 1902. The Matron-in-Chief, Dame Maud McCarthy, was widely regarded as one of the most brilliant members of the senior staff on the Western Front and was joined by a number of Irishwomen, some of whom were killed in action. In the Middle East, Staff Nurse Mary Danaher, from Limerick, was one of these women. She was one of seven non-elite officers from Limerick who never returned from their war service, as identified by the city's library.[89]

Examples such as these illustrate not just the deep entrenchment of the army in Irish society, but also the mass mobilisation of society occasioned by the Great War. Eric Hobsbawm refers to the War as one of the few 'natural breaks' in history, a natural start- or endpoint for discussing historical change.[90] The Irish case is no exception. When the contest for Ireland's national identity was sparked in Easter, 1916, Irish officers could not avoid involvement in the struggles that followed.

CONTESTING THE IRISH MILITARY TRADITION: THE EASTER RISING, 1916

Constitutional nationalist officers were turning away from politics by 1916, due to their preoccupation with the war and their support for conscription, which alienated their erstwhile comrades. According to Martin, 'most nobles, for example Midleton, blamed the government for being too soft on separatist nationalism from 1914 on.'[91] Diverse officers echoed this sentiment.[92] It comes as no surprise that the outbreak of armed rebellion in Dublin provoked shock and outrage amongst the officer corps, as it did among most unionists and nationalists more generally, particularly at a time when Irish soldiers in the Middle East and on the Western Front seemed, through sheer grit and determination, to finally be making a dent in the seemingly indestructible war machines of the Central Powers. Hughes and Richardson argue that not only did the Rising seem like a collapse of the 'home front', but to the Irish officer, 'the rebellion was an injury to his Irishness'.[93] The Rising, and its aftermath, marked a turning point where the mentality of the officer corps and that of the general public further diverged on the national question: the army response provoked public sympathy for the rebels, while the rebellion vindicated certain officers' pre-war views, elucidated by Maurice Moore, that 'in army eyes Nationalists are Sinn Feiners'.[94]

News of the Rising, of course, did not filter through to the fighting soldiers themselves until after the fact, and attempts were made at suppressing the news in the overseas empire in order to avoid negatively affecting morale. The governor of the French Settlements in India, M. Martineau, received a curious request on 30 April from the Viceroy of India to suppress 'the intelligence regarding a riot in Dublin which has just been despatched to India by Reuters Agency' through the French telegraph cable.[95] For those in Dublin at the time, however, it was a different story. An insight into this first-hand experience of what must, to an Irish officer, have been a deeply confusing turn of events can be arrived at by examining three very different officers who recorded their reminiscences of the Rising: Captain E. Gerrard, a professional career soldier; John Clarke MacDermott, an Ulsterman whose experience of the Rising figured in his decision to seek a commission; and Lieutenant Arthur Aston Luce, a volunteer officer and Trinity College academic who had taken an active interest in the College's OTC and other institutions seeking to train his countrymen for war.

Captain Gerrard, an Irish artillery officer stationed in Athlone, heard about the disturbances in Dublin and decided to travel to the city of his own accord. He encountered a chaotic situation. A superior officer, noticing his uniform, ordered him to Beggar's Bush Barracks, which had come under attack by the rebels. Gerrard recounted that the ragtag garrison contained only 'Sir Frederick Shaw, myself, one or two ranker officers, four non-commissioned officers, and about ten men, three of whom were invalids'.[96] The remainder of his regiment arrived later in the day, including his comrades John D'Arcy, 'the son of the Protestant Archbishop of Down' and John O'Beirne, 'who was with me in Clongowes College'.[97] Their artillery pieces were deployed on the quays, and they set to shelling the General Post Office.

For the professional Anglo-Irish middle classes of Howth, Malahide, or Kingstown, the response to the rising was one of ambivalence, a feeling that the insurrection was a minor annoyance but not a matter of any immediate concern.[98] John Clarke MacDermott, a law student at Queen's University, was also from a professional background, although unlike many suburban Dubliners, serendipity would place him at the centre of the Rising. He had been supporting the war effort by working in a munitions factory and was spending the Easter holiday in Dublin. He recalled having lunch on Sackville Street at the time the Rising began outside: 'In the course of [our meal] we heard shooting outside and an explosion … we realised by this time that something highly abnormal was taking place.'[99] However, MacDermott and his companion were able to move about the city unhindered in the following hours, and it was only later that it became apparent to them what was taking place. In the face of intensifying sounds of rifle fire, they elected to leave town, and despite once again crossing Sackville Street—encountering 'a detachment of Lancers, still mounted and looking as though they had passed through some disturbing experience'—had 'no difficulty getting to the station', though by then no trains were running.[100] It is possible that MacDermott's experiences of Dublin during the Rising were part of the reason he later applied for a commission in the army and went to fight at the front.

Lieutenant Arthur Aston Luce, a young Fellow of Trinity College Dublin (commissioned via the College OTC) who was home convalescing after serving with the Royal Irish Rifles, had been out in Dublin on the morning of the Rising and experienced how he and others suddenly became targets simply for wearing the King's uniform. After he 'attended divine service at Christ Church Cathedral', Luce was on his way 'to Nelson's Pillar, the then terminus of the Clontarf tram'. He continues:

> People were looking at my uniform, and over the bridge one man stopped me and said, 'I wouldn't go down there, sir, if I were you. I turned to look at the General Post Office, as it then was. The windows were sand-bagged, and rifles looked out. At that moment a small troop [of] horse cantered up on the far side of the road; rifles rang out, and one or two horses and riders fell.[101]

The first-hand reactions of officers to the Rising, as well as the secondary literature, illustrate that when the crisis began, there was no question of their carrying out their duties (Fig. 7.2).[102] After an initial phase of panic, the response became level-headed and professional, and officers were confident that the majority of the population were on their side: Lieutenant Monk Gibbon remarked that there were 'too many Dubliners fighting with Irish regiments' for such a rebellion to attract widespread support.[103]

Many Irish officers in Dublin during the Rising were temporary or garrison soldiers, with little military experience. Lieutenant Luce eventually found refuge with such a group at Trinity College, including his students

Fig. 7.2 Lt Gen Sir Bryan Mahon (right), Commander of the 10th (Irish) Division, with soldiers entraining for Dublin during the Easter Rising. Mahon's Irishness, like that of the photographer, Captain de Courcy Wheeler, did not pre-clude him from doing his duty in the independence period. Wheeler accepted the surrender of the GPO rebels a week later. *Courtesy of the National Library of Ireland*

in the Dublin University Officers' Training Corps. The corps Adjutant, Major Harris, was out on manoeuvres with the British Army's Volunteer Training Corps (the 'Gorgeous Wrecks', so called because of their generally advanced age and the signifier *Georgius Rex* on their armbands).[104] However, motorcycle messengers had been despatched to cadets living in Dublin, and 'by evening upwards of 40 cadets and ex-cadets of the Corps had reported, many of them at considerable risk, as they were fired upon in passing through the streets. This number was further augmented during the night by various details, e.g. young officers, Colonials and soldiers of various regiments on leave.'[105] There were other cadets, too, who 'could not reach the College' but instead 'reported at the various barracks and military offices where they were attached for duty', suggesting that even approaching the middle of the war, there were still plenty of prospective officers to be found in the OTCs—and underlining the diversity of Irish officers who were present in Dublin during the Rising.[106] The defence of the College was carried out, with few men and fewer rifles, in the face of intermittent sniping from the railway bridge adjoining Westland Row Station and snatches of fighting in College Green. The defenders successfully managed to interdict rebel messengers passing the College on their way between the GPO and Stephen's Green, thereby cutting off rebel communications between the north and the south side of the city. After a tense, sleepless night, army reinforcements arrived from Kingsbridge Station on Tuesday 25th April, officially at midday, though both Harris and Luce 'would put the arrival of the troops rather later in the afternoon'.[107] Nonetheless, the immediate ordeal for those officers caught up in the midst of the Rising was at an end.

Similarly, the members of the University Club were caught out by the Rising. Members were startled when two men, Captain Charles de Burgh Daly, RAMC and lawyer Richard Best, sitting at a first-floor window, were 'potted at by that Countess whats-her-name who only missed him [Daly] by an inch'.[108] This episode is an interesting reminder of the strange intimacy of the Rising and War of Independence—there were combatants on both sides drawn from the same social circles, willing to kill for the sake of contested identity. Officer elites, it seems, were not immune from this phenomenon; in other parts of the country, too, the officer elite presented a visible target of opportunity. In Galway, for example, rebels seized Moyode Castle, home of the Persses, an Anglo-Irish military family.[109]

Despite the War Office being aware of the potential for an insurrection to be staged in Easter week, the particulars of the plan were unknown to them and their initial response was disorganised. The first instinct of the authorities was to follow the pattern of previous incidents which had necessitated the use of the military: cavalry was sent onto the streets in the manner of the Land War unrest. When this failed to have the desired effect, the strategy shifted to that employed in Belfast in 1886, 1907, and 1912, namely, the flooding of the city with police and soldiers, the deployment of pickets and patrols, and the blocking of major roads to limit the insurgents' movements.[110] The unique and unprecedented next step taken in 1916, however, was the declaration of martial law.[111]

The military authorities, who found themselves on the back foot, scrambled to find a response to the crisis. The preliminary question was whom to send to take charge. One officer who was considered was General Ian Hamilton, recently recalled from the Dardanelles, but, as Asquith wrote to Kitchener on 26 April, it was thought wiser to send someone who was not directly involved with Irish soldiers fighting at the front, as 'there is a good deal of bitterness in Ireland about Suvla &c, to which Redmond gave strong expression in the House this afternoon. It is very desirable to send a competent man, who so far as Ireland is concerned has no past record.'[112] The debacle at Suvla Bay, where Irish and ANZAC soldiers had sustained horrific casualties against Ottoman forces, was a highly contentious and unpopular affair in Ireland, and it was thought that Hamilton's appointment would unwisely draw an implicit link between the Rising and the memory of this waste of Irish life. General Lovick Friend, who had been tracking, as far as was possible, the activities of republican nationalists in Ireland since the beginning of the war was the man on the spot as the Rising began. As early as November 1914, he had been advocating for the proclamation of martial law in Ireland to Kitchener, 'and go for these Sinn Féin people'—despite the fact that 'we can only at the present moment organise a small striking force' and 'it would be difficult to enforce martial law—with the military force at our disposal'.[113] The man selected to coordinate the response was General John G 'Conky' Maxwell, and on 26 April Kitchener gave his approval.[114] It was a curious choice; Maxwell had been on service in Cairo at the beginning of 1916 and seemed hardly to have distinguished himself. His comrades, Generals Robertson and Murray, voiced their dismay with him frequently in their correspondence.[115] However, it appears the defining criterion was to select someone who had as little contact with Ireland as possible, presumably in the belief that such a commander would be seen as politically disinterested.[116]

The disorganisation of the military response to the Rising, as illustrated by the ad hoc defences of Beggar's Bush Barracks and Trinity College, amongst other strategic points not only indicates the extent to which the military command had become distracted from the potential for unrest in Ireland during the war, but also gives a glimpse of the diversity of Irish officers who rallied to the colours during the First World War. Those present in Dublin included convalescent or leave-taking officers from a multitude of regiments, both home and colonial; temporary officers drawn from the legal, academic, and business establishments; career officers working alongside erstwhile classmates from the elite Irish schools; and the students and fellows of the Dublin University Officer Training Corps. All of the officers who found themselves in Dublin that Easter responded to the Rising as expected, given the character of the British officer corps and its collective mentality, and did not evince a sense of divided loyalty, as some senior officers feared they might. In subsequent years, some of the officers involved moderated their view of the Rising and, in the face of the beatification of the executed rebels by the public, came to realise its historical importance.[117] On the afternoon itself, however, there was no doubt in any of the officers' minds as to what course of action to follow. The officer's conception of duty to king and emperor was evidently more than rhetoric; the defections of Irish soldiers that the republicans had hoped for, and the British military command had oftentimes feared, did not take place.

However, this is not to say that all officers felt the same way about the Rising after the fact, nor were they uniformly in agreement about the handing of the insurrection by the military command. One incident in particular was illustrative of this multiplicity: the summary execution of Francis Sheehy-Skeffington and other innocent men by the unhinged Irish Captain Bowen-Colthurst. Colthurst's murders, of which he was convicted at an eventual inquiry, were alleged by other involved officers to have initially been the subject of an unsuccessful military cover-up, in order to avoid embarrassment and the possibility of discontent over the authorities' handling of the counter-insurgency operations. The dismissal of his crimes, particularly his murder of an unarmed young man in Rathmines for no apparent reason, aroused the ire of two other Irish officers, Sir Francis Fletcher-Vane and William Monk Gibbon, who sought to publicise the injustice.[118] Vane's testimony was suppressed by the high command, and this incident, he maintained, forced his retirement from the service.[119]

All of these Irish officers expressed strikingly diverse reactions to the shock of the Rising, revealing deep-seated uncertainties about the future of military Irishness. A large part of the explanation for how the Rising subsequently took on such importance was the heavy-handedness of the reprisals. The execution of the rebels cast them as martyrs and inflamed Irish public opinion against the British establishment. The conflation of the various rebellious groups with the Sinn Féin party, who at the outset were not even internally united behind the Rising, by the press and authorities undoubtedly also contributed to their monumental electoral victory in 1918.[120] The Viceroy, Lord Wimborne, realised the potentially febrile nature of the military's response and urged General Maxwell to moderate his policy: 'I was I must admit distressed to learn that three comparatively unknown insurgents were executed this morning.' Wimborne complained, in a letter to Maxwell, that his actions were likely to create an impression of outrage amongst the public:

> I am bound to tell you that [this impression] exists and is capable of producing disastrous consequences ... I must respectfully urge you in the most serious manner that public opinion will not support either here or in England further executions of any bar perhaps one or two *very prominent* and deeply implicated insurgents and that a statement from you of a reassuring character is urgently needed.[121]

While the First World War, rather than the Easter Rising, might have been the more dislocating experience for the Anglo-Irish establishment in general, it appears that—as the examples of Vane, Colthurst, Gibbon, Luce, Gerrard, and others illustrate—the story is rather more complicated for the Irish officer corps, particularly those who saw action in Dublin that Easter. In the face of imperial betrayal and unforgiving reprisal, Irish officers revealed a fundamental tension over their sense of identity and social role as military Irishmen.

The political fallout of the Rising was addressed by the Irish Convention, a meeting of the different political interests in Ireland to decide what form the implementation of Home Rule would take. As reported in the Irish press, the Marquis of Londonderry 'said of the Irish Convention they should all turn their attention to removing any difficulty in the way of those who were endeavouring to maintain the equilibrium of the Empire in the present moment'.[122] Irish officers were deeply involved in the deliberations of the Convention, illustrating the view among military and government elites that Irish officers might be able to exercise moral authority in the Irish context. The argument over the implementation of conscription, which had been debated since 1915, was thus a major consideration of the Convention delegates. One of the Irish Party delegates was Captain John Esmonde, a Clongownian ranker officer from a professional background, who had been on active service in Dublin during the Rising. The Government had requested that he and Captain Willie Redmond, the brother of the Irish Parliamentary leader, as officers and 'prominent members of the Home Rule movement', attend the Convention in the hope that they could establish common ground.[123] Sadly, Willie was killed before the Convention took place. Officers were, however, well represented in the political debate; other nationalist officers, such as Colonel Maurice Moore, played a significant role.[124] Officers of all political stripes tended to advocate the conciliatory position that, so long as Ireland remained part of the imperial Commonwealth, Home Rule might not be such a high price to pay for a return to normality.[125]

In November of 1917, Lieutenant-Colonel Charles Stewart Henry Vane-Tempest Stewart, the Marquess of Londonderry, sat in the Kildare Street Club and ruminated on his role in the Irish Convention. 'I am absolutely convinced', he wrote, 'of one thing and that is that so long as the British Empire exists Ireland must remain politically within the circle of the United Kingdom and whatever path is chosen long or short, or through whatever intermediary stages ... that Ireland will be politically governed in exactly the same manner as England or Scotland or Wales'. Once again, the spectre of imperial collapse underpinned officers' conception of the Irish question. He continues, 'the suggestion of Ireland as a separate national political and fiscal unit has never received support in the Colonies and must present a strategic danger.'[126] Vane-Tempest's approach at the Convention once again bears out the central contention that Irish military officers' support for the union was couched in imperial terms. Theirs was not merely a hyperbolic or rhetorical use of the terms empire and colony; these men had lived and worked in the overseas empire and knew it more intimately than politicians in Britain or Ireland did—they were invested, emotionally, economically, and politically, in the imperial project. During the War, Thomas Spring Rice, the Liberal Unionist politician, wrote that 'I know myself men who call themselves Sinn Féiners who are not irreconcilable. We should shift them from the republicans and find out what would reconcile them to the empire.'

Both of those men, Spring Rice and Vane-Tempest, moderated their unionist stance over the course of the war to accommodate some limited measure of home rule, so long as it was still within the empire. Unionists, too, characterised the political situation as hinging on the reconciliation of imperial and Irish patriotism. Spring Rice's colleague Viscount Powerscourt, who fought with the Irish Guards during the war, wrote in 1916:

There has always been a distinct tendency amongst some of the upper classes in Ireland, to ridicule any outward signs of nationalist Ireland, or sentimental Celtic manifestations and to term them unwarrantable, political, or even disreputable. I contend that this patriotic sentiment cannot and should not be squashed. Owing to the neglect, by the upper classes of seeing the necessity of catering for this, it has fallen into the hands of unprincipled organizers and is at once seized and moulded ... If Irish National sentiment became respectable and was organized by respectable people, who would introduce sound principles into it, it would be a great power for good in our country.[127]

This is a key aspect of the political shift among Irish officers and aristocrats over the course of the First World War from moderate unionism to home rule within the empire, a move made in opposition to the rise of republican nationalism. Before the War, nationalist officers' loyalty was always enunciated in terms of crown and empire, even among self-described socialists like Francis Vane or Jack White.[128] This previously uncontroversial enunciation of imperial cohesion had become contentious, as nationalist opinion increasingly moved towards a rejection of empire.

Even after the embers of the Rising were extinguished and the city of Dublin returned to its workaday routine, the effects of martial law persisted. General Maxwell appeared to consider this necessary, in order to suppress sedition, and because his confidence that Parliament would act was characteristically low.[129] Dubliners resented the long imposition of martial law, however.[130] Irish officers attempted to encourage Irish people back to the cause of the Great War by playing on national identity: Earl Dunraven wrote in a pamphlet of 1917, 'If you won't enlist in British regiments, and fight shoulder to shoulder with brave men fighting and dying in the one great cause, well, fill the Irish Regiments.'[131] The irony that the Irish Divisions, which had been the cause of such apprehension in the War Office, were now being deployed as a corrective after the insurgency speaks volumes about the changed nature of the political reality.

Officers were concerned about the effect of the Rising on the war effort; a serious breakdown of discipline would undoubtedly have occurred had the Rising animated the political passions of the 150,183 Irish soldiers then serving in the Crown forces, as some officers worried it might.[132] Sir Matthew Nathan, the Under-Secretary for Ireland, reported that of the Irish soldiers serving in April 1916, members of the Irish Volunteers numbered 30,161 and 29,617 were members of the UVF.[133] However, it soon became clear that the Irish soldiers were little cause for concern. An acquaintance wrote to Godley, assuring him that 'The situation in Ireland seems to be quieter, but there is no doubt that the rebellion was a serious affair. If Maxwell and the military had not squashed it at once, the majority of the Nationalists would have joined the Sinn Féiners; the dividing line between [the two] … is very thin.'[134]

Rather more surprising was the reaction of one of the Catholic army chaplains serving with the Connaught Rangers—Fr. McRory's diary of 1917, only discovered in 2013, reveals a striking sense of victimisation and anger that is not manifest to the same extent in any other officer source of the period. In response to the events of 1916, McRory, a Donegal man who was commissioned into the chaplaincy at the outbreak of the war, writes that 'few in the regular army … [are] friendly to Ireland', and worries that the army will be prejudicial to Irish soldiers after the 'second Ypres on the Liffey'. McRory advocates strongly for Irish officers leading Irish troops:

> There is one thing and it can't be too forcibly impressed onto the minds of the Irish, whether Catholic or Protestant. And that is to have *no other races* as *officers* in Irish regiments except *Irishmen*. And in time of war have *no generals* … but *Irish generals*, and to keep *all Irish soldiers* exclusively in *Irish divisions* … There is another grave reason why Irish officers should fill every officer's position in Irish regiments. *Anti Irish feeling pervades military circles* … If anti Catholicism be added to race hatred, the results of having such officers in Irish regiments are most disastrous.[135]

McRory's fulminations are interesting for a number of reasons. While he was clearly sympathetic to nationalism, what seems to animate him most is a sense of injustice over the lack of meritocratic advancement in the army (due to 'family influence, assisted with petticoat aid') and the sense that the accomplishments of Irish regiments were being done down by callous English officers. He writes particularly bitterly about how his service in Mesopotamia was misrepresented in the press: 'In Bombay and other parts of India was circulated in very sour language, how the Irish priests would not come to Mesopotamia … At this time there were 16 Irish priests, one French and two English priests in Mesopotamia.'[136] There appear to have been a minority of nationalist Catholic chaplains who served in the First World War, as indicated by McRory and his colleagues, alongside those who followed a more general apolitical posture, such as the well-known chaplains Francis Gleeson, attached to the Munster Fusiliers, and Willie Doyle, attached to the Royal Irish Fusiliers.[137] In expressing a sympathetic and personal reaction to the Rising in an imperial context, McRory provides a fascinating example of this exception to the typical mindset of the Irish officer.

This period has invited a number of interesting historiographical debates on the importance of militarism and masculinity to the conception of the Irish nation. Sarah Benton has argued that the revolutionary movements, most successfully the Irish Republican Brotherhood, co-opted a wide-ranging sense of martial masculinity as the cure for the nation's ills. This sense of martial masculinity, while it was used to great effect by nationalist groups, manifested itself most notably among Protestant populations in Britain and the United States and was in effect a global phenomenon.[138] David Fitzpatrick, too, in his assessment of Irish militarism, cites this idea and argues that it lies behind any understanding of the actions of revolutionary groups.[139] Bartlett and Jeffery have argued that the Easter Rising marked a particular sea change in the parameters of the 'Irish military tradition', where now 'tenacity was valued more than spontaneity, determination more than jocularity, and resoluteness more than impetuosity'—in other words, 'it has been the Irish *paramilitary* tradition which has prevailed.'[140]

However, as we have seen, the two traditions of Irish martial life—the rebel tradition of national risings over the centuries and the soldierly tradition of the global and imperial Irish regiments—contained much the same cultural iconography, inhabited an overlapping mental space, and sought to convince the same Irish public of their legitimacy, invoking imagery ranging from the mythical resonance of Cúchulainn and the Wild Geese to the popular impact of the Boer War.[141] The defining distinction—which the Rising, its suppression, and, as we shall see, its aftermath in the postwar years cast light onto—was the *imperial* tradition. This became the defining point of contention following the First World War.

The reactions of Irish officers to the Rising were wide-ranging and varied based on not only political persuasion but social context and place. The question raised at the beginning of this chapter—of whether the Rising was an 'injury to Irishness' in the minds of Irish officers—thus appears to have numerous, surprising answers. Shane Leslie recorded that Kitchener saw it as a vindication of his stance against purely Irish regiments in the new armies.[142] Presumably he overlooked the contribution of the Dublin Fusiliers and Royal Irish Rifles to putting down the Rising. Colonel Moore lamented that by the end of 1916 recruiting was becoming significantly more difficult, though the causal link with the Rising was not clear. Moore attempted to assuage what he clearly took to be a dangerous situation:

> [A]s most of those who wish to enlist have had ample time and opportunity, it may be taken for granted that the great bulk of men at present in Ireland do not want to go to the war ... many say that they would sooner be shot in Ireland than in France ... As a man of experience in warfare, both regular and irregular, it is my duty to say that ... [armed insurrection] could not be successful in Ireland under present conditions. The first sign of such a situation would be immediately followed by the flooding of Ireland with troops for there are plenty available ... surely neither Ireland nor the Empire would desire so calamitous an episode ... I advise those rash young men who are thinking and talking of armed opposition, of shooting soldiers and policemen and such like desperate actions to consider if they cannot better attain their ends by wiser and more effectual methods.[143]

The year 1916 marked the start of a shift in Irish politics culminating with the 1918 election, but for Irish officers the Great War also marked the deaths of many comrades who predominated in the political and cultural life of the officer corps. Alongside the calamitous casualties suffered by the Irish officer corps on the Western Front and in Africa, Salonika and the Middle East, 1916 also saw the death of Lord Kitchener, one of the most prominent commanders, but also, as we have seen, a key commentator on the military situation in Ireland. Lord Roberts, the popular imperial hero and idol for Irish officers, had died in 1914.[144] On the political side, neither the constitutional nationalism to which officers were gradually becoming inured, nor its major proponent in John Redmond would survive the war. At the end of four hard years of fighting, opposition to British rule would once again come to Ireland, this time by way of the ballot box. The Irish Parliamentary Party, which undoubtedly still commanded the support of nationalist officers, was wiped out by the rise of Sinn Féin and republicanism, and a diminution of the military elite's social role was palpable. At the end of the War the Irish officer corps had seen its social base depleted, its elite position submerged, and its institutional identity increasingly undermined by the escalating political situation. The following years would not be kind to the Irish military officer.

NOTES

1. Windham Wyndham-Quin, "'Ireland Awake", An Open Letter to his Fellow Countrymen', Dublin, June 1917 (Dublin, 1917), p. 15.
2. Ronan Fanning, *Fatal Path: British Government and Irish Revolution, 1910–1922* (London, 2013), p. 176; 'Recruiting in Ireland. Sir E. Carson's Analysis of the Figures', *The Times*, 13 October 1916; 'Recruiting in Ireland', *The Times*, 11 May 1916; 'Recruiting in Ireland', *The Times*, 14 April 1917.
3. Letter from Capt. W. B. Rennie, HQ 16th Division, Mallow, n.d. (1914). Moore papers, NLI.
4. Tom Johnstone, *Orange, Green and Khaki: The Story of the Irish Regiments in the Great War, 1914–18* (Dublin, 1992), p. 195.
5. Doherty and Truesdale, *Irish Winners of the Victoria Cross*, p. 102.
6. Australia also claims credit for the first engagement of the war, when a shore battery at Melbourne harbour fired a warning shot at a departing German freighter shortly after receiving notification of the declaration of war in the early hours of 5th August (it was still the evening of the 4th in Europe), forcing it to return to port for impounding.
7. Edward Spiers, *The Army and Society 1815–1914* (London, 1980), p. 288.
8. Tom Johnstone, *Orange, Green and Khaki: The Story of the Irish Regiments in the Great War, 1914–18* (Dublin, 1992) passim.; Steven O'Connor, *Irish Officers in the British Forces, 1922–1945* (London, 2014), p. 76; Jill Bender, 'Ireland and Empire' in Bourke and McBride, *The Princeton History of Modern Ireland* (Princeton, 2016), p. 348.
9. Shane Leslie, *The Irish Tangle for English Readers* (London, 1946), p. 159.
10. 'Not to be Turned into a Militia', *Irish Independent*, 19 August 1914.
11. Peter Martin, 'Dulce et Decorum: Irish Nobles in the Great War, 1914–19', in Gregory, Adrian, and Senia Pašeta, eds., *Ireland and the Great War: 'A War to Unite Us All'?* (Manchester. 2002), p. 32.
12. Trevor Royle, *The Kitchener Enigma* (London, 1985), p. 272.
13. Diary of Shane Leslie, 17 November 1915. Leslie papers, NLI.
14. Lord Meath to Kitchener, 14 August 1914. Kitchener papers, TNA; Percy Illingsworth to Kitchener, 7 August 1914. Kitchener papers, TNA.
15. Royle, *The Kitchener Enigma*, p. 273.
16. Berkeley to Moore, 2 September 1914. Berkeley papers, CCA.
17. Cf. Peter Martin, 'Dulce et Decorum', p. 35.
18. John Redmond to Lord Meath, 19 August 1914. Kitchener papers, TNA; Bryan Mahon, fwd. to Cooper, *The Tenth (Irish) Division in Gallipoli* (Dublin, 1993), pp. 11–14; 'Confidential', G Coy., Royal Engineers to George Berkeley, 31 July 1914. Berkeley papers, CCA.

19. John Redmond, foreword to Bryan Cooper, *The Tenth (Irish) Division in Gallipoli* (Dublin, 1993), p. 6.
20. See Jane McGaughey, *Ulster's Men: Protestant Unionist Masculinities and Militarization in the North of Ireland, 1912–1923* (Montreal, 2012), p. 63.
21. Earl Dunraven, *No Army, No Empire* (n.d.), p. 6; Colonel R. Pope Hennessy, 'A Letter to a Fellow Countryman', 1920. Berkeley papers, CCA; Vane, *On Certain Fundamentals*, p. 8; Basil Brooke to Rev. Macanway, 6 November 1915. Bernard papers, British Library.
22. Myers, *The Great War and Memory*, p. 176.
23. Philip Orr, 'The Somme Legacy', *The Linen Hall Review* 4 (1987), pp. 5–7.
24. Peter Simkins, *Kitchener's Army: The Raising of the New Armies, 1914–16* (Manchester, 1988), pp. 70–71; Hughes, *Fighting Irish*, p. 26.
25. Godley in McGaughey, *Ulster's Men*, p. 115.
26. Ibid. p. 274.
27. Nora Robertson, *Crowned Harp: Memories of the Last Days of the Crown in Ireland* (Dublin, 1960), p. 129.
28. Maurice Moore, typescript of article, 1914. Moore papers, NLI.
29. Tomás Irish, *Trinity in War and Revolution* (Dublin, 2015), p. 87.
30. Roger Willoughby, *A Military History of the University of Dublin and its Officers Training Corps, 1910–1922* (Dublin, 1983), p. 12.
31. Toby Moore to Col. Maurice Moore, London, 30 May 1915. Moore papers, NLI.
32. Edward M. Spiers, *The Army and Society 1815–1914* (New York, 1980), p. 297.
33. Lord Roberts to Kitchener, 10 August 1914. Kitchener papers, TNA; Capt. Kemmis to his father, 17 December 1915. Kemmis papers, LUL.
34. Letter from Capt. W. B. Rennie, ADC, HQ 16th Division, Mallow, n.d. (1914), Moore papers, NLI. Emphasis mine.
35. Gavin Hughes, *Fighting Irish: The Irish Regiments in the First World War* (Sallins, 2015), p. 29. Parsons was not himself a nationalist, and he appears, like many of his fellow officers, to have tolerated nationalist influence in the army so long as there was no detrimental effect on discipline.
36. Spiers, *Army and Society*, pp. 7–8; P. E. Razzell, 'Social Origins of Officers in the Indian and British Home Army: 1958–1962', *British Journal of Sociology* 14 (1963), p. 258.
37. Simkins, *Kitchener's Army*, pp. 217–221.
38. War Office, 'Description of Recruiting Since Mobilisation', 1915. Kitchener papers, TNA.

39. Nicholas Perry, 'The Irish Landed Class and the British Army, 1850–1950', *War in History* 18 (2011), pp. 324–326.

40. David Fitzpatrick, 'The Logic of Collective Sacrifice: Ireland and the British Army, 1914–1918', *Historical Journal* 38 (1995), p. 1017.

41. Anthony Morton, 'Sandhurst and the First World War: The Royal Military College 1902–1918', Sandhurst Occasional Paper No. 17 (2014), p. 4.

42. Paul Usherwood, 'Elizabeth Thompson Butler: The Consequences of Marriage', *Women's Art Journal* 9 (1988), pp. 30–34.

43. Peter Simkins, *Kitchener's Army: The Raising of the New Armies, 1914–16*, (Manchester, 1988), p. 221.

44. Irish, *Trinity in War and Revolution*, p. 94; Edward Littleton Vaughan, *List of Etonians Who Fought in the Great War, 1914–1919* (London, 1921).

45. RHMS officers constituted only a small proportion of the total number of RHMS students who served in the First World War.

46. Spiers, *Army and Society*, p. 8.

47. Martin, 'Dulce et Decorum', p. 29.

48. Ibid. p. 39.

49. Razzell, 'Social Origins', pp. 254, 259.

50. *Times of India*, 26 January 1893.

51. O'Connor, *Irish Officers*, pp. 84–86; Cook, 'The Irish Raj', pp. 509, 520.

52. Frank P. Crozier, *Five Years Hard* (London, 1932), p. 217. Crozier was a typical frontier colonial officer who regarded the advance of 'civilisation' as detrimental to the perceived benefits of the natural, sporting, outdoor life of the African coloniser. Such individuals regarded colonial life as a liberation from the strictures and responsibilities of army discipline and Edwardian society. See Gann and Duignan, *The Rulers of British Africa*.

53. Anthony Kirk-Greene, *Symbol of Authority: The British District Officer in Africa* (London, 2006), p. 20; Gann and Duignan, *British Africa*, p. 208.

54. Heather Streets, *Martial Races: The Military, Race, and Masculinity in British Imperial Culture, 1857–1914* (Manchester, 2004), p. 158.

55. Frank Younghusband to Lord Castletown, The Residency, Kashmir, 15 July 1907. Castletown papers, NLI.

56. Jennifer Regan-Lefebvre, *Cosmopolitan Nationalism in the Victorian Empire: Ireland, India and the Politics of Alfred Webb* (London, 2009), p. 74; Maurice Collis, *The Journey Outward* (London, 1952).

57. Captain William Kemmis to his father, Muttra, 30 October 1913. Kemmis papers, LUL.

58. Bubb, 'The Life of an Irish Soldier in India', p. 804; Cf. Grimshaw, *Indian Cavalry Officer*, p. 28.

59. *Times of India*, 19 February 1917; *Times of India*, 21 August 1917.

60. Confidential Reports on Indian Officers granted King's Commissions, 13 September 1918. India Office records, British Library.
61. Streets, *Martial Races*, pp. 98–101.
62. *The Times*, 20 August 1917. Repington had been chastised while in the officer corps by Henry Wilson for carrying on an affair with Lady Garstin, the wife of an Indian civil servant. After breaking his parole to Wilson and continuing the affair, he was forced to resign his commission.
63. Ibid.
64. Ibid.
65. Cf. Robertson, *Crowned Harp*, p. 26.
66. *The Times*, 29 September 1915.
67. Sir Michael O'Dwyer, 'India's Man-Power in the War', *Army Quarterly* 2 (1921), p. 359; Letter to Viscount Cross, Secretary of State for India, from Dufferin, Roberts, Hope, Chesney, Scobie, Peile and Westland, Simla, 12 August 1887. India Office Records, British Library; *The Times*, 18 November 1914; *Times of India*, 19 February 1917.
68. Streets, *Martial Races*, p. 158.
69. That is, the use of the .303 British Army cartridge to put down dissent. This was famously the answer of Lieutenant Harry 'Breaker' Morant during his court martial for murdering prisoners and civilians in the South African War, when asked by the prosecutor under which rule he had carried out the executions.
70. William Kemmis to his father, Hera, 8 January 1914. Kemmis papers, LUL.
71. William Kemmis to his father, France, 24 May 1916. Kemmis papers, LUL.
72. Roly Grimshaw, *Indian Cavalry Officer 1914–15* (Tunbridge Wells, 1986), p. 28.
73. Maj. Gen. Partap Narain, *Subedar to Field Marshal* (Delhi, 1999), p. 42.
74. Kitchener papers, August–December 1914. TNA.
75. *Hibernia: Quarterly Magazine of the Royal Hibernian Military School*, vols. 4–5. British Library.
76. Letter from Sapper J. Wright, 15th Co. Royal Engineers, BEF, France, *Hibernia*, October 1916, p. 29. British Library.
77. Based on a death rate for Irish soldiers of between 13% and 26%. Cf. Martin, '*Dulce et Decorum*', p. 40.
78. Michael Duffy, 'Tom Hazell', firstworldwar.com, 2009.
79. Peter Martin, '*Dulce et decorum*', pp. 39–40.
80. Patrick Maume, 'O'Gowan, Eric Edward Dorman (Eric Edward Dorman-Smith), ("Chink")', DIB.
81. Tom Johnstone, *Orange, Green and Khaki: The Story of the Irish Regiments in the Great War, 1914–18* (Dublin, 1992), p. 14.

82. Anthony Seldon and David Walsh, *Public Schools and the Great War: The Generation Lost* (Barnsley, 2013), p. 67.

83. For the many other professional institutions that evinced a continuity in pre- and post-independence Ireland, see Campbell, *The Irish Establishment*, p. 27; McBride, *Greening*, p. 11.

84. Military Secretary, 1892; 'Irish Officers for Irish Regiments', *Kerry Sentinel*, 21 August 1915.

85. Anthony P. Quinn, *Wigs and Guns: Irish Barristers in the Great War* (Dublin, 2006), p. 48.

86. John Clarke MacDermott, typescript account of the Easter Rising, 1979, p. 57. Liddell Hart Centre for Military Archives, KCL.

87. Ibid. p. 66.

88. Ibid. p. 62.

89. Liam Hogan, register of Limerick's First World War graves, Limerick City Library.

90. Eric Hobsbawm, *The Age of Empire 1875–1914* (London, 2013), p. 6.

91. Martin, '*Dulce et decorum*', p. 43.

92. Jeffery, *Henry Wilson*, p. 198; Niamh Puirseil, 'War, Work and Labour', in Horne, *Our War* p. 193.

93. Hughes, *Fighting Irish*, p. 102; Richardson, *According to Their Lights*, p. 393–394; Richard S. Grayson and Fearghal McGarry, eds., *Remembering 1916: The Easter Rising, the Somme, and the Politics of Memory in Ireland* (Cambridge, 2016).

94. Maurice Moore, quoted in Ó Corráin, p. 106.

95. Chelmsford to Martineau, Simla, 30 April 1916. Seely correspondence, British Library.

96. Captain E. Gerrard, ADC 5th Division, 'Defence of Beggars Bush Barracks by British, Easter Week, 1916', BMH witness statement WS348.

97. Ibid.

98. Brian Inglis, *West Briton* (London, 1962), p. 14.

99. MacDermott, typescript account of the Easter Rising, p. 54.

100. Ibid. p. 55.

101. A. A. Luce, 'Recollections of Easter Monday 1916', 1965. Luce Papers, TCD.

102. Neil Richardson, *According to Their Lights: Stories of Irishmen in the British Army, Easter 1916* (Dublin, 2015), pp. 12–20; Hughes, *Fighting Irish*, pp. 101–103; Paul Taylor, *Heroes or Traitors? Experiences of Southern Irish Soldiers Returning from the Great War 1919–1939* (Manchester, 2015), pp. 10–11.

103. Hughes, *Fighting Irish*, p. 104.

104. The Volunteer Training Corps was an official militia formation constituted of men who were too old to enlist, or proscribed from doing so due

to occupation—not to be confused with the National- or Ulster Volunteers.
105. Major G. A. Harris, Report on the Defence of Trinity College, May 1916, p. 19; Irish, *Trinity in War and Revolution*, pp. 131–134.
106. Ibid. p. 20.
107. Luce, Recollections of Easter 1916, TCD.
108. Eileen Irwin to her sister-in-law, Dorothy Evans-Price, Burma, about the Easter Rising in Dublin, April, 1916. Sir Alfred Irwin papers, NLI; R. B. McDowell, *Land and Learning: Two Irish Clubs* (Dublin, 1993), p. 142.
109. Fergus Campbell, 'The Easter Rising in Galway', *History Ireland* 14:2 (2006), pp. 24–25.
110. MacDermott, typescript account of the Easter Rising, p. 57.
111. Ronan Fanning, *Fatal Path: British Government and Irish Revolution, 1910–1922* (London, 2013), pp. 222–227.
112. Asquith to Kitchener, 26 April 1916. Kitchener papers, TNA.
113. General Friend to Kitchener, 16 November 1914. Kitchener papers, TNA.
114. Kitchener to Robertson, 26 April 1916. Kitchener papers, TNA.
115. Robertson to Murray, 26 January 1916; Murray to Robertson, 15 February 1916. General Murray correspondence, British Library.
116. Fanning, *Fatal Path*, pp. 141–142.
117. Gerrard, BMH witness statement, p. 8; 'MP Rescued by Sinn Féiners—Strong Escort Disarmed in a Dublin Street', *Daily Sketch*, 13 February 1920.
118. 'The Belfast Inquiry: Colthurst's Statements', *Irish Independent*, 26 August 1916.
119. Leah Levenson and Jerry Natterstad, *Hannah Sheehy-Skeffington: Irish Feminist* (Syracuse, 1986), p. 97; Francis Vane, *Agin the Governments: Memories and Adventures of Sir Francis Fletcher Vane, Bt.* (London, 1929), p. 257. Fletcher-Vane had a fractious relationship with his commander, Lawrence Parsons, throughout his war service which led him to be removed from front-line service and stationed in Dublin. Parsons regarded Vane as too 'political', particularly in the delicate context of the 16th Division.
120. R. F. Foster, *Modern Ireland 1600–1972* (London, 1988), pp. 488–489; Miller, *Queen's Rebels*, p. 107.
121. Lord Wimborne to Maxwell, 8 May 1916. British Library.
122. 'Irish Convention', *Irish Examiner*, 14 December 1917.
123. Richardson, *According to Their Lights*, p. 90.
124. Daithí Ó Corráin, '"A Most Public-spirited and Unselfish Man": The Career and Contribution of Colonel Maurice Moore, 1854–1939', *Studia Hibernica* 40 (2015), p. 109.

125. Earl Dunraven, 'Ireland Awake! An Open Letter to his Fellow Countrymen', 1917, Dunraven papers, LUL, p. 15.
126. Vane-Tempest to mother, 27 November 1917. Vane-Tempest papers, PRONI; See also Lord Roberts to H. H. Asquith, 20 March 1914, in Ian F. Beckett, *The Army and the Curragh Incident 1914* (London, 1986), p. 55.
127. Powerscourt to Spring Rice, 1917. Monteagle papers, NLI.
128. Vane, *On Certain Fundamentals*, p. 12; Leo Keohane, *Captain Jack White: Imperialism, Anarchy & the Irish Citizen Army* (Sallins, 2014), p. 191.
129. Maxwell to Bernard, 11 July 1916. Bernard papers, British Library.
130. *Irish Examiner*, 14 February 1917.
131. Dunraven, 'Ireland Awake'.
132. *The Spectator*, 28 July 1916; 'Irish Officer Court-Martialled', *Irish Examiner*, 24 November 1917; Murray to Robertson, Egypt, 26 May 1916. Murray-Robertson correspondence, British Library; Denman, *Ireland's Unknown Soldiers*, p. 148.
133. *The Times*, 1 August 1916. Nathan's figures are higher than those collected by the Ministry of Pensions, which showed Irish recruitment to 1916 numbering 90,505, and still being under 100,000 by April. See Taylor, *Heroes or Traitors*, p. 8.
134. Wigram to Godley, 18 May 1916. Godley papers, KCL.
135. Chaplain McRory diary, 1917. PRONI.
136. Ibid.
137. Niamh A. Gallagher, 'Irish Civil Society and the Great War, 1914–1918', unpublished PhD thesis, University of Cambridge (2014), pp. 239–240.
138. Sarah Benton, 'Women Disarmed: The Militarisation of Politics in Ireland, 1913–23', *Feminist Review* 50 (1995), pp. 151–152.
139. Fitzpatrick, 'Militarism', p. 383.
140. Bartlett and Jeffery, 'An Irish Military Tradition?', pp. 22–25.
141. Fitzpatrick, 'Militarism', p. 379; Silvestri, *Ireland and India*, p. 126; Karsten, 'Suborned', pp. 32–34; Verney, *The Micks*, p. 4.
142. Shane Leslie diary, 17 November 1916. Leslie papers, NLI.
143. Draft of a letter from Maurice Moore, 9 December 1916. Moore papers, NLI.
144. *Illustrated London News*, 21 November 1914.

CHAPTER 8

The Irish Military Elite and the War of Independence 1918–22

*[U]p to the day when the Union Jack was hauled down at the Royal
Hospital in Dublin in 1922, I endeavoured to keep an open mind on
the various kaleidoscopic aspects of Irish politics. Throughout my
professional career I have held the view that so long as a soldier
continues to serve on the active list it is no business of his to mix himself
up in any way with the political views of whatever government might be
in power at the time.*
—Memoirs of General Nevil Macready, 1923

As the political situation eroded in the war years, the Irish military elite's
attempts to resist 'politicisation' drew them into successive crises which
eroded their social position. As the above quotation from the Commander-
in-Chief in Ireland from 1920 to 1922 suggests, the same was true of the
period of the Irish revolution.[1] Irish officers once again found themselves
inhabiting an unwelcome position, at the centre of a revolutionary situation in which the social institutions from which they derived their authority stood to be stripped away. As Matthew Potter puts it in his study of
landed elites in the Shannon estuary area, 'they found themselves squeezed
between nationalism and unionism; gradually excluded from the emerging
sense of Irishness; and derided for their identity of being both Irish and
British.'[2]

© The Author(s) 2019
L. Sweeney, *Irish Military Elites, Nation and Empire, 1870–1925*,
https://doi.org/10.1007/978-3-030-19307-2_8

Taylor holds that 'It was not service to the British crown that divided society; rather it was the Civil War that split families and communities'; the British Army as an institution, ubiquitous in the Edwardian era and touching nearly every family in Ireland during the Great War, is thus reduced to background music for the main action, the political contest over the future of the Free State.[3] A number of questions remain, however, concerning the effect of the War of Independence and the partition of Ireland on the officers that, up until that point, had constituted the military establishment of Ireland. It is of great significance to the history of this period to examine the role of their affective ties to the country, how this governed their relationship with the new states, and the extent to which the experiences of officers were substantively different from those of the over 100,000 enlisted Irishmen returning from the Great War into the revolutionary situation.[4]

The vast majority of Irish officers were linked by a shared experience of trauma following the Great War, from the young officers who joined up in 1914–18, to the elderly officers who did service as recruiting majors or with the Red Cross. The same cannot be said of the group that now opposed them in arms. The Irish Republican Army (IRA), which, as we have seen, constituted a counter-elite group with little to no overlap with the *ancien régime*, lacked fighters with experience of drill to inject some professionalism into the guerrilla force. John Duggan has found that there was a sense of resentment in the IRA between those who repudiated the call to arms in 1914, and those who enlisted, who had the asset of military experience but also the considerable liability of having served in the British Army.[5] The militaristic 'moment' in Irish politics as it had existed before the First World War was sustained in 1918–19 by the armed opposition to British rule, and officers found themselves once again on the frontline in answering multifaceted political, social, confessional, generational and class challenges to their existence and identity, this time with the added complication of martial law under the governance of General Nevil Macready.[6]

Macready was ambivalent about Ireland, though he had been posted to Belfast during the Easter Rising, and remembered the disorganisation and administrative chaos of the military response. He had also been a police commissioner and was wary about the effectiveness and legitimacy of deploying troops against citizens, even during times of unrest.[7] When he was appointed Commander-in-Chief in Ireland in 1920, however, he found himself once again in a quagmire of administrative ambiguities, which hampered his ability to operate in the extremely delicate situation of military rule. He feared, correctly as it would transpire, that the government in London and the Dublin Castle administration would regard the army as a 'quick fix', as they had done in the past. Sir Warren Fisher had just completed an assessment of the efficacy of the Castle administration and issued a prophetic warning about the 'tendency of the Castle as a whole … to lean on GHQ and avoid responsibility'.[8]

Into this rudderless and volatile political situation came thousands of demobilised soldiers from the First World War. While alienated by their experience of warfare and their long absence from their communities, the majority were able to successfully reintegrate into society—Taylor notes that only an extremely small proportion of the estimated 100,000–150,000 ex-servicemen in the 26 counties were targeted by, or joined in with, violence on either side, while the British Legion lobbied in support of house building and training in trades for army pensioners, often with the support of officers.[9] Others without networks of support or the prospect of work struggled. Some of these had been wartime officers, 'temporary gentlemen' who now had to readjust to the undistinguished, middle-class life from whence they had come. Such men drew frequent comment in the metropolises of Great Britain, but in Ireland their voices, until recently, had been drowned out by the birth pains of the Irish republic.[10]

This chapter illustrates the fragmentation of the Irish officer corps, and the differing directions and locations in which officers were pushed as their social order fragmented. Many gentlemen, temporary or otherwise, found themselves driven, either by inclination or economic necessity, into the ranks of the Auxiliary Division of the Royal Irish Constabulary (RIC) (total strength 2214), the paramilitary force of special constables set up by Major-General Hugh Tudor and constituted of ex-British officers under the command of Frank P. Crozier.[11] The Auxiliaries' decidedly 'ungentlemanly' conduct during the War of Independence was the subject of considerable outrage, both among the general public and within the officer corps, and this has caused historians to question whether this body was indeed drawn uniformly from the officer class.[12] The indication is that the Auxiliaries comprised a fair cross section of the British officer corps as it existed at the end of the First World War, including its proportion of Irish officers. At the outset, it was intended to be, as advertised in the *Times*, a 'corps d'elite for ex-officers' and appears to have recruited largely, if not exclusively, from that pool.[13]

The officer corps, as well as directing the counterinsurgency operations and seeking to maintain the King's authority in Ireland, also found themselves directly targeted by the IRA. In particular, those aristocratic and gentry officers who had the reputation of not being 'good landlords', or came from families that had failed to live up to this standard in the past, found themselves the recipients of death threats, theft, extortion, and arson attacks as the War of Independence progressed. This took a particularly heavy toll on officers who resided in Ireland, although some of the old officer elite sustained and continued to live in Ireland through the worst days of the violence.

The 'Temporary Gentleman' in Revolutionary Ireland, 1919–21

As in Britain, the end of the war led to the rapid demobilisation of tens of thousands of men in Ireland, ill-equipped to deal with civilian life, some without homes or jobs to return to. Because of the high mortality rate of officers on the Western Front, many temporary commissions were issued—as we have seen in Chap. 7, this initially stemmed from the traditional enclave of the experienced and regimentally socialised sergeants-major, but increasingly after 1916 officers were commissioned from less traditional backgrounds.[14] After the war, having experienced the privileges of the aristocratic milieu of the officers' mess (Fig. 8.1), many of these 'temporary gentlemen' were dissatisfied at returning to humdrum peacetime employment.[15] This, coupled with the lack of other employment opportunities, induced Irishmen of all social conditions to continue to flock to the British Army, from north and south. This formed a major component of the economic migration of the period: in 1919–21, twice as many men from the south, and four times as many from the north, joined the army than had done so in the pre-war period.[16] In 1921–22 Irish officers increasingly sought transfers to the Northern Ireland District, sensing that the writing was on the wall for the southern regiments.[17]

Those who remained in Ireland were not immune from the political situation. Like many of the rank and file, nationalist ex-officers were also increasingly incensed at the delay to the implementation of Home Rule, which was popularly but unfairly blamed on feckless and intransigent Westminster MPs. A letter to the editor of the *Freeman's Journal* from a demobilised soldier asserts: 'this is a larger question and a cause of more grievous discontent amongst those who have returned from the army than people imagine ... when they saw what had happened in the betrayal of

Fig. 8.1 Group of junior officers at Waterford Barracks, 1915. The enthusiasm of the Irish response to the call to arms during the First World War concealed an increasingly perilous position for the officer corps in Ireland. Officers who enthusiastically embarked for the front returned to a greatly changed social position in 1918. *Courtesy of the National Library of Ireland*

our dead leader [John Redmond], by the usual broken promises of British statesmen, [they] were turning towards Sinn Féin.'[18] Colonel Moore estimated that upwards of 60,000 of the returning soldiers (somewhere around one half of the ex-servicemen in the 26 counties) were supportive of the nationalist movement and would be 'ready and willing to fight for the freedom of Ireland'.[19] In the event, ex-soldiers who took up arms numbered in the hundreds, rather than the tens of thousands. In the most recent study of Irish ex-soldiers, Paul Taylor notes that the degree of support for Sinn Féin differed vastly in various parts of the country, though he identifies a general change in attitudes, as enunciated by a Cork unionist: 'Everybody's taken a step to the left. Your old Nationalists have joined pacifist Sinn Féin; pacifist Sinn Féin has become active Republican. We Unionists take our stand on the old Nationalism.'[20] As we have seen in previous chapters, this shift in public attitudes was a continuation of the general trend before the First World War. In the light of this societal shift, officers increasingly endorsed the movement for Dominion Home Rule (DHR) as an acceptable compromise between the unionist and republican positions. Veterans reflected the general political trends of society, in that the political divide was generational, confessional, urban and rural, southwest and northeast: younger, Catholic, rural southwesterners were more likely to support independence; older, Protestant, urban northeasterners were more likely to defend the Union.[21]

While the 'temporary gentlemen' faced the prospect of reacclimatising to life outside the elite, career officers faced a dislocating experience of a different kind in 1922. In that year, the six Irish regiments with recruiting areas in Leinster, Munster, and Connacht were disbanded, and their colours deposited at Windsor Castle where they remain to this day.[22] As well as the intense upset experienced by these men, whose martial Irish identity rested heavily on the regimental connection, there were practical problems to securing a transfer to a new regiment. While, according to a notice in the *Times*, 'It is intended, as a general rule, to transfer officers to other regiments in which their seniority and service will correspond as far as possible', this did not always transpire in practice; promotion from outside the regiment was generally discouraged, as the implication was that there were no suitable candidates for the post internally.[23] Further, the reduction in the size of the army in 1922 meant a reduction in status was likely for transferring officers. The *Times* later reported that 'some [officers] are … to be allowed to volunteer for transfer, to other infantry regiments, or to the Royal Engineers or Corps of Signals. Those who cannot thus be provided for have a very strong case for inclusion in one or other of the promised schemes of Empire settlement.'[24] One such scheme, in Canada, received a large number of Irish ex-officers in the 1920s.[25]

Captain William Kemmis wrote to Field Marshal Haig in 1923 seeking patronage, and received the following reply:

> You say 'help me to get some kind of job'—the Army is the missing word, inside or outside or what? ... Now look here, I know of no job in the Army to suit you, you know what a run there is on staff jobs of any kind & outside the Army you know what amount of unemployment there is ... why don't you exchange or transfer to a regt. who has another 2 years abroad.[26]

This was easier said than done, though service in active war zones—Somalia, Iraq, or Russia—was an option. Another was the colonial police, which was also popular with former Royal Irish Constabulary officers. The forces of the new British mandates in the Middle East, particularly the Palestine Gendarmerie, were popular destinations for Irish officers.[27]

A remarkable feature of the revolutionary period, in fact, was that Irish representation in the British Army did not decline substantially, and its social profile remained similar to the years before the First World War. According to O'Connor, the lack of other opportunities forms a large part of the explanation: over 20,000 Irishmen joined the British Army between 1919 and 1921, a time when unemployment was much worse in Ireland than elsewhere in the United Kingdom, even discounting the exacerbating effects of the guerrilla campaign.[28] This was a welcome development to the War Office, who faced a crisis in officer recruitment following the First World War. A government report on the situation found that a number of factors—including frequent moves of regiments and the unpopularity of overseas service, postwar cuts in the regimental establishments, high fees at the military academies, and 'special factors arising out of the late war'—had significantly depressed the numbers of young men presenting for examinations. Further, the report noted: 'parents do not like to send their sons into the Army until they are satisfied that it will provide an attractive career with definite prospects.'[29] The peacetime army thus returned rapidly to its pre-war social structure: the percentage of officers who had been commissioned from the ranks fell from 41% during the war to 5% by the 1930s, barely an improvement on the officer corps of the 1890s or the Edwardian period.[30] One solution proposed to expand access was to revive the system of university nominations, which had proved so successful at the outbreak of the War, but had since provided only ten officers: Lord Haldane called for the system to be 'applicable to the Dominions, including the whole of Ireland'.[31] However, the Dublin University OTC was disbanded in 1922.

The social position of the Irish officer was becoming increasingly tenuous after the First World War, exacerbated by economic factors such as the ineligibility of officers for army unemployment insurance.[32] While ex-enlisted men were eligible for an army pension, demobilised temporary officers had no such fall-back.[33] Ex-officers sought out other means of maintaining a gentlemanly existence: Trinity College Dublin enthusiastically embraced schemes for admitting ex-servicemen, and between 1919 and 1921 matriculated ninety-six new students with a service background. In the same period other Irish colleges and universities saw an increase in admissions of 73%.[34] The University of Cambridge ran schemes training veterans in agriculture, and along with other universities trained applicants for the colonial civil service examinations.[35] One of the few boons of military rule in Ireland was that the new Lord Lieutenant, Field Marshal French, was determined to do what he could for returning servicemen, and felt that the state owed them a debt of gratitude. The internal divisions and external pressures on his administration, however, meant that little relief was actually delivered to the returning soldiers.[36]

MARTIAL LAW, 1920–22

Irish officers, on active service and otherwise, could not avoid being caught up in the War of Independence. The Indian Army officer Gerald Little, with an officer's typical wry understatement, wrote to his brother, who had been wounded in the War of Independence, in July 1920: 'Have just heard from Father you stopped one in Dublin. I was very sorry to hear it indeed … You must be having some exciting times in Dublin these days if all the papers say is true. I wonder how it will end.'[37] It was a detached response to a situation that, in reality, was deeply dislocating for the officer class.

A significant difficulty with the administration of martial law was the aforementioned ambivalence with which military officers greeted the task of governing. Field Marshal John French, whose career had a distinct Irish component throughout the previous five decades, had the distinction of being the penultimate Lord Lieutenant of Ireland, and the last to hold the position substantively. His successor, Viscount Fitzalan, was appointed in 1921 as a caretaker during the transfer of government from the British to the Irish, and from the military to civilians. Lord Dunraven encapsulated his tenure thus: 'I had the pleasure and honour of [John French's] friendship when he was Lord Lieutenant of Ireland. He was too much of a soldier, too fond of saying, "I am a plain soldier and obey orders." I could wish he had asserted himself more when he was responsible for Ireland in very critical times.'[38] According to Martin Thomas, the increasing imperial instability that followed the First World War emphasised the inadequacy of standard reactions to civil unrest. It was becoming clear that some middle ground between everyday policing practices and the vigorous coercion of martial law was required to deal with civil disorder, while still preserving the integrity of the empire.[39] Ireland was proving a resonant example of these very failings of military administration.

The proclamation of martial law over increasingly large swathes of the country in 1920–21 represented another erosion of the moral authority of the officer corps, which, even during the Curragh incident, had characterised its apolitical nature as a defining feature of its identity. Military officers were unsuited to civil governance, and the administration of martial law was accordingly heavy-handed. Officers, in particular those with no prior experience of operations in Ireland, did not fully appreciate that colonial counterinsurgency tactics could not be imported wholesale to an Irish context, as General Maxwell had learned in 1916.[40] Certain officers, like Wilson and Macready, expressed their frustration at the situation by adopting a greater animosity towards the Irish, as Kitchener had done in 1914.[41] British military officers, in some cases appointed to the Irish Command for their supposed disinterest in Irish affairs, unsurprisingly had little or no experience of the country, failed to understand local conditions, and adopted an attitude of hostility and paranoia.[42] Irish officers on the other hand, attempted to conciliate: in extreme cases, like the aforementioned cases of William Monk Gibbon and Henry Vane, the officers were condemned as Sinn Féin supporters and sanctioned.[43] According to Charles Townshend, the constant castigation of the military government in the press, and the growing tensions between the army and society, had a heavily demoralising effect on officers.[44]

Martial law came into effect in the counties of Cork, Tipperary, Kerry, and Limerick on 27 December 1920, with the commanders of the 6th, 16th, 17th and 18th Divisions and the Kerry Infantry Brigade being appointed military governors for their districts.[45] The CO of 6th Division, General Sir Peter Strickland, was not an Irishman and echoed the line adopted by General Maxwell in 1916: in an interview for the *Evening*

Standard, Strickland insisted: 'the politics of the country are not my business. The work we have to do at present in Ireland is disliked by every soldier engaged in it.'[46] His introduction to the country was a harsh one: he recorded in July 1920 that a local functionary had been assassinated while sitting in his club. Shocked, he wrote in his diary, '14 men went in and shot him. *What* a country'.[47] In the *Standard* interview he goes on to address the efficacy of martial law: 'nothing is accomplished in these attacks. In all cases they are easily beaten off.' Strickland also responded to the poor public perception of the army and anxieties over the institution of courts martial: 'I do not think there is a trace of bitterness in the attitude of the officers in these courts ... [they do not] come into contact or conflict with the prisoners. In fact, there is a special corps of court-martial officers being established.'[48] Once again the officer corps was characteristically confident in its abilities, though its particular ways of doing things would prove, fundamentally, a poor fit for the conditions in Ireland.

As during the Easter Rising, the divisions wrought by the War of Independence could hit uncomfortably close to home. Sir John French discovered this for himself when he had the embarrassment of driving past a hostile crowd which was being whipped up against the government by none other than his own sister, Charlotte Despard, and Maud Gonne.[49] Once again, the social network in which Irish officers operated found itself split by opposing political allegiances.

French's tenure as Lord Lieutenant was an exercise in attempting to make the best of a bad job. However, while many of the officers in senior positions in Ireland suffered, like Macready, from a lack of interest or knowledge of Ireland and the Irish, French's self-described Irishness gave him the opposite problem: according to Richard Holmes, 'He cherished two fatal misconceptions: firstly, that his own deep personal commitment to Ireland gave him a special insight into the country's problems; and secondly that Sinn Féin survived only by terrorising the population.'[50] French's priorities during his tenure were neutralising Sinn Féin, preparing the ground for the granting of Home Rule, and centralising the authority of Dublin Castle in the face of the 'extraordinary lack of method of co-ordination in thought' that prevailed in the Irish administration.[51] The latter he was able to accomplish to an extent; the other two priorities presented insurmountable difficulties. While French has been described as 'a virtual dictator' by Costello, he found his latitude for action severely curtailed by a lack of reliable information, poor discipline, and an unhelpful attitude from London.[52] Despite his efforts at conciliation between unionists and nationalists and his attempt to get a clear picture of the state of the country with the establishment of various advisory councils, French underestimated the popularity and capacity of Sinn Féin. He succeeded, according to his critics in the press, only in getting a clear picture of the interior of the Kildare Street Club from his elite, out-of-touch advisors.[53] His first and foremost duty as he and his superiors in London saw it was the pacification of the country, and his concentration on reacting to outbreaks of violence instead of taking initiative and, for example, establishing a satisfactory intelligence network or seeking to attenuate underlying social tensions in the country, effectively stalled his administration from the start.[54]

Erskine Childers argued from an officer's perspective against the imposition of martial law in an article of 1920, 'as one who lives under that regime, and also as a soldier with a varied experience of war and an instinctive regard for its decencies and chivalries'. Childers characterised the atrocities of the army as dragging Britain into a conflict which could not be morally supported: 'It is impossible for those who levy such a war to make it respectable ... because it is waged by the strong against the weak for a base and selfish end', supported by a government from which 'emanates a stream of proclamations proscribing anything and everything with a national tendency'. Childers also considers the injustices of the controversial military courts then in operation: 'lastly, the court-martial ... soldiers have no business with law; they are not trained for it; they could not do impartial justice if they would ... This Irish war, small as it may seem now, will, if it is persisted in, corrupt and eventually ruin not only your Army, but your nation and your Empire itself.'[55] These views were largely out of step with those of the military authorities and the War Office, not least the Chief of the Imperial General Staff, Henry Wilson, who held that the resolution of any Irish difficulty was simply a matter of employing a greater number of troops.[56] He took a dim view of conciliation, holding that nothing but 'determined *shooting* would be of any use'—a view which was reinforced by his experiences of Victorian Ireland, the Boer War, and the First World War.[57] Wilson became the last British Field Marshal to die 'in combat', when he was murdered outside of his residence in London in February 1922, by two ex-servicemen who had joined the IRA, as he was drawing his sword to defend himself.[58]

In campaigning in support of Dominion Home Rule in 1920, Colonel Pope Hennessy counter-argued the popular Sinn Féin position with words which foreshadowed, in a rather exaggerated way, the coming campaigns:

> An Irish republic is unattainable as a practical proposition because it can only be brought about ... by the complete defeat of Great Britain in a war which disrupts the British Empire ... what is left of Western Civilization would founder finally, whoever won.
>   ... The reconquest of Ireland would not take very long, and this is a subject on which I am competent to express an opinion, having both studied war and practised it ... Fighting, properly so called, might last three weeks, guerrilla warfare another two months. By the end of that time I imagine that although those towns would still be standing in which no organised resistance has been offered, about a quarter of the villages in the country would have been burnt, not to mention every farmhouse in the neighbourhood of which a shot had been fired.[59]

At the same time, even though partition was already an inevitability, Pope Hennessy attempted to resist the sundering of the country through his writing, arguing that separation from the Empire would betray the men who had died for the cause of Home Rule:

> Men do not die, as Irishmen had died, for three-quarters of a country ... By complete severance from the Empire, Ireland would not only expose her produce to the possibility of hostile tariffs in her main market [i.e. Britain], but would lose her share in whatever Imperial Preference might be established.[60]

This was the position of many Irish officers at the outbreak of the War of Independence, including Major Gerald Dease, Nugent Everard, Stephen Gwynn, the Earl of Fingall, Lt. Col. Thomas Myles, and Major G. B. O'Connor, men from across the social spectrum of Irish officers. The Irish Dominion League, led by Sir Horace Plunkett, was supported by a number of these officers, and Captain George Berkeley believed that Dominion home rule (DHR) was the natural outcome to Ireland's difficulties: 'the Irish Question could be perfectly well settled if Lloyd G would agree to treat w Sinn Fein on the basis of finding a halfway house—that wd be DHR ... Personally I loathe parties and I loathe deals ... But they are inevitable.'[61]

'FORMER BRITISH ARMY OFFICERS ... [WHO] FOUND DIFFICULTY IN SETTLING DOWN': THE AUXILIARY DIVISION OF THE ROYAL IRISH CONSTABULARY

One of the darkest chapters of the Irish War of Independence was the brutality and terror inflicted by the Auxiliary Division of the Royal Irish Constabulary, a group of former commissioned officers who were employed as paramilitary police cadets. Supposedly constituted entirely of officers in order to ensure the suitability of recruits, it instead became one of the worst examples of the hard rule of the military, a byword for oppression. Despite this, the Auxiliaries remain relatively poorly understood, particularly compared to the more widely known 'Black and Tans' with whom they are sometimes conflated. It remains unclear, for example, whether the policy of recruiting only officers persisted; there were men who never held a commission among the Auxiliaries, though it is uncertain how widespread this was.[62] The anecdotal evidence suggests that many Auxiliaries did not conform to the demographic characteristics of the traditional British officer corps. The majority came from England, though a sample of the RIC register by Lowe found that as many as 10% of the Auxiliary corps might have been constituted of Irish officers—Lowe uncovers 17 Catholic officers and 29 Protestants from Ireland.[63] John MacDermott, a northern Irish wartime officer commissioned from the ranks in 1917, recalls friends of his from Belfast becoming Auxiliaries, including one Willie Crossley, who went through officer training with him. MacDermott records his impressions of the corps: 'They were recruited mainly from former British Army officers ... drawn from a class which had found difficulty in settling down after the excitements of war service and were, in general, intelligent and well educated ... Willie's Auxiliary friend turned out to be the son of a high ranking soldier.'[64] Far from being exclusively constituted of 'temporary gentlemen', as some commentators seeking to explain their ungentlemanly behaviour held, the Auxiliaries seem to have been drawn from all sections of the officer corps, and all parts of the United Kingdom (Fig. 8.2).[65]

2
26   L. SWEENEY

Fig. 8.2 Members of the Auxiliary Division of the Royal Irish Constabulary, a force ostensibly constituted of ex-British officers, notorious for their brutality during the Irish War of Independence. Many colonial officers and temporary wartime officers were drawn to the Division. *Courtesy of the National Library of Ireland*

Officers had a conflicted view of the Auxiliaries. The Irish Catholic General Edward Bulfin declined the Inspector-Generalship of the RIC, the job which would eventually go to Hugh Tudor, on the grounds that it was 'distasteful' and not of a 'military character'.[66] A.D. Harvey characterises the Auxiliary Division as 'generally men who had been more accustomed to giving than to receiving orders, leavened by a considerable number of long-serving NCOs who had years of experience of obeying only as much of their officers' orders as suited them'—an assessment which could just as easily be applied to the British officer corps of the First World War.[67]

The opinion of others in the army was far from laudatory: *The Times* reported: 'considerable animosity now exists between the Regulars and the Auxiliary Division of the Royal Irish Constabulary, the former being incensed at the licence and indiscipline of the latter and resenting the discredit which has been reflected upon themselves.'[68] Regular army officers, both British and Irish, as well as the men of the RIC considered the actions of the Auxiliaries to be particularly shocking and 'rough' because the division was constituted of officers.[69] Dublin Castle functionaries referred to the Auxiliaries as 'officers' or 'supposed officers' in inverted commas, implicitly contrasting the activities of 'Tudor's Toughs' with the popular image of the British officer as restrained and gentlemanly.[70]

Their conduct in Ireland, however, would not have seemed out of place in an outfit like the Royal West African Frontier Force (WAFF), in which the Auxiliary Division's commander, the Irishman Frank Percy Crozier, had served as a junior officer. Crozier had made a career in the colonial forces, where he had managed to distinguish himself as a soldier and support himself on his pay. He had also spent a significant portion of his career in Ireland. Despite attending the prestigious and military-oriented Wellington College, Crozier found himself entering the military via one of the common 'back door' methods—a volunteer regiment—as he did not satisfy the height requirement for the regular army. When on leave from his posting in the WAFF, he travelled extensively through Ireland, visiting his geographically diffuse extended family of resident magistrates and minor gentry. Crozier resigned his commission in 1908 to try his hand at civilian life in Canada, but he returned in 1912 and involved himself heavily in the developing volunteer movement, eventually commanding a brigade of the Ulster Volunteers in Belfast. Following service in the First World War, he found himself in Ireland once again, at the head of a corps of officers brutalised by war and imperial service, pullulating with the miasma of colonialism. According to one historian of the Auxiliary Division, A.D. Harvey, 'It would have been an outstanding leader who could have got such men properly under control: Crozier ... found the task beyond him.'[71]

Like Crozier, the other senior officers were deeply influenced by their colonial experience. The officer who implemented the Auxiliary scheme, Major-General Hugh Tudor, had also served in the empire, in India, Egypt, and South Africa, while the other commander on the ground, Brigadier-General E.A. Wood, had served previously in the British South Africa Police.[72] Tudor's second-in-command and chief of intelligence in Ireland, Ormonde Winter, had worked to build up a criminal investigation department in India and also had a background in military intelligence during the war—Ireland, he recalled, resembled much more the former than the latter.[73] D.M. Leeson and Michael Foy characterise the Auxiliary commanders as adopting a strategy of coercion based on the attrition of the First World War, though considering the colonial service of Crozier and Tudor, as well as regular Auxiliary cadets like Lieutenant Colonel F.H.W. Guard (a former officer of the Gold Coast Volunteer Corps) and Lieutenant Frank Fitch (a ranker officer who served in India and South Africa), the inheritance of these officers' imperial experiences also cannot be ruled out here.[74] For instance, around a quarter of the officers recruited as Auxiliary cadets in 1920 were old enough to have served in the Boer War.[75] The inheritance of this conflict might be read into officers' proposal to combat the rebels by 'dividing the twenty-six counties "into sections by means of blockhouses and barbed wire"', the same way Lord Roberts defeated the Boers two decades before.[76] The RIC had been cited as a significant influence on colonial police and paramilitary forces; the backgrounds of these Auxiliary officers illustrate that the relationship worked in the opposite direction as well.[77] Their colonial experience had not prepared them for the intimacy, claustrophobia, and paranoia of fighting a hidden guerrilla war in a small country, however.

The Auxiliaries were regarded, even at the outset, as rather below the salt by the elite circle of Irish officers.[78] For example, in 1920 the committee of the Kildare Street Club, which during the First World War had happily welcomed wartime officers as temporary members, decided that Commander Crozier was not eligible for membership.[79] This is unsurprising for one remembered as 'if not exactly a soldier of fortune, hardly [conforming] to the type of British regular officer'.[80] Crozier was, however, characteristic of officers in his belief that the downfall of the military regime in Ireland was more to do with meddling by politicians than with the effect of martial law on a resentful public: 'In the "bad eighties"—amidst murder and repression the task of keeping order was left to gentlemen aided by military and police … in 1920, against a far more deadly foe, a Cabinet of civilians saw fit to shelve General Shaw's military measure in favour of a make-believe quasi-military regime doomed to fail in advance.'[81] Considering the role of the Auxiliaries and other officers in enforcing coercion on the spot, and in carrying out so tenaciously the government's policy of reprisals, the blame cannot be entirely shifted to the politicians, however.[82] It is also unlikely that Shaw's plan of flooding Ireland with ten military battalions in order to extinguish the rebellion, which Crozier alludes to, would have led to a less chaotic or controversial outcome.[83] As Charles Townshend argues about the first chaotic imposition of martial law in the aftermath of the Rising, the commanders can neither 'be held entirely responsible for British policy', nor could the commander on the ground 'be seen as a mere unthinking soldier'.[84] So it was with the military regime of 1920–21. If the officers of the Auxiliary Division 'behaved with greater license' than the RIC or Black and Tans, and were less likely to be punished, as Leeson puts it 'this was merely the privilege of rank'.[85] In the aftermath of one of the official reprisals, one auxiliary wrote home displaying his own conflicted feelings about the actions of his unit: 'I have never experienced such orgies of murder, arson and looting as I have witnessed during the past sixteen days with the RIC Auxiliaries. It baffles description. And we are supposed to be officers and gentlemen.'[86]

Crozier, while shocked at the outrages committed by the men under his command, never wavered in his idea of the righteousness of his cause, and insisted that his personal responsibility was limited:

> The plan ought to have worked well and could have done so had it not been for sinister influences in the background over which I had no control but which were eventually to wreck the whole policy of resolute action by the secret employment of irregular reprisals (murders etc.) carried out by the 'Wardens of the Law' yet placed to the credit of the 'other side', to their shame.[87]

Crozier claimed also that when he took action, dismissing over fifty officers for looting, murder, desertion, and other misconduct, this was seen as an impertinent interference calculated to undermine the war effort: he received anonymous telephone calls warning him: 'Don't be a fool ... if you continue to stick your toes in you'll miss the "honours" list at the end of this show ... you can have a KBE in June. These men if they are not reinstated will play hell with London and upset the Cabinet altogether.'[88] Crozier and one of his senior Irish officers, Lt.-Col. Kirkwood, certainly felt a pang of guilt for their role, even while obviating any sense of personal responsibility, citing the imperfect circumstances under which they worked. Eventually, their disgust at the actions of the Auxiliaries led both men to resign from the corps in protest.[89] Overall, however, the argument that their latitude for action was hamstrung by dithering politicians does not stand up against the actions of Auxiliary officers, which only appeared outside the norm for officers because of the extraordinary circumstance of their being accorded a wide degree of agency within the United Kingdom, as opposed to on the colonial frontier.

That the Auxiliary Corps was drawn from a wide spectrum of Irish as well as British former officers and NCOs illustrates the multiplicity of Irish reactions to the extraordinary conditions of the War of Independence, and underlines the extent to which it reached its most bitter expression as a civil conflict between Irishmen.[90] The story of Irish officers after the First World War was one of decline and marginalisation across the board: from the 'temporary gentlemen' frozen out of the elite, and thrust into a dangerous mixture of unemployment and civil unrest, to the traumatised colonial officer given licence to vent his anger on the innocent, to the perplexed aristocratic officer, suddenly confronted with challenges to his social authority while simultaneously expected to operate as an instrument of government under martial law. In many cases, these men's religious affiliation began to mark them as targets, as the national struggle took on an increasingly sectarian bent. Edward Pearce characterises the elite, Conservative, Protestant establishment as increasingly inclined to circle the wagons around the Unionist heartland in the north: 'Southern Protestants in the Conservative Party, like Lord Lansdowne, a Fitzmaurice and a Kerry landowner, came to realize that nothing would be done for the southern Protestants. Too few, too scattered, asking too much in the way of reasonable demands', their claim to moral authority continued to erode as 'the argument was shifting, retreating into the redoubt of Ulster, an Ulster waiting to be defined'.[91] The Irish officer corps thus constituted a central component of the increasingly delicate membrane connecting Ireland to Great Britain and the Empire. After independence, Irish officers would therefore play an integral part in the construction of two new Irish states, and in defining their future relationship with that empire.

NOTES

1. Nevil Macready, *Annals of an Active Life* (London, 1923), p. 171.
2. Matthew Potter, '"The Most Perfect Specimen of Civilized Nature": The Shannon Estuary Group—Elite Theory and Practice', in O'Neill, Ciaran, ed., *Irish Elites in the Nineteenth Century* (Dublin, 2013), p. 124.
3. Paul Taylor, *Heroes or Traitors? Experiences of Southern Irish Soldiers Returning from the Great War 1919–1939* (Manchester, 2015), p. 248.
4. Recent studies which make reference to the experience of ex-servicemen include Taylor, *Heroes or Traitors*, Jane McGaughey, *Ulster's Men: Protestant Unionist Masculinities and Militarization in the North of Ireland, 1912–1923* (Montreal, 2012); Gavin Hughes, *Fighting Irish: The Irish Regiments in the First World War* (Sallins, 2015); Neil Richardson,

According to their Lights: Stories of Irishmen in the British Army, Easter 1916 (Dublin, 2015); Leo Keohane, *Captain Jack White: Imperialism, Anarchism and the Irish Citizens Army* (Dublin, 2014); Steven O'Connor, *Irish Officers in the British Forces, 1922–1945* (London, 2014).

5. John P. Duggan, *A History of the Irish Army* (Dublin, 1991), p. 130. There is some discussion over the significance of ex-servicemen's representation in the IRA; Fitzpatrick and Leonard suggest that hundreds of ex-servicemen joined after the Great War, as commanders, drill instructors, and in the flying columns. Local studies find smaller numbers of ex-servicemen in particular brigades, while 109 IRA ex-servicemen can be traced through the Bureau of Military History statements. See Taylor, *Heroes or Traitors*, pp. 14–15.

6. Charles Townshend, *Easter 1916: The Irish Rebellion* (London, 2005), p. 334.

7. Colm Campbell, *Emergency Law in Ireland,1918–1925* (Oxford, 1994), p. 135.

8. Warren Fisher, quoted in Keith Jeffery, *The British Army and the Crisis of Empire* (Manchester, 1984), p. 82.

9. Taylor, *Heroes or Traitors?*, pp. 24–26, 87, 96.

10. See, for example, Martin Petter, ' "Temporary Gentlemen" in the Aftermath of the Great War: Rank, Status and the Ex-officer Problem', *Historical Journal* 37 (1994), pp. 127–152.

11. A. D. Harvey, 'Who Were the Auxiliaries?', *Historical Journal* 35 (1992), p. 665.

12. Ibid., passim.

13. *The Times*, 2 November 1920.

14. Ian F. W. Beckett and Keith Simpson, *A Nation in Arms: A Social Study of the British Army in the First World War* (Manchester, 1985), pp. 73–76.

15. Petter, 'Temporary Gentlemen', p. 133.

16. Karsten, 'Suborned', p. 49.

17. W. B. Buckley to W. D. O. Kemmis, Cairo, 21 May 1923. Kemmis papers, LUL.

18. J. F. Magee to the editor, *Freeman's Journal*, 10 March 1919.

19. Maurice Moore, note, Dublin n.d. Moore papers, NLI.

20. Taylor, *Heroes or Traitors*, p. 83.

21. Ibid. pp. 82–85.

22. These were the Royal Irish Regiment, the Leinster Regiment, the Royal Dublin Fusiliers, the Royal Munster Fusiliers, the South Irish Horse, and the Connaught Rangers.

23. *The Times*, 30 May 1922.

24. *The Times*, 9 June 1922.

25. MacDermott, typescript account of the Easter Rising, p. 140. KCL.; Jason R. Myers, *The Great War and Memory in Irish culture, 1918–2010* (Palo Alto, 2013), p. 14; Stephen Garton, 'The Dominions, Ireland, and India', in Gerwarth, Robert, and Erez Manela, eds., *Empires at War 1911–1923* (Oxford, 2014), p. 70.

26. William Haig to Kemmis, Brighton, 29 April 1923. Kemmis papers, LUL.

27. See Georgina Sinclair, 'The "Irish" Policeman and the Empire: Influencing the Policing of the Empire-Commonwealth', *Irish Historical Studies* 36 (2008), pp. 173–187; Jeffery A. Rudd, 'Origins of the Transjordan Frontier Force', *Middle Eastern Studies* 26 (1990), p. 162.

28. O'Connor, *Irish Officers*, p. 10.

29. HM Stationery Office, 'Report of the Committee on the Education and Training of Officers', 1924. National Archives of Ireland.

30. O'Connor, *Irish Officers*, p. 16

31. 'Report of the Committee on the Education and Training of Officers'. A further thirty officers had been commissioned from the universities by direct entry between 1919 and 1922.

32. Petter, 'Temporary gentlemen', p. 128.

33. Taylor, *Heroes or Traitors*, pp. 111–119. Ex-servicemen in the Free State encountered numerous difficulties in claiming this pension throughout the 1920s.

34. Irish, *Trinity in War and Revolution*, pp. 203–204.

35. Anthony Kirk-Greene, *Symbol of Authority: The British District Officer in Africa* (London, 2006), p. 46.

36. Richard Holmes, *The Little Field Marshal: The Life of Sir John French* (London, 2004), p. 344

37. Gerald Little quoted in Alexander Bubb, 'The Life of the Irish Soldier in India: Representations and Self-Representations, 1857–1922', *Modern Asian Studies* 46:4 (2012), p. 808.

38. Earl Dunraven, *Past Times and Pastimes*, vol. 1 (1921), p. 178.

39. Martin Thomas, '"Paying the Butcher's Bill": Policing British Colonial Protest after 1918', *Crime, Histoire & Sociétés/Crime, History & Societies* 15 (2011), p. 59.

40. Fanning, *Fatal Path*, p. 142.

41. See Keith Jeffery, *Field Marshal Sir Henry Wilson: A Political Soldier* (Oxford, 2006), pp. 264–266; Charles Townshend, *The British Campaign in Ireland, 1919–1921* (London, 1975), p. 20.

42. Jeffery, *Henry Wilson*, p. 271; Townshend, *The British Campaign in Ireland*, p. 20; Keith Jeffery, *The British Army and the Crisis of Empire, 1918–22* (Manchester, 1984), p. 77.

43. Vane, *Agin the Governments*, p. 257.

44. Townshend, *The British Campaign in Ireland*, p. 158.

45. Proclamation of martial law, *Kilkenny People* 18 December 1920.
46. *Evening Standard*, 25 January 1921.
47. Strickland's pocket diary, 18 July 1920. Strickland papers, IWM.
48. *Evening Standard*, 25 January 1921.
49. Richard Holmes, *The Little Field Marshal: The Life of Sir John French* (London, 2004), p. 17.
50. Ibid. pp. 338–339.
51. Ibid. pp. 338–341.
52. Costello, *A Most Delightful Station*, p. 317.
53. Holmes, *The Little Field Marshal*, p. 342.
54. P. Bew, *Ireland*, pp. 400–404.
55. Erskine Childers, 'Military Rule in Ireland. What it Means', *Daily News*, 29 March 1920.
56. Jeffery, *Crisis of Empire*, pp. 89–91.
57. Jeffery, *Henry Wilson*, p. 263.
58. Jeffery, *Crisis of Empire*, p. 94.
59. Colonel R. Pope Hennessy DSO, 'The Irish Dominion: A Method of Approach to a Settlement', London, 1920. Berkeley papers, CCA.
60. Ibid.
61. Berkeley, notes on Dominion Home Rule, June 1920. CCA.
62. D. M. Leeson, *The Black and Tans* (Oxford, 2011), p. 106. One of the difficulties in ascertaining more definite information is the Auxiliaries' poor recordkeeping.
63. W. J. Lowe, 'Who were the Black and Tans?' *History Ireland* 12:3 (2004), pp. 48–49.
64. MacDermott, Typescript Account of the Easter Rising, pp. 138–140. KCL.
65. Jon Lawrence, 'Forging a Peaceable Kingdom: War, Violence and Fear of Brutalization in Post-First World War Britain', *Journal of Modern History* 75 (2003), p. 580.
66. Jeffery, *Crisis of Empire*, p. 82.
67. Harvey, 'Who were the Auxiliaries?', p. 669.
68. *The Times*, 1 January 1921.
69. Leeson, *The Black and Tans*, p. 37.
70. Fanning, *Fatal Path*, p. 247; Leeson, *The Black and Tans*, pp. 112–118. Leeson also identifies the Auxiliaries as more likely to take part in indiscriminate violence, as opposed to a series of targeted reprisals.
71. Harvey, 'Who were the Auxiliaries?' p. 669.
72. Leeson, *The Black and Tans*, pp. 32–33.
73. Ormonde Winter, *Winter's Tale* (London, 1955), p. 293.
74. Leeson, *The Black and Tans.*, pp. 112–114.
75. Ibid. p. 105.

76. Cabinet Irish Committee, quoted in Jeffery, *Crisis of Empire*, p. 91; see also Omissi and Thompson, *The Impact of the South African War*, p. 280.
77. See David Anderson and Daivd Killingray, eds., introduction to *Policing the Empire: Government, Authority, and Control, 1830–1940* (Manchester, 1991).
78. Harvey, 'Who were the Auxiliaries?', p. 668.
79. McDowell, *Land and Learning*, p. 94.
80. *The Times* obituary of Crozier, quoted in Clifford, introduction to *The Men I Killed*, p. 11.
81. F. P. Crozier, *Ireland For Ever* (n.p., 1930) p. 69.
82. Jeffery, *Crisis of Empire*, p. 85.
83. Ibid., p. 79.
84. Townshend, *Easter 1916*, p. 300.
85. Leeson, *The Black and Tans*, p. 223.
86. Aideen Carroll, *Seán Moylan: Rebel Leader* (Cork, 2010), p. 72.
87. Crozier, *Ireland For Ever*, p. 71.
88. Ibid. p. 90.
89. Harvey, 'Who were the Auxiliaries?', p. 667.
90. Leeson, *The Black and Tans*, p. 191.
91. Edward Pearce, *Lines of Most Resistance: The Lords, the Tories, and Ireland, 1886–1914* (St Ives, 1999), p. 418.

CHAPTER 9

Barriers Broken: Partition, the Free State, and Empire, 1922–25

In these days it is neither necessary nor desirable to confine the selection of officers to any one class or community … barriers, social and intellectual, have been daily and continue to be broken down.
—Ramsay MacDonald to T.M. Healy, 1924

With the Anglo-Irish Treaty came the partition of Ireland, and the establishment of two new sovereign entities at Dublin and Stormont. The Irish officer corps constituted a bridging link across this divide, and certain senior officers, including many who had been involved in pre-war volunteering, made contributions to the new governments, north and south. For northern officers, the preservation of the Union did not necessarily mean a return to the status quo; the upsets of the previous decade, and the uncertainties created by partition, impelled military officers to take a leading role in the Northern Irish government. In the north as in the south, there were nonetheless some continuities. The Irish link to the British Empire continued to be expressed in terms of military Irishness, and serving and retired officers continued to play a social role within the 'Protestant Free State'—as Ian D'Alton has dubbed the self-contained, pillarised world of post-Partition southern Protestants.[1] In the governing structures of the Free State, however, officers of the *ancien régime* had comprehensively ceded their claim to the legitimate narrative of military Irishness, to new bodies that evinced very little overlap with the old structures.

© The Author(s) 2019
L. Sweeney, *Irish Military Elites, Nation and Empire, 1870–1925*,
https://doi.org/10.1007/978-3-030-19307-2_9

According to Bill Kissane, 'the fact that the civil war was preceded by a nationalist revolution in which constitutional and military methods were conjoined ... predisposed [Sinn Féin] to see the military divisions of 1922–23 in constitutional terms ... military divisions became party political divisions.'[2] In other words, the marginalisation of the old Irish military elite was an integral part of the Irish revolution.

Irish officers attempted to continue inhabiting the patrician roles they had grown used to, although the Civil War had made them a target, and many officers chose to leave Ireland for Britain or the empire rather than risking their lives. For those that remained, the post-war problems of unemployment and cultural obsolescence did not abate. The perspectives and experiences of diverse examples of Irish officers illustrate the extent to which the First World War and Irish revolution, in the words of Dunraven, 'killed society'.[3] For officers, the contestation over diverging Irish identities in this period rang the death-knell for the military Irishness forged in the Victorian period.

CIVIL WAR AND PARTITION, 1920–23

Many officers and their families (including the brother of Field Marshal Henry Wilson) were targeted in the campaign of house burnings, hundreds of which took place in the years 1920–23. Before 1922, British military authorities considered assisting loyalists who sought to leave Ireland, and instituting special protection measures for those determined to 'stick it out'; however, the commander of the Dublin district found such plans to be impractical, and simply advised loyalists who considered themselves at risk of attack to leave the country.[4] The withdrawal of British active service units in 1922 did not cause reprisals against representatives of the old order to abate. House burnings, mainly concentrated in the rural parts of Munster and Connacht, particularly Counties Tipperary, Cork, and Galway, were carried out for a number of reasons, from local grievances to political intimidation. Some were burned by the IRA, if they viewed the inhabitants as being either 'pro-English' or connected in some way with the Free State government—the houses of four senators, three of whom also had connections to the British Army, were deliberately targeted.[5] Others were burned in reprisal for the actions of the Black and Tans and Auxiliaries, or for reasons revolving around land distribution and rents—the same old cause of agrarian unrest which recalled the struggles of 20 years previous.

The end of the War of Independence did not stop the burnings; when Durrow Abbey in County Offaly was burned in early 1923, the perpetrators claimed an anti-imperial agenda in destroying the property of those allied to the Free State. Ironically, Durrow was one of the few big houses to be rebuilt after the Civil War, when its owners returned to Ireland—an example of the powerful and compelling ties of Irishness which were under contestation in this period.[6] Irish gentry officers, like Maurice Moore, found themselves doubly targeted, for being both landlords and soldiers. A particularly shocking incident in the targeting of ex-officers was the case of General Beauchamp Doran, who was beaten by assailants claiming the authority of the Provisional Government in Rosslare in 1922. The incident provoked calls in the House of Commons for government assistance to re-settle ex-soldiers outside of Ireland, and Winston Churchill noted that in the five months since the signing of the Anglo-Irish Treaty, ten serving or former officers had been killed in Ireland.[7] Remarkably enough, even while the threat of house burnings and physical harm provided a strong inducement to leave Ireland, the reactions of inhabitants of the big houses were restrained. Where one would expect anger and resentment at the destruction of centuries of tradition and the wiping out of an entire way of life, letters discussing fire damage, written in reflection after the heat of the moment had dissipated, tend to express only mild sympathy and a general sense of resignation.[8] A common theme of uncertainty and despair, rather than anger or frustration, pervades the correspondence of the jobless and homeless officers in this period.

Ex-officers, mainly 'temporary gentlemen' and oftentimes known personally to the assailants, were often targeted. However, it appears that simply having been an officer was not enough on its own to place these men in harm's way. Paul Taylor's recent work on army veterans in Ireland found that there was no systematic campaign against ex-servicemen, although many were targeted for being loyalists, rendering assistance to the British Army or police, or for no personal reason as part of campaigns of extortion or the seizing of weapons. One ex-British Army soldier in Cork was assassinated apparently because he had joined the Free State Army.[9] Reasons for violence, and the degree of violence meted out, varied widely: some ex-officers were executed; others, like Captain Timothy Collins of Co. Cork, were 'as a result of my service in H.M. Forces ... practically boycotted'; at the other end of the spectrum, Thomas Glynne of Co. Longford complained that the IRA had stolen his bicycle.[10] Even between garrison towns there was variation: Fermoy evinced high levels of intimidation, while Birr was, in the words of one officer, a 'placid oasis in the heart of stormy Ireland'.[11]

Some officers who remained in Ireland were characterised by strong links of affinity and paternalism like Bryan Cooper, who encapsulated a sense of *noblesse oblige*, explaining 'there were times when an officer must be prepared to run what would otherwise appear unnecessary risks' in order to set an example.[12] Others who remained were content to live quiet lives, attempting to make themselves invisible. The experiences of such officers, either through fear or embarrassment, constitute a historical silence. Those who remained relied on a community network in places where this still functioned after 1922, though it was many years before the acrimony, suspicion, and apprehension borne of the backlash against the landlord class and other pre-independence social elites abated.[13]

Officers who departed oftentimes did so for pragmatic reasons, seeking employment in the empire. Colonel Richard Pope Hennessy, whose background included multiple generations of imperial service, recorded that he was motivated by 'my individual feeling of loyalty as a soldier to the King and my belief that, in the main, the British Empire—with all its faults … is the most potent human instrument for good'.[14] The vast majority of officers were sympathetic with such views.

Historical scholarship has tended to focus on religious difference and the phenomenon of Protestant depopulation, but other factors, such as class, have been under-emphasised.[15] According to Hart, the majority of targets were local figures, mostly of the middle class with comparatively few high-profile landowners targeted.[16] Targeted reprisals were an urban as well as rural phenomenon, and, as was always the case in Ireland, the significant factor here was the *threat* of violence, which was far more extensively employed than were actual acts of violence. After the Treaty, which popular loyalist thought viewed as capitulation, strings of furniture vans from across the country, conveying the belongings of departing families, and the accrued *matériel* of dozens of military stations large and small, became a familiar sight.[17] Large landowners felt an inducement to leave, having faced a declining social role in Ireland since the 1880s.[18] Such people also found it much easier to depart, as they might have family or other properties in Britain where they could weather the storm. Those more atypical middle-class officers who faced higher levels of violence, including many 'temporary gentlemen', had little choice but to attempt to melt back into civilian society, or perhaps to try their luck in the colonies.

A fellow officer wrote to General Godley from India in 1921, in sympathy for the plight of officers in Ireland, which encapsulates the experience of dislocation following a revolution which, for Irish officers in particular, had taken on the characteristics of a civil war:

> It is too sad to think of the horrible time you are having as regards Ireland, and one does feel sorry for the regiments in that country. They must lead a dog's life of it and often, I daresay, wish they were back in the trenches where they knew exactly who were friends and who were enemies—while they can never know this in Ireland.[19]

The unfortunate undercurrent running through these officers' experiences is the extent to which, in hindsight, the military administration was the agent of its own downfall, as much as the victim of forces beyond its control. As in 1914, officers fled from political responsibilities, allowing the implicit prejudices of an eroding elite to impair their judgment in prosecuting the War of Independence. The sympathetic attitude of many individual Irish officers toward their countrymen on both sides of the conflict could not overcome this institutional inertia.

On the question of partition, which had been instituted with the Government of Ireland Act in 1920, Irish officers were hesitant and equivocal. While northern Unionist leaders had accepted the necessity of partition as the cost of their survival even before the First World War, certain officers still hoped in 1920 that the inevitable sundering of the island could be avoided.[20] The rump of the Irish officer class continued to inhabit an elevated social role in the Northern Irish government of Craig, whom hundreds of officers had backed since 1912–13, and in the new Senate of Southern Ireland. Officers thus represented an enduring link between North and South in the ensuing period, and were reluctant partitioners. Colonel J. G. Vaughan-Hart, for example, was a landowner whose grandfather, also a military officer, had settled in County Donegal in the early nineteenth century. During the deliberations over the boundary he lobbied unsuccessfully for Donegal to be included within Northern Ireland, for the dual reasons that it was 'the most northerly county in Ireland' and because, as the majority of the business of his estate had to be transacted in Derry, the new border would represent significant 'inconvenience and delay through customs'. Vaughan-Hart held that 'in this case the wishes of a proportion of the inhabitants should not outweigh the Geographic and Economic conditions'.[21] Conversely, Captain Riciardo in Co. Tyrone thought a 'really neutral chairman of Bound. Comm.' would 'lop off the areas where local govt. is in the hands of a nationalist majority … we [in Sion Mills] should join our 3 county friends & personally I should not be sorry—but the N. area would be reduced to absurdity.'[22] In the face of the complex situation in the borderlands, inertia carried the day and the *de facto* county border was made permanent.

Economic considerations and patronage, as before, continued to operate between officers even across the border. Captain Jack White, who had become disillusioned with the cause of the Irish workers that he had championed since 1913, wrote to his friend the equally controversial Captain Wilfrid Spender, who for his aforementioned high-profile resignation from the army on unionist principles had been rewarded with the post of Secretary to the Cabinet of Northern Ireland. Because of their affinity as troublemaking officers and their burgeoning friendship, White requested help in finding 'a job', adding that he 'would be willing to serve a modest apprenticeship'. Spender's reply is indicative of the continuing lack of opportunity for Irish officers in the post-war era: 'We are absolutely overwhelmed with applications for our Civil Service, and have been obliged to decline the offers of a very large number of people, including a Brigadier General.'[23]

In other ways, regimental affinity and shared experience contributed to the maintenance of cross-border links. Southern officers who had served in the Inniskilling Dragoons or other northern regiments maintained strong connections with their comrades.[24] The few former officers elected to the Free State Senate, as the 'official' representation of the old officer establishment, were able to discuss with their counterparts in Northern Ireland with a pre-existing sense of military regard. These officer senators, despite constituting representatives of both the gentry and aristocracy, Catholic and Protestant, were conflated as a single entity— the *ancien régime*. In the north, however, in the words of McConville, 'Ascendency rule lasted with the almost automatic election of prime ministers from patrician families until a businessman, Mr. Brian Faulkner, succeeded Captain Chichester Clarke in 1971.'[25] The definition of 'patrician' is, of course, open to interpretation: Northern Ireland's first prime minister, Lord Craigavon, served as an officer in the Boer War, and though his background was eminently respectable, it was that of an industrialist: distilling was the family business. It was not until the third holder of the office, Basil Brooke, that we find a leader who was cut from the familiar cloth of the traditional gentry officer. The civil service that these men presided over was well stocked with Irish officers, such as the Co. Wexford native Arthur Solly-Flood, who developed the northern state's own, new manifestation of military Irishness: the B-Specials, a corps of armed special constables imbued with what Bew, Gibbon, and Patterson call a 'pseudo-military' character.[26]

The experience of gentry officers in Northern Ireland, in the words of Olwen Purdue, 'rather than being a romantic story of decline and isolation … was more often the pragmatic one of adjustment and survival'.[27] The upheavals, social and political, of land and Home Rule agitation in 1879–1914 had impacted upon the northern landlords just as it had done the southern. The area of the new border had been, and continued to be, a particularly fertile breeding ground for Irish officers, from whence a number of the senior Irishmen in this study hailed.[28] Landed families in the new Northern Ireland had the security of a stronger economy, and a continuing role within that economy; enduring links to employment channels in Britain; and, vitally important, 'the continued political and social role that many of them played in the state of Northern Ireland … allowing and encouraging them to survive as a cohesive social group, and behave as an elite well into the twentieth century'.[29] Their continuing social role can be discerned by contrasting the different rituals of war commemoration in both jurisdictions: in contrast to the Irish Free State's downplayed, delayed, and marginalised national war memorial at Islandbridge, dedications of memorials in the north were seized upon enthusiastically by the government. While dedicating the Coleraine war memorial, James Craig exhorted his audience, in the name of the fallen, to 'stand firm, and to give away none of Ulster's soil'.[30] Commemoration of the British Army retained an official public role in the north, and was an important tool in the creation and reinforcement of state legitimacy.

Despite these momentous changes in the political and social life of Ireland, it is remarkable that in general the life courses of officers in this period continued as normal into the middle decades of the twentieth century. Certainly, southern Irish military elites were less visible in 1923 than they had been in 1914—a combination of the devastating losses of the war, the IRA raids, and the potential attraction of upping sticks and moving near to English cousins had diminished the gentry officer stock by an appreciable degree.[31] Many military families also settled on a semi-permanent basis in north-western India, as many Irish officers had done since the early nineteenth century. However, many others remained rooted in Ireland, constituting a liminal, semi-concealed Protestant space where the performativity of the old order could persist behind closed doors.[32] Lennox Robinson, in his biography of the Sligo landowner, Unionist MP, British Army officer, and Free State Senator Bryan Cooper, characterises the changes thus: 'It must be insisted again and again that two changes are taking place: the passing of power, and, curiously with it, the realisation by a few sensitive and intelligent landowners like Bryan Cooper that their life and interests are inseparably woven in with the Irish people.'[33] Irish officers maintained a condition of 'shabby gentility' in Ireland, and imagined themselves 'like passengers on a ship seized by mutineers, the members of old Ascendancy families continued … as if determined to give an example to the lascars who had come up from the bilges to take over the ship, who might otherwise disgrace themselves by panic or excess'.[34]

DEPARTURES AND RETURNS: IRELAND AND THE BRITISH EMPIRE IN THE 1920s

Irish officers continued to look to the empire, though some clearly felt the pull of national affinity drawing them to Ireland even after independence.[35] The preservation of a connection to the overseas empire is evidenced by the continuing popularity of imperial service: in the 1920s, one-third of the Indian Medical Service was still staffed by Irish officers, a testament to the continuing role of Trinity College and the Royal College of Surgeons as important centres for professional training. Further professionalisation of the army after the First World War contributed to the continuing slow colonisation of the British officer corps by the middle classes, an elite corps being regarded by the Labour prime minister Ramsay MacDonald as 'neither necessary nor desirable'.[36] While the Irish regiments with recruiting areas in the southern counties were disbanded in 1922, Irish officers continued to exploit imperial opportunities for professional migration.[37] There were compelling economic reasons to explain this form of occupational migration, though after 1922 officers' accounts are also infused with a tangible feeling of rootlessness, of inhabiting a sense of Irishness that no longer existed.

Conditions that governed who stayed and who went were manifold; from the aforementioned sense of Ireland as 'home' or one of the multifaceted conceptions of Irish nationality, to more mundane reasons of family or economic necessity. Imperial service remained at the centre of these inducements, being integral both to the officer's sense of self and to his livelihood. For those officers formerly of the southern Irish regiments who found themselves cut loose, the imperial connection became even more important. The Indian Army always required experienced officers, but there were also other opportunities to be seized. After some lean years William Kemmis was successful in receiving the patronage he had long sought from Field Marshal Haig: 'The Maharajah of Baroda asked me to recommend to him some reliable officer who would undertake the duty of supplying him with horses. I at once thought of you, as the work would not only be interesting but should be profitable.'[38]

British imperial officers continued to roam the world, though they were seemingly of a more diverse and peripatetic type than had previously been the case. There were those in the 'Wild Geese' tradition, like Jack White and John Henry Patterson, who had initially embarked on an imperial career for adventure and advancement, and had found a cause while overseas. In White's case, it was revolution and trade unionism; in Patterson's, Zionism. White's imperialism was dashed by his experiences in the Boer War, leading him to join the Irish Citizen Army. The post-war condition of Ireland, however, demoralised him and his departure, though inflected by his socialist ideals, echoes the sectarian worries of his compatriots in the 'Protestant Free State': he 'worked for political and economic freedom in Catholic Ireland, and is proud of having done so; [but] … till Southern Ireland is freed from the enslaving elements of Roman Catholicism she cannot gain independence'.[39] White's radicalism led to his imprisonment and banishment from his home in Northern Ireland in 1931, when he was ordered (unconstitutionally) by the government to absent himself from the state. He landed in London, where he became part of a cosmopolitan anti-imperial network of left-wing revolutionaries from as far afield as Ceylon and the United States, and went on to fight in the Spanish Civil War on the republican side.[40] Also fighting with the International Brigades was Henry Kelly, who had been achieved the rank of major in both the British and Free State armies. White did not directly serve the empire again until the outbreak of the Second World War, when he made an unlikely alliance with General Hubert Gough in an attempt to promote recruitment to the British Army from both parts of Ireland.[41] White's life was potentially the most extreme expression of the dislocation of the Irish officer in the early twentieth century.

John Henry Patterson was a Protestant ranker officer from a humble background in Co. Westmeath. He garnered a degree of social cachet through service in the Indian military works department, though he became well-known mainly for his heady written accounts of life in the colonies, including 1907s *The Man-Eaters of Tsavo*.[42] Briefly returning to Ireland between imperial sojourns in 1913, he commanded a UVF battalion in Belfast. His command of the Jewish Legion during the First World War developed in him an impassioned Zionism, and he spent many years subsequently campaigning for the formation of a Jewish state while living in England and the United States.[43] The British Empire was the making of these two men, and while they continued to express a sense of Irishness, neither felt truly at home in post-war Ireland, north or south. Other officers, like Edward Bellingham, saw their life in the Free State as akin to retirement—while sitting in Seanad Éireann he devoted his spare time to maintaining his estate as a gentleman farmer—and only returned to active duty in the RAF at the outbreak of the Second World War.[44] Others still, like the middle-class Derry-born Joseph Aloysius Byrne, a long-time veteran of the Irish Command, found their careers blocked after garnering a reputation as 'political' officers in the eyes of the British officer establishment. Byrne's Catholicism and his plans for utilising special forces during the War of Independence were points of contention to the army command of 1920. After independence he elected to leave the army and seek his fortune in the empire, becoming Governor of Sierra Leone in 1927.[45]

There were Irish officers of the more conventional type, too, who continued to dominate regiments of the British and Indian armies—men from military families like Colonel Kendal Chavasse, whose connections secured him a commission in the Royal Irish Fusiliers. In Bombay in the 1930s, he encountered a community of Irishmen whose conception of military Irishness was still predominantly an imperial one, inflected with the national touches of Jameson whiskey and recordings of Irish reels in the officers' mess.[46] According to Alexander Bubb, 'the romance of the wandering Irish mercenary has survived the passing of empire, because he has changed to a figure of discontent, resistance [and] victimhood from one of loyalty, imperial aspiration and hope of social advancement.'[47]

Those who took part in these faraway manifestations of Irishness were unable to distance themselves, however, from the situation in Ireland any more than their forebears of a generation previous. The impact of Irish political realities on the overseas empire was demonstrated most dramatically with the mutiny of sixty-nine soldiers of the Connaught Rangers in 1920, in a curious inversion of the Curragh incident six years earlier.[48] This time, the soldiers protesting against conditions in Ireland were rankers in a self-identified 'Catholic Irish Regiment', with the attendant nationalist connotations that such an alignment increasingly brought to mind in the early 1920s.[49] Initially, the Rangers officers were uncertain how to deal with the mutiny, which seemed to be limited enough in scope: initially, soldiers ran up an Irish flag over the cantonment, and then voluntarily submitted themselves for arrest. However, after an attempt to seize weapons from the armoury the authorities cracked down, and one soldier—Private Daly—was executed for his role in organising the mutineers.[50] Over half of the mutineers joined the Civic Guard or the National Army on their release.[51]

It was perhaps unsurprising that the conduct of the British Army in Ireland would resonate through the large body of Irish soldiers serving around the globe—one can easily imagine, as a contrite Frank Crozier imagined, 'the men of Connaught, who had fought in the Great War for Empire, opening their Irish mail under the burning sun … acting as the stone wall of British imperialism, reading of the Black and Tan atrocities in the West of Ireland.'[52] As the correspondent of the London *Times* remarked, it was a sign that '[t]he situation is altered. War in Ireland will mean war on Ireland, and it may do mischief past reckoning':

> The effect on many Loyalists is apparent. Such fighting would threaten the Army. Reports from the Connaught Rangers in India show that there is a storm brewing. Here were Irishmen as completely as possible away from the contact of Sinn Fein. News came in which they presumably took to mean that the British Army was being used for such purposes in Ireland that they could not remain part of it. No such mentality disclosed itself anywhere among Irish troops in 1916.[53]

However, the perhaps remarkable reality was that, as Peter Karsten contends, the Connaught Rangers mutiny was a sole exception to the general pattern of 'business as usual' in the army.[54]

It was, curiously enough, the middle-class professional officers whose way of life changed the least. According to Brian Inglis, life in the leafy suburbs of Dublin carried on much as it had done in previous decades: the old regimental banners and war memorials telling the deeds of generations of the prominent local families remained a visible manifestation of the imperial connection in the quiet naves of the Church of Ireland throughout the country, and middle-class life remained inflected with the exotic influences of colonial service and military pomp. Manifestations of the 'empire at home' were still tangible in commodities, attitudes, and popular culture. Brian Inglis writes of interwar Malahide:

It was in fact, quite a typical English village. It could have had a Miss Mitford for chronicler, a John Betjeman as its poet laureate. But Malahide was in … that part of Ireland which had severed itself from the United Kingdom. In India too, I believe, a few English colonies stayed on after the country of their adoption gained its independence, continuing to behave exactly as they had done under the British Raj; not out of calculated defiance but simply because they could not believe that their world could be overturned by the signatures of English politicians they despised and local nationalist leaders they detested. So it was in Malahide, because the members of the old Protestant Ascendency were so firmly established there, they could live their lives almost as they had before the Treaty of 1921.[55]

The general studies of officer demography by Spiers and others all agree that the social composition of the officer corps did not change significantly until the 1950s.[56] This, coupled with anecdotal evidence from Irish officers in the 1920s, suggests that officers from Irish military families continued to make up a large percentage of officers, while the Irish middle class did not see much of a change. Steven O'Connor finds that Irish officers in the 1920s still 'generally came from better-off backgrounds as indicated by their exclusive education'.[57] The 1920s saw a reversal of pre-war trends which had seen increasing upper middle-class representation in the officer corps, with 16.8% coming from this background compared to 36.9% of officers coming from the traditional military families which had dominated Irish recruitment since the late nineteenth century.[58] Interestingly enough, officers from Irish elite schools made up a greater percentage of Irish officers in the interwar period than Irishmen from an English public school background—35.7% versus 22.5%.[59] This adds plausibility to the argument that there was a thriving, imperially focussed dimension to the 'Protestant Free State'. The National Army, by contrast, attracted few former British officers; the middle class, as in the British forces, also constituted but a small constituency in the national forces, again with the exception of the technical branches.[60]

Outside of the imperial lifeboat of the 'Protestant Free State', the Anglo-Irish, who either self-identified as such or had the moniker applied to them by others, became increasingly aware of their difference: the moderate Nationalist MP Stephen Gwynn observed, 'all my life I have been spiritually hyphenated without knowing it.'[61] This partitioning of the mind and the country may have led Irish officers to ascribe an even greater significance to regimental affinity and imperial service as markers of identity. When these men returned home in British uniform, the majority did not face discrimination from their fellow countrymen.[62] However, according to no less divisive a figure than Frank Crozier, there was a real or imagined frisson of tension which was tangible to the officer class in the post-independence south: 'make no mistake about it, the Irish hotel proprietor, waiter, jarvey, gillie or railway porter has not yet lost his sense of judgment and discrimination—he can tell the difference between the "gentleman" of 1932 and 1914 at a glance. That is why he was so "shocked" in 1920 and 1921 when he heard about "love", yet knew there was "no love lost."'[63] Crozier struggles to express the intangible, unsettling feeling of homelessness and dislocation that accompanied the loss of officers' social position as a component of the Irish elite. This fundamentally altered emotional landscape made it all the more difficult for officers to continue living under a political regime many of them had actively sought to prevent coming into being.[64]

In the more anonymous urban setting, according to Jane Leonard, this feeling of othering could express itself more violently: 'interwar Dublin was an extremely unnerving and dangerous place to wear service medals and poppies. Parading veterans were heckled and beaten up.'[65] Those who had been involved in the military administration were also unlikely to return—John French, who had left the Irish Command and the Lord Lieutenancy in 1921, had hoped to return to Ireland in his old age, but Viscount Fitzalan informed him in no uncertain terms: 'your presence in Ireland would now be a disturbing factor … [if] the Republicans win … neither you nor I nor any of our friends can stay here.'[66] It was a harsh reality check, although in the event it transpired that once again the apprehension was worse than the reality—officers did remain and eked out a life for themselves in the Free State, even as an unlucky handful endured the targeting of the IRA.[67] They constituted a continuity, an institutional memory, though they regarded themselves as a spent force. Dunraven provided a succinct epitaph for the Irish military elite: 'the war killed society. The old order passes.'[68]

'THE OLD ORDER PASSES': MILITARY IRISHNESS IN THE FREE STATE

The 'old order' was not heavily represented in the newly developing traditions of military Irishness: the National Army and the anti-treaty IRA. Considering the very small proportion of officers who supported republican nationalism, as well as the aforementioned targeting of serving and former British officers by the IRA, it is unsurprising that few, if any, officers found themselves in that sort of company.[69] On the other side, the attractiveness of the National Army to former officers, or to prospective young officers from the same social backgrounds, could not compare to the opportunities and rewards of imperial service. While the National Army sought out Irishmen with First World War experience, these were almost entirely men who had been private soldiers or NCOs; Jane Leonard's work on Irish soldiers in this period identifies only a handful of ex-British officers, though there certainly were more.[70] Among the officers examined in this study, too, very few had a connection to the National Army, and as a group they shared few commonalities. Commentators in the *Times* of London remarked on this change in social composition, judging the new army as being of 'dubious character', though the presence of a small number of senior officers who 'gained [their] experience in the service of the Crown' was cited as a positive influence.[71]

Other scholars, notably Taylor, have examined in-depth the prevalence of British Army ex-servicemen in the uniform of the Free State, though without differentiating between former officers and enlisted men. The evidence seems to suggest that, of a peak National Army officer corps establishment of **3500**, as many as **50%** may have been former British soldiers—though ex-British officers made up a very small proportion of this group, which Taylor finds was mainly composed of former enlisted men. There will always be a degree of ambiguity here, however; even the Free State government itself did not appear entirely certain how many former British servicemen, particularly former Great War veterans, there were in the National Army.[72]

The seemingly low numbers of officers 'crossing over' into the National Army is unsurprising, considering the persistently strong representation of Irishmen in the British Army officer corps in the 1920s, and the imperial outlook retained by Irishmen from military families; Irishmen who sought careers in the British officer corps before 1922 simply continued to do so afterwards. This further suggests that 'temporary gentlemen' with war experience, who were after all, mostly drawn from the professional middle classes, tended to return to their former employment instead of continuing into the officer corps of the National Army. As a further confirmation of the dramatic demographic shift between the British and National

armies, Taylor identifies 'several hundred' former National Volunteer officers in the National Army—only a small percentage of the thousands of
Volunteer officers who took up arms in Ireland's pre-First World War militaristic moment.[73]

Those few former British officers who held commissions in the
National Army came from a diverse range of backgrounds, as illustrated
by William Richard English-Murphy and Eric Dorman-Smith. The former, a temporary officer commissioned in 1915, joined the IRA before
being commissioned into the Free State Army as a general in 1922. Like
so many FSA officers and soldiers, he only served until the end of the
Civil War, though he was rewarded for his service with the post of
Commissioner of the Dublin Metropolitan Police. Dorman-Smith on the
other hand was a scion of the Catholic gentry and was already a Sandhurst
cadet at the outbreak of the First World War. He personally hauled down
the Union flag at Carlow barracks during the British withdrawal in 1922,
and his illustrious career in the British Army took him across the empire
before he retired as a Brigadier in 1944. He had a deep sense of Irish
nationality, and in his retirement he actively supported and was often
consulted by the Irish army. His true allegiance, rather peculiarly, was to
irredentist republicanism, and in an odd parallel of the Ireland of 40
years' previous, he drilled IRA fighters in the grounds of his estate during
the northern campaign of the 1950s.[74] In any case, compared to the
intake of elite Irishmen to the British Army after 1922, the Free State
officers drawn from this social provenance were merely a drop in the
ocean. The soldiers of the National Army joked that these men had been
'left behind' by the British in order to introduce Free State officers to the
old Curragh traditions.[75]

Many of the Free State officers did, however, come from an Irish elite
school background, particularly from Clongowes and Belvedere Colleges,
institutions which, as we have seen, were able to ride the wave of Irish
independence, and this coupled with the officers who had experience of
the British Army as enlisted men combined to create an atmosphere which
would not have been unrecognisable to a British officer. According to
David Fitzpatrick, one such officer who was hosted by the Free State Army
in 1926 reported that the senior officers 'held their liquor well' and the
juniors would generally 'be socially acceptable to a British officers' mess'.[76]
Other gentry officers of the old school, such as Colonel Hutcheson-Poë
and Captain Henry de Courcy Wheeler, the Irish officer who accepted the

surrender of the 1916 rebels, remained broadly supportive and interested in the development of the new army.[77] There was a certain regard for the Free State fighters (Fig. 9.1): when Irish troops came to replace the British in the Curragh, they found they could not hoist the new flag of the State as, by tradition, all the flagpoles had been cut down—but they also found the grates blackened, the billiard tables ironed, and the cues re-tipped.[78] It is also worth noting that, among Irishmen of a military persuasion who did join the Free State Army, the prospect of transferring across the water in order to pursue a military career in the British Army could be discussed without taboo by the mid-1920s—this suggests a fundamentally professional outlook prevailed.[79]

Fig. 9.1   Major General Seán Mac Eoin of the National Army (centre) takes command of Athlone Barracks from a British officer, 1922. There was little continuity between the officer corps of the *ancien régime* and that of the Free State. However, many Free State officers had fought as enlisted men during the First World War. *Courtesy of the National Library of Ireland*

All of these indications suggest that, for middle-class professionals, Catholic and Protestant, unionist and nationalist, the Irish revolution was not as significant a cause of long-term upheaval as it was for the landed class—or, indeed, for the Protestant working class.[80] While middle-class career officers and 'temporary gentlemen' were disproportionately targeted in the revolutionary period, their material conditions, and thus opportunities for employment, did not change dramatically. Civilian professions, which had been associated with moderate Nationalism before the Great War, found themselves able to weather the upheavals of the revolutionary period and to persist in their social role, even after the Irish Parliamentary Party lost its political relevance. Following the Civil War and the normalisation of conditions in Ireland, middle-class officers continued to embody the connection between Ireland and the overseas empire, while elite Irish schools found a niche producing ecumenical officer material, to be found in both Irish and imperial armies.

There was a degree of official collaboration between the British Army and the Free State Army as well, despite the vocal protests of some unionist officers. By the late 1920s, it was a fairly commonplace occurrence for National Army officers to travel to England for courses of instruction at Woolwich or Aldershot. Between 1927 and 1931, 25 such officer exchanges had taken place, and the officers involved seemed to have given a good account of themselves and avoided controversy.[81] National Army officers also attended courses in the United States in this period, at training institutions such as Fort Benning and Fort Leavenworth.[82]

While the majority of nationalist officers generally faded from public life after the end of the militaristic political 'moment'—roughly from the foundation of the volunteer movements in 1913 to the end of martial law in 1922—there were some who returned to public life in the Free State, and even those who, in the realignment of post-war Irish politics, became converts to Sinn Féin. It is interesting also to note that the only two non-Unionist army veterans to be elected in 1918, both for Sinn Féin, were officers from landed backgrounds: Robert Barton and Captain William Archer Redmond.[83] Robert Childers Barton came from a County Wicklow Protestant landowning background. He developed nationalist sympathies through shared experiences with his friend and cousin, Erskine Childers, and after devoting his early years to the development of the family estate he gained a commission in the Royal Dublin Fusiliers in 1914.[84] Stationed in Dublin during the Easter Rising, his experiences guarding prisoners caused his sympathy towards the republican movement to grow, and in 1917 he resigned his commission and joined Sinn Féin, eventually standing successfully as their candidate for Wicklow West in the 1919 election.[85] In the same year he was charged by the military courts then operating in Ireland for making seditious speeches calculated to cause unrest, and gave only the standard defence: 'I am a soldier of the Irish Republic and I repudiate your authority, so I refuse to answer any question', which the prosecution was unaccustomed to hearing from an officer:

> Capt. Wallis [the prosecutor] contended that such words coming from a man of the standing of the accused were calculated to have more effect and be much more dangerous than coming from some irresponsible person. He submitted that the present unhappy state of the country was very largely due to that sort of encouragement of crime by Mr. Barton and other responsible persons.[86]

Barton's example illustrates that, as in the pre-war period, officer status did not preclude political involvement, nor was the military establishment all of one mind during the period of martial law.

Other former officers found a much more natural home in the new establishment politics. The Cosgrave government earned the respect of the old elite through conciliation and goodwill.[87] Lord Dunraven became, and remained, a supporter of Cumann na nGaedeal and dutifully carried out his role as landlord and senator under the new regime.[88]

The departure of the large British Army garrisons from Ireland had a hugely detrimental effect on the life of the social elite, both in Dublin and in the former garrison towns. With the falling off in officer memberships, the Kildare Street Club lost a significant amount of prestige, and saw a corresponding decline in memberships from landlords and civilian elites as well.[89] This suggests that, in addition to officer status constituting an avenue for social advancement and socialisation into pre-war elite social circles, it was also the glue that held these circles together. Without this intrinsic component, the Irish elite as it had existed before the war splintered into pieces. However, the handful of ex-officers who had been nominated to the Free State Senate, in official recognition and partial deference to the interests of this group—Sir Walter Nugent, Sir William Hickie, Sir Edward Bellingham, Sir John Keane, Lord Dunraven, Bryan Mahon and Bryan Cooper—as well as many of their senatorial colleagues, persisted as members of the Kildare Street Club, which saved it from declining to total obscurity.[90]

Existence in the Free State, with its new mythologies and identity, required a degree of soul-searching from officers. Captain Berkeley, one of the pro-Irish Volunteer officers, appended some marginalia to his old papers in the aftermath of southern independence, perhaps out of embarrassment for his views at the time. In a letter to Maurice Moore dated 2 September 1914, he complained that the Belfast Volunteers had passed a resolution against Redmond's call for enlistment, which 'seems to me extremely injudicious … unless you or someone in authority stop it … it was proposed by a conceited young ass called Connolly.' To this Berkeley later added, 'a better man than I thought, far better.'[91]

Enthusiastic nationalists and Gaelic revivalists like Shane Leslie perforce took on the role of ambassadors for their fellow Anglo-Irishmen remaining in the country, casting a history of military service (among other distinctions) as evidence of a contribution to the glory of Ireland as a whole: writing in 1946, Leslie asked 'the triumphant Catholic nationalists to consider whether a case can be made for Protestant patriotism and landlord beneficence in the past'. Leslie talked of the contribution of the remaining patrician families of his home county of Monaghan: 'each of the four families surviving accomplished something noteworthy for Ireland in their day … All four families have been represented in the World Wars, which is typical of all Anglo-Irish surviving.'[92] The traditional metaphors that demarcated military Irishness had changed, however—even as the traditional occupational structure of the corps persisted. No longer were Irish officers in the British Army to be counted in the tradition of the 'Wild Geese' as they had been seen by officers and cultural nationalists before the Great War—they had become no more than servants of a foreign power.

'THE WAR KILLED SOCIETY'

Irish officers conceived of the 'imperial connection' as vital to Ireland, and from the first stirrings of republican rebellion they saw their priority as protecting it: Lord Monteagle outlined the myriad 'points of contact between Ireland and Empire—army, foreign affairs, post, telegraphs, railways, ports'.[93] Its vision of a 'greater Britain'—a feeling, in Dunraven's words, 'that England was everywhere'—was central to Irish officers' identity.[94] The preservation of the imperial connection in the 1920s allowed them to continue to play the role of 'imperial Irishmen' even as the military establishment was marginalised in Irish society.

Was Dunraven right that 'the war killed society'? In terms of its terrible human cost, the Great War undoubtedly took a heavy toll.[95] However, the political salience of the War of Independence and the effect of southern independence and partition on the officer class cannot be discounted. Irish officers of the old military establishment found themselves in the minority and, as with any minority in the newly partitioned Irelands, they suffered consequences: resentment, loss of status, and segregation from public life.[96] However, their retreat from political salience meant that officers could interact apolitically after 1922, recalling the conditions of the Victorian era. There was little resentment or animosity directed against officers in general, though certain individuals like Crozier still contrite about his role in the Auxiliaries, felt with embarrassment: 'The British Crown was "let down" by disloyal men operating in a uniform known, the world over, with respect.'[97] The Irish officer class(es) in the Free State faced a dilemma between two facets of their identity. When Ireland had been part of the United Kingdom, officers 'did not regard their nationality as integral to their military experience'.[98] However, in the contentious period of nationalist upheaval and civil war, in the long Irish revolutionary decade, the question of nationality was unavoidable. These officers who for so long had been regarded, and had regarded themselves, as the centre of an imperial social life, became irreversibly marginalised. The various niches that minorities of officers found for themselves after 1922—in the Northern Ireland government, the overseas empire and Imperial mandates, the Irish Senate, the National Army, and the partial continuities of 'Protestant Free State'—suggest that if their 'society' was killed by the war, its ashes were scattered wide by the peace.

Notes

1. Ian d'Alton, 'The "Protestant Free State" and the Church of Ireland's Patrician celebrations, 1932", in Hill, J., and M. Lyons, eds., *Representing Irish Religious Histories: Historiography, Ideology, and Practice* (London, 2016); Ian d'Alton and Ida Milne, eds., *Protestant and Irish: The Minority's Search for a Place in Independent Ireland* (Cork University Press, 2019).
2. Bill Kissane, *The Politics of the Irish Civil War* (Oxford, 2007), p. 2.
3. Earl Dunraven, *Past Times and Pastimes*, vol. 2 (1922), p. 198.
4. Con Costello, *A Most Delightful Station: The British Army on the Curragh of Kildare, 1855–1922* (Cork, 1996), p. 324.

5. Maurice Moore and Sir John Keane were examples of officers who suffered this form of reprisal.
6. Ciarán J. Reilly, 'The Burning of Country Houses in Co. Offaly during the Revolutionary Period, 1920–3', in Dooley, Terence, and Christopher Ridgeway, eds., *The Irish Country House: Its Past, Present and Future* (Dublin, 2011), pp. 127–128.
7. Hansard, 30 May 1922, vol. 154 cc 1888–1889.
8. Haig to Kemmis, 3 June 1923. Kemmis papers, LUL; Lt-Col. W. B. Buckley to Kemmis, 20 September 1923. Kemmis papers, LUL; Reilly to Maurice Moore, 1 February 1923. Moore papers, NLI.
9. Paul Taylor, *Heroes or Traitors? Experiences of Southern Irish Soldiers Returning from the Great War 1919–1939* (Manchester, 2015), pp. 67–70.
10. Ibid. pp. 71–72.
11. Wilfrid Ewart, quoted in Taylor, *Heroes or Traitors*, p. 82.
12. Bryan Cooper, *The Tenth (Irish) Division in Gallipoli* (Dublin, 1993), p. 79.
13. A good example of this is the town of Skibbereen in west Cork, home of the Somerville, Townshend, and Coghill military families, a place which retained a strong link to the British armed forces for many years after independence. Violence eventually visited itself on the village when Admiral Somerville was murdered by the IRA in 1936.
14. Pope-Hennessy, 'The Irish Dominion'. Berkeley papers, CCA.
15. See David Fitzpatrick, 'Protestant Depopulation and the Irish Revolution', *Irish Historical Studies* 38 (2013), p. 647
16. Peter Hart, *The IRA and its Enemies* (Oxford, 1998), p. 286.
17. Tomás Irish, *Trinity in War and Revolution* (Dublin, 2015), p. 221.
18. Reilly, 'The burning of country houses', pp. 110–114.
19. W. Birdie to Godley, Murree, 6 July 1921. Godley papers, KCL.
20. Capt. Henry Harrison MC, 'The Irish Peace Conference 1920 and its Betrayal: Does the Government Want a Genuine Peace?' Irish Dominion League, Dublin, 1921. Berkeley papers, CCA.
21. J. G. Vaughan Hart, notes on County Donegal Protestant Registration Association, n.d. Lieut. Col J. G. Vaughan Hart papers, PRONI.
22. Riciardo to Nugent, Sion Mills, Co. Tyrone, 1921. Nugent papers, PRONI.
23. Spender quoted in Leo Keohane, *Captain Jack White: Imperialism, Anarchism, and the Irish Citizen Army* (Dublin, 2014), p. 213.
24. The regimental journal of the Royal Inniskilling Dragoons reported the deaths of two widely known southern ex-officers in 1965: The aforementioned Captain William Kemmis from Co. Wicklow, and Major C. A. Fleury Teulon of Glenwood Estate, Co. Cork. Kemmis papers, LUL.
25. Michael McConville, *Ascendency to Oblivion: The Story of the Anglo-Irish* (London, 1986), p. 262.

26. Paul Bew, Peter Gibbon and Henry Patterson, *Northern Ireland 1921/2001: Political Forces and Social Classes* (London, 2002), pp. 28–29.
27. Olwen Purdue, '"Ascendancy's… Last Big Jamboree": Big House Society in Northern Ireland, 1921–69', in Dooley and Ridgeway, p. 135.
28. Ibid. p. 137.
29. Purdue, 'Ascendency', p. 140.
30. James Craig, quoted in Keith Jeffery, 'Irish Varieties of Great War Commemoration', in Horne, John, and Edward Madigan, eds., *Towards Commemoration: Ireland in War and Revolution, 1912–1923* (Dublin, 2013), p. 119; Leonard, 'Lest we forget', p. 66.
31. Enda Delaney, *Demography, State and Society: Irish Migration to Britain, 1921–1971* (Liverpool, 2000), pp. 42, 70.
32. D'Alton, 'The "Protestant Free State"'.
33. Lennox Robinson, *Bryan Cooper* (London, 1931), p. 49.
34. Brian Inglis, *West Briton* (London, 1962), p. 13.
35. Maurice Collis, *Trials in Burma* (London, 1937), p. 208.
36. Downing Street to T. M. Healy, 7 February 1924. National Archives of Ireland, S.3592.
37. Steven O'Connor, *Irish Officers in the British Forces, 1922–1945* (London, 2014), p. 84.
38. Haig to Kemmis, 26 June 1927. Kemmis papers, LUL.
39. White quoted in Keohane, *Captain Jack White*, p. 207.
40. Ibid. p. 232.
41. Ibid. pp. 238–239.
42. Yanky Fachler, 'Patterson, John Henry', *Dictionary of Irish Biography*. Paterson's experience in Tsavo was the subject of the 1996 film 'The Ghost and the Darkness'. He is also commemorated in a mural on Northumberland Street in west Belfast.
43. Yanky Fachler, 'The Zion Mule Corps—and its Irish commander', *History Ireland* 11:4 (2003), pp. 36–37.
44. Richard Hawkins, 'Bellingham, Sir Edward', DIB.
45. Paul Rouse, 'Byrne, Sir Joseph Aloysius', DIB.
46. Alexander Bubb, 'The Life of the Irish Soldier in India: Representations and Self-representations, 1857–1922', *Modern Asian Studies* 46:4 (2012), p. 811.
47. Ibid. p. 811.
48. *The Times*, 25 November 1920.
49. Michael Silvestri, *Ireland and India: Nationalism, Empire and Memory* (Cambridge, 2006), p. 182.
50. Karsten, 'Suborned', p. 51.
51. Silvestri, *Ireland and India*, p. 148.
52. F. P. Crozier, *Ireland For Ever* (London, 1930), p. 103.
53. *The Times*, 7 July 1920.
54. Karsten, 'Suborned', p. 49.

55. Inglis, *West Briton*, p. 12; see also McDowell, *Land and Learning*, p. 37.
56. Razzell, 'Social Origins', p. 259; Otley, 'Militarism', p. 334.
57. O'Connor, Irish Officers, p. 15.
58. Ibid. p. 17.
59. Ibid. p. 17.
60. John P. Duggan, *A History of the Irish Army* (Dublin, 1991), p. 338; O'Connor, *Irish Officers*, p. 93; Taylor, *Heroes or Traitors?*, p. 212.
61. Stephen Gwynn, quoted in Christopher Fauske, 'A Life Merely Glimpsed: Louis MacNeice at the End of the Anglo-Irish Tradition', *The Canadian Journal of Irish Studies* 20:1 (1994), p. 19.
62. Michael McConville, *Ascendency to Oblivion: The Story of the Anglo-Irish* (London, 1986), p. 263.
63. Crozier, *Ireland For Ever*, p. 64.
64. Maume, 'Windham Thomas Wyndham-Quin', DIB; Paul Bew, *Conflict and Conciliation in Ireland 1890–1910. Parnellites and Radical Agrarians* (Oxford, 1987), p. 4; Fergus Campbell, 'Irish Popular Politics and the Making of the Wyndham Land Act, 1901–1903', *Historical Journal* 45:4 (2002), p. 756.
65. Jane Leonard, 'The Twinge of Memory: Armistice Day and Remembrance Sunday in Dublin since 1919', in English, Richard, and Graham Walker, eds., *Unionism in Modern Ireland: New Perspectives on Politics and Culture* (Basingstoke, 1996), p. 103.
66. Fitzalan quoted in Holmes, *The Little Field Marshal*, p. 363.
67. Taylor, *Heroes or Traitors*, p. 70.
68. Dunraven, *Past Times*, p.198.
69. Hart, *The IRA and its Enemies*, p. 287.
70. Leonard, 'Survivors', p. 219; Duggan, *A history of the Irish Army*, pp. 116–119.
71. *The Times*, 12 March 1923.
72. T. M. Healy to the Duke of Devonshire, 1 September 1923, 'Proposed Reciprocal Arrangements for Exchange of Information Regarding Ex-members of Imperial Forces enlisted or desiring to enlist in the National Army'. National Archives of Ireland, S.2140.
73. Taylor, *Heroes or Traitors*, p. 14.
74. Patrick Maume, 'O'Gowan, Eric Edward Dorman-Smith', DIB.
75. Costello, *A Most Delightful Station*, p. 347.
76. David Fitzpatrick, 'Unofficial Emissaries: British Army Boxers in the Irish Free State', *Irish Historical Studies* 30 (1996), pp. 215–216.
77. Duggan, *History of the Irish Army*, p. 129; Neil Richardson, *According to Their Lights: Stories of Irishmen in the British Army, Easter 1916* (Cork, 2015), pp. 385–386.
78. Costello, *A Most Delightful Station*, p. 38.

79. Fitzpatrick, 'Unofficial Emissaries', p. 213.
80. See Eugenio Biagini, 'The Protestant Minority in Southern Ireland', *Historical Journal* 55 (2012).
81. Department of External Affairs, Irish Free State, 'Army, Courses of Instruction for IFS Army Officers in England'. National Archives of Ireland, S.5401.
82. Ibid.
83. Leonard, 'Survivors', p. 220.
84. Pauric J. Dempsey and Sean Boylan, 'Barton, Robert Childers', DIB.
85. *Daily Sketch,* 1 May 1920.
86. Newspaper cutting, 'Speeches in Wicklow. Allegations against Mr. R. C. Barton MP. Courtmartial in Dublin', n.d. [1919]. Barton papers, NLI.
87. Inglis *West Briton*, p. 30.
88. Cosgrave to Dunraven, Dublin, 19 January 1933. Dunraven papers, LUL.
89. R. B. McDowell, *Land and Learning: Two Irish Clubs* (Dublin, 1993), p. 38.
90. Ibid. p. 96.
91. Berkeley to Moore, Belfast, 2 September 1914. Berkeley papers, CCA.
92. Shane Leslie, *The Irish Tangle for English Readers* (London, 1946), pp. 150–151.
93. Monteagle to Archbishop Bernard, Kildare Street Club, 19 August 1916. Bernard papers, British Library.
94. Dunraven, *Past Times*, p. 98; Cf. Andrew Thompson and Meghan Kowalsky, 'Social Life and Cultural Representation: Empire in the Public Imagination', in Thompson, Andrew, ed. *Britain's Experience of Empire in the Twentieth Century* (Oxford, 2012), pp. 253–254.
95. See Martin, 'Dulce et Decorum' passim.
96. David Fitzpatrick, *The Two Irelands 1912–1939* (Oxford, 1998), p. 6.
97. Crozier, *Ireland For Ever*, p. 99.
98. O'Connor, *Irish Officers*, p. 35.

CHAPTER 10

Conclusion

Perhaps more than any other citizens of the Empire, Irishmen are able to adapt themselves to altered circumstances. The problems of the new India … although different, may prove to be not less fruitful than those of the India where so many of their fathers won fame and fortune.
—Lord Meston addressing students of Trinity College Dublin. Irish Times, *28 February 1925*

Allegations having been made that ex-Service men had been victimised by the Irish Free State Government, a meeting, presided over by General Sir Bryan Mahon, was held … He understood that a number of ex-Service men who were in His Majesty's Forces have lost their jobs … General W.B. Hickie said that he was rather doubtful about the allegations … He believed that the Committee now about to be formed would help to allay a great deal of dissatisfaction
—Irish Times, *28 March 1925*

It was the position of the officer corps at the intersection of Ireland and the British Empire, as well as its deep interconnections with the old landed interest, that ultimately led to its marginalisation in the Irish revolutionary period. This was a long-standing and inevitable conclusion for an officer corps with a heavy representation of Irishmen in the late nineteenth century, which had, as Hew Strachan reminds us, increasingly taken on 'the features of a hereditary class' in the early twentieth century.[1] The social classes which were the driving force behind Irish republicanism, and

© The Author(s) 2019
L. Sweeney, *Irish Military Elites, Nation and Empire, 1870–1925*,
https://Doi.org/10.1007/978-3-030-19307-2_10

accordingly became its major beneficiaries, were never those which viewed the British officer corps as an attainable or acceptable career option. This led to the seemingly contradictory position of the post-independence British officer corps in the south, where many Irishmen continued to aspire to an officer's career, but at the same time the social position of British officers in Irish society had diminished precipitously. Following independence, the social dynamic changed once again: the inter-war British Army appeared to lose its sectarian connotations by and large and can be seen in the context of a more general trend of occupational migration to the United Kingdom and the overseas empire. While the memory of the First World War, conflated as it was with the Easter Rising, remained a point of contention, the army itself largely escaped the negative reputation of the Royal Irish Constabulary, which had a much longer popular memory of oppression attached to it, due to its comparative 'closeness' to communities compared to highly mobile army regiments in the years of the Land War, Home Rule riots, and the War of Independence.

While Irish officers continued to seek opportunities in the overseas empire for economic and professional migration, the cultural resonance of military Irishness was diminished because the pervasive public presence the army had in Ireland before the War had vanished entirely outside the treaty ports and the Six Counties: No longer did columns of khaki-coated regulars march to and fro in the garrison towns; no more did the ballrooms of the Irish gentry play host to dashing men in crimson; in the Kildare Street Club, only a mere handful of the old officers who used to dominate its membership held on. While the institution had departed and the performance of social distinction had ended, however, the individual officers who fought for the empire were still there, concealed on the margins of polite society.

The post-war condition of Ireland, like that of many newly formed European polities, was marked by the development of new 'communities of violence' around contested cultural borders. After 1918, all across the continent new 'small democracies' emerged from the ashes of the old European empires. This entailed a recalibration of state power, and thus of military elite authority. The successor states of Austria-Hungary had, like Ireland, emerged from a long history of national agitation, emboldened by Wilson's declaration concerning the self-determination of peoples.[2] In Russia, revolution had given way to a long and intensely bloody civil war.[3] In the fractured *Kaiserreich*, the 'imperial vacuum and disputed borders' led to a horrific cycle of violence between ethno-national groups on the

German-Polish border, as recounted in Tim Wilson's important comparative analysis.[4] In all of these places, newly empowered communities of violence contributed not only to the continuation of armed conflict, but also prefaced the emergence of authoritarian governments and state terror in the 1930s. By contrast, the marginalisation of military Irishness as a community of violence reveals a relatively successful democratic revolution in Ireland, without mainstream recourse to reactionary imperialism or fascism in the twentieth century. The generally localised, small-scale nature of the violence surrounding Irish independence, and the essential robustness of the Irish partition through successive testing moments of crisis, has led Eugenio Biagini to call Ireland's case 'the revolution that succeeded' after the First World War.[5] However, the decline of the military establishment as a social lodestone also allowed for other important social forces, such as religion, to establish primacy as sites of contestation and conflict.

This book has sought to sketch a social portrait of a specific elite identity at a time when the relationship between Irish nationality and the Irish political landscape was undergoing a fundamental change. It has argued for a definition of the Irish officer which is based on first-hand interaction with the culture and society of Ireland. It examined the mentalities and actions of those for whom Irishness was not an abstraction, but a fact of life—for whom the island of Ireland was home, or the seat of ancestral inheritance. For them, the truly dislocating experience of the early twentieth century was the stripping away of the certainties of their existence and, in some cases, the complete destruction of their way of life. In such a circumstance, continuing to actively engage with the empire seems a natural course of action. Adopting this definition of military Irishness has allowed for a more in-depth analysis than hitherto of the class make-up of the officer corps, and an assessment of the extent to which in the late nineteenth century it was subject to increasing middle-class incursion and concurrent 'greening'. The evidence suggests that there was little manifestation of increasing nationalist thought or sympathy in the officer corps, and the nationalists who were officers did not generally have middle-class backgrounds; it was mainly officers of the gentry, who were secure in their position and possessed high social capital, who felt the freedom to harbour more transgressive opinions, while middle-class officers felt more pressure to 'play the game' and conform to type.

Middle-class professionals were in the nineteenth century mainly confined to the technical regiments: the Engineers, Artillery, chaplaincies, and Royal Army Medical Corps. While there was a tentative widening of access in the Edwardian period, officers from military families were still privileged for selection and advancement, which constituted a barrier to middle-class officers in particular. Concerted efforts were made, beginning in the 1890s, to attract a class of officer from the universities, leading in 1908 to the establishment of officer training corps, though in Ireland these made little impact on the overall demographics of the officer corps as they were few in number and existed in already-established centres for technical training of officers: Trinity College Dublin and Queen's University Belfast. OTCs were established in much larger numbers in the English public schools, ensuring that even with this change between one fifth and one quarter of officers continued to come through the traditional route of Eton and Sandhurst, and further ensuring that other elite English public schools would continue to be well represented. Other mechanisms by which officer elites were reproduced throughout the period, as we have seen, were the systems of patronage and seniority which led in the final quarter of the nineteenth century to the domination of the military establishment by the gallant Victorian Irishmen, Garnet Wolseley, and Frederick Roberts.

The Wolseley and Roberts rings seem, however, to have been a result of historical conditions as opposed to a radical new departure in the operation of socialisation in the officer corps, and there is little evidence for a tightly knit Irish mafia directing the policy of the army, even with the predominance of Irish officers during the Second Boer War. While having an Irish commanding officer was clearly noteworthy enough to be remarked upon, and provided a sense of reassurance and admiration among Irish soldiers, it does not seem to have particularly helped or hindered in the pursuit of patronage or favour. The one potential exception to this might have been in the recruitment of Irish officers for Irish regiments, of which Wolseley, despite his own ambivalence about his nationality, was an enthusiastic supporter. The situation of Irish officers commanding Irish regiments remained a rare one throughout the period and even into the First World War, however, and as the recurring references to this fact by military commentators and the contemporary press illustrate, no-one seemed to be able to find a good reason why this was the case.[6] The army command seemingly saw no reason to enunciate a specific nationality policy to address this matter in the manner of the Austro-Hungarian army, even after the Childers Reforms established specific territorial links for battalions in the 1880s. Thus, it is evident that, in the army command's mentality, the cultural identity of the British officer was much stronger than the pull of national feeling. In the event, as illustrated by the responses of officers during the war years, they were largely correct.

An important change from the 1870s to the 1920s was the increasing apprehensiveness surrounding the perceived 'politicisation' of the army in Ireland. This did not operate in a straightforward manner: Frederick Roberts's tenure as Commander-in-Chief in Ireland, despite being marked by close association with Dublin Castle, was regarded as apolitical and Roberts was considered a unifying figure during Ireland's imperial moment. The 'constructive unionism' of landlords and politicians like Edward Saunderson, and the activities of gentry officers in defending their class interests during the Land War, were likewise regarded as simply the disinterested actions of the army in aid of the civil power; nothing more controversial than the maintenance of the status quo and the keeping of the Queen's peace. This changed with the advent of the mass unionist political movement in opposition to Home Rule, which inflected its message with the rhetoric of loyalty, allegiance to the Crown, and celebration of the British Empire.[7] This rhetorical space, which had traditionally been occupied by the British Army, lost its political neutrality and the ability of the army to act disinterestedly was permanently compromised. This situation degenerated into a serious crisis with the Curragh incident, where there was a tangible difference between the popular reception garnered by the aristocratic cavalry officers who rebelled, and the 'political soldier' Henry Wilson at the War Office. The conflation of politicisation with professionalism may have restricted the extent to which the officer corps was able to professionalise, before the challenges of the First World War made it unavoidable.

The Curragh incident was indicative of a wide array of institutional crises that affected the social position of the Irish officer: the decline of the landed interest, the pervasive sense of imperial decline wedded to the rise of Britain's imperial rivals in Europe, and the increasingly contentious and adversarial debate over Home Rule which threatened to escalate into civil war in 1914. All of these considerations choked off attempts at reform and reinforced the traditional aristocratic, gentlemanly character of military masculinity in the pre-war officer corps.

However, an analysis of the condition of the officer corps in early 1914 reveals that, while moderate unionism and traditional aristocratic values were the majority view, there was still space for other forms of opinion. A small handful of officers were open to conciliation with nationalists, even at this most critical and polarised time. A number of serving and former officers were prominent members of the Irish Volunteers in this period, and while many of them have not thus far appeared in any other study of the Irish military establishment, and the testimony of such officers as Colonel Cotter, Captain Berkeley, Lord Dunraven, and others present a unique insight into the boundaries of the officer corps and the depth of its connections to multiple segments of Irish society. The information which was collected on the religious affiliation of officers, and on their avenues of socialisation and educational attainments has tended to support the conclusions of other scholars, though it has also identified the importance of Irish elite schools to officer socialisation. This accounts for the smaller proportion of 'typical' officers with an Eton-Sandhurst background in Ireland than in the rest of the United Kingdom, and presents us with yet another intriguing continuity between pre- and post-independence Ireland.

Further to the analysis of the role of education in socialising Irish officers into the elite establishment, the mainly field-commissioned output of the Royal Hibernian Military School (RHMS)—another segment of the Irish military establishment which has been underemphasised by historians—cannot be ignored. These ranker officers illustrate three important realisations. First, that in periods of warfare in which officer attrition outstripped demand, the army would first look to traditional sources of new officers: experienced non-commissioned officers and the ex-pupils of military schools. Second, officers promoted from the ranks were more likely to be Irishmen, due to the size and prominence of the RHMS, its policy of privileging the applications of Irish pupils, and the disproportionate rate of commissioning of its old boys compared to the ranks as a whole. Third, it illustrates the possibility of military families entering the precincts of the officer corps over more than one generation—an important realisation considering the dominance of military families in the Irish officer corps towards the end of the nineteenth century. Colonel Edmond Cotter, one of the Irish officers who has been heretofore neglected by historical scholarship on the military in Ireland, is an important example, his father having been an NCO in the Buffs who encouraged his successful route to a commission through Woolwich.

A recurring theme in the writings of officers both in Ireland and the overseas empire is the importance of women in arbitrating the interface between the officer corps and elite society more broadly. Ann Laura Stoler and others have written of the 'gate-keeping' role played by elite women, which in relation to the officer corps also raises important questions about the relation between polite society, social distinction, and violence.[8] The accounts of women during the officer corps' crisis of identity in 1914, as recounted in Chaps. 5–6, reveal the role of gendered proscriptions operating in various contexts to restrain access to social capital, as well as to sanction and arbitrate social acceptance. This was also true in the self-consciously masculine sphere of the overseas empire, and indeed at war, where conceptions of self-sufficiency and frontier manliness constituted an aspect of the ideal officer's identity. The presence of women was resisted by officers, who defined this self-sufficient masculinity in opposition to the supposed 'femininity' of civilisation, which included, interestingly enough, the professionalised officialdom that accompanied colonial infrastructure.[9] It is also noteworthy in the Irish context that officers' moral authority, and thus their legitimacy as Irish social elites, was the subject of vocal challenges by a number of prominent women in this period, such as Maud Gonne, Constance Markievicz, Charlotte Despard, and Hannah Sheehy-Skeffington.

Despite the important interconnections between the officer corps and the volunteer movements (the connections between officers and the UVF, as we have seen, were much more extensive than with the Irish Volunteers), the make-up of these paramilitary bodies nonetheless constituted a counter-elite that would seek to supersede and marginalise the officer class. While professionals in the engineering and medical disciplines from the Irish universities were strongly represented in the officer corps, disproportionately so in the Indian Army and Indian Medical Service, it was nonetheless the middle class who stood to gain most from the Irish revolution. As the demographic studies by Cohan and others have shown, the membership of the IRA and Free State Army officer corps was constituted of these men, either drawn from the university-educated urban middle class or the sons of large private farmers (who incidentally also harboured long-standing grievances against the landed gentry). The studies of the officer corps, this one included, have all found little evidence of these social classes in the British officer corps. The sole exception to this was the strong representation, in less fashionable regiments, of sons of the Protestant clergy, who nonetheless represented something of an elite position within rural life.[10]

It has become a well-established realisation that Ireland, like Britain, reacted enthusiastically to the outbreak of the First World War. However, still striking is the extent to which a large and diverse group of Irishmen sought officer commissions throughout the war. The significant contribution of the Trinity College OTC, in particular, is noteworthy—not least because many of its members found themselves in combat with their fellow Irishmen during the Easter Rising. It is evident by the minority of Irish Volunteers who rejected Redmond's call to join the Irish Divisions that in the view of the majority of Irish people in 1914, there was no particular sectarian dimension to joining the army, in common with previous decades. However, following the developments of 1913–14, senior officers like Kitchener remarkably, and unjustly, began to regard Irish soldiers as potential fifth-columnists. Even during the War of Independence, there was a large Irish representation among British Army recruits, so there is little evidence to suggest Irish military disloyalty during this contentious period.

Following the war, it is clear that the question of 'politicisation' in the army had not disappeared, and that the rapidly changing political situation in Ireland was coming to a head. Even some officers who had been strong Unionists at the outbreak of the war felt it necessary to moderate their views to fall in line with the officers supporting dominion home rule, who had attempted to direct events at the Irish Convention. In response to the 1918 election, the increasing radicalisation of the populace and the destruction of the Irish Parliamentary Party's majority, officers found themselves increasingly publicly advocating for a form of Home Rule within the empire. Additionally, there were calls in the press from Irish officers for a separate Irish representation at the Versailles Peace Conference.[11] Clearly, even as the country was beginning to destabilise, there was still a space for officers of atypical political convictions, and Irish officers' attitudes were, in general, geared toward conciliation.

Perhaps this is unsurprising considering the integral role played by the officer corps in binding together the Irish establishment, particularly through the gentlemen's clubs in Dublin and other towns and cities. Their status as officers and gentlemen gave them a unique degree of social cachet which persisted throughout the late nineteenth and early twentieth century, and peaked during the period of popular imperialism following the Boer War. This in turn played a role in reinforcing the aristocratic character of the officer corps, and facilitated their socialisation with the landed class in the rooms of the Kildare Street Club. With the marginalisation of the British officer corps from the Irish establishment in the 1920s, the Kildare Street Club and Dublin United Services Club lost their relevance for the military establishment, and became *endroits* for middle-class socialisation.

Following the war, the experience of demobilised 'temporary gentle-men' as well as more established career officers has been overshadowed in many histories of the revolutionary period. This is curious considering the important role played by military officers from the declaration of martial law until the withdrawal of the British Army in 1922. While a large num-ber of 'temporary gentlemen' probably voted for Sinn Féin in 1918 along with their countrymen, economic conditions and a sense of loss of status drew many of them, along with many former enlisted men, back into the army in 1919–22 and afterwards. Many more Irish ex-officers than had previously been assumed also joined the Auxiliary Division of the RIC, though others had clear reservations about associating with such a corps. In the context of this body's frontline position in the contest over Irishness that was the War of Independence, it is remarkable that the Auxiliary com-mander, Frank Percy Crozier, wrote so extensively and introspectively about his own sense of Irishness and the outlook of the Irish officers he encountered throughout his career, both in the West African Frontier Force and closer to home. Perhaps more than any other officer, Crozier illustrates the seeming contradiction surrounding identity and nationality that Irish officers were presented with in the revolutionary period, and the multiplicity of responses thus provoked from the Irish officer corps.

One of the persistent questions about this period in Irish history is the extent to which the Irish revolution overshadowed the historical impor-tance of the First World War, both in terms of memory and remembrance, as well as in the realm of politics and society more widely. The Anglo-Irish and the landed elite, it is argued, were 'outflanked by Easter Week' and their monumental sacrifice for the cause of Ireland and empire on the Western Front was undermined by the symbolic sacrifice of the Easter Rising.[12] For the officer corps, it is difficult to say which was the more significant event. Certainly, a greater number of officers took part in the First World War, and the experience of four years of brutal warfare had a monumental impact on their lives. However, it is worth noting that more Irishmen fought in Dublin that Easter wearing a British Army uniform than did as insurrectionists. Naturally, they were simply doing their duty as opposed to fighting for a romantic cause, but the effect of undertaking active operations in their own capital city must surely have had a deep effect on them. For professional officers, in particular, the usual mental blinders that operated in the execution of their duties—the demonisation and othering of the enemy, or the dehumanising racial structures of the overseas empire—fell away when the enemy to be engaged were their own countrymen. Some Irish officers, as we have seen, were horrified by the brutality of the martial authorities in bringing the insurrection to an end, and later by the activities of their brother officers in the Auxiliary Division, in a way that they would not have been in the context of India, South Africa, or Flanders. For the Irish officers who took an active part, then, the Rising may well have been the more significant event simply because of the different context and scale compared to previous service conditions in Ireland. This accounts for the remarkable difference in tone with which Captain Gerrard or Colonel Pope Hennessy, who fought in the Rising and were deeply affected by it, remembered their experiences, compared to the way in which the event was dismissed out of hand by Captain Kemmis, who was on active service on the Western Front in 1916.

After 1922, the social position of officers in Northern Ireland remained largely the same—although the political role played by the army from the Edwardian period onward would cast a long shadow over the Six Counties. In the overseas empire, where many Irish officers from North and South continued to serve throughout the 1920s, the pace of life continued largely as normal; the Irishness of officers appeared to be no more or less a matter of comment than it had been before the First World War. The constant sense of apprehension that senior officers held concerning the potential disloyalty of Irish soldiers was only vindicated once, in 1920, when a small number of men of the Connaught Rangers mutinied while on service in India. In many ways this was the exception that proved the rule: that, on the one hand, service in the British Army was not particularly seen as a sectarian statement, and on the other, that Irish officers as a self-selecting group were not prone to mutiny against the empire. Indeed, the enlisted Connaught Ranger mutineers did not seek during their mutiny to challenge the legitimacy of the British Empire, to make common cause with Indian nationalists, or to remove themselves from the colonial mindset in any other way. The officers who dealt with them, likewise, demonstrated a familiar mixture of leniency and severity. Most of the soldiers who took part were let off with little more than a slap on the wrist, while the ring-leader, Daly, became the last British soldier to be executed for mutiny.[13]

The defining aspect of military Irishness was empire, both for professional and sentimental reasons. The preservation of the imperial connection was crucial for officers' livelihood, their worldview and their sense of self, and officers were able to reconcile an imperial military identity with their sense of 'hyphenated Irishness'.[14] While in this period comparisons were drawn between the Irish question and the aims of colonial nationalist movements, these were made mainly by civilian colonial administrators, not officers. Of course, officers made comparisons between Ireland and the overseas empire in order to make sense of their experiences, but in the main these tended to be superficial, emphasising the connectivity of the component parts of the British empire. The lack of seriously considered comparison between Ireland and the overseas empire can be discerned in the disastrous attempts by military officers like Maxwell, Macready, and Crozier to import colonial counter-insurgency tactics into the Irish context in 1916 and 1920.

A sense of imperial decline was a constant feature of the British imperial mentality, and a sense of glory departed was indeed persistent and resonant amongst the self-defined Anglo-Irish after 1922, who found themselves isolated as 'Protestants in a Catholic state' and yearned nostalgically for the glory days of empire.[15] The belief that Ireland was naturally and inevitably bound to the British empire was maintained in these communities, alongside the implication, originally formulated in the era of pre-war nationalism, that any serious unrest or deterioration of the condition of Ireland would, in some intangible way, have a calamitous effect on the imperial enterprise as a whole. Following independence, and the calls for the Free State to leave the Commonwealth in the 1930s and 1940s, some officers, like Crozier and Gough, clearly still believed it.[16]

While it is apparent that the old Irish officer corps had very little to do in general with the army of the Free State, there were once again exceptions: retired officers like Hutcheson-Poë retained an interest in the new army, and there is evidence to suggest that there were certainly at least a smattering more former British Army officers serving in the National Army than the five or so that Jane Leonard has identified.[17] There were clearly minor overlaps between the old imperial officer corps and their National Army replacements who now occupied the Victorian barracks peppering Ireland, in terms of the culture and organisation of the new officer corps. However, by and large the segment of Irish society that had contributed material to the British Army's officer corps continued to be found in that organisation after 1922.

The myriad ways in which the old imperial officer corps intersected with Irish society leads to the conclusion that, in general, a sense of cultural nationality and Irish affinity was a more significant component of the British military establishment than has previously been assumed. Deeply held Irish cultural and political nationalism was not incompatible with holding a commission in the British Army in the Victorian era, nor was it up to and during the First World War or, seemingly, in the later 1920s after the embers of civil war were extinguished. Military Irishness was sustained by a sense of *noblesse oblige* that could only operate within established class parameters. For the period between 1916 and 1922, the story is slightly more complicated. In this period, Irish officers attempted to conciliate with nationalists, to mitigate the radicalising effects of careless and poorly appraised non-Irish military commanders, and a distracted political leadership. They were not afraid to protest against the brutality of martial law, and in some cases they paid the price by being forced to resign their commissions. However, their livelihood, and their essential sense of self, depended on their connection with the empire, and it was this political sticking point that put them increasingly out of touch with the flavour of republican nationalism that was then developing. In the changed political landscape of partitioned Ireland, officers once again looked to the overseas empire for certainty, employment, and status.

One of the themes which comes through very strongly in the examination of Irish officers' letters, reminiscences, diaries, and various published materials is their engagement with Irishness, and how it interacted with military identities. While certain officers, like Crozier, Dunraven, Godley, Wolseley, and Butler, pontificate at length about the various characteristics of their and others' Irishness, and its importance to their own lives, the majority of officers hardly mention it at all until some particular event occurs that causes them to consider it. Clearly, the general day-to-day atmosphere in the officers' mess of an Irish regiment, or on campaign in the empire, or even interacting socially with non-Irish officers, were situations in which Irishness was little more than a superficial characteristic, not an integral or problematic aspect of officers' lives. However, when officers were forced to confront their Irishness—whether in discussions over Home Rule, or in carrying out operations in Ireland, or in the inescapable situation of 1919–22—they displayed a sensitive and deeply felt Irish identity, and the impression that is portrayed is of something fundamental and very important to these men.

The effect of this deeply held sense of Irishness is, of course, impossible to quantify. The incompleteness of the official sources and the ambiguities surrounding the identification of Irish officers make it very difficult to make substantive statements concerning the interaction between Irishness and the British Army. I have attempted to steer a middle path, collecting and collating as far as is practicable the available information for a slice of the Irish officer corps, in order to achieve a general picture of its social characteristics. I have deliberately sought out the marginal and transgressive elements within this slice, in order to demarcate the boundaries and fault lines of officer identity and reveal aspects of the Irish officer corps that have thus far been overlooked. In the process, many of the unexamined categories which had previously been employed to assess this group, like 'Anglo-Irish', have been problematised, and the many Irish officers who do not fit these categories have been foregrounded in the analysis. Further, the many continuities pertaining to the 'departure of the British army' from Ireland have been employed to illustrate the continuing linkages between Ireland and its old officer class. Many of the departing Regiments were filled with Irishmen and officered by Irishmen, who would be returning, in uniform, to Ireland on their next period of leave.

The Irish officers examined in this text were an organic component of the elite establishment, with a sense of Irish identity that was socialised in an era before the advent of democratic republicanism. The officer corps' mechanisms of socialisation, patronage, and advancement placed officers in a reactionary position, faced with the increasing irrelevance of their moral authority, and the political challenge of Irish nationalism which hastened their marginalisation in Irish society. Many aspects of this pre-independence Irish military establishment have been overlooked, or referenced only in passing in prior studies of this period. The Royal Hibernian Military School, which sat in the Phoenix Park at the very centre of the Irish military establishment for 151 years, is hardly mentioned at all in the histories of British rule in Ireland or the military. The accounts and testimony of such diverse officers as William Bent, William Armstrong, J.G. Vaughan-Hart, William Kemmis, Edmond Cotter, Thomas Hazzell, F. R. Logan, and many others have not yet featured in a single published history of Irish soldiers, and each has contributed a new perspective and an invaluable insight into the mentalities and identities of the Irish officer corps.

The importance and uniqueness of the Irish officer corps was the way in which it drew in and reflected many strands of Irish elite opinion, playing a central role in pre-independence Irish society. The marginal status of officers in the period following southern independence illustrates both the extent to which the landed elite and the imperial connection were displaced in the revolutionary period, and also the extent to which the Irish revolution was a civil contest, between an Irishness based on membership of a multiethnic empire with an aristocratic and hierarchical worldview, and the advance of a sense of democratic localism, in which militarism became problematic and other.

NOTES

1. Hew Strachan, *The Politics of the British Army* (Oxford, 1997), p. 15.
2. Peter Haslinger, 'Austria-Hungary' in Gerwarth, Robert, and Erez Manela, eds., *Empires at War 1911–1923* (Oxford, 2014), p. 87.
3. Joshua Sanborn, 'The Russian Empire', in Ibid. pp. 104–105; Jane McGaughey, *Ulster's Men: Protestant Unionist Masculinities and Militarization in the North of Ireland, 1912–1923* (Montreal, 2012), p. 176.
4. Heather Jones, 'The German Empire', in Ibid. p. 71; Tim Wilson, 'Ghost Provinces, Mislaid Minorities: The Experience of Southern Ireland and Prussian Poland Compares, 1918–23', *Irish Studies in International Affairs* 13 (2002), passim.
5. Biagini and Mulhall, eds., preface to *The Shaping of Modern Ireland: A Centenary Assessment* (Sallins, 2016), pp. v–vi.
6. *Belfast News-Letter*, 6 June 1888; *Kerry Sentinel*, 21 August 1915; *Irish Examiner*, 18 August 1915.
7. Michael Silvestri, *Ireland and India: Nationalism, Empire and Memory* (Cambridge, 2006), pp. 125–126.
8. Frederick Cooper and Ann Laura Stoler, *Tensions of Empire: Colonial Cultures in a Bourgeois World* (Berkeley, 1997); Susan Meyer, *Imperialism at Home: Race and Victorian Women's Fiction* (London, 1996); Anne McClintock, *Imperial Leather: Race, Gender, and Sexuality in the Colonial Context* (New York, 1995).
9. F. P. Crozier, *Five Years Hard* (London, 1932), p. 217; Chaplain McRory, diary of 1917, PRONI.
10. Edward Spiers, *The Army and Society 1815–1914* (London, 1980), p. 8.
11. *Freeman's Journal*, 11 March 1919.
12. Dan Finlay, 'Outflanked by Easter Week: Death in the Flemish Mud', *Books Ireland* 226 (1999), p. 311.
13. Silvestri, *Ireland and India*, p. 158; Thomas Bartlett, 'The Connaught Rangers Mutiny in India, 1920', *History Ireland* 6:1 (1998), pp. 6–7.
14. Gwynn, quoted in Christopher Fauske, 'A Life Merely Glimpsed: Louis MacNeice at the End of the Anglo-Irish Tradition', *Canadian Journal of Irish Studies* 20 (1994), p. 19.
15. J. G. Darwin, 'Fear of Falling: British Politics and Imperial Decline since 1900', *Transactions of the Royal Historical Society* 36 (1986), pp. 27–43.
16. Hubert Gough, *Soldiering On* (London, 1954); F. P. Crozier, *Ireland For Ever* (London, 1930). Dunraven, writing in *Past Times*, encapsulates the early remembrances of the independence period succinctly, calling 1921 a 'year of disgrace'.
17. Jane Leonard, 'Survivors', in Horne, John, ed., *Our War: Ireland and the Great War* (Dublin, 2008), p. 219.

BIBLIOGRAPHY

PRIMARY MANUSCRIPT SOURCES

BRITISH LIBRARY

Add MS 42829 Letter-Books of Lord Strathnairn, 1870.

Add MS 49802 Balfour Papers, Correspondence with Charles Vane-Tempest Stewart, 6th Marquess of Londonderry, 1887–1909.

Add MS 49807 Balfour Papers, Correspondence with General Sir Redvers Buller.

Add MS 49821 Balfour Papers, Correspondence with Sir John Ross-of-Bladensburg, 1887–1914.

Add MS 52461 General Murray, Corresp. With General Robertson.

Add MS 58372 Miscellaneous Letters and Papers, General Maxwell Corresp.

Add MS 60823 Carnarvon Papers, Miscellaneous Correspondence, 1868–1888.

Add MS 60830 Carnarvon Papers, General Irish Correspondence, 1885–1889.

Add MS 77075 Althorp Papers, Correspondence with Gen. Thomas Steele, C-in-C Ireland 1880–85, and Garnet Wolseley, C-in-C Ireland, 1890–1995.

Add MS 77091 Althorp Papers, Letters from Sir John Foster George Ross of Bladensburg, 1882–1887, 1902–1910.

IOR 19017 Confidential reports on Indian Officers granted King's Commissions.

IOR 7023 Proposal (by Roberts, Dufferin et al.) to Raise Two New Regiments to be Officered by Native Gentlemen.

IOR/L/PS/11 Seely Correspondence.

© The Author(s) 2019
L. Sweeney, *Irish Military Elites, Nation and Empire, 1870–1925*,
https://doi.org/10.1007/978-3-030-19307-2

Ms 49820-21 Balfour Papers.
Ms 52782 Bernard Papers.
Mss Eur A108 Frederick Sleigh Roberts Papers, 1883–1891.
Mss Eur A203 Frederick Sleigh Roberts Papers, 1912.
Mss Eur B329 Frederick Sleigh Roberts Papers, 1892.
Mss Eur D567 Letters of Brigadier-General Thomas Baker Rel. to 2nd Afghan War.
Mss Eur F108 Papers of George Stuart White.
Mss Eur F/118 IOR Reading (Private) Collection: Lists of Correspondents.
Mss Eur F143/33-38 Sir Walter Lawrence Papers, 1895–1914.

BUREAU OF MILITARY HISTORY

WS50 Hobson.
WS262 Hawes.
WS287 Flannery.
WS316 Folan.
WS348 Gerrard.
WS509 McCarty.
WS625 Handley.
WS1045 Roberts.
WS1307 Ibbertson.
WS1449 Whelan.
WS1604 Desborough.
WS1770 O'Sheil.

CAMBRIDGE UNIVERSITY LIBRARY

Add MS 7490 Mayo Papers.

CORK COUNTY ARCHIVES

CCCA/PR12 Captain George Berkeley Collection.

GLUCKSMAN LIBRARY, LIMERICK UNIVERSITY

P6/1138-1417 Armstrong Papers.
D3196 Dunraven Papers.
P6/1473-1613 Kemmis Papers.

Imperial War Museum

73/20 Brigadier General J. J. H. Nation, Private Papers.
85/7 Brigadier General T. A. Andrus, Private Papers.
P363 General Sir Peter Strickland, Private Papers.

Liddell Hart Centre for Military Archives, King's College London

KCLMA Godley Papers.
KCLMA MacDermott. John Clarke MacDermott, Manuscript Remembrances of 1916 (1979).

Manuscripts and Archives Research Library, Trinity College Dublin

IE TCD Ms 11425/3/4/1/2 John Wray Correspondence.
IE TCD Ms 4456 Account of Events during the Easter Rising.
IE TCD Ms 5956/5 Papers Rel. to Captain George Kinkead, Only Son of Professor R. J. Kinkead.
IE TCD Ms 5955 Letters of William HM Bent.
IE TCD Ms 9308 Miscellaneous Autographs; Letters Describing Dublin during the 1916 Easter Rising.

National Archives of Ireland

S.2048 Royal Hibernian Military School, Control and Maintenance.
S.2087 British Army Officers Permits to Carry Firearms in Saorstat Eireann.
S.2140 Ex Members of British Forces in National Army.
S.2217 Royal Hibernian Military School and Royal Hospital Kilmainham—Applicability of Adaptation of Charters Act 1926.
S.2983 Evacuation of Houses Rented by the British Army in Limerick, 1922.
S.2991 Conscience Money.
S.2992 British Army, Firing of Field Guns, Armistice Day, 1922.
S.3592 Education and Training of Officers.
S.3644 Deserters from the British Army, 1924.
S.3829 Officers Kidnapped at Macroom.
S.4405 Deposit of Colours of Disbanded Irish Regiments.
S.4507 Supersession of Officers of the British Army.
S.4930 British Army Estimates 1929, 1930.
S.4945 British Army Council's Proposal to Carry Out a Survey of Lough Swilly.

S.5401 Army, Courses of Instruction for Irish Free State Army Officers in England.
S.14050 Conscription in Ireland. British Government Report 1916.

NATIONAL ARMY MUSEUM

'A General Group'. *Vanity Fair*, 29 November 1900.
6807 Chelmsford Papers Relating to the 6th Kaffir War, 1877–1878.
7112–38 Coghill Papers.

NATIONAL LIBRARY OF IRELAND

Ms 122 Monteagle Papers.
Ms 3124 Studdart Family Papers.
Ms 8489 Maurice Moore Papers, 1886–1936.
Ms 10556 Moore Family Papers.
Ms 10561 Maurice Moore Correspondence.
Ms 10575 Maurice Moore Diaries.
Ms 13415 Documents Relating to the Irish Peace Conference, 1920.
Ms 16888 Newspaper Cuttings Rel. to Robert Barton.
Ms 19972 Mahon Papers.
Ms 22110 Evelyn French Papers.
Ms 24283 Nora Robertson Papers.
Ms 22863 Shane Leslie Diaries.
Ms 34169 Doneraile Papers.
Ms 34172 Castletown Papers Rel. to Land Agitation.
Ms 34173 Castletown Papers Rel. to Home Rule.
Ms 34174 Doneraile Correspondence.
Ms 49670 Diaries and Correspondence of Sir Alfred Irwin, 1878–1921.
P8129 Miscellaneous Letters Rel. Army matters, 1891–1994.

PUBLIC RECORDS OFFICE, NORTHERN IRELAND

D623 Abercorn Papers.
D627 Montgomery Papers.
D654 Charles Vane-Tempest Letters.
D1071 Papers of the 1st Marquess of Dufferin.
D1295 Wilfrid Spender Papers.
D1447 Correspondence of Lieutenant Edmund De Wind VC.
D1449 Lennox Conyngham Papers.
D1507 Carson Papers.
D1567 Staples Papers.

D1868 Father McRory Diaries.
D2004 Ross of Bladensburg Papers.
D3004 Brookeborough Papers.
D3019 Kelso Papers.
D3044 Clanwilliam Meade Papers.
D3077 Lieutenant Colonel J. G. Vaughan Hart Papers.
D3122 Lieutenant Colonel E. J. Gordon-Tucker Papers.
D3835 Sir Oliver Nugent Papers.
D4190 Papers of Brigadier John Alexander Sinton.
MIC204 Queen's University OTC Papers.
T2419 Sir James Acheson Papers.
T2996 Saunderson Papers.
T3778 Joseph McCullough Letters.

QUEEN MARY UNIVERSITY OF LONDON ARCHIVAL COLLECTIONS

NL Lyttelton Family Papers.

THE NATIONAL ARCHIVES, KEW

CO 904 Dublin Castle Records.
PRO 30/57 Kitchener Papers Rel. to Ireland.
WO 159/18 Kitchener Papers, 1914.
WO 159/19 Kitchener Papers, 1915.

PRIMARY PRINTED SOURCES

Anonymous (Cairnes, William), *Social Life in the British Army* (London, 1900).
Arthur, George (ed.), *The Letters of Lord and Lady Wolseley* (London, 1922).
Becker, Bernard, *Disturbed Ireland: Being the Letters Written during the Winter of 1880–81* (London, 1881).
Butler, William F., *Sir William Butler: An Autobiography* (London, 1911).
Cassidy, Martin, *The Inniskilling Diaries, 1899–1903* (Barnsley, 2001).
Collis, Maurice, *Somerville and Ross: A Biography* (London, 1968).
Collis, Maurice, *The Journey Outward* (London, 1952).
Cooper, Bryan, *The Tenth (Irish) Division in Gallipoli* (Dublin, 1993).
Crozier, F. P., *A Brass Hat in No Man's Land* (Belfast, 1932a).
Crozier, F. P., *Five Years Hard* (London, 1932b).
Crozier, F. P., *Impressions and Recollections* (1930a).
Crozier, F. P., *Ireland For Ever* (London, 1930b).

Crozier, F. P., *The Men I Killed* (1937).

Cullen, Clara (ed.), *The World Upturning: Elsie Henry's Wartime Diaries, 1913–1919* (Sallins, 2013).

de Vere White, Terence, *The Anglo-Irish* (London, 1972).

Godley, Alexander John, *The Life of an Irish Soldier: Reminiscences of General Sir Alexander Godley* (London, 1939).

Gough, Hubert, *Soldiering On* (London, 1954).

Grimshaw, Roly, *Indian Cavalry Officer 1914–15* (Tunbridge Wells, 1986).

Inglis, Brian, *West Briton* (London, 1962).

Leslie, Shane, *The Irish Tangle for English Readers* (London, 1946).

Maclean, A. H. H., *Public Schools and the War in South Africa, 1899–1902* (London, 1903).

Macready, Nevil, *Annals of an Active Life* (London, 1923).

Montgomery-Cuninghame, Thomas Andrew, *Dusty Measure: A Record of Troubled Times* (London, 1939).

Moody, T. W., and Richard Hawkins with Margaret Moody (eds.), *Florence Arnold-Forster's Irish Diary* (Oxford, 1988).

Morris, A. J. A. (ed.), *The Letters of Lieutenant Colonel Charles á Court Repington CMG, Military Correspondent of The Times 1903–1918* (Stroud, 1999).

Preston, Adrian (ed.), *In Relief of Gordon: Lord Wolseley's Campaign Journal of the Khartoum Relief Expedition, 1884–1885* (London, 1967).

Robertson, Nora, *Crowned Harp: Memories of the Last Years of the Crown in Ireland* (Dublin, 1960).

Robson, Brian (ed.), *Roberts in India: The Military Papers of Field Marshal Lord Roberts 1876–1893* (Stroud, 1993).

Turner, Alfred, *Sixty Years of a Soldier's Life* (London, 1912).

Vane, Francis Fletcher, *Agin the Governments: Memories and Adventures of Sir Francis Fletcher Vane Bt.* (1929).

Vane, Francis Fletcher, *On Certain Fundamentals* (1909).

Vane, Francis Fletcher, *Pax Britannica* (1905).

Vane, Francis Fletcher, *Principles of Military Art* (1916).

White, Major E. (ed.), *The Irish Military Guide*, March 1892.

Winter, Ormonde, *Winter's Tale* (London, 1955).

Wolseley, Garnet, *The Soldier's Pocket-book for Field Service* (1869).

Wolseley, Garnet, *The Soldier's Pocket-book for Field Service* (1871).

Wolseley, Garnet, *The Soldier's Pocket-book for Field Service* (1882).

Wolseley, Garnet, *The Soldier's Pocket-book for Field Service* (1886).

Wolseley, Garnet, *The Story of a Soldier's Life*, 2 vols. (London, 1903).

Wyndham-Quin, Windham, 4th Earl Dunraven, '"Ireland Awake!" An Open Letter to his Fellow Countrymen' (1917).

Wyndham-Quin, Windham, 4th Earl Dunraven, *No Army, No Empire* (n.d.).

Wyndham-Quin, Windham, 4th Earl Dunraven, *Past Times and Pastimes*, 2 vols. (1921–1922).
Wyndham-Quin, Windham, 4th Earl Dunraven, *The Crisis in Ireland* (1905).
Wyndham-Quin, Windham, 4th Earl Dunraven, *The Outlook in Ireland: The Case for Devolution and Conciliation* (1907).

LSE Selected Pamphlets

MacVeagh, Jeremiah, 'A Sketch of the Donegal Land War', 1889.

Newspapers/Periodicals

An T-Oglach.
Army Quarterly.
Ballymena Observer.
Butte Independent.
Daily Chronicle.
Daily News.
Daily Sketch.
Freeman's Journal.
Hibernia: Quarterly Magazine of the Royal Hibernian Military School.
Irish Examiner.
Irish Independent.
Kerry Evening Post.
Kerry Sentinel.
Kildare Observer.
Kilkenny People.
Killarney Echo and South Kerry Chronicle.
Leinster Express.
Morning Post.
The Belfast News-Letter.
The Irish Times.
The London Gazette.
The Spectator.
The Standard and *Evening Standard.*
The Times of India.
The Times of London.
Tuam Herald.
United Service Gazette.
Vanity Fair.
Westminster Gazette.

SECONDARY SOURCES

Allen, Charles, *Soldier Sahibs: The Men Who Ruled the North-West Frontier* (London, 2000).

Anderson, Benedict, *Imagined Communities* (London, 1983).

Anderson, David M., and David Killingray (eds.), *Policing the Empire: Government, Authority and Control, 1830–1940* (Manchester, 1991).

Attridge, Steve, *Nationalism, Imperialism and Identity in Late Victorian Culture: Civil and Military Worlds* (Basingstoke, 2003).

Banerjee, Sikata, *Muscular Nationalism: Gender, Violence and Empire in India and Ireland, 1914–2004* (New York, 2012).

Barth, Volker (ed.), *Imperial Co-operation and Transfer, 1870–1930: Empires and Encounters* (London, 2015).

Bartlett, Thomas, and Keith Jeffery (eds.), *A Military History of Ireland* (Cambridge, 1996).

Barton, Brian, *Brookeborough: The Making of a Prime Minister* (Belfast, 1988).

Barua, Pradeep P., *Gentlemen of the Raj: The Indian Army Officer Corps, 1917–1949* (London, 2003).

Bayly, Chris, *Imperial Meridian: The British Empire and the World, 1780–1830* (London, 1989).

Beckett, Ian F., and Keith Simpson, *A Nation in Arms: A Social Study of the British Army in the First World War* (Barnsley, 2014).

Beckett, Ian F., *Johnnie Gough, VC: A Biography of Brigadier-General Sir John Edmond Gough, VC, KCB* (London, 1989).

Beckett, Ian F., *The Army and the Curragh Incident 1914* (London, 1986).

Beckett, Ian F., 'Women and Patronage in the Late Victorian Army', *History* 85:279 (2000), pp. 463–480.

Bender, Jill, *The 1857 Indian Uprising and the British Empire* (Cambridge, 2015).

Benton, Sarah, 'Women Disarmed: The Militarisation of Politics in Ireland, 1913–23', *Feminist Review* 50 (1995), pp. 148–172.

Bew, John, *The Glory of Being Britons: Civic Unionism in Nineteenth-Century Belfast* (Dublin, 2009).

Bew, Paul, *Conflict and Conciliation in Ireland 1890–1910. Parnellites and Radical Agrarians* (Oxford, 1987).

Bew, Paul, *Ideology and the Ulster Question: Ulster Unionism and Irish Nationalism, 1912–1916* (Oxford, 1994).

Bew, Paul, *Ireland: The Politics of Enmity 1789–2006* (Oxford, 2007).

Bew, Paul, Peter Gibbon, and Henry Patterson, *Northern Ireland 1921/2001: Political Forces and Social Classes* (London, 2002).

Biagini, Eugenio, and Clare Daly (eds.), *The Cambridge Social History of Modern Ireland* (Cambridge, 2017).

Biagini, Eugenio, and Dan Mulhall (eds.), *The Shaping of Modern Ireland: A Centenary Assessment* (Sallins, 2016).

Biagini, Eugenio, *British Democracy and Irish Nationalism 1876–1906* (Cambridge, 2007).

Biagini, Eugenio, 'Power Politics, Imperial Strategies, and Local Elites', *The Historical Journal* 45:3 (2002), pp. 679–687.

Biagini, Eugenio, 'The Protestant Minority in Southern Ireland', *The Historical Journal* 55 (2012), pp. 1161–1184.

Black, Jeremy, *A Military History of Britain* (London, 2006).

Black, Jeremy, 'Popular Politics in a Changing World', *Victorian Review* 20:2 (1994), pp. 162–165.

Blunt, Alison, 'Imperial Geographies of Home: British Domesticity in India, 1886–1925', *Transactions of the Institute of British Geographers* 24:4 (1999), pp. 421–440.

Bond, Brian, *The Victorian Army and the Staff College 1854–1914* (London, 1972).

Bordieu, Pierre, *Distinction* (Cambridge, MA, 1984).

Bourke, Richard, and Ian McBride (eds.), *The Princeton History of Modern Ireland* (Princeton, 2016).

Bowman, Timothy, and Mark Connelly, *The Edwardian Army: Recruiting, Training, and Deploying the British Army, 1902–1914* (Oxford, 2012).

Bowman, Timothy, *Carson's Army: The Ulster Volunteer Force, 1910–22* (Manchester, 2007).

Boyce, David George, and Alan O'Day (eds.), *The Making of Modern Irish History: Revisionism and the Revisionist Controversy* (Abingdon, 1996).

Bredin, Brigadier A. E. C., *A History of the Irish Soldier* (Belfast, 1987).

Brendon, Piers, *The Decline and Fall of the British Empire, 1781–1997* (London, 2007).

Brewer, John D., 'Max Weber and the Royal Irish Constabulary: A Note on Class and Status', *The British Journal of Sociology* 40 (1989), pp. 82–96.

Bruce, Anthony, *The Purchase System in the British Army, 1660–1871* (London, 1980).

Bubb, Alexander, 'The Life of the Irish Soldier in India: Representations and Self-representations, 1857–1922', *Modern Asian Studies* 46:4 (2012), pp. 769–813.

Buckland, Patrick, *James Craig Lord Craigavon* (Dublin, 1980).

Bushnell, John, 'The Tsarist Officer Corps, 1881–1914: Customs, Duties, Inefficiency', *The American Historical Review* 86 (1981), pp. 753–780.

Butler, William, *The Irish Amateur Tradition in the British Army, 1854–1992* (Manchester, 2016).

Cameron, Ewen A., 'Internal Policing and Public Order, c.1797–1900' in Spiers, Edward M., Jeremy A. Crang, and Matthew J. Strickland (eds.), *A Military History of Scotland* (Edinburgh, 2012), pp. 436–457.

Campbell, Colm, *Emergency Law in Ireland, 1918–1925* (Oxford, 1994).

Campbell, Fergus, 'Irish Popular Politics and the Making of the Wyndham Land Act, 1901–1903', *Historical Journal* 45:4 (2002), pp. 755–773.

Campbell, Fergus, *Land and Revolution: Nationalist Politics in the West of Ireland 1891–1921* (Oxford, 2005).

Campbell, Fergus, 'The Easter Rising in Galway', *History Ireland* 14 (2006), pp. 22–25.

Campbell, Fergus, *The Irish Establishment, 1879–1914* (Oxford, 2009a).

Campbell, Fergus, 'The Social Composition of the Senior Officers of the Royal Irish Constabulary, 1881–1911', *Irish Historical Studies* 36 (2009b), pp. 522–541.

Campbell, Fergus, 'Who Ruled Ireland? The Irish Administration, 1879–1914', *The Historical Journal* 50 (2007), pp. 623–644.

Cannadine, David, *The Decline and Fall of the British Aristocracy* (London, 1996).

Casey, P. J., K. T. Cullen, and J. P. Duignan, *Irish Doctors in the First World War* (Dublin, 2015).

Cassar, George H., *The Tragedy of Sir John French* (Newark, 1985).

Clark, Christopher, *Iron Kingdom: The Rise and Downfall of Prussia, 1600–1947* (London, 2007).

Clark, Christopher, *The Sleepwalkers: How Europe Went to War in 1914* (London, 2012).

Clarke, Howard R., *A New History of the Royal Hibernian Military School (1765–1924) Phoenix Park, Dublin* (Cleveland, Yorks, 2011).

Clarke, Joseph, and John Horne (eds.), *Militarized Cultural Encounters in the Long Nineteenth Century: Making War, Mapping Europe* (Basingstoke, 2018).

Cohan, A. S., *The Irish Political Elite* (Dublin, 1972).

Collett, Nigel, *The Butcher of Amritsar: General Reginald Dyer* (London, 2007).

Cook, S. B., 'The Irish Raj: Social Origins and Careers of Irishmen in the Indian Civil Service, 1855–1914', *Journal of Social History* 20 (1987), pp. 507–529.

Cooper, Frederick, and Ann Laura Stoler, *Tensions of Empire: Colonial Cultures in a Bourgeois World* (Berkeley, 1997).

Costello, Con, *A Most Delightful Station: The British Army on the Curragh of Kildare, Ireland, 1855–1922* (Cork, 1996).

Craig, Gordon A., *The Politics of the Prussian Army, 1640–1945* (London, 2007).

Cronin, Mike, 'The Socio-economic Background and Membership of the Blueshirt Movement, 1932–5', *Irish Historical Studies* 29 (1994), pp. 234–249.

Crosbie, Barry, *Irish Imperial Networks: Migration, Social Communication and Exchange in Nineteenth-Century India* (Cambridge, 2012).

Crossman, Virginia, 'The Army and Law and Order in the Nineteenth Century' in Bartlett, Thomas, and Keith Jeffery (eds.), *A Military History of Ireland* (Cambridge, 1996).

Crowley, John, Donal Ó Drisceoil, Mike Murphy, and John Borgonovo (eds.), *Atlas of the Irish Revolution* (Cork, 2017).

Cullen, Fintan, 'Marketing National Sentiment: Lantern Slides of Evictions in Late Nineteenth Century Ireland', *History Workshop Journal* 54 (2002), pp. 162–179.

d'Alton, Ian, and Ida Milne (eds.), *Protestant and Irish: The Minority's Search for a Place in Independent Ireland* (Cork, 2019).

d'Alton, Ian, 'The "Protestant Free State" and the Church of Ireland's Patrician Celebrations, 1932', in Hill, J., and M. Lyons (eds.), *Representing Ireland's Religious Histories: Historiography, Ideology and Practice* (London, 2016).

Das, Santanu, *Race, Empire and First World War Writing* (Cambridge, 2011).

Darwin, J. G., 'The Fear of Falling: British Politics and Imperial Decline Since 1900', *Transactions of the Royal Historical Society* 36 (1986), pp. 27–43.

Daunton, Martin, and Rick Halpern (eds.), *Empire and Others: British Encounters with Indigenous Peoples, 1600–1850* (London, 1999).

Deak, Istvan, *Beyond Nationalism: A Social and Political History of the Habsburg Officer Corps, 1848–1918* (Oxford, 1990).

Delaney, Enda, and Donald M. MacRaild (eds.), *Irish Migration, Networks and Ethnic Identities Since 1750* (London, 2007).

Delaney, Edna, *Demography, State and Society: Irish Migration to Britain, 1921–1971* (Liverpool, 2000).

Delaney, Enda, *The Irish in Post-War Britain* (Oxford, 2007).

de Nie, Michael, 'Ulster will Fight? The British Press and Ulster, 1885–1886', *New Hibernia Review/Iris Éireannach Nua* 12 (2008), pp. 18–38.

Denman, Terence, 'The Catholic Irish Soldier and the First World War: The "Racial Environment"', *Irish Historical Studies* 27 (1991), pp. 352–365.

Doherty, Richard, and David Truesdale (eds.), *Irish Winners of the Victoria Cross* (Dublin, 2000).

Donaldson, Peter, *Remembering the South African War* (Liverpool, 2013).

Dooley, Terence, and Christopher Ridgeway (eds.), *The Irish Country House: Its Past, Present, and Future* (Dublin, 2011).

Dooley, Thomas P., *Irishmen or English Soldiers? The Times and World of a Southern Catholic Irishman (1876–1916) Enlisting in the British Army during the First World War* (Liverpool, 1995).

Dooney, Laura, 'Trinity College and the War', in Fitzpatrick, David (ed.), *Ireland and the First World War* (Dublin, 1988).

Duggan, John P., *A History of the Irish Army* (Dublin, 1991).

Dungan, Miles, *Irish Voices from the Great War* (Dublin, 1998).

English, Richard, and Graham Walker (eds.), *Unionism in Modern Ireland: New Perspectives on Politics and Culture* (Basingstoke, 1996).

Fachler, Yanky, 'The Zion Mule Corps—And Its Irish Commander', *History Ireland* 11 (2003), pp. 34–48.

Fanning, Ronan, *Fatal Path: British Government and Irish Revolution, 1910–1922* (London, 2013).

Farwell, Byron, *Eminent Victorian Soldiers* (London, 1986).

Fauske, Christopher, 'A Life Merely Glimpsed: Louis MacNeice at the End of the Anglo-Irish Tradition', *The Canadian Journal of Irish Studies* 20 (1994), pp. 17–29.

Finlay, Dan, 'Outflanked by Easter Week: Death in the Flemish Mud', *Books Ireland* 226 (1999), pp. 311–312.

Fitzpatrick, David (ed.), *Ireland and the First World War* (Dublin, 1988).

Fitzpatrick, David, 'Militarism in Ireland, 1900–1922' in Bartlett, Thomas, and Keith Jeffery (eds.), *A Military History of Ireland* (Cambridge, 1996a).

Fitzpatrick, David, 'Protestant Depopulation and the Irish Revolution', *Irish Historical Studies* 38 (2013), pp. 643–670.

Fitzpatrick, David, 'The Logic of Collective Sacrifice: Ireland and the British Army, 1914–1918', *The Historical Journal* 38 (1995), pp. 1017–1030.

Fitzpatrick, David, *The Two Irelands 1912–1939* (Oxford, 1998).

Fitzpatrick, David, 'Unofficial Emissaries: British Army Boxers in the Irish Free State', *Irish Historical Studies* 30 (1996b), pp. 206–232.

Foster, R. F., *Modern Ireland, 1600–1972* (London, 1988).

Foster, R. F., *Vivid Faces: The Revolutionary Generation in Ireland, 1890–1923* (London, 2014).

Fraser, T. G., 'Ireland and India' in Jeffery, Keith (ed.), *An Irish Empire? Aspects of Ireland and the British Empire* (Manchester, 1996).

French, David, *Military Identities: The Regimental System, the British Army, and the British People, c.1870–2000* (Oxford, 2005).

Gann, L. H., and Peter Duignan, *The Rulers of British Africa 1870–1914* (London, 1978).

Gannon, Seán, *The Irish Imperial Service: Policing Palestine and Administering the Empire, 1922–1966* (London, 2018).

Garton, Stephen, 'The Dominions, Ireland, and India', in Gerwarth, Robert, and Erez Manela (eds.), *Empires at War 1911–1923* (Oxford, 2014), pp. 152–177.

Geppert, Dominik, William Mulligan, and Andreas Rose (eds.), *The Wars Before the Great War: Conflict and International Politics Before the Outbreak of the Great War* (Cambridge, 2015).

Gerwarth, Robert, and Erez Manela (eds.), *Empires at War 1911–1923* (Oxford, 2014).

Gerwarth, Robert, and John Horne (eds.), *War in Peace: Paramilitary Violence in Europe after the Great War* (Oxford, 2012).

Graham, Colin, *Deconstructing Ireland* (Edinburgh, 2001).

Gray, Peter, *Victoria's Ireland? Irishness and Britishness, 1837–1901* (Dublin, 2004).

Grayson, Richard, and Fearghal McGarry (eds.), *Remembering 1916: The Easter Rising, the Somme, and the Politics of Memory in Ireland* (Cambridge, 2016).
Grayson, Richard, *Dublin's Great Wars: The First World War, the Easter Rising, and the Irish Revolution* (Cambridge, 2018).
Grayson, Richard, 'Veterans as Victims: The Experiences and Rediscovery of Irish Nationalists in the British Military in 1914–18' in Lelourec, Lesley, and Grainne O'Keefe (eds.), *Ireland and Victims* (Oxford, 2012).
Gregory, Adrian, and Senia Pašeta (eds.), *Ireland and the Great War: 'A War to Unite Us All'?* (Manchester, 2002).
Gruzinsky, Oscar, 'Career Patterns and Characteristics of British Naval Officers', *British Journal of Sociology* 26 (1975), pp. 35–51.
Haire, David N., 'In Aid of the Civil Power 1868–90' in Lyons, F. S. L., and R. A. J. Hawkins (eds.), *Ireland under the Union: Varieties of Tension* (Oxford, 1980).
Hart, Peter, *The IRA and Its Enemies* (Oxford, 1998).
Hart, Peter, 'The Social Structure of the Irish Republican Army, 1916–1923', *THJ* 42 (1999), pp. 207–231.
Harvey, A. D., 'Who were the Auxiliaries?', *The Historical Journal* 35 (1992), pp. 665–669.
Harvey, Dan, and Gerry White, *The Barracks: A History of Victoria/Collins Barracks, Cork* (Cork, 1997).
Haslinger, Peter, 'Austria-Hungary', in Gerwarth, Robert, and Erez Manela (eds.), *Empires at War 1911–1923* (Oxford, 2014), pp. 73–90.
Hay, Marnie, 'Moulding the Future: Na Fianna Éireann and Its Members, 1909–1923', *Studies: An Irish Quarterly Review* 100 (2011), pp. 441–454.
Heller, Michael, 'Work, Income and Stability: The Late Victorian and Edwardian London Male Clerk Revisited', *Business History* 50 (2008), pp. 253–271.
Hobsbawm, Eric, *The Age of Empire 1875–1914* (London, 2013).
Holmes, Richard, *The Little Field Marshal: The Life of Sir John French* (London, 2004).
Hoppen, K. Theodore, *Ireland Since 1800: Conflict and Conformity* (Harlow, 1999).
Horne, John, and Edward Madigan (eds.), *Towards Commemoration: Ireland in War and Revolution, 1912–1923* (Dublin, 2013).
Horne, John (ed.), *Our War: Ireland and the Great War* (Dublin, 2008).
Hughes, Gavin, *Fighting Irish: The Irish Regiments in the First World War* (Sallins, 2015).
Hutchinson, John, 'The Irish Revival, Elite Competition and the First World War' in O'Neill, Ciaran (ed.), *Irish Elites in the Nineteenth Century* (Dublin, 2013).
Hyam, Robert, *Understanding the British Empire* (Cambridge, 2010).
Irish, Tomás, *Trinity in War and Revolution* (Dublin, 2015).
Jackson, Alvin, *Colonel Edward Saunderson: Land and Loyalty in Victorian Ireland* (Oxford, 1995).

Jackson, Major General Louis C., *History of the United Service Club* (London, 1937).

James, David, *Lord Roberts* (London, 1954).

Jeffery, Keith (ed.), *An Irish Empire? Aspects of Ireland and the British Empire* (Manchester, 1996).

Jeffery, Keith, *Field Marshal Sir Henry Wilson: A Political Soldier* (Oxford, 2006).

Jeffery, Keith, *Ireland and the Great War* (Cambridge, 2011).

Jeffery, Keith, 'Irish Varieties of Great War Commemoration' in Horne, John, and Edward Madigan (eds.), *Towards Commemoration: Ireland in War and Revolution, 1912–1923* (Dublin, 2013).

Jeffery, Keith, *The British Army and the Crisis of Empire, 1918–22* (Manchester, 1984).

Jenkins, Gareth, 'Nationalism and Sectarian Violence in Liverpool and Belfast, 1880s–1920s', *International Labour and Working Class History* 78 (2010), pp. 164–180.

Johnstone, Tom, *Orange, Green and Khaki: The Story of the Irish Regiments in the Great War, 1914–18* (Dublin, 1992).

Johnson, Robert, *British Imperialism* (New York, 2003).

Jones, Heather, 'The German Empire', in Gerwarth, Robert, and Erez Manela (eds.), *Empires at War 1911–1923* (Oxford, 2014), pp. 52–71.

Jordan, Thomas E., 'Queen Victoria's Irish soldiers: Quality of Life and Social Origins of the Thin "Green" Line', *Social Indicators Research* 57 (2002), pp. 73–88.

Karsten, Peter, 'Irish Soldiers in the British Army, 1792–1922: Suborned or Subordinate?', *Journal of Social History* 17 (1983), pp. 31–64.

Kenez, Peter, 'Russian Officer Corps before the Revolution: The Military Mind', *The Russian Review* 31 (1972), pp. 226–236.

Kennedy, Catriona, and Matthew McCormack (eds.), *Soldiering in Britain and Ireland, 1750–1850* (New York, 2013).

Kenny, Kevin, *Ireland and the British Empire* (Oxford, 2004).

Keohane, Leo, *Captain Jack White: Imperialism, Anarchism and the Irish Citizens Army* (Dublin, 2014).

Kirk-Greene, Anthony, *Symbol of Authority: The British District Officer in Africa* (London, 2006).

Kochanski, Halik, *Sir Garnet Wolseley: Victorian Hero* (London, 1999).

Laffan, Michael, *The Partition of Ireland, 1911–1925* (Dublin, 1983).

Lambert, David, and Alan Lester (eds.), *Colonial Lives Across the British Empire: Imperial Careering in the Long Nineteenth Century* (Cambridge, 2006).

Leeson, D. M., *The Black and Tans* (Oxford, 2011).

Leonard, Jane, 'Survivors' in Horne, John (ed.), *Our War: Ireland and the Great War* (Dublin, 2008).

Leonard, Jane, 'The Twinge of Memory: Armistice Day and Remembrance Sunday in Dublin Since 1919', in English, Richard, and Graham Walker (eds.), *Unionism in Modern Ireland: New Perspectives on Politics and Culture* (Basingstoke, 1996).

Lelourec, Lesley, and Grainne O'Keefe, *Ireland and Victims* (Oxford, 2012).

Lewis, Gifford, *Somerville and Ross: The World of the Irish RM* (New York, 1985).

Levenson, Leah, and Jerry Netterstad, *Hannah Sheehy-Skeffington: Irish Feminist* (Syracuse, 1986).

Levine, Philippa, 'Rereading the 1890s: Venereal Disease as "Constitutional Crisis" in Britain and British India', *Journal of Asian Studies* 55:3 (1996), pp. 585–612.

Lowe, W. J., 'Who were the Black and Tans?' *History Ireland* 12 (2004), pp. 47–51.

Lyons, F. S. L., and R. A. J. Hawkins (eds.), *Ireland under the Union: Varieties of Tension* (Oxford, 1980).

Mackenzie, John M., *Propaganda and Empire: The Manipulation of British Public Opinion, 1880–1960* (Manchester, 1986).

Malcolm, Elizabeth, '"Troops of Largely Diseased Women": VD, the Contagious Diseases Acts, and Moral Policing in Late Nineteenth-Century Ireland', *Irish Economic and Social History* 26 (1999), pp. 1–14.

Martin, Peter, 'Dulce et decorum: Irish Nobles in the Great War 1914–19' in Gregory, Adrian, and Senia Pašeta (eds.), *Ireland and the Great War: 'A War to Unite us All'?* (Manchester, 2002).

Marwick, Peter, *The Deluge: British Society and the First World War* (London, 1965).

Maxwell, Leigh, *The Ashanti Ring: Sir Garnet Wolseley's Campaigns 1870–1882* (London, 1985).

McBride, Lawrence, *The Greening of Dublin Castle* (Washington, DC, 1991).

McClintock, Anne, *Imperial Leather: Race, Gender, and Sexuality in the Colonial Context* (New York, 1995).

McConnell, James, 'John Redmond and Irish Catholic loyalism', *English Historical Review* 75 (2010), pp. 83–111.

McConville, Michael, *Ascendency to Oblivion: The Story of the Anglo-Irish* (London, 1986).

McCourt, Edward, *Remember Butler: The Story of Sir William Butler* (London, 1967).

McDowell, R. B., *Land and Learning: Two Irish Clubs* (Dublin, 1993).

McGarry, Fearghal, *The Rising: Ireland, Easter 1916* (Oxford, 2016).

McGaughey, Jane G. V., *Ulster's Men: Protestant Unionist Masculinities and Militarization in the North of Ireland, 1912–1923* (Montreal, 2012).

McInnis, Verity G., 'Indirect Agents of Empire: Army Officers' Wives in British India and the American West, 1830–1875', *Pacific Historical Review* 83:3 (2014), pp. 378–409.

McMahon, Timothy, 'A New Role for Irish Anglicans in the Later Nineteenth Century: The HCMS and Imperial Opportunity' in O'Neill, Ciaran (ed.), *Irish Elites in the Nineteenth Century* (Dublin, 2013).

Meyer, Susan, *Imperialism at Home: Race and Victorian Women's Fiction* (London, 1996).

Miller, David W., *Queen's Rebels: Ulster Loyalism in Historical Perspective* (Dublin, 2007).

Miller, Stephen M., 'Duty or Crime? Acceptable Behaviour in the British Army in South Africa, 1899–1902', *Journal of British Studies* 49:2 (2010), pp. 311–331.

Moore-Bick, Christopher, *Playing the Game: The British Junior Infantry Officer on the Western Front 1914–18* (Solihull, 2011).

Morton, Anthony, 'Sandhurst and the First World War: The Royal Military College 1902–1918', Sandhurst Occasional Paper No. 17 (2014), pp. 1–52.

Muenger, Elizabeth, *The British Military Dilemma in Ireland* (Lawrence, KA, 1991).

Myers, Jason R., *The Great War and Memory in Irish Culture, 1918–2010* (Palo Alto, 2013).

Narain, Major General Partap, *Subedar to Field Marshal* (Delhi, 1999).

Nash, Catherine, Byronie Reid, and Brian Graham (eds.), *Partitioned Lives: The Irish Borderlands* (Farnham, 2013).

O'Connor, Steven, *Irish Officers in the British Forces, 1922–45* (New York, 2014).

Ó Corráin, Daithí, '"A Most Public-Spirited and Unselfish Man": The Career and Contribution of Colonel Maurice Moore, 1854–1939', *Studia Hibernica* 40 (2015), pp. 71–134.

Ollerenshaw, Philip, 'Businessmen and the Development of Ulster Unionism, 1886–1921', *Journal of Imperial and Commonwealth History* 28 (2000), pp. 35–64.

O'Neill, Ciaran (ed.), *Irish Elites in the Nineteenth Century* (Dublin, 2013).

Omissi, David, and Andrew Thompson (eds.), *The Impact of the South African War* (Basingstoke, 2002).

Orr, Philip, 'The Somme Legacy', *Linen Hall Review* 4 (1987), pp. 5–7.

Otley, C. B., 'Militarism and Militarisation in the Public Schools, 1900–1972', *British Journal of Sociology* 29 (1978), pp. 321–339.

Overlack, Peter, '"Easter 1916" in Dublin and the Australian Press: Background and Response', *Journal of Australian Studies* 21 (2009), pp. 188–193.

Parkinson, Alan F., and Eamon Phoenix (eds.), *Conflicts in the North of Ireland, 1900–2000: Flashpoints and Fracture Zones* (Dublin, 2010).

Parsons, Timothy, *The British Imperial Century, 1815–1914: A World History Perspective* (Lanham, MD, 1999).

Patterson, Steven, *The Cult of Imperial Honor in British India* (New York, 2009).

Peers, Douglas M., and Nandini Goptu (eds.), *India and the British Empire* (Oxford, 2012).

Pennell, Catriona, *A Kingdom United: Popular Responses to the Outbreak of the First World War in Britain and Ireland* (Oxford, 2012).

Pennell, Catriona, 'Going to War' in Horne, John (ed.), *Our War: Ireland and the Great War* (Dublin, 2008).

Perkin, Harold, *The Rise of Professional Society: England Since 1880* (London, 1989).

Perry, Nicholas, 'The Irish Landed Class and the British Army, 1850–1950', *War in History* 18 (2011), pp. 304–333.

Petter, Martin, '"Temporary gentlemen" in the Aftermath of the Great War: Rank, Status and the Ex-officer Problem', *The Historical Journal* 37 (1994), pp. 127–152.

Porter, Andrew, 'The South African War and the Historians', *African Affairs* 99 (2000), pp. 633–648.

Potter, Simon J., *Newspapers and Empire in Ireland and Britain: Reporting the British Empire, c.1857–1921* (Dublin, 2004).

Power, Paul, 'The Anglo-Irish Problem: A Matter of Which Question', *Comparative Politics* 26 (1994), pp. 237–250.

Purdue, Olwen, '"Ascendency's... Last Big Jamboree": Big House Society in Northern Ireland, 1921–69' in Dooley, Terence, and Christopher Ridgeway (eds.), *The Irish Country House: Its Past, Present, and Future* (Dublin, 2011).

Quinn, Anthony P., *Wigs and Guns: Irish Barristers in the Great War* (Dublin, 2006).

Radford, Mark, 'Andrew Reed (1837–1914): A Very Civil Policeman', *History Ireland* 13 (2005), pp. 31–35.

Radford, Mark, '"Closely Akin to Actual Warfare": The Belfast Riots of 1886 & the RIC', *History Ireland* 7 (1999), pp. 27–31.

Radford, Mark, *The Policing of Belfast 1870–1914* (London, 2015).

Raugh, Harold E., *The Victorians at War, 1815–1914: An Encyclopaedia of British Military History* (Santa Barbara, 2004).

Razzell, P. E., 'Social Origins of Officers in the Indian and British Home Army: 1758–1962', *British Journal of Sociology* 14 (1963), pp. 248–260.

Regan, John, 'Southern Irish Nationalism as a Historical Problem', *Historical Journal* 50:1 (2007), pp. 197–223.

Regan-Lefebvre, Jennifer, *Cosmopolitan Nationalism in the Victorian Empire: Ireland, India and the Politics of Alfred Webb* (London, 2009).

Reid, Richard, *Frontiers of Violence in North-East Africa: Genealogies of Conflict Since 1800* (Oxford, 2011).

Reilly, Ciarán J., 'The Burning of Country Houses in Co. Offaly During the Revolutionary Period, 1920–3' in Dooley, Terence, and Christopher Ridgeway (eds.), *The Irish Country House: Its Past, Present, and Future* (Dublin, 2011).

Richardson, Neil, *According to their Lights: Stories of Irishmen in the British Army, Easter 1916* (Dublin, 2015).

Robinson, Lennox, *Bryan Cooper* (London, 1931).

Rothenburg, Gunther E., 'Nobility and Military Careers: The Hapsburg Officer Corps, 1740–1914', *Military Affairs* 40 (1976), pp. 182–186.

Royle, Trevor, *The Kitchener Enigma* (London, 1985).

Rudd, Jeffery A., 'Origins of the Transjordan Field Force', *Middle Eastern Studies* 26 (1990), pp. 161–184.

Sanborn, Joshua, 'The Russian Empire', in Gerwarth, Robert, and Erez Manela (eds.), *Empires at War 1911–1923* (Oxford, 2014), pp. 91–108.

Schwarz, Bill (ed.), *Memories of Empire, Volume I: The White Man's World* (Oxford, 2011).

Screen, J. E. O., 'Marshal Mannerheim: The Years of Preparation', *The Slavonic and East European Review* 43 (1965), pp. 293–302.

Seldon, Anthony, and David Walsh, *Public Schools and the Great War: The Generation Lost* (Barnsley, 2013).

Shepard, Christopher, '"I Have a Notion of Going Off to India": Colonel Alexander Porter and Irish Recruitment to the Indian Medical Service, 1855–96', *Irish Economic and Social History* 41 (2014), pp. 36–52.

Silvestri, Michael, *Ireland and India: Nationalism, Empire and Memory* (Cambridge, 2006).

Simkins, Peter, *Kitchener's Army: The Raising of the New Armies, 1914–16* (Manchester, 1988).

Sinclair, Georgina, 'The "Irish" Policeman and the Empire: Influencing the Policing of the Empire-Commonwealth', *Irish Historical Studies* 36 (2008), pp. 173–187.

Sjoberg, Laura, and Sandra Via (eds.), *Gender, War, and Militarism: Feminist Perspectives* (Santa Barbara, 2010).

Smith, Brendan, Jane Ohlmeyer, James Kelly, and Thomas Bartlett (eds.), *The Cambridge History of Ireland*, 4 vols. (Cambridge, 2018).

Spiers, Edward, *The Army and Society 1815–1914* (London, 1980).

Strachan, Hew, *The Politics of the British Army* (Oxford, 1997).

Streets, Heather, *Martial Races: The Military, Race, and Masculinity in British Imperial Culture, 1857–1914* (Manchester, 2004).

Surridge, '"You Soldiers are What We Call Pro-Boer": The Military Critique of the South African War, 1899–1902', *History Ireland* 8 (2000), pp. 582–600.

Taylor, Paul, *Heroes or Traitors? Experiences of Southern Irish Soldiers Returning from the Great War 1919–1939* (Manchester, 2015).

Thomas, Martin, '"Paying the Butcher's Bill": Policing British Colonial Protest After 1918', *Crime, Histoire & Sociétés/Crime, History & Societies* 15 (2011), pp. 55–76.

Thompson, Andrew (ed.), *Britain's Experience of Empire in the Twentieth Century* (Oxford, 2012).

Tobin, Robert, '"Tracing Again the Tiny Snail Track": Southern Protestant Memoir Since 1950', *The Yearbook of English Studies* 35 (2005), pp. 171–185.

Townshend, Charles, *Easter 1916: The Irish Rebellion* (London, 2005).

Townshend, Charles, *The British Campaign in Ireland, 1919–1921* (London, 1975).

Travers, Tim, 'The Hidden Army: Structural Problems in the British Officer Corps, 1900–1918', *Journal of Contemporary History* 17 (1982), pp. 523–544.

Urquhart, Diane, *Ladies of Londonderry: Women and Political Patronage* (London, 2007).

Usherwood, Paul, 'Elizabeth Thompson Butler: The Consequences of Marriage', *Women's Art Journal* 9 (1988), pp. 30–34.

Verney, Peter, *The Micks: The Story of the Irish Guards* (London, 1970).

Vitarbo, Gregory, 'Nationality Policy and the Russian Imperial Officer Corps, 1905–1914', *Slavic Review* 66 (2007), pp. 682–701.

von Zugbach, R. G. L., *Power and Prestige in the British Army* (Aldershot, 1988).

Webster, Wendy, *Englishness and Empire 1939–1965* (Oxford, 2005).

Wessels, Andre, *Lord Roberts and the War in South Africa 1899–1902* (Stroud, 2000).

Wichert, Sabine, 'The Northern Ireland Conflict: New Wine in Old Bottles?', *Contemporary European History* 9 (2000), pp. 307–322.

Willoughby, Roger, *A Military History of the University of Dublin and its Officers Training Corps 1910–1922* (Dublin, 1983).

Wilson, Tim, 'Ghost Provinces, Mislaid Minorities: The Experience of Southern Ireland and Prussian Poland Compared, 1918–23', *Irish Studies in International Affairs* 13 (2002), pp. 61–86.

Yeates, Pádraig, *A City in Wartime: Dublin, 1914–18* (Dublin, 2011).

REFERENCE WORKS

Brown, Judith M., and William Roger Louis, *The Oxford History of the British Empire* vol. IV, the Twentieth Century (Oxford, 1999).

Burke's *Landed Gentry*.

Burke's *Peerage and Baronetage*.

Cambridge Dictionary of Irish Biography.

Hansard.

Hogan, Liam, Register of Limerick's First World War Graves, Limerick City Library.

irishwarmemorials.ie

Kelly's Handbook to the Titled, Landed, and Official Classes 1945.

Oxford Dictionary of National Biography.

Porter, Andrew (ed.), *The Oxford History of the British Empire* vol. III, the Nineteenth Century (Oxford, 1999).

The Indian Army List.
The Monthly Army List.
Vaughan, Edward Littleton, *List of Etonians Who Fought in the Great War, 1914–1919* (London, 1921).
Winter, Jay (ed.), *The Cambridge History of the First World War*, 3 vols. (Cambridge, 2014).
thepeerage.com

PHD THESES

Gallagher, Niamh A., 'Irish Civil Society and the Great War, 1914–1918', unpublished PhD thesis, University of Cambridge, 2014.
Kochanski, Halik, 'Field Marshall Viscount Wolseley, a Reformer at the War Office', unpublished PhD thesis, King's College London, 1996.
Moore-Bick, Christopher James, 'The Development of the Junior British Infantry Officer on the Western Front, 1914–1918', unpublished PhD thesis, University of Cambridge, 2005.
Redman, Lydia, 'Industrial Conflict, Social Reform and Competition for Power under the Liberal Governments 1906–1914', unpublished PhD thesis, University of Cambridge, 2014.
Ridden, Jennifer, 'Making Good Citizens: National Identity, Religion and Liberalism among the Irish Elite c.1800–1850', unpublished PhD thesis, King's College London, 1998.
Watson, Samuel Johnson, 'Professionalism, Social Attitudes, and Civil-Military Accountability in the United States Army Officer Corps, 1815–1846', unpublished PhD thesis, Rice University, 1996.

Index[1]

[1] Note. Page numbers followed by 'n' refer to notes.

© The Author(s) 2019

L. Sweeney, *Irish Military Elites, Nation and Empire, 1870–1925,*

https://doi.org/10.1007/978-3-030-19307-2

CPSIA information can be obtained
at www.ICGtesting.com
Printed in the USA
BVHW020145151019
561132BV00006B/15/P

9 783030 193065